Gopal N. Shenoy

3.2.1 – 3.2.3

2.1
2.2
2.3

3.3

n.1

n.2.1 – n.2.2

4.1

8.2

n. (X.n.4.1)

A First Course in Database Systems

Jeffrey D. Ullman
and
Jennifer Widom

Department of Computer Science
Stanford University

An Alan R. Apt Book

Prentice Hall
Upper Saddle River, New Jersey 07458

Library of Congress Cataloging-in-Publication Data

Ullman, Jeffrey D.
    A First Course in Database Systems/
Jeffrey D. Ullman and Jennifer Widom
        p. cm.
    Includes bibliographical references and index.
    ISBN: 0-13-861337-0
    1. Database management. I. Widom, Jennifer. II. Title.
QA76.9.D3U42 1997
005.74--dc21   97-7762
                                          CIP

Publisher: **ALAN APT**
Editor-in-chief: **MARCIA HORTON**
Managing editor: **BAYANI MENDOZA DE LEON**
Director of production and manufacturing: **DAVID W. RICCARDI**
Creative director: **PAULA MAYLAHN**
Production editor: **IRWIN ZUCKER**
Art director: **HEATHER SCOTT**
Cover designer: **TAMARA NEWNAM CAVALLO**
Manufacturing buyer: **DONNA SULLIVAN**
Editorial assistant: **TONI CHAVEZ**

©1997 by Prentice-Hall, Inc.
Simon & Schuster / A Viacom Company
Upper Saddle River, New Jersey 07458

The author and publisher of this book have used their best efforts in preparing this book. These efforts include the
development, research, and testing of the theories and programs to determine their effectiveness. The author and
publisher make no warranty of any kind, expressed or implied, with regard to these programs or the documentation
contained in this book. The author and publisher shall not be liable in any event for incidental or consequential damages
in connection with, or arising out of, the furnishing, performance, or use of these programs.

Printed in the United States of America

10 9 8 7 6 5 4 3 2 1

ISBN   0-13-861337-0

Prentice-Hall International (UK) Limited, London
Prentice-Hall of Australia Pty. Limited, Sydney
Prentice-Hall Canada Inc., Toronto
Prentice-Hall Hispanoamericana, S.A., Mexico
Prentice-Hall of India Private Limited, New Delhi
Prentice-Hall of Japan, Inc., Tokyo
Simon & Schuster Asia Pte. Ltd., Singapore
Editora Prentice-Hall do Brasil, Ltda., Rio de Janeiro

Preface

This book developed from course notes used in Stanford's CS145 introduction to databases. CS145 is the first in a sequence of five courses.[1] As taught originally by Arthur Keller, it evolved into a course that stresses the aspects of database systems of most use to the majority of computer science students: database design and programming. The course also involves an extensive, running project, in which the students design and then implement a substantial database application. Assignments related to this project, other homework assignments, exams, and other course materials are available from this book's home page; see the section on "Support on the World Wide Web."

Use of the Book

This book is suitable for a one-semester course. In a one-quarter course, such as CS145, we have had to omit or skim some of the material. We'll leave it to the instructor what can best be elided, but obvious possibilities include material on Datalog, advanced aspects of SQL programming, and detailed coverage of SQL3.

If you have a running project as part of the course, then it is important that SQL instruction be moved earlier than it appears in the book. Some of the things that are suitable for postponement include the material on Datalog, SQL3 sections in Chapters 5 and 6, and some of the theory in Chapter 3 (but students need normalization and possibly multivalued dependencies if they are to do a good relational design before starting SQL programming).

Prerequisites

We have used the book at the "mezzanine" level, in a course taken both by advanced undergraduates and beginning graduate students. The formal prerequisites for the course are Sophomore-level treatments of: (1) Data structures, algorithms, and discrete math, and (2) Software systems, software engineering,

---

[1] The four that follow are: database system principles, a project course in database system implementation, transactions and distributed databases, and database theory.

and programming languages. Of this material, it is important that students
have at least a rudimentary understanding of such topics as: algebraic expressions and laws, logic, basic data structures such as search trees, object-oriented
programming concepts, and programming environments. However, we believe
that adequate background is surely acquired by the end of the Junior year in a
typical computer science program.

Exercises

The book contains extensive exercises, with some for almost every section. We
indicate harder exercises or parts of exercises with an exclamation point. The
hardest exercises have a double exclamation point.

Some of the exercises or parts are marked with a star. For these exercises,
we shall endeavor to maintain solutions accessible through the book's web page.
These solutions are publicly available and should be used for self-testing. Note
that in a few cases, one exercise B asks for modification or adaptation of your
solution to another exercise A. If certain parts of A have solutions, then you
should expect the corresponding parts of B to have solutions as well.

Support on the World Wide Web

The book's home page is

```
http://www-db.stanford.edu/~ullman/fcdb.html
```

Here are solutions to starred exercises, errata as we learn of them, and backup
materials. We hope to make available the notes for each offering of CS145 as
we teach it, including homeworks, solutions, and project assignments.

Acknowledgements

Special thanks go to Bobbie Cochrane and Linda DeMichiel, for their help with
aspects of the SQL3 standard. Many others helped us debug the manuscript as
well, including: Donald Aingworth, Jonathan Becker, Larry Bonham, Christopher Chan, Oliver Duschka, Greg Fichtenholtz, Bart Fisher, Meredith Goldsmith, Steve Huntsberry, Leonard Jacobson, Thulasiraman Jeyaraman, Dwight
Joe, Seth Katz, Brian Kulman, Le-Wei Mo, Mark Mortensen, Ramprakash
Narayanaswami, Torbjorn Norbye, Mehul Patel, Catherine Tornabene, Jonathan Ullman, Mayank Upadhyay, Vassilis Vassalos, Qiang Wang, Sundar Yamunachari, and Takeshi Yokukawa. Remaining errors are ours, of course.

J. D. U.
J. W.

Table of Contents

Chapter 1

The Worlds of Database Systems

In this book the reader will learn the effective use of database management systems, including the design of databases and the programming of operations on databases. This chapter serves to introduce a number of important database concepts. After a brief history of the subject, we learn what makes database systems different from other software genres. This chapter also provides background concerning the implementation of the database management systems that support databases and their use. An understanding of what goes on "behind the scenes" is important if we are to have an appreciation of why databases are designed as they are or why there are limits on the way operations can be performed on databases. Finally, we review some ideas, such as object-oriented programming, with which the reader may be familiar but that are essential in the chapters to follow.

1.1 The Evolution of Database Systems

What is a database? In essence a database is nothing more than a collection of information that exists over a long period of time, often many years. In common parlance, the term *database* refers to a collection of data that is managed by a *database management system*, also called a *DBMS*, or just *database system*. A DBMS is expected to:

1. Allow users to create new databases and specify their *schema* (logical structure of the data), using a specialized language called a *data-definition language*.

2. Give users the ability to *query* the data (a "query" is database lingo for a question about the data) and modify the data, using an appropriate language, often called a *query language* or *data-manipulation language*.

1

3. Support the storage of very large amounts of data — gigabytes or more — over a long period of time, keeping it secure from accident or unauthorized use and allowing efficient access to the data for queries and database modifications.

4. Control access to data from many users at once, without allowing the actions of one user to affect other users and without allowing simultaneous accesses to corrupt the data accidentally.

1.1.1 Early Database Management Systems

The first commercial database management systems appeared in the late 1960's. These evolved from file systems, which provide some of item (3) above; file systems store data over a long period of time, and they allow the storage of large amounts of data. However, file systems do not generally guarantee that data cannot be lost if it is not backed up, and they don't support efficient access to data items whose location in a particular file is not known.

Further, file systems do not directly support item (2), a query language for the data in files. Their support for (1) — a schema for the data — is limited to the creation of directory structures for files. Finally, file systems do not satisfy (4). When they allow concurrent access to files by several users or processes, a file system generally will not prevent situations such as two users modifying the same file at about the same time, so the changes made by one user fail to appear in the file.

The first important applications of DBMS's were ones where data was composed of many small items, and many queries or modifications were made. Here are some of these applications.

Airline Reservations Systems

Here, the items of data include:

1. Reservations by a single customer on a single flight, including such information as assigned seat or meal preference.

2. Information about flights — the airports they fly from and to, their departure and arrival times, or the aircraft flown, for example.

3. Information about ticket prices, requirements, and availability.

Typical queries ask for flights leaving about a certain time from one given city to another, what seats are available, and at what prices. Typical data modifications include the booking of a flight for a customer, assigning a seat, or indicating a meal preference. Many agents will be accessing parts of the data at any given time. The DBMS must allow such concurrent accesses, prevent problems such as two agents assigning the same seat simultaneously, and protect against loss of records if the system suddenly fails.

Banking Systems

Data items include names and addresses of customers, accounts, loans, and their balances, and the connection between customers and their accounts and loans, e.g., who has signature authority over which accounts. Queries for account balances are common, but far more common are modifications representing a single payment from or deposit to an account.

As with the airline reservation system, we expect that many tellers and customers (through ATM machines) will be querying and modifying the bank's data at once. It is vital that simultaneous accesses to an account not cause the effect of an ATM transaction to be lost. Failures cannot be tolerated. For example, once the money has been ejected from an ATM machine, the bank must record the debit, even if the power immediately fails. On the other hand, it is not permissible for the bank to record the debit and then not deliver the money because the power fails. The proper way to handle this operation is far from obvious and can be regarded as one of the significant achievements in DBMS architecture.

Corporate Records

Many early applications concerned corporate records, such as a record of each sale, information about accounts payable and receivable, or information about employees — their names, addresses, salary, benefit options, tax status, and so on. Queries include the printing of reports such as accounts receivable or employees' weekly paychecks. Each sale, purchase, bill, receipt, employee hired, fired, or promoted, and so on, results in a modification to the database.

The early DBMS's, evolving from file systems, encouraged the user to visualize data much as it was stored. These database systems used several different data models for describing the structure of the information in a database, chief among them the "hierarchical" or tree-based model and the graph-based "network" model. The latter was standardized in the late 1960's through a report of CODASYL (Committee on Data Systems and Languages).[1] We shall introduce the reader to both the network and hierarchical models in Section 2.7, although today they are only of historical interest.

A problem with these early models and systems was that they did not support high-level query languages. For example, the CODASYL query language had statements that allowed the user to jump from data element to data element, through a graph of pointers among these elements. There was considerable effort needed to write such programs, even for very simple queries.

---

[1] *CODASYL Data Base Task Group April 1971 Report*, ACM, New York.

1.1.2   Relational Database Systems

Following a famous paper written by Ted Codd in 1970,[2] database systems changed significantly. Codd proposed that database systems should present the user with a view of data organized as tables called *relations*. Behind the scenes, there might be a complex data structure that allowed rapid response to a variety of queries. But, unlike the user of earlier database systems, the user of a relational system would not be concerned with the storage structure. Queries could be expressed in a very high-level language, which greatly increased the efficiency of database programmers.

We shall cover the relational model of database systems throughout most of this book, starting with the basic relational concepts in Chapter 3. SQL (Structured Query Language), the most important query language based on the relational model, will be covered starting in Chapter 5. However, a brief introduction to relations will give the reader a hint of the simplicity of the model, and an SQL sample will suggest how the relational model promotes queries written at a very high level, avoiding details of "navigation" through the database.

Example 1.1 : Relations are tables. Their columns are headed by *attributes*, which describe the entries in the column. For instance, a relation named `Accounts`, recording bank accounts, their balance, and type might look like:

accountNo	*balance*	*type*
12345	1000.00	savings
67890	2846.92	checking
. . .	. . .	. . .

Heading the columns are the three attributes: `accountNo`, `balance`, and `type`. Below the attributes are the rows, or *tuples*. Here we show two tuples of the relation explicitly, and the dots below them suggest that there would be many more tuples, one for each account at the bank. The first tuple says that account number 12345 has a balance of one thousand dollars, and it is a savings account. The second tuple says that account 67890 is a checking account with $2846.92.

Suppose we wanted to know the balance of account 67890. We could ask this query in SQL as follows:

```
SELECT balance
FROM Accounts
WHERE accountNo = 67890;
```

For another example, we could ask for the savings accounts with negative balances by:

---

[2]Codd, E. F., "A relational model for large shared data banks," *Comm. ACM*, **13**:6, pp. 377–387.

```
SELECT accountNo
FROM Accounts
WHERE type = 'savings' AND balance < 0;
```

Select-from-where statement

We do not expect that these two examples are enough to make the reader an expert SQL programmer, but they should convey the high-level nature of the SQL select-from-where statement. In principle, they ask the database system to

1. Examine all the tuples of the relation `Accounts` mentioned in the `FROM`-clause,

2. Pick out those tuples that satisfy some criterion indicated in the `WHERE`-clause, and

3. Produce as an answer certain attributes of those tuples, as indicated in the `SELECT`-clause.

In practice, the system must "optimize" the query and find an efficient way to answer the query, even though the relations involved in the query may be very large. □

IBM was an early vendor of both relational and prerelational DBMS's. In addition, new companies were formed to implement and sell relational DBMS's. Today, some of these companies are among the largest software vendors in the world.

1.1.3 Smaller and Smaller Systems

Originally, DBMS's were large, expensive software systems running on large computers. The size was necessary, because to store a gigabyte of data required a large computer system. Today, a gigabyte fits on a single disk, and it is quite feasible to run a DBMS on a personal computer. Thus, database systems based on the relational model have become available for even very small machines, and they are beginning to appear as a common tool for computer applications, much as spreadsheets and word processors did before them.

1.1.4 Bigger and Bigger Systems

On the other hand, a gigabyte isn't much data. Corporate databases often occupy hundreds of gigabytes. Further, as storage becomes cheaper people find new reasons to store greater amounts of data. For example, retail chains often store a *terabyte* (1000 gigabytes, or 10^{12} bytes) or more of information recording the history of every sale made over a long period of time (for planning inventory; we shall have more to say about this matter in Section 1.3.4). Databases no longer focus on storing simple data items such as integers or short character strings. They can store images, audio, video, and many other kinds of data that take comparatively huge amounts of space. For instance, an hour of video consumes about a gigabyte. Databases storing images from satellites are expected, by the year 2000, to hold several *petabytes* (1000 terabytes, or 10^{15} bytes).

Handling such large databases required several technological advances. For example, databases of modest size are today stored on arrays of disks, which are called *secondary storage devices* (compared to main memory, which is "primary" storage). One could even argue that what distinguishes database systems from other software is, more than anything else, the fact that database systems routinely assume data is too big to fit in main memory and must be located primarily on disk at all times. The following two trends allow database systems to deal with larger amounts of data, faster.

Tertiary Storage

The largest databases today require more than disks. Several kinds of *tertiary storage devices* have been developed. Tertiary devices, perhaps storing a terabyte each, require much more time to access a given item than does a disk. While typical disks can access any item in 10-20 milliseconds, a tertiary device may take several seconds. Tertiary storage devices involve transporting an object, upon which the desired data item is stored, to a reading device. This movement is performed by a robotic conveyance of some sort.

For example, compact disks (CD's) may be the storage medium in a tertiary device. An arm mounted on a track goes to a particular CD, picks it up, carries it to a CD reader, and loads the CD into the reader.

Parallel Computing

The ability to store enormous volumes of data is important, but it would be of little use if we could not access large amounts of that data quickly. Thus, very large databases also require speed enhancers. One important speedup is through index structures, which we shall mention in Sections 1.2.1 and 5.7.7. Another way to process more data in a given time is to use parallelism. This parallelism manifests itself in various ways.

For example, since the rate at which data can be read from a given disk is fairly low, a few megabytes per second, we can speed processing if we use many disks and read them in parallel (even if the data originates on tertiary storage, it is "cached" on disks before being accessed by the DBMS). These disks may be part of an organized parallel machine, or they may be components of a distributed system, in which many machines, each responsible for a part of the database, communicate over a high-speed network when needed.

Of course, the ability to move data quickly, like the ability to store large amounts of data, does not by itself guarantee that queries can be answered quickly. We still need to use algorithms that break queries up in ways that allow parallel computers or networks of distributed computers to make effective use of all the resources. Thus, parallel and distributed management of very large databases remains an active area of research and development.

1.2 The Architecture of a DBMS

In this section, we shall sketch the structure of a typical database management system. We shall also look at what the DBMS does to process user queries and other database operations. Finally, we shall consider some of the problems that come up in designing a DBMS that can maintain large amounts of data and process a high rate of queries. The technology for implementing a DBMS is not the subject of this book, however; we concentrate on how databases are designed and used effectively.

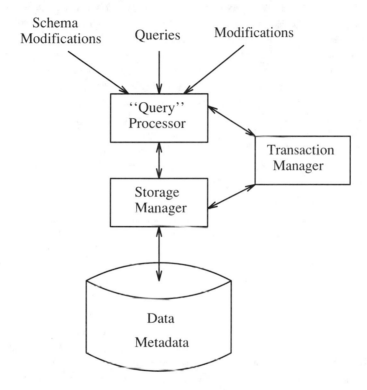

Figure 1.1: Major components of a DBMS

1.2.1 Overview of DBMS Components

Figure 1.1 shows the essential parts of a DBMS. At the bottom, we see a representation of the place where data is stored. By convention, disk-shaped components indicate a place for storage of data. Note that we have indicated that this component contains not only data, but *metadata*, which is information about the structure of the data. For example, if this DBMS is relational, the metadata includes the names of the relations, the names of the attributes of those relations, and the data types for those attributes (e.g., integer or character

---

How Indexes Are Implemented

The reader may have learned in a course on data structures that a hash table is a very efficient way to build an index. Early DBMS's did use hash tables extensively. Today, the most common data structure is called a *B-tree*; the "B" stands for "balanced." A B-tree is a generalization of a balanced binary search tree. However, while each node of a binary tree has up to two children, the B-tree nodes have a large number of children. Given that B-trees normally appear on disk rather than in main memory, the B-tree is designed so that each node occupies a full disk block. Since typical systems use disk blocks on the order of 2^{12} bytes (4096 bytes), there can be hundreds of pointers to children in a single block of a B-tree. Thus, search of a B-tree rarely involves more than three levels.

The true cost of disk operations generally is proportional to the number of disk blocks accessed. Thus, searches of a B-tree, which typically examine only three disk blocks, are much more efficient than would be a binary-tree search, which typically visits nodes found on many different disk blocks. This distinction, between B-trees and binary search trees, is but one of many examples where the most appropriate data structure for data stored on disk is different from the data structures used for algorithms that run in main memory.

---

string of length 20).

Often, a DBMS maintains *indexes* for the data. An index is a data structure that helps us find data items quickly, given a part of their value; the most common example is an index that will find those tuples of a particular relation that have a given value for one of the attributes. For instance, a relation storing account numbers and balances might have an index on account-number, so that we can find the balance, given an account number, quickly. Indexes are part of the stored data, and a description of which attributes have indexes is part of the metadata.

In Fig. 1.1 we also see a *storage manager*, whose job it is to obtain requested information from the data storage and to modify the information there when requested to by the levels of system above it. We also see a component that we have called the *query processor*, although that name is somewhat of a misnomer. It handles not only queries but requests for modification of the data or the metadata. Its job is to find the best way to carry out a requested operation and to issue commands to the storage manager that will carry them out.

The *transaction manager* component is responsible for the integrity of the system. It must assure that several queries running simultaneously do not interfere with each other and that the system will not lose data even if there is a system failure. It interacts with the query manager, since it must know what data is being operated upon by the current queries (in order to avoid conflicting actions), and it may need to delay certain queries or operations so that these conflicts do not occur. It interacts with the storage manager because schemes for protection of data usually involve storing a *log* of changes to the data. By properly ordering operations, the log will contain a record of changes so that after a system failure even those changes that never reached the disk can be reexecuted.

At the top of Fig. 1.1 we see three types of inputs to the DBMS:

1. *Queries.* These are questions about the data. They are generated in two different ways:

   (a) Through a *generic query interface.* For example, a relational DBMS allows the user to type SQL queries that are passed to the query processor and answered.

   (b) Through *application program interfaces.* A typical DBMS allows programmers to write application programs that, through calls to the DBMS, query the database. For example, an agent using an airline reservation system is running an application program that queries the database about flight availabilities. The queries are submitted through a specialized interface that might include boxes to be filled in with cities, times, and so on. One cannot ask arbitrary queries through this interface, but it is generally easier to ask an appropriate query through this interface than to write the query directly in SQL.

2. *Modifications.* These are operations to modify the data. Like queries, they can be issued either through the generic interface or through the interface of an application program.

3. *Schema Modifications.* These commands are usually issued by authorized personnel, sometimes called *database administrators*, who are allowed to change the schema of the database or create a new database. For example, when the IRS started requiring banks to report interest payments along with each customer's Social Security number, a bank may have had to add a new attribute `socialSecurityNo` to a relation that stored information about customers.

1.2.2 The Storage Manager

In a simple database system, the storage manager might be nothing more than the file system of the underlying operating system. However, for efficiency purposes, DBMS's normally control storage on the disk directly, at least under some circumstances. The storage manager consists of two components, the buffer manager and the file manager.

1. The *file manager* keeps track of the location of files on the disk and obtains the block or blocks containing a file on request from the buffer manager. Recall that disks are generally divided into *disk blocks*, which are regions of contiguous storage containing a large number of bytes, perhaps 2^{12} or 2^{14} (about 4000 to 16,000 bytes).

2. The *buffer manager* handles main memory. It obtains blocks of data from the disk, via the file manager, and chooses a page of main memory in which to store that block. The buffer manager may keep a disk block in main memory for a while, but returns it to the disk if its page of main memory is needed for another block. Pages are also returned to disk when the transaction manager requires it; see Section 1.2.4.

1.2.3 The Query Manager

The job of the query manager is to turn a query or database manipulation, which may be expressed at a very high level (e.g., as an SQL query), into a sequence of requests for stored data such as specific tuples of a relation or parts of an index on a relation. Often the hardest part of the query-processing task is *query optimization*, that is, the selection of a good *query plan* or sequence of requests to the storage system that will answer the query.

Example 1.2: Suppose that a bank has a database with two relations:

1. `Customers` is a table giving, for each customer, their name, Social Security number, and address.

2. `Accounts` is a table giving, for each account, its account number, balance, and the Social Security number of its owner. Note that each account has a principal owner, whose Social Security number is used for tax-reporting purposes; there may be other owners of an account, but these cannot be known from the two relations given here.

Suppose also that the query "find the balances of all accounts of which Sally Jones is the principal owner" is asked. The query manager must find a query plan to perform on these relations, a plan that will yield the answer to the query. The fewer steps taken to answer the query, the better the query plan is. In general, the costly steps are those in which a disk block is copied from the disk into a page of the buffer pool by the storage manager, or a page is written back onto the disk. Thus, it is reasonable to count only these disk-block operations in evaluating the cost of a query plan.

In order to answer the query, we need to examine the `Customers` relation to find the Social Security number of Sally Jones (we assume there is only one customer with that name, although in practice there could be several). We then need to examine the `Accounts` relation to find every account with that Social Security number and print the balances of those accounts.

A simple but expensive plan is to examine all the tuples (rows) of the Customers relation until we find one with Sally Jones as the customer name. On average, we shall have to look at half of the tuples before we find the one we want. Since a bank will have many customers, the Customers relation will occupy many disk blocks, and this step will be very expensive. Once we have Sally Jones' Social Security number, we are not yet done. Now we have to look at the Accounts tuples and find those that have the selected Social Security number. Since there may be several such accounts, we have to look at all the tuples. A typical bank will have many accounts, so the Accounts relation will also occupy many disk blocks. Examining them all will be quite expensive.

If there is an index on the customer name for relation Customers, then a better plan exists. Instead of looking at the whole Customers relation, we use the index to find only the disk block containing the tuple for Sally Jones. As we mentioned in the box in Section 1.2.1, a typical B-tree index requires that we look at three disk blocks of the index in order to find what we want.[3] One more block access gets us the tuple for Sally Jones.

Of course we still need to do the second step: finding the accounts with that Social Security number in the Accounts relation. That step will require many disk accesses, typically. However, if there is an index on the Social Security number for relation Accounts, then we can find each of the blocks containing one of the accounts with a given Social Security number by going through this index. To do so, we must make 2 or 3 disk accesses to go through the index, as we discussed for indexed access to the Customers relation. If all the desired tuples are on different disk blocks, then we shall have to access each of these blocks. But there probably aren't too many accounts for one person, so this step probably uses only a few disk accesses. If these two indexes exist, then we can answer the query with perhaps 6–10 disk accesses. If one or both of them do not exist, and we have to use one of the poorer query plans, then the number of disk accesses might be in the hundreds or thousands, as we scan an entire, large relation. □

It might appear from Example 1.2 that all there is to query optimization is to use indexes if they exist. In fact, there is a great deal more to the subject. Complex queries often allow us to reorder operations, and there may be a very large number of possible query plans, often exponentially many in the size of the query. Sometimes we have a choice of two indexes to use, but we cannot use both. A study of this important part of DBMS implementation is beyond the scope of this book.

1.2.4 The Transaction Manager

As we discussed in Section 1.1, there are some special guarantees that a DBMS must make to those performing operations on a database. For example, we

---

[3]In fact, since the root node of the B-tree is used in every search involving that index, its block is often found in main memory, occupying one of the buffer pages, so two disk-block accesses usually suffice.

Transaction — a group of operations that must be executed together

discussed the importance that the effect of an operation never be lost, even in the face of a severe system failure. The typical DBMS allows the user to group one or more queries and/or modifications into a *transaction*, which informally is a group of operations that must appear to have been executed together sequentially, as a unit.

Frequently, a database system allows many transactions to execute concurrently; e.g., something may be going on at each of a bank's ATM machines simultaneously. The role of assuring that all these transactions are executed properly is the job of the *transaction manager* component of the DBMS. In more detail, "proper" execution of transactions requires what are often called the *ACID* properties, after the initials of the four principal requirements on transaction execution. These properties are:

Complete the entire transaction or none of it

- *Atomicity.* We require that either all of a transaction be executed or none of it is. For instance, withdrawal of money from an ATM machine and the associated debit to the customer's account should be a single, atomic transaction. It is not acceptable if the money is dispensed but the debit is not made, or if the debit is made and the money not dispensed.

- *Consistency.* A database generally has a notion of a "consistent state," in which the data meets any expectations we may have. For example, an appropriate consistency condition for an airline database is that no seat be assigned to two different customers. While this condition might be violated for a brief moment during a transaction, as people are moved among seats, the transaction manager must assure that after transactions have completed, the database satisfies any consistency conditions assumed.

- *Isolation.* When two or more transactions run concurrently, their effects must be isolated from one another. That is, we must not see effects caused by the two transactions running at the same time that would not occur if one ran before the other. For instance, when two airline agents are selling seats on the same flight, and only one seat remains, one request should be granted and the other denied. It is unacceptable if the same seat were sold twice or not at all, because of concurrent operations.

- *Durability.* If a transaction has completed its work, its effect should not get lost should the system fail, even if it fails immediately after the transaction completes.

How to implement transactions so that they have the ACID properties could be the subject of a book itself, and we shall not attempt to cover the matter here. However, Section 7.2 discusses how, in the language SQL, one specifies the operations that belong in a transaction, and what guarantees the SQL programmer can expect from having grouped operations into transactions. Also, we shall in this section outline very briefly the common techniques for enforcing the ACID properties.

Granularity of Locks

Different DBMS's may differ on what sorts of items have locks. For instance, one might lock individual tuples of a relation, individual disk blocks, or even whole relations. The bigger the thing that has a lock, the more likely one transaction is to have to wait for another, even when the two transactions really don't access the same data. However, the smaller the lockable item, the larger and more complex the locking mechanism is.

Locking

(Write access control to the same item in the db to prevent concurrent modification of the same item)

The principal cause of nonisolation among transactions is if two or more transactions read or write the same item in the database. For example, if two transactions try to write a new balance for the same account at the same time, one will overwrite the other, and the effect of the first to write will be lost. Thus, in most DBMS's the transaction manager is able to *lock* the items that the transaction accesses. While one transaction has a lock on an item, other transactions cannot access it. Thus, for example, the first transaction to lock the balance on account 12345 would get both to read it and to write the new value, before another transaction would be allowed to access it. A second transaction would read the new balance, rather than the old balance, and the two transactions would not interact badly.

Logging

Written by the transaction manager to a non-volatile medium such as disk.

A "log" of all transactions initiated, the changes to the database caused by each transaction, and the end of each transaction is recorded by the transaction manager. The log is always written to *nonvolatile storage*, that is, a storage medium like disk where the data will survive a power failure. Thus, while the transaction itself may use volatile main memory for part of its work, the log is always written immediately to disk. Logging of all operations is an important factor in assuring durability.

Transaction Commitment

make tentative changes
write log
Then make permanent changes to db (commitment)

For durability and atomicity, transactions are ordinarily done in a "tentative" way, in which the changes to the database are computed but not actually made in the database itself. By the time the transaction is ready to complete, or *commit*, the changes have been copied to a *log*. This log record is first copied to disk. Only then are the changes entered into the database itself.

Even if the system fails in the middle of the two steps, when the system comes back up we can read the log and see that the changes still need to be made to the database. If the system fails before all changes have been entered in the log, we can redo the transaction, sure that we are not accidentally booking an airline seat twice or debiting a bank account twice, for example.

1.2.5 Client-Server Architecture

Many varieties of modern software use a *client-server* architecture, in which requests by one process (the *client*) are sent to another process (the *server*) for execution. Database systems are no exception, and it is common to divide the work of the components shown in Fig. 1.1 into a server process and one or more client processes.

In the simplest client/server architecture, the entire DBMS is a server, except for the query interfaces that interact with the user and send queries or other commands across to the server. For example, relational systems generally use the SQL language for representing requests from the client to the server. The database server then sends the answer, in the form of a table or relation, back to the client. The relationship between client and server can get more complex, especially when answers are extremely large. We shall have more to say about this matter in Section 1.3.3. There is also a trend to put more work in the client, since the server will be a bottleneck if there are many simultaneous database users.

1.3 The Future of Database Systems

There are many currents in the database stream today, and they lead the discipline in a variety of new directions. Some of these are new technologies — object-oriented programming, constraints and triggers, multimedia data, or the World Wide Web, for example — that are changing the nature of conventional DBMS's. Other currents involve new applications, such as warehousing of data or information integration. In this section we give brief introductions to the major trends for future database systems.

1.3.1 Types, Classes, and Objects

Object-oriented programming has been widely regarded as a tool for better program organization and ultimately, more reliable software implementation. First popularized in the language Smalltalk, object-oriented programming received a big boost with the development of C++ and the migration to C++ of much software development that was formerly done in C. More recently, the language Java, suitable for sharing programs across the World Wide Web, has also increased attention on object-oriented programming. The database world has likewise been attracted to the object-oriented paradigm, and several companies are selling DBMS's dubbed "object-oriented." In this section we shall review the ideas behind object orientation.

The Type System

An object-oriented programming language offers the user a rich collection of types. Starting with *base types*, commonly integers, real numbers, booleans, and character strings, one may build new types by using *type constructors*. Typically, the type constructors let us build:

1. *Record structures.* Given a list of types $T_1, T_2, \ldots, T_n$ and a corresponding list of *field names* (called *instance variables* in Smalltalk) $f_1, f_2, \ldots, f_n$, one can construct a record type consisting of n components. The ith component has type T_i and is referred to by its field name f_i. Record structures are exactly what C or C++ calls "structs."

2. *Collection types.* Given a type T, one can construct new types by applying a *collection operator* to type T. Different languages use different collection operators, but there are several common ones, including arrays, lists, and sets. Thus, if T were the base type integer, we might build the collection types "array of integers," "list of integers," or "set of integers."

3. *Reference types.* A reference to a type T is a type whose values are suitable for locating a value of the type T. In C or C++, a reference is a "pointer" to a value, that is, a location in which is held the virtual-memory address of the value pointed to. The model of pointers is often suitable for understanding references. However, in database systems, where data is stored on many disks, perhaps distributed over many hosts, a reference is of necessity something more complex than a pointer. It might, for example, include the name of a host, a disk number, a block within that disk, and a position within the block where the referenced value is held.

Of course, record-structure and collection operators can be applied repeatedly to build ever more complex types. For instance, we might define a type that is a record structure with a first component named `customer` of type string and whose second component is of type set of integers and named `accounts`. Such a type is suitable for associating bank customers with the set of their accounts.

Classes and Objects

A class consists of a type and possibly one or more functions or procedures (called *methods*; see below) that can be executed on objects of that class. The objects of a class are either values of that type (called *immutable objects*) or variables whose value is of that type (called *mutable objects*). For example, if we define a class C whose type is "set of integers," then $\{2, 5, 7\}$ is an immutable object of class C, while variable s could be declared to be of class C and assigned the value $\{2, 5, 7\}$.

Object Identity

Objects are assumed to have an *object identity* (OID). No two objects can have the same OID, and no object has two different OID's. The OID is the value that a reference to the object has. We may often think of the OID as a pointer in virtual memory to the object but, as we discussed in connection with reference types, in a database system the OID may actually be something more complex: a sequence of bits sufficient to locate the object on secondary or tertiary memory of any of a large number of different machines. Further, since data is persistent, the OID must be valid for all time, as long as the data exists.

Methods

Associated with a class there are usually certain functions, often called *methods*. A method for a class C has at least one argument that is an object of class C; it may have other arguments of any class, including C. For example, associated with a class whose type is "set of integers," we might have a method to compute the power set of a given set, to take the union of two sets, or to return a boolean indicating whether or not the set is empty.

Abstract Data Types

In many cases, classes are also "abstract data types," meaning that they *encapsulate*, or restrict access to objects of the class so that only the methods defined for the class can modify objects of the class directly. This restriction assures that the objects of the class cannot be changed in ways that were not anticipated by the implementor of the class. This concept is regarded as one of the key tools for reliable software development.

Class Hierarchies

It is possible to declare one class C to be a *subclass* of another class D. If so, then class C *inherits* all the properties of class D, including the type of D and any functions defined for class D. However, C may also have additional properties. For example, new methods may be defined for objects of class C, and these may be either in addition to or in place of methods of D. It may even be possible to extend the type of D in certain ways. In particular, if the type of D is a record-structure type, then we can add new fields to this type that are present only in objects of type C.

Example 1.3: Consider a class of bank account objects. We might describe the type for this class informally as:

```
CLASS Account = {accountNo: integer;
                 balance: real;
                 owner: REF Customer;
                }
```

Why Objects?

Object-oriented programming offers a number of capabilities of importance in database systems.

- Through a rich type system, we can deal with data in forms that are more natural than relations or earlier data models. Note that the relational model has a rather restricted type system. Relations are sets of records, and these records have a record structure in which the fields (called "attributes" in the relational model) have base types.

- Through classes and a class hierarchy, we can share or reuse software and schemas more readily than with conventional systems.

- Through abstract data types we can protect against misuse of our data by preventing access except through some carefully designed functions that are known to use the data properly.

That is, the type for the `Account` class is a record structure with three fields: an integer account number, a real-number balance, and an owner that is a reference to an object of class `Customer` (another class that we'd need for a banking database, but whose type we have not introduced here).

We would also define some methods for the class. For example, we might have a method

```
deposit(a: Account, m: real)
```

that increases the `balance` for `Account` object a by amount m.

Finally, we might wish to have several subclasses of the `Account` subclass. For instance, a time-deposit account might have an additional field `dueDate`, the date at which the account balance may be withdrawn by the owner. There might also be an additional method for the subclass `TimeDeposit`

```
penalty(a: TimeDeposit)
```

that takes an account a belonging to the subclass `TimeDeposit` and calculates the penalty for early withdrawal, as a function of the `dueDate` field in object a and the current date; the latter would be obtainable from the system on which the method is run. □

We shall consider object-oriented aspects of database systems extensively in this book. In Section 2.1 we introduce the object-oriented database-design language ODL. Chapter 8 is devoted to object-oriented query languages. There we cover both the OQL query language that is becoming a standard for object-oriented DBMS's and the proposed object-oriented features for SQL, the standard query language for relational DBMS's.

1.3.2   Constraints and Triggers

Another recent trend in database systems has been the extensive use of active elements in commercial systems. By "active" we mean that the component of the database is available at all times, ready to execute whenever it becomes appropriate for it to do so. There are two common kinds of active elements found in database systems:

Boolean valued functions

1. *Constraints.* These are boolean-valued functions whose value is required to be true. For instance, we might place in a banking database the constraint that a balance cannot be less than 0. A database modification that violated this constraint, such as a withdrawal that would leave the account negative, is rejected by the DBMS.

P.

2. *Triggers.* A trigger is a piece of code that waits for an *event* to occur; possible events are the insertion or deletion of a certain kind of data item. When the event occurs, an associated sequence of actions is executed, or *triggered.* For instance, an airline reservation system could have a rule whose condition is triggered when a flight status is changed to `cancelled`. The action part of the rule might be a query that asks for the phone number of all customers booked on that flight, so these customers may be notified. A more complex action would be to rebook the customers on alternative flights automatically.

Active elements are not a new idea. They appeared as "ON-conditions" in the programming language PL/I. They have also appeared in artificial-intelligence systems for many years, and they are akin to "daemons" that are used in operating systems. However, when the size of the data on which the active elements operate is very large, or the number of active elements is very large, there are severe technical problems in implementing active elements efficiently. For that reason, active elements did not appear as standard components of a DBMS until the early 1990's. We discuss active elements in Chapter 6.

1.3.3   Multimedia Data

Another important trend in database systems is the inclusion of multimedia data. By "multimedia" we mean information that represents a signal of some sort. Common forms of multimedia data include video, audio, radar signals, satellite images, and documents or pictures in various encodings. These forms have in common that they are much larger than the earlier forms of data — integers, character strings of fixed length, and so on — and of vastly varying sizes.

The storage of multimedia data has forced DBMS's to expand in several ways. For example, the operations that one performs on multimedia data are not the simple ones suitable for traditional data forms. Thus, while one might search a bank database for accounts that have a negative balance, comparing each balance with the real number 0.0, it is not feasible to search a database of pictures for those that show a face that "looks like" a particular image. Thus, DBMS's have had to incorporate the ability of users to introduce functions of their own choosing, which they may apply to multimedia data. Often, the object-oriented approach is used for such extensions, even in relational systems.

The size of multimedia objects also forces the DBMS to modify the storage manager so that objects or tuples of a gigabyte or more can be accommodated. Among the many problems that such large elements present is the delivery of answers to queries. In a conventional, relational database, an answer is a set of tuples. These would be delivered to the client by the database server as a whole.

However, suppose the answer to a query is a video clip a gigabyte long. It is not feasible for the server to deliver the gigabyte to the client as a whole. For one reason it takes too long and will prevent the server from handling other requests. For another, the client may want only a small part of the film clip, but doesn't have a way to ask for exactly what it wants without seeing the initial portion of the clip. For a third reason, even if the client wants the whole clip, perhaps in order to play it on a screen, it is sufficient to deliver the clip at a fixed rate over the course of an hour (the amount of time it takes to play a gigabyte of compressed video). Thus, the storage system of a multimedia DBMS has to be prepared to deliver answers in an interactive mode, passing a piece of the answer to the client on request or at a fixed rate.

1.3.4 Data Integration

As information becomes ever more essential in our work and play, we find that existing information resources are being used in many new ways. For instance, consider a company that wants to provide on-line catalogs for all its products, so that people can use the World Wide Web to browse its products and place on-line orders. A large company has many divisions. Each division may have built its own database of products independently of other divisions. These divisions may use different DBMS's, different structures for information, perhaps even different terms to mean the same thing or the same term to mean different things.

Example 1.4: Imagine a company with several divisions that manufacture disks. One division's catalog might represent rotation rate in revolutions per second, another in revolutions per minute. Another might have neglected to represent rotation speed at all. A division manufacturing floppy disks might refer to them as "disks," while a division manufacturing hard disks might call *them* "disks" as well. The number of tracks on a disk might be referred to as "tracks" in one division, but "cylinders" in another. ☐

Central control is not always the answer. Divisions may have invested large amounts of money in their database long before integration across divisions was recognized as a problem. A division may have been an independent company, recently acquired. For these or other reasons, these so-called *legacy databases* cannot be replaced easily. Thus, the company must build some structure on top of the legacy databases to present to customers a unified view of products across the company.

One popular approach is the creation of *data warehouses*, where information from many legacy databases is copied, with the appropriate translation, to a central database. As the legacy databases change, the warehouse is updated, but not necessarily instantaneously updated. A common scheme is for the warehouse to be reconstructed each night, when the legacy databases are likely to be less busy.

The legacy databases are thus able to continue serving the purposes for which they were created. New functions, such as providing an on-line catalog service through the Web, are done at the data warehouse. We also see data warehouses serving needs for planning and analysis. For example, company analysts may run queries against the warehouse looking for sales trends, in order to better plan inventory and production. *Data mining*, the search for interesting and unusual patterns in data, has also been enabled by the construction of data warehouses, and there are claims of enhanced sales through exploitation of patterns discovered in this way.

1.4   Outline of the Book

Ideas related to database systems can be divided into three broad categories:

1. *Design of databases*. How does one build a useful database? What kinds of information goes into the database? How is the information structured? What assumptions are made about types or values of data items? How do data items connect?

2. *Database programming*. How does one express queries and other operations on the database? How does one use other capabilities of a DBMS, such as transactions or triggers?

3. *Database implementation*. How does one build a DBMS, including such matters as query processing, transaction processing and organizing storage for efficient access?

While database implementation is a major segment of the software industry, the number of people who will design or use databases far exceeds the number that will build them. This book is intended for a first course in database systems, so it is appropriate to concentrate on the first two aspects: design and programming. In this chapter we have tried to give the reader a glimpse of the third aspect — implementation — but we shall not return to the subject in this book. Rather, the remaining chapters of this book divide material on design and programming as follows.

1.4.1 Design

Chapters 2 and 3 cover design. We begin with two high-level notations for expressing database designs in Chapter 2. One, ODL (Object Definition Language), is an object-oriented language for declaring classes. The second, called the E/R or Entity/Relationship model, is a graphical notation for describing the organization of the database.

Neither ODL nor the E/R model is intended to be used directly as the definition of a database's structure, although ODL is very close to a data-definition language if the DBMS is object-oriented. Rather, it is expected that the design rendered in one of these models will be translated into whatever formal notation is used by the data-definition language associated with the DBMS being used. Since most DBMS's are relational, we concentrate on translating ODL or E/R into the relational model. Chapter 3 is thus devoted to the relational model and to the translation process. Then, in Section 5.7 we show how to render relational database schemas formally in the data-definition portion of the SQL language.

Chapter 3 also introduces the reader to the notion of "dependencies," which are formally stated assumptions about relationships among tuples in a relation. Dependencies allow us to decompose relations in beneficial ways, through a process known as "normalization" of relations. Dependencies and normalization are covered in Section 3.5 and the following sections; they are an important part of design for relational databases. The subject is useful both for those who would design their databases directly in the relational model and those who have converted an ODL or E/R design into relations and find some problems with the design.

1.4.2 Programming

Chapters 4 through 8 cover database programming. We start in Chapter 4 with an abstract treatment of queries in the relational model, introducing the family of operators on relations that form "relational algebra." We also discuss an alternative way to describe queries, based on logical expressions and called "Datalog."

Chapters 5 through 7 are devoted to SQL programming. As we mentioned, SQL is the dominant query language of the day. Chapter 5 introduces basic ideas regarding queries in SQL and the expression of database schemas in SQL. Almost all of this chapter and the following two chapters is based on a standard version of SQL called SQL2. However, certain aspects of SQL programming that are found in some commercial systems are not part of SQL2. In those cases, we use a later standard, not yet formally adopted, called SQL3.

Chapter 6 covers aspects of SQL concerning triggers and constraints on the data. Since the capability of SQL2 is limited in these areas, we devote some time to the treatment of constraints and triggers in SQL3 as well as in SQL2.

Chapter 7 covers certain advanced aspects of SQL programming. First, while the simplest model of SQL programming is a stand-alone, generic query interface, in practice most SQL programming is embedded in a larger program that is written in a conventional language, such as C. In Chapter 7 we learn how to connect SQL statements with a surrounding program and to pass data from the database to the program's variables and vice versa. This chapter also covers how one uses SQL features that specify transactions, connect clients to servers, and authorize access to databases by nonowners.

In Chapter 8 we turn our attention to emerging standards for object-oriented database programming. Here, we consider two directions. The first, OQL (Object Query Language), can be seen as an attempt to make C++ compatible with the demands of high-level database programming. The second, which is the object-oriented features found in SQL3, can be viewed as an attempt to make relational databases and SQL compatible with object-oriented programming. To an extent, these two approaches meet on a common ground. However, there are also a number of ways in which they differ substantially.

1.5   Summary of Chapter 1

+ *Database Management Systems*: A DBMS allows designers to structure their information, allows users to query and modify that information, and helps manage very large amounts of data and many concurrent operations on the data.

+ *Database Languages*: There are languages or language components for defining the structure of data (data-definition languages) and for querying and modification of the data (data-manipulation languages).

+ *Relational Database Systems*: Today, most database systems are based on the relational model of data, which organizes information into tables. SQL is the language most often used in these systems.

+ *Object-Oriented Database Systems*: Some current database systems use object-oriented data-modeling ideas, including classes, powerful type systems, object identity, and inheritance of properties by subclasses. In the future most database management systems, including relational ones, are likely to support some or all of these concepts.

+ *Secondary and Tertiary Storage*: Large databases are stored on secondary storage devices, usually disks. The largest databases require tertiary storage devices, which are several orders of magnitude more capacious than disks, but also several orders of magnitude slower.

✦ *Components of a DBMS*: The principal components of a database management system are the query processor, transaction manager, and storage manager.

✦ *The Storage Manager*: The storage manager handles both files of data on secondary storage and the main-memory buffers that hold parts of these files. A database management system normally maintains indexes, which are data structures that support efficient access to data.

✦ *The Query Manager*: An important job of the query manager is to "optimize" queries, that is, to find a good algorithm for answering a given query.

✦ *The Transaction Manager*: Transactions are elementary units of work on the database. The transaction manager allows many transactions to execute concurrently, while making certain that transactions have the ACID properties: atomic, consistent, isolated, and durable.

✦ *Client-Server Systems*: Database management systems usually support a client-server architecture, with major database components at the server and the client used to interface with the user.

✦ *Active Database Elements*: Modern database systems support some form of active elements, usually triggers and/or integrity constraints.

✦ *Future Systems*: Major trends in database systems include support for very large "multimedia" objects such as videos or images and the integration of information from many separate information sources into a single database.

1.6 References for Chapter 1

There are a number of books that cover important aspects of the implementation of database systems. [3] and [5] cover implementation of a transaction manager. Distributed database implementation is treated in these works and [7]. Implementation of a file manager is discussed in [11].

Object-oriented database systems are treated in [2], [4], and [6]. The theory of database systems is covered in [1], [9], and [10]. Many of the research papers that shaped the database field are found in [8].

1. Abiteboul, S., R. Hull, and V. Vianu, *Foundations of Databases*, Addison-Wesley, Reading, MA, 1995.

2. Bancilhon, F., C. Delobel, and P. Kanellakis, *Building an Object-Oriented Database System*, Morgan-Kaufmann, San Francisco, 1992.

3. Bernstein, P. A., V. Hadzilacos, and N. Goodman, *Concurrency Control and Recovery in Database Systems*, Addison-Wesley, Reading, MA, 1987.

4. Cattell, R. G. G., *Object Data Management*, Addison-Wesley, Reading, MA, 1994.

5. Gray, J. N. and A. Reuter, *Transaction Processing: Concepts and Techniques*, Morgan-Kaufmann, San Francisco, 1993.

6. Kim, W. (ed.), *Modern Database Systems: The Object Model, Interoperability, and Beyond*, ACM Press, New York, 1994.

7. Oszu, M. T. and P. Valduriez, *Principles of Distributed Database Systems*, Prentice Hall, Englewood Cliffs, NJ, 1991.

8. Stonebraker, M. (ed.), *Readings in Database Systems*, Morgan-Kaufmann, San Francisco, 1994.

9. Ullman, J. D., *Principles of Database and Knowledge-Base Systems, Volume I*, Computer Science Press, New York, 1988.

10. Ullman, J. D., *Principles of Database and Knowledge-Base Systems, Volume II*, Computer Science Press, New York, 1989.

11. Wiederhold, G., *Database Design*, McGraw-Hill, New York, 1983.

Chapter 2

Database Modeling

The process of designing a database begins with an analysis of what information the database must hold and the relationships among components of that information. Often, the structure of the database, called the *database schema*, is specified in one of several languages or notations suitable for expressing designs. After due consideration, the design is committed to a form in which it can be input to a database management system, and the database takes on physical existence.

In this book, we shall use two design notations. The more traditional approach, called the "entity-relationship" (E/R) model, is graphical in nature, with boxes and arrows representing the essential data elements and their connections. We shall, in parallel, introduce ODL (Object Definition Language), an object-oriented approach to database design that is an emerging standard for object-oriented database systems. This chapter also mentions two other models — the network and hierarchical models — that are primarily of historical interest. They are in a sense restricted versions of ODL, and they were used in commercial database systems that were implemented in the 1970's.

In Chapter 3 we turn attention to the relational model, where the world is represented by a collection of tables. The relational model is somewhat restricted in the structures it can represent. However, the model is extremely simple and useful, and it is the model on which the major commercial database management systems are based today. Often, database designers begin by developing a schema using the E/R or an object-based model, then translate the schema to the relational model for implementation.

Figure 2.1 suggests the design process. We start with ideas about the information we want to model. These ideas will be rendered in some design language; we show entity-relationship and ODL as the two alternatives, although there are others, of course. In the majority of cases, the designs will then be implemented by a relational database management system. If so, then by a fairly mechanical process that we shall discuss in Chapter 3, the abstract design is converted to a concrete, relational database implementation. We also show an alterna-

25

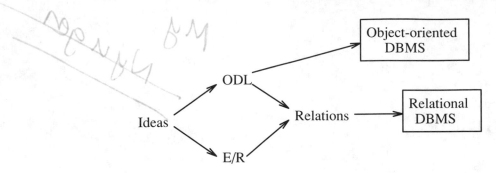

Figure 2.1: The database modeling and implementation process

tive path where an ODL design becomes input to an object-oriented database management system. In that case, the translation is rather automatic, perhaps involving a simple translation from ODL dictions to corresponding dictions in an object-oriented programming language like C++ or Smalltalk.

2.1   Introduction to ODL

ODL (Object Definition Language) is a proposed standard language for specifying the structure of databases in object-oriented terms, as one finds in languages such as C++ or Smalltalk. It is an extension of IDL (Interface Description Language), a component of CORBA (Common Object Request Broker Architecture). The latter is an emerging standard for distributed, object-oriented computing.

The primary purpose of ODL is to allow object-oriented designs of databases to be written and then translated directly into declarations of an object-oriented database management system (OODBMS). Since such systems usually have either C++ or Smalltalk as their primary language, ODL must be translated into declarations of one of these languages. ODL resembles both these languages (but C++ more so), so the translation suggested by Fig. 2.2 is quite straightforward. In comparison, the translation from ODL or entity-relationship designs into declarations suitable for the more common relational database management systems (RDBMS) is considerably more complex.

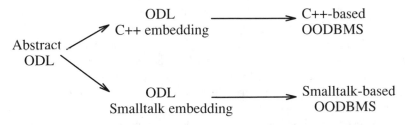

Figure 2.2: Converting ODL designs into declarations for an OODBMS

Schemas and Data

ODL is a language for specifying the schema or structure of a database. It does not provide facilities to specify the actual content of the database, nor does ODL provide for queries or operations on the data. As we mentioned in Section 1.1, schema-specifying languages like ODL are often referred to as *data-definition languages*, while languages that allow us to specify the content of the database or to query and modify that data are similarly called *data-manipulation languages*. We shall not discuss data-manipulation languages until we look at databases from the point of view of the user in Chapter 4. Data-definition languages, on the other hand, are the core of the study of databases from the point of view of the designer.

2.1.1 Object-Oriented Design

In an object-oriented design, the world to be modeled is thought of as composed of *objects*, which are observable entities of some sort. For example, people may be thought of as objects; so may bank accounts, airline flights, courses at a college, buildings, and so on. Objects are assumed to have a unique *object identity* (OID) that distinguishes them from any other object, as we discussed in Section 1.3.1.

To organize information, we usually want to group objects into *classes* of objects with similar properties. The concepts of "object" and "class" in databases are essentially the same as those notions found in object-oriented programming languages such as C++ or Smalltalk (again, recall our discussion of object-oriented concepts in Section 1.3.1). However, when speaking of ODL object-oriented designs, we should think of "similar properties" of the objects in a class in two different ways:

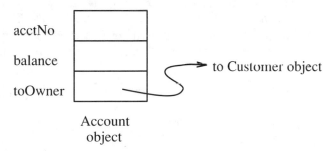

Figure 2.3: An object representing an account

- The real-world concepts represented by the objects of a class should be similar. For instance, it makes sense to group all customers of a bank into

---

The Nature of OID's

As we mentioned in Section 1.3.1, object-oriented databases are often so large that the number of OID's needed far exceeds the number of addresses in an address space. Thus, object-oriented database systems generally have some scheme for creating unique strings associated with each object; often these strings are quite long, perhaps 16 bytes. For example, an object might get as an OID the time of its creation (measured in small enough units that two could not be created by a single machine at one time) together with an identifier for the host that created it (if the database system is distributed over several hosts).

---

one class and all accounts at the bank into another class. It would not make sense to group customers and accounts together in one class, because they have little or nothing in common and play essentially different roles in the world of banking.

- The properties of objects in a class must be the same. When programming in an object-oriented language, we often think of objects as records, like that suggested by Fig. 2.3. Objects have fields or slots in which values are placed. These values may be of common types such as integers, strings, or arrays, or they may be references to other objects. They may also be methods, that is, functions to apply to the object. However, in our study of ODL we shall not emphasize the use of methods, which is similar to their use in any object-oriented programming language. We return to the subject of ODL methods in Section 8.1.

While it is often helpful to think of objects as having a record structure, this chapter is devoted to design at an abstract level. Thus, we shall emphasize the first, more abstract notion of a class and its properties, without concerning ourselves with the details of implementation such as how fields of a record are ordered, or even if an object really is represented by a record structure.

When specifying the design of ODL classes, we describe properties of three kinds:

1. *Attributes*, which are properties whose types are built from primitive types such as integers or strings. Specifically, an attribute has a type that does not involve any class. In ODL, attribute types are limited; we discuss the matter further in Section 2.1.7.

2. *Relationships*, which are properties whose type is either a reference to an object of some class or a collection (e.g., a set) of such references.

3. *Methods*, which are functions that may be applied to objects of the class. As mentioned above, we shall not emphasize the use of methods here.

2.1.2 Interface Declarations

A declaration of a class in ODL, in its simplest form, consists of:

1. The keyword `interface`.

2. The name of the interface (i.e., class).

3. A bracketed list of properties of the class. Recall these properties are attributes, relationships, and methods.

That is, the simple form of an interface declaration is

interface <name> {
  <list of properties>
}

2.1.3 Attributes in ODL

The simplest kind of properties are called *attributes*. These properties describe some aspect of an object by associating with that object a value of some simple type. For example, person objects might each have an attribute `name` whose type is string and whose value is the name of that person. Person objects might also have an attribute `birthdate` that is a triple of integers (i.e., a record structure) representing the year, month, and day of their birth.

Example 2.1: In Fig. 2.4 is an ODL declaration of the class of movies. It is not a complete declaration; we shall add more to it later. Line (1) declares `Movie` to be a class. The keyword `interface` is used in ODL to indicate a class.[1] Following line (1) are the declarations of four attributes that all `Movie` objects will have.

```
1)   interface Movie {
2)       attribute string title;
3)       attribute integer year;
4)       attribute integer length;
5)       attribute enum Film {color,blackAndWhite} filmType;
     };
```

Figure 2.4: An ODL declaration of the class `Movie`

The first attribute, on line (2), is named `title`. Its type is `string`—a character string of unknown length. We expect the value of the `title` attribute

---

[1] Technically, in ODL a class is an interface plus an implementation for the data structures and methods associated with the interface. We shall not discuss implementations of ODL interfaces in this section, but we shall continue to refer to interface declarations as defining "classes."

in any `Movie` object to be the name of the movie. The next two attributes, `year` and `length` declared on lines (3) and (4), have integer type and represent the year in which the movie was made and its length in minutes, respectively. On line (5) is another attribute `filmType`, which tells whether the movie was filmed in color or black-and-white. Its type is an *enumeration*, and the name of the enumeration is `Film`. Values of enumeration attributes are chosen from a list of *literals*, `color` and `blackAndWhite` in this example.

An object in the class `Movie` as we have defined it so far can be thought of as a record or tuple with four components, one for each of the four attributes. For example,

("Gone With the Wind", 1939, 231, color)

is a `Movie` object.   □

Example 2.2 : In Example 2.1, all the attributes have atomic types. We can also have attributes whose types are structures, collections, or collections of structures, as we shall discuss in Section 2.1.7. Here is an example with a nonatomic type.

We can define the class `Star` by

```
1)    interface Star {
2)        attribute string name;
3)        attribute Struct Addr
              {string street, string city} address;
      };
```

Line (2) specifies an attribute `name` (of the star) that is a string. Line (3) specifies another attribute `address`. This attribute has a type that is a *record structure*. The name of this type is `Addr` and the type consists of two fields: `street` and `city`. Both fields are strings. In general, one can define record structure types in ODL by the keyword `Struct` and curly braces around the list of field names and their types.   □

2.1.4   Relationships in ODL

While we can learn much about an object by examining its attributes, sometimes a critical fact about an object is the way it connects to other objects in the same or another class.

Example 2.3 : Now, suppose we want to add to the declaration of the `Movie` class from Example 2.1 a property that is a set of stars. Since stars are themselves a class, as described in Example 2.2, we cannot make this information an attribute of `Movie`, because attribute types must not be classes or built from classes. Rather, the set of stars of a movie is a *relationship* between the classes `Movie` and `Star`. We represent this relationship by a line

```
relationship Set<Star> stars;
```

in the declaration of class Movie. This line may appear in Fig. 2.4 after any of the lines numbered (1) through (5). It says that in each object of class Movie there is a set of references to Star objects. The set of references is called stars. The keyword relationship specifies that stars contains references to other objects, while the keyword Set preceding <Stars> indicates that stars references a set of Star objects, rather than a single object. In general, a type that is a set of elements of some other type T is defined in ODL by the keyword Set and angle brackets around the type T.

In physical terms, we might imagine the set stars to be represented by a list of pointers to Star objects; the Star objects would not appear physically inside the Movie object. However, in the database design phase, the physical representation is not known, and the important aspect of a relationship is that from a Movie object one can find the stars of that movie conveniently. □

In Example 2.3 we saw a relationship that associated a set of objects, the stars, with a single object, the movie. It is also possible to have a relationship that associates a single object with an object of the class being declared. For instance, suppose we had given the type of the relationship in Example 2.3 as Star rather than Set<Star>, in a line such as

```
relationship Star starOf;
```

Then this relationship would associate with each movie a single Star object. That arrangement would not make too much sense here, since typically a movie has several stars. However, we shall see many other examples where a single-valued relationship is appropriate.

2.1.5 Inverse Relationships

Just as we might like to access the stars of a given movie, we might like to know the movies in which a given star acted. To get this information into Star objects, we can add the line

```
relationship Set<Movie> starredIn;
```

to the declaration of class Star in Example 2.2. However, this line and a similar declaration for Movie omits a very important aspect of the relationship between movies and stars. We expect that if a star S is in the stars set for movie M, then movie M is in the starredIn set for star S. We indicate this connection between the relationships stars and starredIn by placing in each of their declarations the keyword inverse and the name of the other relationship. If the other relationship is in some other class, as it usually is, then we refer to that relationship by the name of its class, followed by a double colon (::) and the name of the relationship.

Example 2.4: To define the relationship starredIn of class Star to be the inverse of the relationship stars in class Movie, we revise the declaration of class

Star to be that shown in Fig. 2.5. We see in line (4) not only the declaration of the relationship starredIn but the fact that it has an inverse, Movie::stars. Since relationship stars is defined in another class, the relationship name is preceded by the name of that class (Movie) and a double colon. This notation is used in general when referring to a property of a different class. □

```
1)    interface Star {
2)        attribute string name;
3)        attribute Struct Addr
              {string street, string city} address;
4)        relationship Set<Movie> starredIn
                  inverse Movie::stars;
      };
```

Figure 2.5: Class Star, showing a relationship and its inverse

In Example 2.4 the two inverse relationships each associated an object (a movie or a star) with a set of objects. As we mentioned, there are other relationships that associate an object with a single object of another class. The notion of inverse does not change. As a general rule, if a relationship R for class C associates with object x of class C the set of one or more objects $y_1, y_2, \ldots, y_n$, then the inverse relationship of R associates with each of the y_i's the object x (perhaps along with other objects).

Sometimes, it helps to visualize a relationship R from class C to some class D as a list of pairs, or tuples, of a relation. Each pair consists of an object x from class C and an associated object y of class D, as:

C	D
x_1	y_1
x_2	y_2
$\ldots$	$\ldots$

If R is of type Set<D>, then there may be more than one pair with the same C-value. If R is of type D, then there can be only one pair with a given C-value.

Then the inverse relationship for R is the set of pairs with the components reversed, as:

D	C
y_1	x_1
y_2	x_2
$\ldots$	$\ldots$

Notice that this rule works even if C and D are the same class. There are some relationships that logically run from a class to itself, such as "child of" from the class "Persons" to itself.

About the Requirement for Relationship Inverses

As an abstract design language, ODL requires that relationships have inverses. The interpretation of this requirement is that whenever we have a way to go from an object, say a movie object, to its related objects such as star objects, then it is also possible to go in the opposite direction, from a star to the movies in which they starred. That is, given a star like Charlton Heston, we can examine all the movie objects and check their stars. We may then list those that Heston starred in. ODL requires that this inverse process be given a relationship name.

However, when we turn ODL into real programming language declarations, say in its C++ embedding, we know that it is possible to put references only in the movie objects and not have references to movies in the star objects. Thus, the C++ embedding of ODL allows "one-way" relationships. Since we are concerned here with design, not implementation, we shall expect that relationships have inverses.

2.1.6 Multiplicity of Relationships

It is often significant whether a relationship associates a given object with a unique related object, or whether an object can be related to many other objects. In ODL we can specify these options by using or not using a collection operator like Set in the relationship declaration. When we have an inverse pair of relationships, there are four possible options: the relationship can be unique in either direction, in both directions, or in neither direction.

The relationship between stars and movies that we have been discussing is unique in neither direction. That is, a movie typically has several stars, and a star appears in several movies. The following example is an elaboration of the previous examples, in which we introduce another class, Studio, representing the studio companies that produce movies.

Example 2.5: In Fig. 2.6 we have the declaration of three classes, Movie, Star, and Studio. The first two of these have already been introduced in Examples 2.1 and 2.2. Studio objects have attributes name and address; these appear in lines (13) and (14). Notice that the type of addresses here is a string, rather than a structure as was used for the address attribute of class Star on line (10). There is nothing wrong with using attributes of the same name but different types in different classes.

In line (7) we see a relationship ownedBy from movies to studios. Since the type of the relationship is Studio, and not Set<Studio>, we are declaring that for each movie there is a unique studio that owns it. The inverse of this relationship is found on line (15). There we see the relationship owns from studios to movies. The type of this relationship is Set<Movie>, indicating that

```
1)   interface Movie {
2)       attribute string title;
3)       attribute integer year;
4)       attribute integer length;
5)       attribute enum Film {color,blackAndWhite} filmType;
6)       relationship Set<Star> stars
                    inverse Star::starredIn;
7)       relationship Studio ownedBy
                    inverse Studio::owns;
     };

8)   interface Star {
9)       attribute string name;
10)      attribute Struct Addr
             {string street, string city} address;
11)      relationship Set<Movie> starredIn
                    inverse Movie::stars;
     };

12)  interface Studio {
13)      attribute string name;
14)      attribute string address;
15)      relationship Set<Movie> owns
                    inverse Movie::ownedBy;
     };
```

Figure 2.6: Some ODL classes and their relationships

each studio owns a set of movies—perhaps 0, perhaps 1, or perhaps a large number of movies.   □

The uniqueness requirements for a relationship and its inverse are called the *multiplicity* of the relationships. The three most common multiplicities are:

1. A *many-many* relationship from a class C to a class D is one in which there is a set of D's associated with each C and, in the inverse relationship, a set of C's associated with each D. For example, in Fig. 2.6, stars is a many-many relationship from class Movie to class Star, and starredIn is many-many from Star to Movie. In each direction, it is permitted for the set to be empty; e.g., there might be no stars known for a certain movie.

2. A *many-one* relationship *from* class C *to* class D is one where for each C there is a unique D, but in the inverse relationship there is a set of C's

---

Implications Among Relationship Types

We should be aware that a many-one relationship is a special case of a many-many relationship, and a one-one relationship is a special case of a many-one relationship. That is, any useful property of many-many relationships applies to many-one relationships as well, and a useful property of many-one relationships holds for one-one relationships too. For example, a data structure for representing many-one relationships will work for one-one relationships, although it might not work for many-many relationships.

Notice also that if we say a relationship R is "many-many," we really mean that R has the *freedom* to be many-many. As R changes, it might at some time be many-one or even one-one. Likewise, a many-one relationship R might at some time be one-one.

---

associated with each D. In Fig. 2.6, `ownedBy` is a many-one relationship from `Movie` to `Studio`. We say that the inverse relationship is *one-many* from class D to class C. In Fig. 2.6, relationship `owns` is one-many from `Studio` to `Movie`, for example.

3. A *one-one* relationship from class C to class D is one where each C is related to a unique D and, in the inverse relationship, each D is related to a unique C. For example, suppose we augmented Fig. 2.6 with a class `President` representing the presidents of studios. We expect that each studio has only one president, and no president can be president of more than one studio. Thus, the relationships between studios and their presidents would be one-one in both directions.

There is a subtle point in our use of terms like "unique" or like "one" in many-one or one-one. It is normal to expect that the "unique" or "one" element actually exists. For example, for each movie there really is one owning studio, and for each studio there really is a president. However, in practice, there are reasons why the expected unique object does not exist. For instance, the studio might temporarily be without a president, or we might not know which studio owns a certain movie.

Thus, we shall normally allow that the expected unique value of a related object might be missing. We shall see later that a "null" value is often allowed in a database where a true value is expected. For example, in conventional programming terms we might find a nil pointer where a pointer to a single object was expected. In Section 2.5 we shall take up the subject of integrity constraints and see mechanisms for stipulating that intended unique objects must exist without exception.

2.1.7   Types in ODL

ODL offers the database designer a type system similar to that found in C or
other conventional programming languages. A type system is built from a basis
of types that are defined by themselves and certain recursive rules whereby
complex types are built from simpler types. In ODL, the basis consists of:

1. *Atomic types*: integer, float, character, character string, boolean, and
   enumerations. The latter are lists of names declared to be synonyms for
   integers. We saw an example of an enumeration in line (5) of Fig. 2.6,
   where the names `color` and `blackAndWhite` were defined, in effect, to be
   synonyms for the integers 0 and 1.

2. *Interface types*, such as `Movie`, or `Star`, which represent types that are
   actually structures, with components for each of the attributes and relationships of that interface. These names represent complex types defined
   using the rules below, but we may think of them as basic types.

   These basic types are combined into structured types using the following
type constructors:

1. *Set*. If T is any type, then `Set<T>` denotes the type whose values are
   all finite sets of elements of type T. Examples of using the set type-
   constructor occur in lines (6), (11), and (15) of Fig. 2.6.

2. *Bag*. If T is any type, then `Bag<T>` denotes the type whose values are bags
   or *multisets* of elements of type T. A bag allows an element to appear
   more than once. For example, $\{1, 2, 1\}$ is a bag but not a set, because 1
   appears more than once.

3. *List*. If T is any type, then `List<T>` denotes the type whose values are
   finite lists of zero or more elements of type T. As a special case, the type
   `string` is a shorthand for the type `List<char>`.

4. *Array*. If T is a type and i is an integer, then `Array<T,i>` denotes the
   type whose elements are arrays of i elements of type T. For example,
   `Array<char,10>` denotes character strings of length 10.

5. *Structures*. If $T_1, T_2, \ldots, T_n$ are types, and $F_1, F_2, \ldots, F_n$ are names of
   fields, then

$$\texttt{Struct N \{T}_1 \texttt{ F}_1\texttt{, T}_2 \texttt{ F}_2\texttt{,} \ldots \texttt{, F}_n \texttt{ T}_n\texttt{\}}$$

   denotes the type named N whose elements are structures with n fields.
   The ith field is named F_i and has type T_i. For example, line (10) of
   Fig. 2.6 showed a structure type named `Addr`, with two fields. Both fields
   are of type `string` and have names `street` and `city`, respectively.

Sets, Bags, and Lists

To understand the distinction between sets, bags, and lists, remember that a set has unordered elements, and only one occurrence of each element. A bag allows more than one occurrence of an element, but the elements and their occurrences are unordered. A list allows more than one occurrence of an element, but the occurrences are ordered. Thus, $\{1, 2, 1\}$ and $\{2, 1, 1\}$ are the same bag, but $(1, 2, 1)$ and $(2, 1, 1)$ are not the same list.

The first four types — set, bag, list, and array — are called *collection types*. There are different rules about which types may be associated with attributes and which with relationships.

- The type of an attribute is built starting with either an atomic type or a structure whose fields are atomic types. Then we may optionally apply a collection type to the initial atomic type or structure.

- The type of a relationship is either an interface type or a collection type applied to an interface type.

It is important to remember that interface types may not appear in the type of an attribute and atomic types do not appear in the type of a relationship. It is this distinction that separates attributes and relationships. Also notice that there is a difference in the way complex types are built for attributes and relationships. Each allows an optional collection type as the final operator, but only attributes allow a structure type.

Example 2.6: Some of the possible types of attributes are:

1. `integer`.

2. `Struct N {string field1, integer field2}`.

3. `List<real>`.

4. `Array<Struct N {string field1, integer field2}>`.

Example (1) is an atomic type; (2) is a structure of atomic types, (3) a collection of an atomic type, and (4) a collection of structures built from atomic types. These are the only four possibilities for attribute types.

Now, suppose the interface names `Movie` and `Star` are available basic types. Then we may construct relationship types such as `Movie` or `Bag<Star>`. However, the following are illegal as relationship types:

1. `Struct N {Movie field1, Star field2}`. Relationship types cannot involve structures.

2. `Set<integer>`. Relationship types cannot involve atomic types.

3. `Set<Array<Star>>`. Relationship types cannot involve two applications of collection types (neither can attribute types).

☐

2.1.8   Exercises for Section 2.1

* **Exercise 2.1.1 :** Let us design a database for a bank, including information about customers and their accounts. Information about a customer includes their name, address, phone, and Social Security number. Accounts have numbers, types (e.g., savings, checking) and balances. We also need to record the customer(s) who own an account. Give a description in ODL of this database. Pick appropriate types for all attributes and relationships.

Exercise 2.1.2 : Modify your design of Exercise 2.1.1 in the following ways. Describe the changes; do not write a complete, new schema.

  a) There is only one customer that can be listed as the owner of an account.

  b) In addition to (a), a customer may not have more than one account.

  c) Addresses have three components: street, city, and state. In addition, customers can have any number of listed addresses and phones.

 ! d) Customers can have any number of addresses, which are triples as in (c), and associated with any address is a set of phones. That is, we need to record for each of a customer's addresses, which phones ring at each address. *Note*: be careful of the limitations on types for attributes and/or relationships.

Exercise 2.1.3 : Give an ODL design for a database recording information about teams, players, and their fans, including:

  1. For each team, its name, its players, its team captain (one of its players), and the colors of its uniform.

  2. For each player, his/her name.

  3. For each fan, his/her name, favorite teams, favorite players, and favorite color.

Exercise 2.1.4 : Modify Exercise 2.1.3 to record for each player the history of teams on which they have played, including the start date and ending date (if they were traded) for each such team.

```
1)   interface Ship {
2)       attribute string name;
3)       attribute int yearLaunched;
4)       relationship TG assignedTo inverse TG::unitsOf;
     };

5)   interface TG {
6)       attribute real number;
7)       attribute string commander;
8)       relationship Set<Ship> unitsOf
             inverse Ship::assignedTo;
     };
```

Figure 2.7: An ODL description of ships and task groups

*! **Exercise 2.1.5:** Suppose we wish to keep a genealogy. We shall have one class, Person. The information we wish to record about persons includes their name (an attribute) and the following relationships: mother, father, and children. Give an ODL design for the Person class. Be sure to indicate the inverses of the relationships, which, like mother, father, and children, are also relationships from Person to itself. Is the inverse of the mother relationship the children relationship? Why or why not? Describe each of the relationships and their inverses as sets of pairs.

! **Exercise 2.1.6:** Let us add to the design of Exercise 2.1.5 the attribute education. The value of this attribute is intended to be a collection of the degrees obtained by each person, including the name of the degree (e.g., B.S.), the school, and the date. This collection of structs could be a set, bag, list, or array. Describe the consequences of each of these four choices. What information could be gained or lost by making each choice? Is the information lost likely to be important in practice?

! **Exercise 2.1.7:** Design a database suitable for a university registrar. This database should include information about students, departments, professors, courses, which students are enrolled in which courses, which professors are teaching which courses, student grades, TA's for a course (TA's are students), which courses a department offers, and any other information you deem appropriate. Note that this question is more free-form than the questions above, and you need to make some decisions about multiplicities of relationships, appropriate types, and even what information needs to be represented.

Exercise 2.1.8: In Fig. 2.7 is an ODL definition for the classes Ship and TG (*task group*, a collection of ships). We would like to make some modifications to this definition. Each modification can be described by mentioning a line or lines to be changed and giving the replacement, or by inserting one or more new lines after one of the numbered lines. Describe the following modifications:

a) The type of the attribute `commander` is changed to be a pair of strings, the first of which is the rank and the second of which is the name.

b) A ship is allowed to be assigned to more than one task group.

c) *Sister ships* are identical ships made from the same plans. We wish to represent, for each ship, the set of its sister ships (other than itself). You may assume that each ship's sister ships are `Ship` objects.

*!! Exercise 2.1.9: Under what circumstances is a relationship its own inverse? *Hint*: Think about the relationship as a set of pairs, as discussed in Section 2.1.5.

*! Exercise 2.1.10: Can a type ever be legal as both the type of an ODL attribute and the type of an ODL relation? Explain why or why not.

2.2   Entity-Relationship Diagrams

There is a graphical approach to database modeling, called *entity-relationship diagrams*, that bears a significant resemblance to the ODL object-oriented approach. Entity-relationship (or E/R) diagrams have the same three principal components as appeared in our initial discussion of ODL (although both the E/R and ODL models have additional features that we shall discuss later). These components are:

1. *Entity sets*, which are analogous to classes. *Entities*, which are members of an entity set, are analogous to objects in ODL.

2. *Attributes*, which are values describing some property of an entity. Thus, attributes in E/R and ODL are essentially the same concept.

3. *Relationships*, which are connections among two or more entity sets. Relationships in the E/R model are quite similar to relationships in ODL. However:

   (a) In the E/R model we give one name to a relationship in both directions, while in ODL we separately specify a relationship and its inverse. For example, the inverse relationships `Movie::stars` and `Star::starredIn` of Fig. 2.6 would be represented in the E/R model by a single relationship.

   (b) Relationships in the E/R model can involve more than two entity sets, while ODL relationships involve at most two classes.

Example 2.7: In Fig. 2.8 is an E/R diagram that represents the same real-world information as the ODL declarations of Fig. 2.6. The entity sets are *Movies*, *Stars*, and *Studios*. We shall name entity sets in the plural, while classes are often given singular names, which explains the slight difference in names between here and Fig. 2.6.

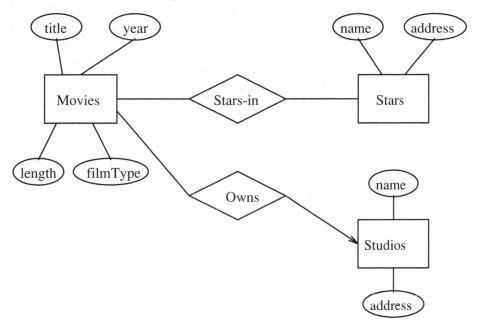

Figure 2.8: An entity-relationship diagram for the movie database

The *Movies* entity set has the same four attributes that class Movie has in Fig. 2.6: *title*, *year*, *length*, and *filmType*. Similarly, the other two entity sets have the name and address attributes that were declared for their corresponding ODL classes.

We also see in Fig. 2.8 E/R relationships corresponding to the relationships in the ODL declarations of Fig. 2.6. One relationship is *Stars-in*, which embodies the information in the pair of inverse relationships stars and starredIn from the ODL classes Movie and Star, respectively. The E/R relationship Owns in Fig. 2.8 represents the ODL inverse relationships Movie::ownedBy and Studio::owns. The arrow pointing to entity set *Studios* in Fig. 2.8 indicates that each movie is owned by a unique studio. We shall discuss issues of multiplicity in E/R diagrams next. □

2.2.1 Multiplicity of E/R Relationships

As we saw in Example 2.7, arrows can be used to indicate the multiplicity of a relationship in an E/R diagram. If a relationship is many-one from entity set

---

Visualizing E/R Relationships

It is often helpful to represent E/R relationships by a table or relation, with each row representing a pair of entities participating in the relationship. For instance the *Stars-in* relationship could be visualized as a table with pairs such as:

Movies	*Stars*
Basic Instinct	Sharon Stone
Total Recall	Arnold Schwarzenegger
Total Recall	Sharon Stone

Of course, there is no particular way that relationships must be implemented, either in ODL or in the E/R model.

This table is sometimes called the *relationship set* for the relationship. The members of the relationship set are the rows of the table. Rows can be represented as tuples, with components for each participating entity set. For instance,

(Basic Instinct, Sharon Stone)

is a tuple in the relationship set for relationship *Stars-in*.

E to entity set F, then we place an arrow entering F. The arrow indicates that each entity in set E is related to exactly one entity in set F. However, an entity in F may be related to many entities in E.

Following this principle, a one-one relationship between entity sets E and F is represented by arrows pointing to both E and F. For example, Fig. 2.9 shows two entity sets, *Studios* and *Presidents*, and the relationship *Runs* between them (attributes are omitted). We assume that a president can run only one studio and a studio has only one president, so this relationship is one-one, as indicated by the two arrows, one entering each entity set.

Figure 2.9: A one-one relationship

2.2.2 Multiway Relationships

Unlike ODL, the E/R model makes it convenient to define relationships involving more than two entity sets. However, in practice, ternary (three-way) or higher-degree relationships are rare. A multiway relationship in an E/R diagram is represented by lines from the relationship diamond to each of the involved entity sets.

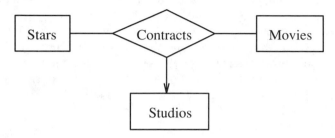

Figure 2.10: A three-way relationship

Example 2.8 : In Fig. 2.10 is a relationship *Contracts* that involves a studio, a star, and a movie. This relationship represents that a studio has contracted with a particular star to act in a particular movie. In general, the value of an E/R relationship can be thought of as a relationship set of tuples whose components are the entities participating in the relationship, as we discussed in the box on "Visualizing E/R Relationships." Thus, relationship *Contracts* can be described by 3-tuples of the form

$$\text{(studio, star, movie)}$$

In multiway relationships, an arrow pointing to an entity set E means that if we select one entity from each of the other entity sets in the relationship, those entities are related to a unique entity in E. (Note that this definition simply generalizes the notion of multiplicity we used for two-way relationships.) In Fig. 2.10 we have an arrow pointing to entity set *Studios*, indicating that for a particular star and movie, there is only one studio with which the star has contracted for that movie. However, there are no arrows pointing to entity sets *Stars* or *Movies*. A studio may contract with several stars for a movie, and a star may contract with one studio for more than one movie. □

2.2.3   Roles in Relationships

It is possible that one entity set appears two or more times in a single relationship. If so, we draw as many lines from the relationship to the entity set as the entity set appears in the relationship. Each line to the entity set represents a different *role* that the entity set plays in the relationship. We therefore label the edges between the entity set and relationship by names, which we call "roles."

Example 2.9 : In Fig. 2.11 is a relationship *Sequel-of* between the entity set *Movies* and itself. Each relationship is between two movies, one of which is

---

Limits on Arrow Notation in Multiway Relationships

There are not enough choices of arrow or no-arrow on the lines attached to a relationship with three or more participants. Thus, we cannot describe every possible situation with arrows. For instance, in Fig. 2.10, the studio is really a function of the movie alone, not the star and movie jointly, since only one studio produces a movie. However, our notation does not distinguish this situation from the case of a three-way relationship where the entity set pointed to by the arrow is truly a function of both other entity sets. In Section 3.5 we shall take up a formal notation — functional dependencies — that has the capability to describe all possible alternatives.

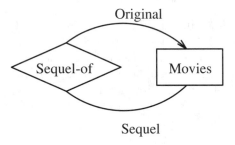

Figure 2.11: A relationship with roles

the sequel of the other. To differentiate the two movies in a relationship, one line is labeled by the role *Original* and one by the role *Sequel*, indicating the original movie and its sequel, respectively. We assume that a movie may have many sequels, but for each sequel there is only one original movie. Thus, the relationship is many-one from *Sequel* movies to *Original* movies, as indicated by the arrow in the E/R diagram of Fig. 2.11.   □

Example 2.10: As a final example that includes both a multiway relationship and an entity set with multiple roles, in Fig. 2.12 is a more complex version of the *Contracts* relationship introduced earlier in Example 2.8. Now, relationship *Contracts* involves two studios, a star, and a movie. The intent is that one studio, having a certain star under contract, may further contract with a second studio to allow that star to act in a particular movie. Thus, the relationship is described by 4-tuples of the form

$$(\text{studio1, studio2, star, movie}),$$

meaning that studio2 contracts with studio1 for the use of studio1's star by studio2 for the movie.

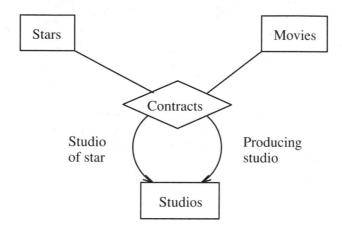

Figure 2.12: A four-way relationship

We see in Fig. 2.12 arrows pointing to *Studios* in both of its roles, as "owner" of the star and as producer of the movie. However, there are not arrows pointing to *Stars* or *Movies*. The rationale is as follows. Given a star, a movie, and a studio producing the movie, there can be only one studio that "owns" the star. (We assume a star is under contract to exactly one studio.) Similarly, only one studio produces a given movie, so given a star, a movie, and the star's studio, we can determine a unique producing studio. Note that in both cases we actually needed only one of the other entities to determine the unique entity—for example, we need only know the movie to determine the unique producing studio—but this fact does not change the multiplicity specification for the multiway relationship.

There are no arrows pointing to *Stars* or *Movies*. Given a star, the star's studio, and a producing studio, there could be several different contracts allowing the star to act in several movies. Thus, the other three components in a relationship 4-tuple do not necessarily determine a unique movie. Similarly, a producing studio might contract with some other studio to use more than one of their stars in one movie. Thus, a star is not determined by the three other components of the relationship. □

2.2.4 Attributes on Relationships

Sometimes, it is convenient to associate attributes with a relationship, rather than with any one of the entity sets that the relationship connects. For example, consider the relationship of Fig. 2.10, which represents contracts between a star and studio for a movie. We might wish to record the salary associated with this contract. However, we cannot associate it with the star; a star might get different salaries for different movies. Similarly, it does not make sense to associate the salary with a studio (they may pay different salaries to different

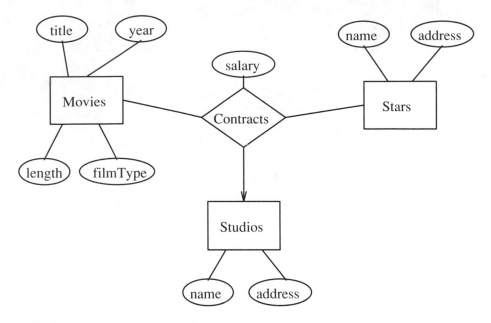

Figure 2.13: A relationship with an attribute

stars) or with a movie (different stars in a movie may receive different salaries).
However, it is appropriate to associate a salary with the

(star, movie, studio)

triple in the relationship set for the *Contracts* relationship. In Fig. 2.13 we
see Fig. 2.10 fleshed out with attributes. The relationship has attribute *salary*,
while the entity sets have the same attributes that we showed for them in
Fig. 2.8.

It is never necessary to place attributes on relationships. We can instead
invent a new entity set, whose entities have the attributes ascribed to the relationship. If we then include this entity set in the relationship, we can omit the
attributes on the relationship itself.

Example 2.11: Let us revise the E/R diagram of Fig. 2.13, which has the
salary attribute on the *Contracts* relationship. Instead, we create an entity
set *Salaries*, with attribute *salary*. *Salaries* becomes the fourth entity set of
relationship *Contracts*. The whole diagram is shown in Fig. 2.14.   □

2.2.5   Converting Multiway Relationships to Binary

Recall that, unlike the E/R model, ODL limits us to binary relationships. However, any relationship connecting more than two entity sets can be converted to

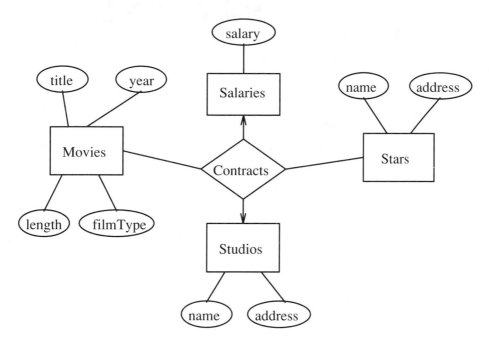

Figure 2.14: Moving the attribute to an entity set

a collection of binary, many-one relationships without losing any information. In the E/R model, we can introduce a new entity set whose entities we may think of as tuples of the relationship set for the multiway relationship. We call this entity set a *connecting* entity set. We then introduce many-one relationships from the connecting entity set to each of the entity sets that provide components of tuples in the original, multiway relationship. If an entity set plays more than one role, then it is the target of one relationship for each role.

Example 2.12: The four-way *Contracts* relationship in Fig. 2.12 can be replaced by an entity set that we may also call *Contracts*. As seen in Fig. 2.15, it participates in four relationships. If the relationship set for the relationship *Contracts* has a 4-tuple

(studio1, studio2, star, movie)

then the entity set *Contracts* has an entity *e*. This entity is linked by relationship *Star-of* to the entity *star* in entity set *Stars*. It is linked by relationship *Movie-of* to the entity *movie* in *Movies*. It is linked to entities *studio1* and *studio2* of *Studios* by relationships *Studio-of-star* and *Producing-studio*, respectively.

Note that we have assumed there are no attributes of entity set *Contracts*, although the other the entity sets in Fig. 2.15 have unseen attributes. However, it is possible to add attributes, such as the date of signing, to entity set *Contracts*. □

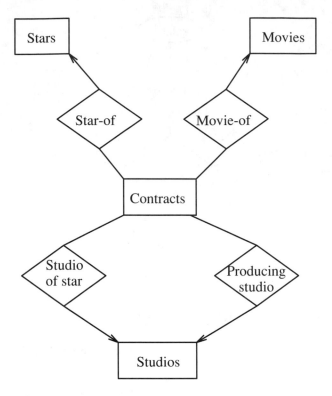

Figure 2.15: Replacing a multiway relationship by an entity set and binary relationships

In ODL we would represent a multiway relationship like Fig. 2.12 in a manner similar to the transformation described above for the E/R model. However, since there are no multiway relationships in ODL, the transformation is not optional; it is essential.

Example 2.13: Assume we have classes `Star`, `Movie` and `Studio`, corresponding to each of the three entity sets in Fig. 2.12. To represent the four-way relationship *Contracts*, we introduce a new class, say `Contract`. This class has no attributes, but it has four relationships corresponding to the four components of the E/R relationship. The ODL declaration is shown in Fig. 2.16; inverse relationships are omitted. Each 4-tuple in the E/R relationship *Contracts* corresponds to an object in the ODL class `Contract`. □

2.2.6   Exercises for Section 2.2

* **Exercise 2.2.1:** Render the bank database of Exercise 2.1.1 in the E/R model. Be sure to include arrows where appropriate, to indicate the multiplicity of a relationship.

```
interface Contract {
   relationship Studio ownerOfStar;
   relationship Studio producingStudio;
   relationship Star star;
   relationship Movie movie;
};
```

Figure 2.16: Representing contracts in ODL

Exercise 2.2.2: Modify your solution to Exercise 2.2.1 to account for the changes suggested in Exercise 2.1.2:

a) Change your diagram so an account can have only one customer.

b) Further change your diagram so a customer can have only one account.

! c) Change your original diagram of Exercise 2.2.1 so that a customer can have a set of addresses (which are street-city-state triples) and a set of phones. Remember that we do not allow attributes to have collection types in the E/R model, although they are permitted in ODL under limited circumstances.

! d) Further modify your diagram so that customers can have a set of addresses, and at each address there is a set of phones.

Exercise 2.2.3: Render the teams/players/fan database of Exercise 2.1.3 in the E/R model. Remember that a set of colors is not a suitable attribute type for teams. How can you get around this restriction?

! **Exercise 2.2.4:** Suppose we wish to add to the schema of Exercise 2.2.3 a relationship *Led-by* among two players and a team. The intention is that this relationship set consists of triples

(player1, player2, team)

such that player 1 played on the team at a time when some other player 2 was the team captain.

a) Draw the modification to the E/R diagram.

b) Replace your ternary relationship with a new entity set and binary relationships.

! c) Are your new binary relationships the same as any of the previously existing relationships? Note that we assume the two players are different, i.e., the team captain is not self-led.

Exercise 2.2.5: Modify your E/R diagram from Exercise 2.2.3 to include the player's history, as in Exercise 2.1.4.

! **Exercise 2.2.6:** Render the people database of Exercises 2.1.5 and 2.1.6 in the E/R model. Include relationships for mother, father, and children; do not forget to indicate roles when an entity set is used more than once in a relationship. Also include information about degrees obtained by each person, as described in Exercise 2.1.6. Indicate the multiplicity for each relationship. Do you need separate relationships for mother, father, and children? Why or why not?

Exercise 2.2.7: An alternative way to represent the information of Exercise 2.1.5 is to have a ternary relationship *Family* with the intent that a triple in the relationship set for *Family*

(person, mother, father)

is a person, their mother, and their father; all three are in the *People* entity set, of course.

* a) Draw this diagram (no education information is required). Place arrows on edges where appropriate.

  b) Replace the ternary relationship *Family* by an entity set and binary relationships. Again place arrows to indicate the multiplicity of relationships.

Exercise 2.2.8: Render your design of the university database from Exercise 2.1.7 in the E/R model.

2.3 Design Principles

We have yet to learn many of the details of the ODL or E/R models, but we have enough to begin study of the crucial issue of what constitutes a good design and what should be avoided. In this section, we shall try to enunciate and elaborate upon some useful principles.

2.3.1 Faithfulness

First and foremost, the design should be faithful to the specifications. That is, classes or entity sets and their attributes should reflect reality. You can't attach an attribute `number-of-cylinders` to `Star`, although it would make sense for an entity set or class `Automobile`. Whatever connections are asserted should make sense given what we know about the part of the real world being modeled.

Example 2.14: If we define a relationship *Stars-in* between *Star* and *Movie*, it should be a many-many relationship. The reason is that an observation of the real world tells us that stars can appear in more than one movie, and movies can have more than one star. It is incorrect to declare the relationship `Stars-in` to be many-one in either direction or to be one-one. □

Redundancy and Inverse Relationships

We might think that the use of a relationship and its inverse in ODL is an example of redundant design. However, we should not assume that the relationship and its inverse will be represented by two different data structures, such as pointers in one direction and pointers in the other direction. Recall the definition of relationships and their inverses merely reflected the fact that one can, in principle, traverse a relationship in either direction.

If we do, however, elect to implement the relationship by two separate data structures, then we indeed run the risks associated with redundancy. Since the underlying pointers are expected to be maintained consistently as the data changes, the implementors of an ODL-based DBMS must be careful how they execute database modifications. However, that is a system-level issue, and there is a presumption that the implementors will (eventually) get it right. There is thus less risk associated with redundancy at the implementation level, and the existence of pointers in both directions could result in a great improvement in the speed with which the relationship can be traversed.

2.3.2 Avoiding Redundancy

We should be careful to say everything once only. For instance, we have used a relationship *Owns* between movies and studios. We might also choose to have an attribute *studioName* of entity set *Movies*. While there is nothing illegal about doing so, it is dangerous for several reasons.

1. The two representations of the same owning-studio fact take more space than either representation alone.

2. If a movie were sold, we might change the owning studio to which it is related by *Owns* but forget to change the value of its *studioName* attribute, or vice versa. Of course one could argue that one should never do such careless things, but in practice, errors are frequent, and by trying to say the same thing in two different ways, we are inviting trouble.

These problems will be described more formally in Section 3.7, and we shall also learn there some tools for redesigning database schemas so the redundancy and its attendant problems go away.

2.3.3 Simplicity Counts

Avoid introducing more elements into your design than are absolutely necessary.

Example 2.15: Suppose that instead of a relationship between *Movies* and *Studios* we postulated the existence of "movie-holdings," the ownership of a single movie. We might then create another class or entity set *Holdings*. A one-one relationship *Represents* could be established between each movie and the unique holding that represents the movie. A many-one relationship from *Holdings* to *Studios* completes the picture shown in Fig. 2.17.

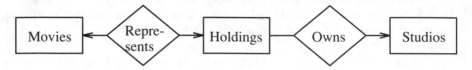

Figure 2.17: A poor design with an unnecessary entity set

Technically, the structure of Fig. 2.17 truly represents the real world, since it is possible to go from a movie to its unique owning studio via *Holdings*. However, *Holdings* serves no useful purpose, and we are better off without it. It makes programs that use the movie-studio relationship more complicated, wastes space, and encourages errors. □

2.3.4   Picking the Right Kind of Element

Sometimes we have options regarding the type of design element used to represent a real-world concept. Many of these choices are between using attributes and using classes or entity sets. In general, an attribute is simpler to implement than either a class/entity set or a relationship. However, making everything an attribute will usually get us into trouble.

Example 2.16: Let us consider a specific problem. In Fig. 2.6 or Fig. 2.8, were we wise to make studios a class or entity set? Should we instead have made the name and address of the studio be attributes of movies and eliminated the studio class or entity set? One problem with doing so is that we repeat the address of the studio for each movie. That leads to redundancy; in addition to the disadvantages of redundancy discussed in Section 2.3.2, we also face the risk that, should we not have any movies owned by a given studio, we lose the studio's address.

On the other hand, if we did not record addresses of studios, then there is no harm in making the studio name an attribute of movies. We do not have redundancy due to repeating addresses. The fact that we have to say the name of a studio like `Disney` for each movie owned by Disney is not true redundancy, since we must represent the owner of each movie somehow, and saying the name is a reasonable way to do so. □

In general, we suggest that if something has more information associated with it than just its name, it probably needs to be an entity set or class. However, if it has only its name to contribute to the design, then it probably is better made an attribute. This distinction is closely related to the question of "normalization" of schemas in the relational model that we shall take up in Section 3.7.

Example 2.17: Let us consider a point where there is a tradeoff between using a multiway relationship and using a connecting entity set with several binary relationships. We saw a four-way relationship *Contracts* among a star, a movie, and two studios in Fig. 2.12, and in Fig. 2.15 we mechanically converted it to an entity set *Contracts*. Does it matter which we choose?

In an ODL design, we really have no choice, because we do not have multiway relationships. In the E/R model, either is appropriate. However, should we change the problem just slightly, then we are almost forced to choose a connecting entity set. Let us suppose that contracts involve one star, one movie, but any set of studios. This situation is more complex than the one in Fig. 2.12, where we had two studios playing two roles. In this case, we can have any number of studios involved, perhaps one to do production, one for special effects, one for distribution, and so on. Thus, we cannot assign roles for studios.

It appears that a relationship set for the relationship *Contracts* must contain triples of the form

(star, movie, set-of-studios)

and the relationship contracts itself involves not only the usual *Stars* and *Movies* entity sets, but a new entity set whose entities are *sets of* studios. While this approach is permissible, it seems unnatural to think of sets of studios as basic entities, and we do not recommend it.

A better approach is to think of contracts as an entity set. As in Fig. 2.15, a contract entity connects a star, a movie and a set of studios, but now there must be no limit on the number of studios. Thus, the relationship between contracts and studios is many-many, rather than many-one as it would be if contracts were a true "connecting" entity set. Figure 2.18 sketches the E/R diagram. Note that a contract is associated with a single star and a single movie, but any number of studios.

The same design strategy matches ODL well. For instance, the following ODL interface declaration:

```
interface Contract {
    relationship Star theStar;
    relationship Movie theMovie;
    relationship Set<Studio> studios;
};
```

is suitable. Here, contracts objects have three relationships, to a single star, a single movie, and a set of studios. Inverse relationships are omitted. □

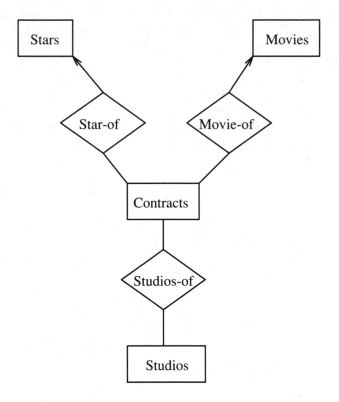

Figure 2.18: Contracts connecting a star, a movie, and a set of studios

```
interface Address {
    attribute string addr;
    relationship Set<Customer> residents
        inverse Customer::livesAt;
};

interface Customer {
    attribute string name;
    relationship Address livesAt
        inverse Address::residents;
    relationship AcctSet accounts
        inverse AcctSet::owner;
};

interface Account {
    attribute real balance;
    relationship Set<AcctSet> memberOf
        inverse AcctSet::members;
};

interface AcctSet {
    attribute string ownerAddress;
    relationship Customer owner
        inverse Customer::accounts;
    relationship Set<Accounts> members
        inverse Account::memberOf;
};
```

Figure 2.19: A poor design for a bank database

2.3.5 Exercises for Section 2.3

* **Exercise 2.3.1:** In Fig. 2.19 is an ODL design of a bank database involving customers and accounts. Assume the meaning of the various relationships and attributes are as expected, given their names. Criticize the design. What design rules are violated? Why? What modifications would you suggest?

!! **Exercise 2.3.2:** In this and following exercises we shall consider two design options in the E/R model for describing births. At a birth, there is one baby (twins would be represented by two births), one mother, any number of nurses, and any number of doctors. Suppose, therefore, that we have entity sets *Babies*, *Mothers*, *Nurses*, and *Doctors*. Suppose we also use a relationship *Births*, which connects these four entity sets, as suggested in Fig. 2.20. Note that a tuple of the relationship set for *Births* has the form

(baby, mother, nurse, doctor)

If there is more than one nurse and/or doctor attending a birth, then there will be several tuples with the same baby and mother, one for each combination of nurse and doctor.

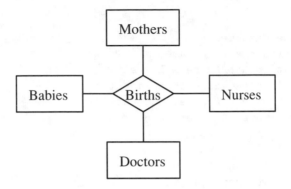

Figure 2.20: Representing births by a multiway relationship

There are certain assumptions that we might wish to incorporate into our design. For each, tell how to add arrows or other elements to the E/R diagram in order to express the assumption.

a) For every baby, there is a unique mother.

b) For every combination of a baby, nurse, and doctor, there is a unique mother.

c) For every combination of a baby and a mother there is a unique doctor.

! **Exercise 2.3.3:** Another approach to the problem of Exercise 2.3.2 is to connect the four entity sets *Babies*, *Mothers*, *Nurses*, and *Doctors* by an entity set *Births*, with four relationships, one between *Births* and each of the other entity sets, as suggested in Fig. 2.21. Use arrows (indicating that certain of these relationships are many-one) to represent the following conditions:

a) Every baby is the result of a unique birth, and every birth is of a unique baby.

b) In addition to (a), every baby has a unique mother.

c) In addition to (a) and (b), for every birth there is a unique doctor.

!! **Exercise 2.3.4:** Suppose we change our viewpoint to allow a birth to involve more than one baby born to one mother. How would you represent the fact that every baby still has a unique mother using the approaches of Exercises 2.3.2 and 2.3.3?

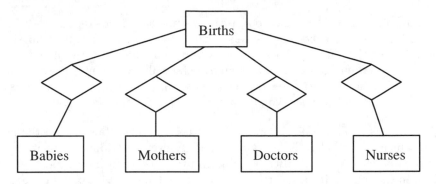

Figure 2.21: Representing births by an entity set

! **Exercise 2.3.5:** Recast the E/R designs of Exercises 2.3.2 and 2.3.3 in ODL. Which of the conditions of these exercises do you find it easy to enforce in ODL? Which cannot be enforced? How would you modify your design to allow multiple births as in Exercise 2.3.4?

2.4 Subclasses

Often, a class contains certain objects that have special properties not associated with all members of the class. If so, we find it useful to organize the class into *subclasses*, each subclass having its own special attributes and/or relationships, in addition to those of the class as a whole. ODL has a simple way to declare subclasses, which we shall discuss next. Then we shall see how the E/R model represents class-subclass hierarchies using special relationships called "isa" relationships (i.e., "an A is a B" expresses an "isa" relationship from subclass A to class B).

2.4.1 Subclasses in ODL

Among the kinds of movies we might store in our example database are cartoons, murder mysteries, adventures, comedies, and many other special types of movies. For each of these movie types, we could define a subclass of the class Movie that we introduced in Example 2.1. We define one class C to be a subclass of another class D by following the name C in its declaration with a colon and the name D.

Example 2.18: We can declare Cartoon to be a subclass of Movie, and therefore Movie to be a *superclass* of Cartoon, with the following ODL declaration:

```
1)   interface Cartoon: Movie {
2)      relationship Set<Star> voices;
     };
```

Here, line (1) declares `Cartoon` to be a subclass of `Movie`. Line (2) says that all `Cartoon` objects have a relationship `voices`, the people who speak the voices of the cartoon characters. We have not indicated the name of the inverse of relationship `voices`, although technically we should do so. Notice that relationship `voices` does not make sense for all movies, only cartoons, so we would not want to make `voices` a relationship for the class `Movie`. □

A subclass *inherits* all the properties of its superclass (also called the class from which the subclass is *derived*). That is, every attribute or relationship of the superclass is automatically an attribute or relationship of the subclass. Thus, in Example 2.18 each cartoon object has attributes `title`, `year`, `length`, and `filmType` inherited from `Movie` (recall Fig. 2.6), and it inherits relationships `stars` and `ownedBy` from `Movie`, in addition to its own relationship `voices`.

2.4.2   Multiple Inheritance in ODL

A class may have more than one subclass, with each subclass inheriting properties from its superclass as described in Section 2.4.1. Furthermore, subclasses may themselves have subclasses, yielding a hierarchy of classes where each class inherits the properties of its ancestors. It also is possible for a class to have more than one superclass. The following examples illustrate the potential and problems of multiple superclasses.

Example 2.19: We might define another subclass of `Movie` for murder mysteries by:

```
1)   interface MurderMystery: Movie {
2)      attribute string weapon;
     };
```

Thus, all murder mysteries have an attribute indicating the murder weapon, as well as the four attributes and two relationships possessed by all movies.

Now, consider a movie like *Who Framed Roger Rabbit?*, which is both a cartoon and a murder mystery. These movies should have both the relationship `voices` and the attribute `weapon`, as well as the usual `Movie` properties. We can describe this situation by declaring another subclass `Cartoon-MurderMystery`, which is a subclass of both `Cartoon` and `MurderMystery`. The declaration is:

```
interface Cartoon-MurderMystery: Cartoon, MurderMystery {};
```

Thus, a cartoon-murder-mystery object is defined to have all the properties of both subclasses `Cartoon` and `MurderMystery`. We have not declared any attributes or relationships belonging exclusively to cartoon-murder-mysteries. Objects of class `Cartoon-MurderMystery` inherit the attribute `weapon` from class `MurderMystery` and the relationship `voices` from `Cartoon`. In addition, since classes `MurderMystery` and `Cartoon` both inherit the four attributes and two relationships from class `Movie`, class `Cartoon-MurderMystery` inherits these six properties as well. Class `Cartoon-MurderMystery` does not, however, inherit two copies of these six properties; rather, it inherits the properties from `Movie` via either of its two immediate superclasses. Figure 2.22 illustrates the subclass-superclass relationships involving these four classes. □

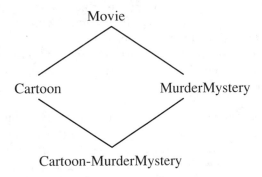

Figure 2.22: Diagram showing multiple inheritance

In general, we may declare a class C to be a subclass of any number of other classes by following the declaration of the interface name C by a colon and a list of those other classes. The declaration of `Cartoon-MurderMystery` in Example 2.19 illustrates this form. When a class C inherits from several classes, there is the potential for *conflicts* among property names. Two or more of the superclasses of C may have an attribute or relationship of the same name, and the types of these properties may differ.

Example 2.20 : Suppose we have subclasses of `Movie` called `Romance` and `Courtroom`. Further suppose that each of these subclasses has an attribute called `ending`. In class `Romance`, attribute `ending` draws its values from the enumeration {`happy`, `sad`}, while in class `Courtroom`, attribute `ending` draws its values from the enumeration {`guilty`, `notGuilty`}. If we create a further subclass, `Courtroom-Romance`, that has as superclasses both `Romance` and `Courtroom`, then the type for inherited attribute `ending` in class `Courtroom-Romance` is unclear. □

Although ODL itself does not define a specific syntax, implementations of ODL will provide at least one of the following mechanisms so that users can specify how to handle conflicts that arise from multiple inheritance:

1. Telling which of the two definitions of the property applies to the subclass. For instance, in Example 2.20 we may decide that in a courtroom romance we are more interested in whether the movie has a happy or sad ending than we are in the verdict of the courtroom trial. In this case, we would specify that class `Courtroom-Romance` inherits attribute `ending` from superclass `Romance`, and not from superclass `Courtroom`.

2. Giving a new name in class C for the other property with the same name. For instance, in Example 2.20, if `Courtroom-Romance` inherits attribute `ending` from superclass `Romance`, then we may specify that class `Courtroom-Romance` has an additional attribute called `verdict`, which is a renaming of the attribute `ending` inherited from class `Courtroom`.

3. Redefining for class C some properties that are defined in one or more of its superclasses. For instance, in Example 2.20 we may decide that attribute `ending` should not be inherited directly from either superclass. Rather, for courtroom romances, we redefine attribute `ending` to be an integer value, representing a satisfaction rating for the movie's ending from an audience poll.

Note that even in Example 2.19 there are conflicts: `Cartoon-MurderMystery` inherits from each of its immediate superclasses (`Cartoon` and `MurderMystery`) all six properties, such as `title` and `stars`, that these two classes inherited from class `Movie`. However, since the definitions of `title` and the other properties are identical in both superclasses `Cartoon` and `MurderMystery`, any means of choosing which definition to use is acceptable.

2.4.3 Subclasses in Entity-Relationship Diagrams

Recall that classes in ODL are analogous to entity sets in the E/R model. Suppose class C is a subclass of class D. To express this notion in the E/R model, we relate the entity sets corresponding to classes C and D by a special relationship called *isa*. We draw the usual boxes for entity sets C and D. Any attributes or relationships that pertain only to C entities are attached to the C box. Attributes that apply to both C and D are placed at D.

An *isa* relationship is indicated by edges with a triangle in the middle. A vertex of the triangle should point to the superclass. The word "isa" may optionally be placed in the triangle.

Example 2.21: The entity set *Movies* and two of its subclasses *Cartoons* and *Murder-Mysteries* are shown in Fig. 2.23. This subclass structure is similar to the one shown for ODL in Example 2.19. Triangles labeled *isa* point from *Cartoons* and from *Murder-Mysteries* to the superclass *Movies*. We have not shown the relationships *Stars-in* and *Owns* that relate *Movies* to *Stars* and *Studios*, and we have only suggested the relationship *Voices* that connects *Cartoons* to *Stars*. □

2.4.4 Inheritance in the E/R Model

There is a subtle difference between the concept of inheritance in ODL or other object-oriented models and inheritance in the E/R model. In ODL, an object must be a member of exactly one class. Thus, for instance, we needed in

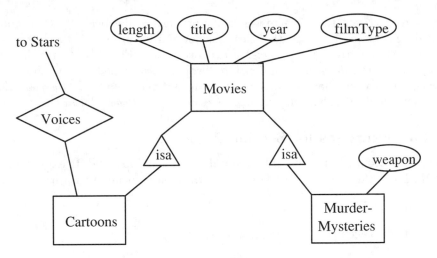

Figure 2.23: Isa relationships in an E/R diagram

Example 2.19 to define the class `Cartoon-MurderMystery` to contain those objects that were both cartoons and murder mysteries. We could not, for example, place the *Roger Rabbit* object in both the `Cartoon` and `MurderMystery` classes.

In the E/R model, we shall view an entity as having components belonging to several entity sets that are part of a single isa-hierarchy. The components are connected into a single entity by the *isa* relationships. The entity has whatever attributes any of its components has, and it participates in whatever relationships its components participate in.

In general the effect of this viewpoint is the same as that of ODL, since inheritance of properties gives an object the same attributes and relationships that its corresponding entity would collect from its components. However, there is a difference that we discuss in Example 2.22, and in Section 3.4 we shall see another difference when we convert ODL and E/R designs to the relational model.

Example 2.22: Notice that in Fig. 2.23 we do not need an entity set corresponding to cartoon-murder-mysteries. The reason is that such an entity, like *Roger Rabbit*, has components that belong to all three of the entity sets *Movies*, *Cartoons*, and *Murder-Mysteries*. The three components are connected into one entity by the *isa* relationships. Together, these components give the *Roger Rabbit* entity all four attributes of *Movies* (and the two relationships of *Movies* that are not shown in Fig. 2.23), plus the attribute *weapon* of entity set *Murder-Mysteries* and the relationship *Voices* of entity set *Cartoons*. These are exactly the properties that the *Roger Rabbit* object, in class `Cartoon-MurderMystery` inherits from its superclasses `Movie`, `Cartoon`, and `MurderMystery` in Example 2.19. □

Note, however, that if there were some properties that belonged to cartoon-murder-mysteries, but to neither cartoons nor murder-mysteries, then we would need a fourth entity set *Cartoon-MurderMysteries* in Fig. 2.23, to which these properties (attributes and relationships) would be attached. Then, the *Roger Rabbit* entity would have a fourth component that belonged to *Cartoon-Murder-Mysteries* and provided these new properties for the *Roger Rabbit* entity.

2.4.5   Exercises for Section 2.4

* **Exercise 2.4.1:** Let us consider a database of warships, and its expression in ODL. Each warship has the following information associated with it:

1. Its name.

2. Its displacement (weight), in tons.

3. Its type, e.g., battleship, destroyer.

In addition, there are the following special kinds of ships that have some other information:

1. *Gunships* are ships that carry large guns, such as battleships or cruisers. For these ships, we wish to record the number and bore of the main guns.

2. *Carriers* hold aircraft. For these we wish to record the length of the flight deck and the set of air groups assigned to them.

3. *Submarines*, which can travel under water. For these we wish to record their maximum safe depth. You may assume no gunship or carrier is a submarine.

4. *Battlecarriers* are both gunships and carriers, and have all the information associated with either.[2]

Answer the following questions:

a) Give the ODL design for this hierarchy of classes.

b) Show how the battlecarrier *Ise* would be represented. It had a displacement of 36,000 tons, mounted 8 14-inch guns, had a 200-foot flight deck, and carried air groups "1 and 2."

!! **Exercise 2.4.2:** For certain subclasses, such as `Battlecarrier` in Exercise 2.4.1, there is only one possible type, while for others, such as `Gunship` there are several, e.g., battleship and cruiser. Does this situation create a form of redundancy? If so, what can be done to eliminate the redundancy?

---

[2]In case anyone wonders, there really was such a thing. The *Ise* and *Hyuga* were two Japanese battleships that were converted in 1943 to have a flight deck and airplane hangar covering their rear halves.

* **Exercise 2.4.3 :** Repeat Exercise 2.4.1 for the E/R model.

! **Exercise 2.4.4 :** Modify your "people" database design of Exercise 2.1.5 to include the following special types of people:

1. Females.

2. Males.

3. People who are parents.

You may wish to distinguish certain other kinds of people as well, so relationships connect appropriate subclasses of people. Render your design in

a) ODL.

b) The E/R model.

2.5 The Modeling of Constraints

We have seen so far how to model a slice of the real world using ODL classes and their properties — both attributes and relationships — or using entity sets and relationships in the E/R model. Much of the structure we are interested in modeling can be expressed in either of these notations. However, there are some other important aspects of the real world that we cannot model with the tools seen so far. This additional information often takes the form of *constraints* on the data that go beyond the structural and type constraints imposed by the definitions of classes, attributes, and relationships.

The following is a rough classification of commonly used constraints. We shall not cover all of these constraint types here. Additional material on constraints is found in Section 4.5 in the context of relational algebra and in Chapter 6 in the context of SQL programming.

1. *Keys* are attributes or sets of attributes that uniquely identify an object within its class or an entity within its entity set. No two objects in a class may agree in their values for each of a set of attributes that constitutes a key.

2. *Single-value constraints* are requirements that the value in a certain role be unique. Keys are a major source of single-value constraints, since they require that associated with value(s) for the key attribute(s) are unique values of the other attributes of the class or entity set. However, there are other sources of single-value constraints, as we shall see.

3. *Referential integrity constraints* are requirements that a value referred to by some object actually exists in the database. Referential integrity is analogous to a prohibition against dangling pointers in conventional programs.

4. *Domain constraints* require that the value of an attribute must be drawn from a specific set of values or lie within a specific range. We shall cover domain constraints for SQL in Section 6.3.

5. *General constraints* are arbitrary assertions that are required to hold in the database. For example, we might wish to require that no more than ten stars be listed for any one movie. We shall see general constraint-expression languages in Sections 4.5 and 6.4.

There are several ways these constraints are important. They tell us something about the structure of those aspects of the real world that we are modeling. For example, keys allow the user to identify objects or entities without confusion. If we know that attribute `name` is a key for objects in class `Studio`, then when we refer to a studio object by its name we know we are referring to a unique object. In addition, knowing a unique value exists saves space and time, since storing a single value is easier than storing a set, even when that set has exactly one member.[3] Referential integrity and keyness also support certain storage structures that allow faster access to certain objects.

2.5.1 Keys

In ODL, a *key* for a class is a set K of one or more attributes such that given any two distinct objects O_1 and O_2 in the class, O_1 and O_2 cannot have identical values for each of the attributes in the key K. In the E/R model, a *key* is exactly the same, but with "class" replaced by "entity set" and "object" replaced by "entity."

Example 2.23: Let us consider the class `Movie` from Example 2.1. One might first assume that the attribute `title` by itself is a key. However, there are several titles that have been used for two or even more different movies, for example, *King Kong*. Thus, it would be unwise to declare that `title` by itself is a key. If we did so, then we would not be able to include information about both *King Kong* movies in our database.

A better choice would be to take the set of two attributes `title` and `year` as a key. We still run the risk that there are two movies made in the same year with the same title (and thus both could not be stored in our database), but that is unlikely.

For the other two classes, `Star` and `Studio`, introduced in Section 2.1, we must again think carefully about what can serve as a key. For studios, it is reasonable to assume that there would not be two movie studios with the same name, so we shall take `name` to be a key for class `Studio`. However, it is less clear that stars are uniquely identified by their name. Surely name does not distinguish among people in general. However, since stars have traditionally chosen "stage names" at will, we might hope to find that `name` serves as a key

---

[3]In analogy, note that in a C program it is simpler to represent an integer than it is a linked list of integers, even when that list contains only one integer.

Constraints Are Part of the Schema

We could look at the database as it exists at a certain time and decide erroneously that an attribute forms a key because no two objects have identical values for this attribute. For example, as we create our movie database we might not enter two movies with the same title for some time. Thus, it might look as if `title` were a key for class `Movie`. However, if we decided on the basis of this preliminary evidence that `title` is a key, and we designed a storage structure for our database that assumed `title` is a key, then we might find ourselves unable to enter a second *King Kong* movie into the database.

Thus, key constraints, and constraints in general, are part of the database schema. They are declared by the database designer along with the structural design (e.g., entities and relationships). Once a constraint is declared, insertions or modifications to the database that violate the constraint are disallowed.

Hence, although a particular instance of the database may satisfy certain constraints, the only "true" constraints are those identified by the designer as holding for all instances of the database that correctly model the real-world. These are the constraints that may be assumed by users and by the structures used to store the database.

---

for class `Star` too. If not, we might choose the pair of attributes `name` and `address` as a key, which would be satisfactory unless there were two stars with the same name living at the same address. □

Example 2.24: Our experience in Example 2.23 might lead us to believe that it is difficult to find keys or to be sure that a set of attributes forms a key. In practice the matter is usually much simpler. In the real-world situations commonly modeled by databases, people often go out of their way to create what are effectively keys for important classes. For example, companies generally assign employee ID's to all employees, and these ID's are carefully chosen to be unique numbers. One purpose of these ID's is to make sure that in the company database each employee can be distinguished from all others, even if there are several employees with the same name. Thus, the employee-ID attribute can serve as a key for employees in the database.

In US corporations, it is normal for every employee to also have a Social Security number. If the database has an attribute that is the Social Security number, then this attribute can also serve as a key for employees. Note that there is nothing wrong with there being several choices of key for a class, as there would be for a class of employees having both employee ID's and Social Security numbers.

The idea of creating an attribute whose purpose is to serve as a key is quite widespread. In addition to employee ID's, we find student ID's to distinguish students in a university. We find drivers' license numbers and automobile registration numbers to distinguish drivers and automobiles, respectively, in the Department of Motor Vehicles. The reader can undoubtedly find more examples of attributes created for the primary purpose of serving as keys.   □

2.5.2   Declaring Keys in ODL

In ODL we declare one or more attributes to be a key for a class by using the keyword key or keys (it doesn't matter which) followed by the attribute or attributes forming keys. If there is more than one attribute in a key, the list of attributes must be surrounded by parentheses. The key declaration must appear immediately after the interface declaration, before the opening curly brace, or any attributes or relationships. The declaration itself is surrounded by parentheses.

Example 2.25 : To declare that the set of two attributes title and year form a key for class Movie, we repalce line (1) of Fig. 2.6 by:

```
interface Movie
    (key (title, year))
{
```

We could have used keys in place of key, even though only one key is declared. Similarly, if name is a key for class Star, then we add

```
(key name)
```

before the curly brace in line (8) of Fig. 2.6.   □

It is possible that several sets of attributes are keys. If so, then following the word key(s) we may place several keys separated by commas. As usual, a key that consists of more than one attribute must have parentheses around the list of its attributes, so we can disambiguate a key of several attributes from several keys of one attribute each.

Example 2.26 : As an example of a situation where it is appropriate to have more than one key, consider a class Employee, whose complete set of attributes and relationships we shall not describe here. However, suppose that two of its attributes are empID, the employee ID, and ssNo, the Social Security number. Then we can declare each of these attributes to be a key by itself with

```
(key empID, ssNo)
```

Because there are no parentheses around the list of attributes, ODL interprets the above as saying that each of the two attributes is a key by itself. If we put parentheses around the list (empID, ssNo), then ODL would interpret the two attributes together as forming one key. That is, the implication of writing

```
(key (empID, ssNo))
```

is that no two employees could have both the same employee ID and the same Social Security number, although two employees might agree on one of these attributes. □

2.5.3 Representing Keys in the E/R Model

An entity set, being in essence a class, can have keys in exactly the same sense that ODL classes do. If a set of attributes forms a key for an entity set, then we cannot have two entities in that set whose values agree for each of the attributes of the key. In our E/R diagram notation, we underline the attributes belonging to a key for an entity set. For example, Fig. 2.24 shows the entity set *Movies* from Fig. 2.8 with attributes *title* and *year* serving together as the key.

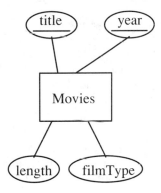

Figure 2.24: Movies entity set with key indicated

In situations where there is more than one key, in the E/R model we do not provide a formal notation to indicate all keys. It is customary to designate one key the *primary key*, and to treat this set of attributes as if it were the only key for the entity set. While the primary key is indicated by underlining in the E/R model, other keys, called *secondary keys*, would either not be indicated or would be listed in a side comment attached to the diagram.

There is an uncommon, but possible, situation, where the key for an entity set does not belong to the entity set itself. We shall defer this matter, called "weak entity sets," until Section 2.6.

2.5.4 Single-Value Constraints

Often, an important property of a database design is that there is at most one value playing a particular role. For example, we assume that a movie object has a unique title, year, length, and film type, and that a movie is owned by a unique studio. In ODL, we have no trouble declaring those assumptions, since each attribute has a type. If the type is not a collection type (e.g., set), then there can be only one value for that attribute or only one related object for a relationship. On the other hand, if an attribute or relationship is defined to have a collection type, such as the type `Set<Star>` for the relationship `stars` on line (6) of Fig. 2.6, then we permit more than one star to be related to a given movie. Such a relationship is called a *multivalued* relationship.

We must also differentiate between a situation where there is at most one value for an attribute or relationship and the situation where there must be *exactly* one value. When there is a relationship that connects objects in one class to single objects of another class, and the latter object is required to exist, we have a constraint called "referential integrity," which we discuss next in Section 2.5.5. When there is an attribute with a single value, we have two choices.

1. We can require that the value of that attribute exist.

2. We can allow the value to be optional.

If an attribute forms part of the key for a class, then we generally require that the value exist in each object. For other attributes, we could invent a *null value* for that attribute, to serve in place of an actual value when no value exists. Then, a non-null value for this attribute would be optional.

Example 2.27 : For the class `Movie`, whose key we decided in Example 2.23 was `title` and `year`, let us require that these two attributes exist in all movie objects. On the other hand, attribute `length` optionally could be missing. We could use −1, for example, as a null value for `length`, since no movie could have a negative length. If we did not know the length of a movie, we would set the value of attribute `length` to −1. Similarly, we could add a third value to the enumeration that defines the possible values for attribute `filmType`. In addition to values `color` and `blackAndWhite`, we could choose a value such as `NULL` or `Unknown` to indicate that no information about the film type was available.   □

The entity/relationship model also offers ways to express single-value constraints. By implication, each attribute of an entity set has a single value. We generally assume that it is possible for a value to be null. An attribute that could not be null would be so indicated as a side remark.

The arrows that indicate many-one or one-one relationships also express single-value constraints. That is, if a relationship has an arrow to an entity set E, then there is at most one entity of set E associated with a choice of entities from each of the other related entity sets.

2.5.5 Referential Integrity

While single-value constraints assert that at most one value exists in a given role, a *referential integrity constraint* asserts that exactly one value exists in that role. We could see a constraint that an attribute have a non-null, single value as a kind of referential integrity requirement, but "referential integrity" is more commonly used to refer to relationships among classes.

Let us consider the relationship `ownedBy` from `Movie` to `Studio` in the ODL declarations of Fig. 2.6, line (7). One might ask how it would be possible for there to be a studio object as the value of `ownedBy` and yet that studio object not exist. The answer is that in an implementation of ODL, the relationship `ownedBy` will be represented by a pointer or reference to a studio object, and it will be possible that at some time the studio object is deleted from the class `Studio`. In that case, the pointer becomes *dangling*; it no longer points to a real object.

A referential integrity constraint on relationship `ownedBy` would require that the referenced studio object must exist. There are several ways this constraint could be enforced.

1. We could forbid the deletion of a referenced object (a studio in our example).

2. We could require that if a referenced object is deleted, then all objects that reference it are deleted as well. In our example, this approach would require that if we delete a studio, we also delete from the database all movies owned by that studio.

In addition to one of these policies about deletion, we require that when a movie object is created, it is given an existing studio object as the value of its relationship `ownedBy`. Further, if the value of that relationship changes, then the new value must also be an existing object. Enforcing these policies to assure referential integrity of a relationship is a matter for the implementation of the database, and we shall not discuss the details here.

2.5.6   Referential Integrity in E/R Diagrams

We can extend the arrow notation in E/R diagrams to indicate whether a relationship is expected to support referential integrity in one or more directions. Suppose R is a relationship from entity set E to entity set F. We shall use a rounded arrowhead pointing to F to indicate not only that the relationship is many-one or one-one from E to F, but that the entity of set F related to a given entity of set E is required to exist. The same idea applies when R is a relationship among more than two attributes.

Example 2.28: Figure 2.25 shows some appropriate referential integrity constraints among the entity sets *Movies*, *Studios*, and *Presidents*. These entity sets and relationships were first introduced in Figs. 2.8 and 2.9. We see a rounded arrow entering *Studios* from relationship *Owns*. That arrow expresses the referential integrity constraint that the studio owning a movie must always be present in the *Studios* entity set.

Figure 2.25: E/R diagram showing referential integrity constraints

Similarly, we see a rounded arrow entering *Studios* from *Runs*. That arrow expresses the referential integrity constraint that if a president runs a studio, then that studio exists in the *Studios* entity set.

Note that the arrow to *Presidents* from *Runs* remains a pointed arrow. That choice reflects a reasonable assumption about the relationship between studios and their presidents. If a studio ceases to exist, its president can no longer be called a (studio) president, so we would expect the president of the studio to be deleted from the entity set *Presidents*. Hence the rounded arrow to *Studios*. On the other hand, if a president were deleted from the database, the studio would continue to exist. Thus, we place an ordinary, pointed arrow to *Presidents*, indicating that each studio has at most one president, but might have no president at some time.   □

2.5.7   Other Kinds of Constraints

As mentioned at the beginning of this section, there are other kinds of constraints one could wish to enforce in a database. We shall only touch briefly on these here, with the meat of the subject appearing in Chapter 6.

Domain constraints restrict the value of an attribute to be in a limited set. ODL requires a type for each attribute, and this type is a rudimentary form of domain constraint. For example, if attribute `length` is of type `integer`, then the value of `length` cannot be 101.5 or any other non-integer. However, ODL does not support more restrictive limits, such as that the length be between 60 and 240. We shall see that SQL does support such constraints in Section 6.3.

There are also more general kinds of constraints that do not fall into any of the categories mentioned in this section. For example, there are constraints on the degree of a relationship, such as that a movie object or entity cannot be connected by relationship `stars` to more than 10 star objects/entities. In the E/R model, we can attach a bounding number to the edges that connect a relationship to an entity set, indicating limits on the number of entities that can be connected to any one entity of the related entity set. In ODL, we could limit the number of stars by making the type of the `stars` attribute of `Movie` an array of length 10. There is, however, no way to specify that a set can have at most 10 elements.

Example 2.29 : Figure 2.26 shows how we can represent the constraint that no movie have more than 10 stars in the E/R model. As another example, we can think of the arrow as a synonym for the constraint "≤ 1," and we can think of the rounded arrow of Fig. 2.25 as standing for the constraint "= 1."   □

Figure 2.26: Representing a constraint on the number of stars per movie

2.5.8   Exercises for Section 2.5

Exercise 2.5.1: Select and specify keys for your ODL designs of:

* a) Exercise 2.1.1.

  b) Exercise 2.1.3.

* c) Exercise 2.1.5.

  d) Exercise 2.4.1.

Exercise 2.5.2: For your E/R diagrams of:

* a) Exercise 2.2.1.

  b) Exercise 2.2.3.

  c) Exercise 2.2.6.

  d) Exercise 2.4.3.

(i) Select and specify keys, and (ii) Indicate appropriate referential integrity constraints.

! **Exercise 2.5.3:** We may think of relationships in the E/R model as having keys, just as entity sets do. Let R be a relationship among the entity sets $E_1, E_2, \ldots, E_n$. Then a *key* for R is a set K of attributes chosen from the attributes of $E_1, E_2, \ldots, E_n$ such that if $(e_1, e_2, \ldots, e_n)$ and $(f_1, f_2, \ldots, f_n)$ are two different tuples in the relationship set for R, then it is not possible that these tuples agree in all the attributes of K. Now, suppose $n = 2$; that is, R is a binary relationship. Also, for each i, let K_i be a set of attributes that is a key for entity set E_i. In terms of E_1 and E_2, give a smallest possible key for R under the assumption that:

  a) R is many-many.

* b) R is many-one from E_1 to E_2.

  c) R is many-one from E_2 to E_1.

  d) R is one-one.

!! **Exercise 2.5.4:** Consider again the problem of Exercise 2.5.3, but with n allowed to be any number, not just 2. Using only the information about which arcs from R to the E_i's have arrows, show how to find a smallest possible key K for R in terms of the K_i's.

! **Exercise 2.5.5:** Give other examples (besides that of Example 2.24) from real life of attributes created for the primary purpose of being keys.

2.6   Weak Entity Sets

There is an odd but plausible condition in which an entity set's key is composed of attributes some or all of which belong to another entity set. Such an entity set is called a *weak entity set*.

2.6.1   Causes of Weak Entity Sets

There are two principal sources of weak entity sets. First, sometimes entity sets fall into a hierarchy. If entities of set E are subunits of entities in set F, then it is possible that the names of E entities are not unique until we take into account the name of the F entity to which the E entity is subordinate.

Example 2.30: Some examples of hierarchies that lead to weak entity sets are:

1. A movie studio might have several film crews. The crews might be designated by a given studio as crew 1, crew 2, and so on. However, other studios might use the same designations for crews, so the attribute *number* is not a key for crews. Rather, to name a crew uniquely, we need to give both the name of the studio to which it belongs and the number of the crew. The situation is suggested by Fig. 2.27. The key for weak entity set *Crew* is its own *number* attribute and the *name* attribute of the unique studio to which the crew is related by the many-one *Unit-of* relationship.[4]

2. A species is designated by its genus and species names. For example, humans are of the species *Homo sapiens*; *Homo* is the genus name and *sapiens* the species name. In general, a genus consists of several species, each of which has a name beginning with the genus name and continuing with the species name. Unfortunately, species names are not unique. Two or more genera may have species with the same species name. Thus, to designate a species uniquely we need both the species name and the name of the genus to which the species is related by a *Member-of* relationship connecting the species to its genus. *Species* is a weak entity set whose key comes partially from its containing genus.

□

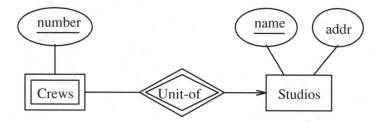

Figure 2.27: A weak entity set and its connections

The second common source of weak entity sets is the connecting entity sets that we introduced in Section 2.2.5 as a way to eliminate a multiway relationship.[5] These entity sets often have no attributes of their own. Their key is formed from the attributes that are the key attributes for the entity sets they connect.

Example 2.31: In Fig. 2.28 we see a connecting entity set *Contracts* that replaces the ternary relationship *Contracts* of Example 2.8. *Contracts* has an attribute *salary*, but this attribute does not contribute to the key. Rather, the key for a contract consists of the name of the studio and the star involved, plus the title and year of the movie involved. □

2.6.2 Requirements for Weak Entity Sets

We cannot obtain key attributes for a weak entity set indiscriminately. Rather, if E is a weak entity set then each of the entity sets F that supplies one or more of E's key attributes must be related to E by a relationship R. Moreover, the following conditions must be obeyed:

1. R must be a binary, many-one relationship[6] from E to F.

2. The attributes that F supplies for the key of E must be key attributes of F.

3. However, if F is itself weak, then the key attributes of F supplied to E may be attributes of some entity set to which F is connected by a many-one relationship.

4. If there are several many-one relationships from E to F, then each relationship may be used to supply a copy of the key attributes of F to

---

[4]The double diamond and double rectangle will be explained in Section 2.6.3.

[5]Note that there is no requirement in the E/R model to eliminate multiway relationships, although in ODL as well as some older models such as the network and hierarchical models discussed in Section 2.7, we must replace multiway relationships.

[6]Remember that a one-one relationship is a special case of a many-one relationship. When we say a relationship must be many-one, we always include one-one relationships as well.

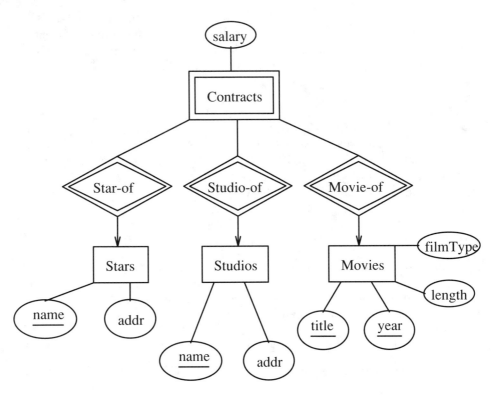

Figure 2.28: Connecting entity sets are weak

Why Are There No "Weak Classes" in ODL?

The issue of how to find a key never arises in ODL or any object-oriented model. As we saw in Section 2.5.2, we can declare an attribute or attributes to form a key, but there is no requirement that we do so. Objects have an "object identity," in effect an address where they can be found, and the object ID uniquely distinguishes objects from one another, even if their attribute values or relationships fail to distinguish two objects. On the other hand, the E/R model is "value oriented," and entities are only distinguished by their associated attribute values. Thus, we have to be careful in E/R designs that entities of any entity set can be distinguished from one another by values alone, without appeal to any "object identity."

---

help form the key of E. Note that an entity e from E may be related to different entities in F through different relationships from E. Thus, the keys of several different entities from F may appear in the key values identifying a particular entity e from E.

The intuitive reason why these conditions are needed is as follows. Consider an entity in a weak entity set, say a crew in Example 2.30. Each crew is unique, abstractly. In principle we can tell one crew from another, even if they have the same number but belong to different studios. It is only the data about crews that makes it hard to distinguish crews, because the number is not enough. The only way we can associate additional information with a crew is if there is some deterministic process that generates additional values that make the designation of a crew unique. The only way we can find a unique value associated with a crew entity is if either.

1. The value is an attribute of the *Crew* entity set, or

2. We can follow a relationship from a crew entity to a unique entity of some other entity set, and that other entity has a unique associated value of some kind. That is, the relationship followed must be many-one (or one-one as a special case) to the other entity set F, and the associated value must be a key for F.

2.6.3 Weak Entity Set Notation

We shall adopt the following conventions to indicate that an entity set is weak and to declare its key attributes.

1. If an entity set is weak, it will be shown as a rectangle with a double border. Examples of this convention are *Crews* in Fig. 2.27 and *Contracts* in Fig. 2.28.

2. If an entity set is weak, then the many-one relationships that connect it to the other entity set or sets that supply its key attributes will be shown as diamonds with a double border. Examples of this convention are *Unit-of* in Fig. 2.27 and all three relationships in Fig. 2.28.

3. If an entity set supplies any attributes for its own key, then those attributes will be underlined. An example is in Fig. 2.27, where the number of a crew participates in its own key, although it is not the complete key for *Crews*.

We can summarize these conventions with the following rule:

- Whenever we see an entity set that has a double border, it is weak. Its key consists of those of its own attributes that are underlined, if any, plus the key attributes of those entity sets to which the weak entity set is connected by many-one relationships with a double border.

2.6.4   Exercises for Section 2.6

* **Exercise 2.6.1:** One way to represent students and the grades they get in courses is to use entity sets corresponding to students, to courses, and to "enrollments." Enrollment entities form a "connecting" entity set between students and courses and can be used to represent not only the fact that a student is taking a certain course, but the grade of the student in the course. Draw an E/R diagram for this situation, indicating weak entity sets and the keys for the entity sets. Is the grade part of the key for enrollments?

Exercise 2.6.2: Modify Exercise 2.6.1 so that we can record grades of the student for each of several assignments within a course. Again, indicate weak entity sets and keys.

Exercise 2.6.3: For your E/R diagram of Exercise 2.3.3, indicate weak entity sets and keys.

Exercise 2.6.4: Draw E/R diagrams for the following situations involving weak entity sets. In each case indicate keys for entity sets.

a) Entity sets *Courses* and *Departments*. A course is given by a unique department, but its only attribute is its number. Different departments can offer courses with the same number. Each department has a unique name.

*! b) Entity sets *Leagues*, *Teams*, and *Players*. League names are unique. No league has two teams with the same name. No team has two players with the same number. However, there can be players with the same number on different teams, and there can be teams with the same name in different leagues.

2.7 Models of Historical Interest

In this section we shall introduce the reader to two additional models and some of their terminology. The "network" and "hierarchical" models were both early attempts to provide a foundation for database systems. They were used in the first commercial database systems, dating from the late 1960's and 1970's. They were supplanted by systems based on the relational model, which is the subject of Chapter 3. However, several of their ideas live on in the newer object-oriented approaches to database design.

2.7.1 The Network Model

We may think of the *network model* as the E/R model restricted to binary, many-one relationships. The two principal elements of the network model are:

1. *Logical record types.* These are similar to entity sets; they consist of a name for the type and a list of attributes. The members of the logical record type are called *records*; they are analogous to entities in the E/R model.

2. *Links.* These are many-one, binary relationships. They connect two entity sets, one of which is the *owner* type and the other of which is the *member* type. The link is many-one from the member type to the owner type. That is, each record of the member type is assigned to exactly one record of the owner type, and each record of the owner type "owns" zero, one, or more records of the member type.

Example 2.32: Let us work our example of movies, stars and the movies in which they star in the network model. Stars and movies each form a logical record type. However, the "stars-in" relationship between movies and stars is many-many, so we cannot use a single link to represent this relationship in the network model. Rather, we must create a new logical record type, which we shall call `StarsIn`, that serves as a "connecting" logical record type, similar to the connecting entity sets that we introduced in Section 2.2.5. Think of each `StarsIn` record as representing a star-movie pair, such that the star appeared in the movie. Then the three logical record types for our network design are:

```
Stars(name, address)
Movies(title, year, length, filmType)
StarsIn()
```

The `Stars` logical record type has two attributes: the name and address of the star, while the `Movies` type has attributes for the title, year, length, and film type of the movie. We do not represent the studio associated with movies, although a complete design would represent that connection by a link. The connecting type `StarsIn` has no attributes in our design, although it could be given attributes if appropriate. For example, if we recorded the amount the star was paid for a particular movie, then this amount is a function of the movie-star pair and would be an attribute of StarsIn. In this example, however, the effect of StarsIn records is only through the links it participates in. □

There are two links in our design. One link is from Stars to StarsIn; that is, Stars is the owner type and StarsIn is the member type. This link, which we shall call TheStar, connects a star to each of the movie-star pairs in which the star participates. The second link is TheMovie, with owner type Movies and member type StarsIn. Each movie record owns the movie-star pairs with that movie. Note that both links are many-one. A StarsIn pair (m, s) is owned by the Movies record for movie m and by the Stars record for star s.

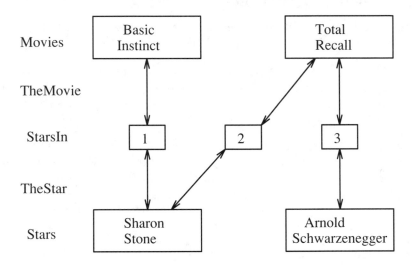

Figure 2.29: Records and their links

Figure 2.29 illustrates how records of the three logical record types are connected by the links. This diagram is not a schema. Rather, it shows individual records themselves and the ways they are connected to other records through links. We see three StarsIn records. Number 1 represents the fact that Sharon Stone was a star in the movie *Basic Instinct*. Number 2 represents the Sharon Stone/*Total Recall* pair, and number 3 represents the Arnold Schwarzenegger/*Total Recall* pair. The numbers are not actually part of these records, but are used so we can refer to StarsIn records. Note that the StarsIn records are members in both links, and the other records are owners.   □

2.7.2   Representing Network Schemas

In diagrams representing the logical record types and links, we generally show logical record types by ovals and links by named arrows. The arrows go from the member type to the owner type.

Example 2.33: The schema diagram for the three logical record types and two links of Example 2.32 is shown in Fig. 2.30. □

Figure 2.30: The network schema for the movies example

2.7.3 The Hierarchical Model

The hierarchical model can be thought of as a restriction of the network model, where the logical record types and links form a forest (collection of trees). That is, if we regard each link as saying that the owner type is the parent of the member type, then the logical record types form a forest. The problem with this requirement is that it may be impossible to achieve for some networks. For example, we see from Fig. 2.30 that logical record type StarsIn would need two parents, Stars and Movies, in the hierarchy. Thus, Fig. 2.30 is not a forest.

Recall that the StarsIn logical record type is really a connecting type for the many-many relationship between stars and movies. In the hierarchical model, we represent many-many relationships by creating a *virtual* copy of each of the related types. We can think of the virtual type as representing a pointer to a record of the real type. Virtual types make it possible to represent any network as a hierarchy.

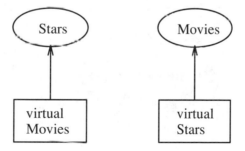

Figure 2.31: The hierarchical schema for the movies example

Example 2.34: Figure 2.31 shows a hierarchical schema for the movies-and-stars example. There are two simple trees in the forest. The first has root Stars and child virtual-Movies, while the second has root Movies with child virtual-Stars.

We can visualize the actual data represented by the schema of Fig. 2.31 as in Fig. 2.32. In the schema, the type Stars has child virtual-Movies. Thus, each

---

Why Hierarchies?

One might wonder why the strange requirements of the hierarchical model were once a significant force in the database industry. The simplest argument is that by organizing data in a hierarchy, with virtual record types only when absolutely necessary, one could store the data by clustering records with their parents in a sequential file. Thus, we might store the data suggested by Fig. 2.32 with a record like Sharon Stone followed by all its "owned" records, in this case the virtual-`Movies` pointers shown below that record. On the assumption that one tends to access information working down the tree, one would tend to find the needed information nearby in the file, as one travels from parent to children records, thus reducing the time it takes to retrieve desired information off a disk.

In this example, there is little benefit, because following the pointer represented by the virtual types would take us to some random place on the disk where the movie information was stored. However, except for many-many relationships, there is often significant improvement in efficiency of query execution resulting from a hierarchical organization.

---

record of type `Stars` has children of type virtual-`Movies`; the virtual records are represented by boxes with the word "to" in them.

For instance, we see the `Stars` record Sharon Stone with two children. Each is a pointer to a `Movies` record, in this case the records for *Basic Instinct* and *Total Recall*. To follow the underlying many-many relationship between stars and movies, we can start at a `Stars` record such as that for Sharon Stone, go from there to the children virtual-`Movies` records, and from each of them to the corresponding real `Movies` record.   □

2.7.4   Exercises for Section 2.7

Exercise 2.7.1: Render in the network model the designs described in:

* a) Exercise 2.1.1.

  b) Exercise 2.1.3.

  c) Exercise 2.1.5.

  d) Exercise 2.3.2.

Exercise 2.7.2: Repeat Exercise 2.7.1 in the hierarchical model.

*! **Exercise 2.7.3:** Suppose we have an entity-relationship diagram with n entity sets and m binary relationships. If we convert this diagram to a network-model design, what are the largest and smallest number of links we might need? Remember that each relationship may be many-many, many-one, or one-one.

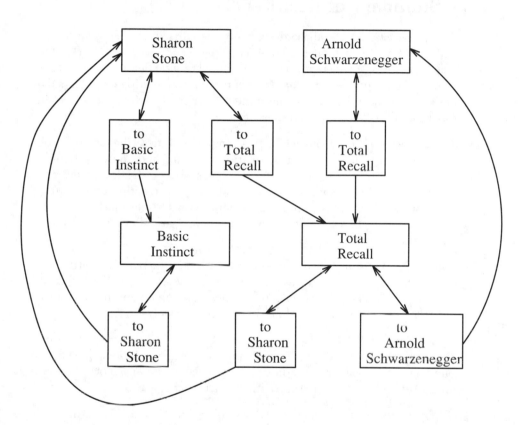

Figure 2.32: Hierarchical representation of movie/star facts

‼ Exercise 2.7.4: Suppose we have an entity-relationship diagram with n entity sets and m binary relationships. Give the largest and smallest number of virtual record types necessary if this diagram is rendered in the hierarchical model?

! Exercise 2.7.5: How do your answers to Exercises 2.7.3 and 2.7.4 change if the relationships are k-ary for some $k > 2$?

2.8   Summary of Chapter 2

✦ *Design Notations*: Database design often is carried out using either the Entity/Relationship model or an object-oriented model such as ODL (Object Description Language). The E/R model is intended to be translated into the model of a real database system, often the relational model. ODL designs can either be treated the same way or serve as (almost) direct input to an object-oriented database system.

✦ *Object Description Language*: In this language we describe classes of objects by giving their attributes, relationships and methods. Attributes are described by their data type. The type system of ODL includes conventional base types such as integers and type construction by formation of record structures, sets, bags, lists, and arrays. Relationships are described by the class to which they connect and are allowed to be either single-valued or multivalued.

✦ *Entity/Relationship Diagrams*: In the E/R model we describe entity sets, their attributes, and relationships among entity sets. Members of entity sets are called entities. We use rectangles, diamonds, and ovals to draw entity sets, relationships, and attributes, respectively.

✦ *Multiplicity of Relationships*: In either ODL or E/R, it is useful to distinguish relationships by their multiplicity. Binary relationships can be one-one, many-one, or many-many. Relationships among more than two entity sets (classes) are permitted in E/R but not in ODL.

✦ *Weak Entity Sets*: An occasional complication that arises in the E/R model is a weak entity set that requires attributes of some related entity set(s) to identify its own entities. A special notation involving diamonds and rectangles with double borders is used to distinguish weak entity sets.

✦ *Good Design*: Designing databases effectively requires that we use our chosen notation (ODL or E/R, e.g.) to represent the real world faithfully, using appropriate elements (e.g., relationships, attributes), and that we avoid redundancy — saying the same thing twice or saying something in an indirect or overly complex manner.

✦ *Subclasses*: Both ODL and E/R support a way to describe special cases of classes or entity sets. ODL has subclasses and inheritance, while E/R uses a special relationship *isa* to represent the fact that one entity set is a special case of another.

✦ *Keys*: Both ODL and E/R allow sets of attributes to be declared keys, meaning that their values uniquely define an object or entity. ODL also has a notion of object identifiers, which are values that uniquely identify objects but are not accessible to the user.

✦ *Network Model*: This model is rarely used today. It is similar to E/R diagrams restricted so that relationships are all binary and many-one.

✦ *Hierarchical Model*: This model also appears infrequently today. It resembles the E/R model with entity sets arranged in a forest and with many-one relationships from parent to child only.

2.9 References for Chapter 2

The original paper on the Entity/Relationship model is [3]. References [4] and [1 cover entity-relationship design extensively as well as some other models useful for design.

The manual defining ODL is [2]. It is the ongoing work of ODMG, the Object Data Management Group. This organization offers electronic access for updated materials on ODL through their email address info@odmg.org and through their Web page: http://www.odmg.org.

1. Batini, C., S. Ceri, and S. B. Navathe, *Conceptual Database Design*, Benjamin/Cummings, Redwood City, CA, 1992.

2. Cattell, R. G. G. (ed.), *The Object Database Standard: ODMG-93 Release 1.2*, Morgan-Kaufmann, San Francisco, 1996.

3. Chen, P. P., "The entity-relationship model: toward a unified view of data," *ACM Trans. on Database Systems* **1**:1, pp. 9–36, 1966.

4. El Masri, R. and S. B. Navathe, *Fundamentals of Database Systems*, Benjamin Cummings, Menlo Park, 1994.

Chapter 3

The Relational Data Model

While the object-oriented and entity-relationship approaches to data modeling that we discussed in Chapter 2 are useful and appropriate ways to describe the structure of data, today's database implementations are almost always based on another approach, called the *relational model*. The relational model is extremely useful because it has but a single data-modeling concept: the "relation," a two-dimensional table in which data is arranged. We shall see in Chapter 5 how the relational model supports a very high-level programming language called SQL (structured query language). SQL lets us write simple programs that manipulate in powerful ways the data stored in relations.

On the other hand, it is often easier to design databases using one of the models we learned in Chapter 2. Thus, our first goal is to see how to translate designs from ODL or E/R notation into relations. We shall then find that the relational model has a design theory of its own. This theory, often called "normalization" of relations, is based primarily on "functional dependencies," which embody and expand the concept of "key" discussed informally in Section 2.5.1. Using normalization theory, we often improve our choice of relations representing a particular database design.

3.1 Basics of the Relational Model

The relational model gives us a single way to represent data: as a two-dimensional table called a *relation*. Figure 3.1 is an example of a relation. The name of the relation is Movie, and it is intended to hold the same sort of information as is found in the simple ODL Movie class definition of Fig. 2.4 from Example 2.1, which we reproduce here as Fig. 3.2. Note that this definition was not the final definition of the Movie class and has only the attributes title, year, length and filmType.

title	year	length	filmType
Star Wars	1977	124	color
Mighty Ducks	1991	104	color
Wayne's World	1992	95	color

Figure 3.1: The relation Movie

3.1.1 Attributes

Across the top of a relation we see *attributes*; in Fig. 3.1 the attributes are
title, year, length, and filmType. Attributes of a relation serve as names
for the columns of the relation. Usually, the attribute describes the meaning of
entries in the column below. For instance, the column with attribute length
holds the length in minutes of various movies.

```
1)   interface Movie {
2)       attribute string title;
3)       attribute integer year;
4)       attribute integer length;
5)       attribute enumeration(color,blackAndWhite) filmType;
     };
```

Figure 3.2: An ODL description of the class Movie

Notice that the attributes of the relation Movie in Fig. 3.1 correspond to the
structure elements called "attributes" in the ODL definition of Fig. 2.4. This
approach to selecting attributes for a relation is quite common. However, in
general there is no requirement that attributes of a relation correspond to any
particular components of an ODL or E/R description of data.

3.1.2 Schemas

The name of a relation and the set of attributes for a relation is called the
schema for that relation. We show the schema for the relation with the relation
name followed by a parenthesized list of its attributes. Thus, the schema for
relation Movie of Fig. 3.1 is

Movie(title, year, length, filmType)

Remember that, while the attributes in a relation schema are a set, not a list,
in order to talk about relations we often must specify a "standard" order for
the attributes. Thus, whenever we introduce a relation schema as above, with a

list of attributes, we shall take this ordering to be the standard order whenever we display the relation or any of its rows.

In the relational model, a design consists of one or more relation schemas. The set of schemas for the relations in a design is called a *relational database schema*, or just a *database schema*.

3.1.3 Tuples

The rows of a relation, other than the header row containing the attributes, are called *tuples*. A tuple has one *component* for each attribute of the relation. For instance, the first of the three tuples in Fig. 3.1 has the four components `Star Wars`, 1977, 124, and `color` for attributes `title`, `year`, `length`, and `filmType`, respectively. When we wish to write a tuple in isolation, not part of a relation, we normally use commas to separate components, and we use parentheses to surround the tuple. For example,

(<code>Star Wars</code>, 1977, 124, <code>color</code>)

is the first tuple of Fig. 3.1. Notice that when a tuple appears in isolation, the attributes do not appear, so some indication of the relation to which the tuple belongs must be given. We shall always use the order in which the attributes were listed in the relation schema.

Often, one can think of tuples as representing objects, while the relation to which they belong represents their class. Surely that is the case for our example relation; each tuple represents a movie object. The components of our tuples and the properties of movie objects described by Fig 3.2 are identical. However, we should be aware that objects have identity, while tuples do not. That is, in principle an object-oriented representation of movies could have two different movie objects with the same values in all attributes, although as we argued in Example 2.23 we would not expect that to be the case for movies.

Relations, however, are sets of tuples, and it is not possible for a tuple to appear more than once in a given relation. Thus, if a relation is to represent a class of objects, we must be sure that the relation has a sufficient set of attributes, so that no two objects could have the same values for all attributes of the relation. In the case of movies, we claimed in Example 2.23 that we would not expect two movies to have both the same title and year. However, in the worst case we may need to create an attribute that is an artificial representation of the object itself. For example, we could give each movie a unique integer "movie ID" and add `movieID` to the set of attributes for our example relation.

3.1.4 Domains

The relational model requires that each component of each tuple be atomic; that is, it must be of some elementary type such as integers or strings. It is not permitted for a value to be a record structure, set, list, array, or any other type that can reasonably have its values broken into smaller components. This requirement is one of the ways that attributes in ODL may not be translatable directly into single attributes of a relation. For example, if an ODL attribute name has type

```
Struct Name {string first, string last}
```

then there must be two attributes, first and last, in the corresponding relation. The matter is discussed more fully in Section 3.2.2.

It is further assumed that associated with each attribute of a relation is a *domain*, that is, a particular elementary type. The components of any tuple of the relation must have, in each component, a value that belongs to the domain of the corresponding column. For example, tuples of the Movie relation of Fig. 3.1 must have a first component that is a string, second and third components that are integers, and a fourth component whose value is one of the constants color and blackAndWhite.

3.1.5   Equivalent Representations of a Relation

As we learned, both the schema and the tuples for a relation are sets, not lists. Thus the order in which they are presented is immaterial. For example, we can list the three tuples of Fig. 3.1 in any of their six possible orders, and the relation is "the same" as Fig. 3.1.

Moreover, we can reorder the attributes of the relation as we choose, without changing the relation. However, when we reorder the relation schema, we must be careful to remember that the attributes are column headers. Thus, when we change the order of the attributes, we also change the order of their columns. When the columns move, the components of tuples change their order as well. The result is that each tuple has its components permuted in the same way as the attributes are permuted.

For example, Fig. 3.3 shows one of the many relations that could be obtained from Fig. 3.1 by permuting rows and columns. These two relations are considered "the same." More precisely, these two tables are different presentations of the same relation.

Notice the effect that permuting the attributes and columns has on tuples in isolation.

Example 3.1: The tuples

$$\text{(Star Wars, 1977, 124, color)}$$

from Fig. 3.1 and

$$\text{(1977, Star Wars, color, 124)}$$

from Fig. 3.3 represent the same object. Yet we can only be sure of their equivalence if we know the order of the attributes for their respective relations. Thus, it is generally advisable to select an order for the attributes of a relation and retain this one ordering for as long as the relation is used.   □

The Formal Notion of a Tuple

While we shall in this book express tuples as lists, with an understood ordering for the attributes of each relation, there is a formal notion of a tuple that allows us to avoid fixing the attribute order. A tuple may be thought of as a function from the attributes of its relation's schema to values — the components of that tuple for those attributes. For instance, the tuple represented two ways in Example 3.1 may be thought of as the function:

$$\texttt{title} \rightarrow \texttt{Star Wars}$$
$$\texttt{year} \rightarrow \texttt{1977}$$
$$\texttt{length} \rightarrow \texttt{124}$$
$$\texttt{filmType} \rightarrow \texttt{color}$$

---

year	title	filmType	length
1991	Mighty Ducks	color	104
1992	Wayne's World	color	95
1977	Star Wars	color	124

Figure 3.3: Another presentation of the relation `Movie`

3.1.6 Relation Instances

A relation about movies is not static; rather, relations change over time. We expect that these changes involve the tuples of the relation, such as insertion of new tuples as movies are added to the database, changes to existing tuples if we get revised or corrected information about a movie, and perhaps deletion of tuples for movies that are expelled from the database for some reason.

It is less common for the schema of a relation to change. However, there are situations where we might want to add or delete attributes. Schema changes, while possible in commercial database systems, are very expensive, because each of the perhaps millions of tuples need to be rewritten to add or delete components. If we are adding an attribute, it may be difficult or even impossible to find the correct values for the new component of tuples.

We shall call a set of tuples for a given relation an *instance* of that relation. For example, the three tuples shown in Fig. 3.1 form an instance of relation `Movie`. Presumably, the relation `Movie` has changed over time and will continue to change over time. For example, in 1980, `Movie` did not contain the tuples for `Mighty Ducks` or `Wayne's World`. However, a conventional database system maintains only one version of any relation: the set of tuples that are in the

---

Schemas and Instances

Let us not forget the important distinction between the schema of a relation and an instance of that relation. The schema is the name and attributes for the relation and is relatively immutable. An instance is a set of tuples for that relation, and the instance may change frequently.

The schema/instance distinction is common in data modeling. For example, in Chapter 2 we distinguished between ODL interface definitions, which define the structure for a class of objects, and the set of objects in that class. The interface definition is analogous to a schema, and a set of objects of the defined class is an instance. Similarly, entity set and relationship descriptions are the E/R model's way of describing a schema, while sets of entities and relationship sets form an instance of an E/R schema. Remember, however, that when designing a database, a database instance is not part of the design. We only imagine what typical instances would look like, as we develop our design.

---

relation "now." This instance of the relation is called the *current instance*.

3.1.7 Exercises for Section 3.1

Exercise 3.1.1: In Fig. 3.4 are instances of two relations that might constitute part of a banking database. Indicate the following:

a) The attributes of each relation.

b) The tuples of each relation.

c) The components of one tuple from each relation.

d) The relation schema for each relation.

e) The database schema.

f) A suitable domain for each attribute.

g) Another equivalent way to present each relation.

!! **Exercise 3.1.2:** How many different ways (considering orders of tuples and attributes) are there to represent a relation instance if that instance has:

* a) Three attributes and three tuples, like the relation Accounts of Fig. 3.4?

b) Four attributes and five tuples?

c) n attributes and m tuples?

acctNo	type	balance
12345	savings	12000
23456	checking	1000
34567	savings	25

The relation Accounts

firstName	lastName	idNo	account
Robbie	Banks	901-222	12345
Lena	Hand	805-333	12345
Lena	Hand	805-333	23456

The relation Customers

Figure 3.4: Two relations of a banking database

3.2 From ODL Designs to Relational Designs

Let us consider the process whereby a new database, such as our movie database, is created. We begin with a design phase, in which we answer questions about what information will be stored, how information elements will be related to one another, what constraints such as keyness or referential integrity may be assumed, and so on. This phase may last for a long time, while options are evaluated and opinions are reconciled.

The design phase is followed by an implementation phase using a real database system. Since the great majority of commercial database systems use the relational model, we might suppose that the design phase should use this model too, rather than the object-oriented ODL model or the E/R model that we discussed in Chapter 2.

However, in practice it is often easier to start with one of the models from Chapter 2, make our design, and then convert it to the relational model. The primary reason for doing so is that the relational model, having only one concept — the relation — rather than several complementary concepts (e.g., entity sets and relationships in the E/R model) has certain inflexibilities that are best handled after a design has been selected.

In this section we shall consider how to convert ODL designs into relational designs. We discuss the conversion from the E/R model to the relational model in Section 3.3. Then Section 3.4 will take up the matter of subclasses. Because ODL and the E/R model treat subclasses (isa-relationships) somewhat differently, their conversions to relations are also slightly different.

Often, we include constraints as part of a database schema. Constraints in ODL or the E/R model, such as key constraints and referential integrity constraints, can also be expressed in the relational model. An important class of constraints, called "functional dependencies" in the relational model, is deferred to Section 3.5. The study of other kinds of constraints on relations begins in Section 4.5.

3.2.1 From ODL Attributes to Relational Attributes

As a starting point, let us assume that our goal is to have one relation for each class and for that relation to have one attribute for each property. We shall see many ways in which this approach must be modified, but for the moment, let us consider the simplest possible case, where we can indeed convert classes to relations and properties to attributes. The restrictions we assume are:

1. All properties of the class are attributes (not relationships or methods).

2. The types of the attributes are atomic (not structures or sets).

Example 3.2: Figure 3.2 is an example of such a class. There are four attributes and no other properties. These attributes each have an atomic type; `title` is a string, `year` and `length` are integers, and `filmType` is an enumeration of two values.

We create a relation with the same name as the class, `Movie` in this case. The relation has four attributes, one for each attribute of the class. The names of the relational attributes can be the same as the names of the corresponding class attributes. Thus, the schema for this relation is

`Movie(title, year, length, filmType)`

as indicated in Section 3.1.1.

An object of the class has values for each of the four class attributes. We may form a tuple for this object by using each attribute's value as a component of the tuple. We have already seen the result of this conversion. Figure 3.1 was an example of the conversion of some `Movie` objects to tuples. □

3.2.2 Nonatomic Attributes in Classes

Unfortunately, even when a class' properties are all attributes we may have some difficulty converting the class to a relation. The reason is that attributes in ODL can have complex types such as structures, sets, multisets, or lists. On the other hand, a fundamental principle of the relational model is that a relation's attributes have an atomic type, such as numbers and strings. Thus, we must find some way of representing nonatomic attribute types as relations.

Record structures, whose fields are themselves atomic, are the easiest to handle. We simply expand the structure definition, making one attribute of the relation for each field of the structure. The only possible problem is that two structures could have fields of the same name, in which case we have to invent new attribute names to distinguish them in the relation.

```
interface Star {
    attribute string name;
    attribute Struct Addr
        {string street, string city} address;
};
```

Figure 3.5: Class with a structured attribute

Representing Enumerations and Dates

ODL has some atomic types — enumerations and dates in particular — that are not representable directly in the standard relational model. However, these types do not present fundamental problems. For example, an enumeration is really a list of aliases for the first few integers. Thus, an ODL enumeration type for the days of the week could be represented by an attribute of type integer, with only the numbers 0 through 6 used. Alternatively, an attribute of string type could be used, with days represented by strings "Mon", "Tues", and so on. Similarly, dates in ODL can be represented in the relational model by an attribute of type string. When we discuss the relational query language SQL in Chapter 5 we shall find that this language supports attribute types that are enumerations or dates, just as ODL does.

Example 3.3 : Consider the preliminary definition of the class Star from Example 2.3, which we reproduce here as Fig. 3.5. The attribute name is atomic, but attribute address is a structure with two fields, street and city. Thus, we can represent this class by a relation with three attributes. The first attribute, name, corresponds to the ODL attribute of the same name. The second and third attributes we shall call street and city; they correspond to the two fields of the address structure and together represent an address. Thus, the schema for our relation is

$$\text{Star}(\text{name, street, city})$$

An example instance of this relation with some possible tuples is shown in Fig. 3.6. □

However, record structures are not the most complex kind of attribute that can appear in ODL class definitions. Values can also be built using type constructors Set, Bag, Array, and List. Each presents its own problems when migrating to the relational model. We shall only discuss the Set constructor, which is the most common, in detail.

name	street	city
Carrie Fisher	123 Maple St.	Hollywood
Mark Hamill	456 Oak Rd.	Brentwood
Harrison Ford	789 Palm Dr.	Beverly Hills

Figure 3.6: A relation representing stars

A Note About Data Quality :-)

While we have endeavored to make example data as accurate as possible, we have used bogus values for addresses and other personal information about movie stars, in order to protect the privacy of members of the acting profession, many of whom are shy individuals who shun publicity.

One approach to representing a set of values for an attribute A is to make one tuple for each value. That tuple includes the appropriate values for all the other attributes besides A. Let us first see an example where this approach works well, and then we shall see a pitfall.

Example 3.4: Suppose that class `Star` were defined so that for each star we could record a set of addresses. The ODL class definition would look like Fig. 3.7. Suppose next that Carrie Fisher also has a beach home, but the other two stars mentioned in Fig. 3.6 have only one home. Then we may create two tuples with `name` attribute equal to `"Carrie Fisher"`, as shown in Fig. 3.8. Other tuples remain as they were in Fig. 3.6. □

The reader should be aware, however, that this technique of expanding a set into several tuples can lead sometimes to a relation that is poorly designed. In Section 3.7 we shall consider the problems that can arise and also learn how to redesign the database schema. For the moment, let us simply consider an example of the problems that can arise.

```
interface Star {
    attribute string name;
    attribute Set<
            Struct Addr {string street, string city}
        > address;
};
```

Figure 3.7: Stars with a set of addresses

name	street	city
Carrie Fisher	123 Maple St.	Hollywood
Carrie Fisher	5 Locust Ln.	Malibu
Mark Hamill	456 Oak Rd.	Brentwood
Harrison Ford	789 Palm Dr.	Beverly Hills

Figure 3.8: Allowing a set of addresses

Atomic Values: Bug or Feature?

It seems that the relational model puts obstacles in our way, while ODL is more flexible in allowing structured values as properties. One might be tempted to dismiss the relational model altogether or regard it as a primitive concept that has been superseded by more elegant "object-oriented" approaches such as ODL. However, the reality is that database systems based on the relational model are dominant in the marketplace. One of the reasons is that the simplicity of the model makes possible elegant and powerful programming languages for querying databases. We shall introduce abstract programming languages — Relational Algebra and Datalog — in Sections 4.1 and 4.2. Perhaps more important is their embodiment in SQL, the standard language used in most of today's database systems.

Example 3.5 : Suppose that we add `birthdate` as an attribute in the definition of the `Star` class; that is, we use the definition shown in Fig. 3.9. We have added to Fig. 3.7 the attribute `birthdate` of type `Date`, which is one of ODL's atomic types. The `birthdate` attribute can be an attribute of the `Star` relation, whose schema now becomes:

$$\text{Star(name, street, city, birthdate)}$$

Let us make another change to the data of Fig. 3.8. Since a set of addresses can be empty, let us assume that Harrison Ford has no address in the database. Then the revised relation is shown in Fig. 3.10.

Two bad things have happened in Fig. 3.10. First, Carrie Fisher's birthdate has been repeated in each tuple. There is thus redundancy in the information contained in this relation. Note that her name is also repeated, but that repetition is not true redundancy, because without the name appearing in each tuple we could not know that both addresses were associated with Carrie Fisher. The difference is that the star's name is a key for the objects being represented by the relation and therefore should appear in each tuple representing that star. In contrast, the birthdate is data about the star and is not part of a key for the represented object, so repeating the birthdate is redundant.

```
interface Star {
    attribute string name;
    attribute Set<
            Struct Addr {string street, string city}
        > address;
    attribute Date birthdate;
};
```

Figure 3.9: Stars with a set of addresses and a birthdate

name	street	city	birthdate
Carrie Fisher	123 Maple St.	Hollywood	9/9/99
Carrie Fisher	5 Locust Ln.	Malibu	9/9/99
Mark Hamill	456 Oak Rd.	Brentwood	8/8/88

Figure 3.10: Adding birthdates

The second problem is that because Harrison Ford has an empty set of addresses, we have lost all information about him. In particular, his birthdate is not part of the relation, even though it would appear in the Star object for Ford. Again, the reader should remember that neither of these problems is fatal to our methodology for converting from ODL schemas to relational schemas. However, we must be aware of problems such as these and fix the relational schema by "normalization" methods described in Section 3.7.   □

When there are several attributes of a class that have a collection type (which we shall call a *multivalued* attribute), the number of tuples we need to represent a single object can multiply. We need to create a tuple for each combination of values for the multivalued attributes. We shall return to this problem in Section 3.2.5 in the context of relationships with a collection type.

3.2.3   Representing Other Type Constructors

Besides record structures and sets, an ODL class definition could use Bag, Array, or List to construct values. To represent a bag (multiset), in which a single object can be a member of the bag n times, we cannot simply introduce into a relation n identical tuples.[1] Instead, we could add to the relation

---

[1] To be precise, we cannot introduce identical tuples into relations of the abstract relational model described in this chapter. However, SQL-based relational DBMS's *do* allow duplicate tuples; i.e., relations are bags rather than sets in SQL. See Sections 4.6 and 5.4. If counts of tuples are significant, we advise using a scheme such as that described here, even if your DBMS allows duplicate tuples.

schema another attribute `count` representing the number of times that each element is a member of the bag. For instance, suppose that `address` in Fig. 3.7 were a bag instead of a set. We could say that 123 Maple St., Hollywood is Carrie Fisher's address twice and 5 Locust Ln., Malibu is her address 3 times by

name	street	city	count
Carrie Fisher	123 Maple St.	Hollywood	2
Carrie Fisher	5 Locust Ln.	Malibu	3

A list of addresses could be represented by a new attribute `position`, indicating the position in the list. For instance, we could show Carrie Fisher's addresses as a list, with Hollywood first, by:

name	street	city	position
Carrie Fisher	123 Maple St.	Hollywood	1
Carrie Fisher	5 Locust Ln.	Malibu	2

Finally, a fixed-length array of addresses could be represented by attributes for each position in the array. For instance, if `address` were to be an array of two street-city structures, we could represent `Star` objects as:

name	street1	city1	street2	city2
Carrie Fisher	123 Maple	Hollywood	5 Locust	Malibu

3.2.4 Representing Single-Valued Relationships

Often, one ODL class definition will contain relationships to other ODL classes. As an example, let us consider the full definition of the class `Movie` from Fig. 2.6, which we reproduce here as Fig. 3.11.

```
interface Movie {
    attribute string title;
    attribute integer year;
    attribute integer length;
    attribute enumeration(color,blackAndWhite) filmType;
    relationship Set<Star> stars
            inverse Star::starredIn;
    relationship Studio ownedBy
            inverse Studio::owns;
};
```

Figure 3.11: The complete definition of the `Movie` class

Let us focus first on the relationship ownedBy, which connects each movie to the studio that produced it. Our first thought might be that a relationship is like an attribute. We could create a relational attribute or attributes to represent objects of the related class, in analogy to the way we represent an ODL attribute whose value is a structure or a set of structures. In the case of relationship ownedBy, we would put in the schema for relation Movie one attribute for each property of the Studio class.

One problem with this approach is that Studio objects have a property owns, which is a relationship back to the Movie class. To represent this relationship, each movie tuple would have to contain within it information about all the other movies that its studio made. In principle, the information about each of those movies includes its studio, which invites us to include all the information about that studio's movies again. Clearly this solution involves great complication, if it is feasible at all.[2]

A better approach is seen if we think about how objects are really stored in a computer's memory. When an object O_1 contains within it a reference to another object O_2, we do not copy O_2 into O_1. Rather, there is a "pointer" within O_1 that points to O_2.

However, the relational model does not have the notion of a pointer or anything closely resembling pointers. Instead, we must simulate the effect of pointers by values that represent the related objects. What we need is a set of attributes of the related class that form a key. If we have one, we treat the relationship as if it were the key attribute or attributes of the related class. An example will illustrate the technique.

Example 3.6 : Let us suppose that name is a key for class Studio, whose ODL definition from Fig 2.6 is:

```
interface Studio {
   attribute string name;
   attribute string address;
   relationship Set<Movie> owns inverse Movie::ownedBy;
};
```

We may modify our relation schema for relation Movie, from Fig 3.1, to include an attribute that represents the owning studio. We shall arbitrarily choose studioName to be this attribute. In Fig. 3.12 we see the addition of attribute studioName and some sample tuples.   □

---

[2]While the chains of movies and studios never get outside one studio's movies, a similar approach to the relationship stars and its inverse starredIn would get us from a movie to its stars, to all the movies they starred in, to all the stars of those movies, and so on, quickly taking us to almost all the stars and movies in the database.

title	year	length	filmType	studioName
Star Wars	1977	124	color	Fox
Mighty Ducks	1991	104	color	Disney
Wayne's World	1992	95	color	Paramount

Figure 3.12: Relation `Movie` with new attribute representing the owning studio

3.2.5 Representing Multivalued Relationships

The relationship `stars` in Fig. 3.11 presents a problem not seen when we considered the relationship `ownedBy`. When the type of a relationship is a class, we say that relationship is *single-valued*. Relationship `ownedBy`, whose type is `Studio`, is an example of a single-valued relationship. However, when the type of a relationship is some collection type applied to a class, we say that the relationship is *multivalued*. For instance, `stars` is multivalued, because its type is `Set<Star>`. Put another way, any one-many or many-many relationship from class *A* to class *B* is a multivalued relationship from *A* to *B*.

To represent a multivalued relationship we need to use a combination of two techniques:

1. As for single-valued relationships, we must find a key to represent each related object.

2. As for attributes with set values, we need to represent a set of related objects by creating one tuple for each value. Also like set-valued attributes, this approach leaves us open to redundancy because other attributes of the relation will have their values repeated once for each member of the set. This problem will be fixed in Section 3.7, but we shall accept this defect for the moment.

title	year	length	filmType	studioName	starName
Star Wars	1977	124	color	Fox	Carrie Fisher
Star Wars	1977	124	color	Fox	Mark Hamill
Star Wars	1977	124	color	Fox	Harrison Ford
Mighty Ducks	1991	104	color	Disney	Emilio Estevez
Wayne's World	1992	95	color	Paramount	Dana Carvey
Wayne's World	1992	95	color	Paramount	Mike Meyers

Figure 3.13: The relation `Movie` with star information

Example 3.7: Let us assume that `name` is a key for class `Star`. Then we may extend the relation we designed for class `Movie` by adding an attribute, say starName, in which we shall put the name of one of the stars of each movie. A movie is thus represented by as many tuples as it has stars listed in the database. Some example data is shown in Fig. 3.13. Notice the redundancy; all the other information about each movie is repeated once for each star of that movie. □

Occasionally, a class will have more than one multivalued relationship. In that case, the number of tuples needed to represent a single object of the class explodes. Suppose there are multivalued relationships $R_1, R_2, \ldots, R_k$ for a class C. Then the relation for class C has attributes corresponding to all the attributes of C and attributes representing the keys of all the single-valued relationships of C. It also has attributes representing the keys of the target classes for $R_1, R_2, \ldots, R_k$, as usual.

Suppose one particular object o of class C is connected to n_1 objects through relationship R_1, n_2 objects through relationship R_2, and so on. Then for every choice of an object for R_1, and object for R_2, and so on, we create one tuple corresponding to object o. As a result, there are $n_1 \times n_2 \times \cdots \times n_k$ tuples for this object in the relation constructed for class C.

Example 3.8 : Suppose the class C has a set of single-valued attributes X and two multivalued relationships R_1 and R_2. Let these relationships connect class C to classes whose key attributes are sets Y and Z respectively. Now consider an object c of class C that is related by relationship R_1 to objects with keys y_1 and y_2 and related by relationship R_2 to objects with keys z_1, z_2, and z_3. Also, let x represent the values of object c in the set of attributes X.

Then object c is represented in the relation constructed from class C by six tuples. We can think of these tuples as

$$(x, y_1, z_1) \quad (x, y_1, z_2) \quad (x, y_1, z_3)$$
$$(x, y_2, z_1) \quad (x, y_2, z_2) \quad (x, y_2, z_3)$$

That is, the keys from Y are paired with the keys from Z in all possible ways. □

3.2.6   What If There Is No Key?

An object-oriented model like ODL permits two objects in a class to have exactly the same values for all properties. We thus must be prepared to cope with problems such as two stars that have the same name. If so, then **name** is not a key for class **Star**, and we couldn't use it to represent stars in tuples of the **Movie** relation. Perhaps we could add other attributes of stars to make a key, but in principle there would be no guarantee that there could never be two stars with the same name, born on the same day, living at the same address, and so on for whatever other properties of stars we included in the database.

The only solution that is guaranteed to work is to invent a new attribute representing the "object identifier" of an object in the class that corresponds to the relation. For example, if we were not sure that name was a key for stars, we could invent a "certificate number" for each star that might be their membership number in the Actors' Guild. Certificate numbers are unique because a central authority is responsible for handing them out and keeping track of what numbers have been used.

Example 3.9: If we adopted the approach of inventing a unique certificate number for each star and using the certificate number as a key to represent a star in relationships, then the Movie relation would look like:

title	*year*	*length*	*filmType*	*studioName*	*cert#*
Star Wars	1977	124	color	Fox	12345

Here, we have shown only one tuple, and we suppose 12345 is the certificate number for Carrie Fisher. The relation Star would have to include the certificate number attribute as well as all other information about stars that is present in the Star ODL class definition. For instance,

cert#	*name*	*street*	*city*	*starredIn*
12345	Carrie Fisher	123 Maple St.	Hollywood	Star Wars

suggests the relation schema and one of several tuples for Carrie Fisher. □

3.2.7 Representing a Relationship and Its Inverse

In principle, when translating directly from ODL to the relational model, we represent a relationship twice, once in each direction. Thus in Example 3.7 we stored each star for a movie in a tuple that had that movie's title. If we designed a relation for class Star, we would represent the starredIn relationship by creating for each star as many tuples as the movies they starred in, with the title and year of each movie in one of those tuples (recall that title and year together form the key for movies).

However, representing both the stars relationship and its inverse is redundant. Either provides all the information that the other provides. Thus, for example, we could omit starredIn information altogether from the Star relation. Alternatively, we could leave this information in the Star relation and delete the attribute starName from the Movie relation. We shall see in Section 3.3.2 a third approach, in which the relationship and its inverse are separated out as a new relation. Sometimes, although not always, this approach is preferable. However, when a separate relation for the relationship is the best choice, the "normalization" process to be discussed in Section 3.7 will force us to separate out the relationship into its own relation, even if we did not do so in the initial relational design.

Note that in the ODL model, the relationship and its inverse are both needed, because they imply pointers from movies to their stars and from stars to their movies. One cannot follow a pointer "backwards," so pointers in both

---

Representing Relationships in One Direction

When we have a binary relationship between two entity sets, there is a choice of relation in which the relationship could appear: the relation for either entity set. Does it matter which we choose? If the relationship is many-many or one-one, probably not. But if the relationship is many-one, we recommend including the relationship with the "many"; i.e., with the entity set of which many may be associated with one entity of the other entity set. The reason is that we thereby avoid redundancy.

For example, the relationship *Owns* between *Movies* and *Studios* is best placed with *Movies*. That way, the relation for *Movies* is given an attribute for the name of the owning studio, and each tuple is extended with that studio name. In contrast, if we added the relationship to the relation for *Studios* we would have to expand each studio tuple into many tuples, one for each movie the studio owned. As a result, all the other information about each studio would be duplicated, once for each movie it owned.

---

directions are needed.[3] However, the relational model, like the E/R model, represents relationships by associating values (the keys). Tuples containing pairs of associated keys — for example, the title and year from a movie and the name of a star — can be used to follow the relationship in either direction.

3.2.8 Exercises for Section 3.2

Exercise 3.2.1: Convert your ODL designs from the following exercises to relational database schemas.

* a) Exercise 2.1.1.

  b) Exercise 2.1.2 (include all four of the modifications specified by that exercise).

  c) Exercise 2.1.3.

  d) Exercise 2.1.4.

* e) Exercise 2.1.5.

  f) Exercise 2.1.6.

---

[3]Of course one cannot be certain that a given ODL implementation will represent these "pointers" in the expected manner, so an implementation might in fact have a single representation for the pair of inverse relationships.

Pointers: Feature or Bug?

ODL relationships are presumably implemented by pointers or references from each object to its related object or objects. That implementation is very convenient, because it lets us get from an object to related objects quickly. In comparison, the relational model, which represents "objects" by the value of their key rather than by a pointer, seems to require slower navigation from an object to related objects.

For example, a `Movie` object was represented in Example 3.7 by having one tuple for each star of a movie; that tuple contained only the name of the star, not all the information about the star. If we want to find the addresses of the stars of *Wayne's World*, we need to take the name of each star and look in the `Star` relation for the tuple or tuples for that star. There we shall find the address.

One might think therefore that the absence of pointers in the relational model was a "bug" of that model. However, in practice, we can build indexes on relations that allows us to search very efficiently for tuples having a given value in a given component (see Sections 1.2.1 and 5.7.7). Thus, little is lost by not using pointers in practice. Moreover, while pointers are very useful in programs that run in main memory and whose executions exist for seconds at most, databases are very different from such programs. Implementing pointers among objects that exist for years and that may be distributed across many secondary storage devices attached to widely distributed computer systems is much more difficult. Thus, a strong case can be made for the no-pointers approach of the relational model.

Exercise 3.2.2: Convert the ODL description of Fig. 2.7 to a relational database schema. How does each of the three modifications of Exercise 2.1.8 affect your relational schema?

! **Exercise 3.2.3:** In Fig. 3.14 is an ODL definition of a class of customers. In objects of this class we keep a set of phones of different type (e.g., home, office, fax) and a set of "referrals," in which a customer is given credit for introducing other customers to the business. Convert this ODL specification to a relational database schema.

3.3 From E/R Diagrams to Relational Designs

Translation from an entity/relationship diagram to a database schema is similar to the translation from an ODL design to a database schema. However, in

```
interface Customer {
    attribute Struct Name
        {string first, string last} name;
    attribute Set<
            Struct Phone {string type, int number}
        > phones;
    relationship Customer referredBy inverse referrals;
    relationship Set<Customer> referrals
        inverse referredBy;
};
```

Figure 3.14: Customer records

a sense, the E/R model represents an intermediate form between an object-oriented design and a relational design. Thus, in starting from an E/R diagram, some of the hard work has been done for us already. Two important differences are:

1. In the E/R model, relationships are extracted as a separate concept, rather than being embedded as properties of classes. This difference helps us avoid the sort of redundancy that we found in Section 3.2.2 when we chose to embed a multivalued relationship like stars in tuples representing Movie objects.

2. In ODL, attributes can have any collection type such as <Set>. The E/R model, while being somewhat vague about what sorts of types are permitted, is generally regarded as permitting structured values but not sets or other collection type constructors.[4] As a result, a set-valued attribute, such as a set of addresses for a star discussed in Example 3.4, would force us, in the E/R model, to treat addresses as an entity-set and define a relationship Lives-at to connect stars and their addresses.

3. In the E/R model, relationships are permitted to have attributes. In ODL, there is no corresponding notion.

3.3.1   From Entity Sets to Relations

Let us first consider entity sets that are not weak. We shall take up the modifications needed to accommodate weak entity sets in Section 3.3.3. For each non-weak entity set, we shall create a relation of the same name and with the same set of attributes. This relation will not have any indication of the relationships in which the entity set participates; we'll handle relationships with separate relations, as discussed in Section 3.3.2.

---

[4]However, there are some formulations of the E/R model that use exactly the same restrictions on attribute types that ODL has: a collection of structures or anything simpler.

Example 3.10: Consider the three entity sets Movies, Stars and Studios from Fig. 2.8, which we reproduce here as Fig 3.15. The attributes for the Movies entity set are title, year, length, and filmType. As a result, the relation Movies looks just like the relation Movie of Fig. 3.1 with which we began Section 3.1. □

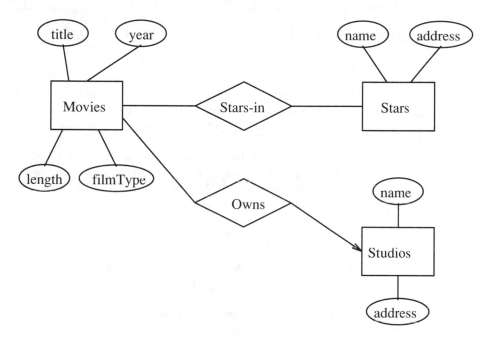

Figure 3.15: E/R diagram for the movie database

Example 3.11: Now consider the entity set Stars from Fig. 3.15. There are two attributes, name and address. Thus, we would expect the corresponding Stars relation to look like

name	address
Carrie Fisher	123 Maple St., Hollywood
Mark Hamill	456 Oak Rd., Brentwood
Harrison Ford	789 Palm Dr., Beverly Hills

This relation resembles the relation Star of Fig. 3.6 that we constructed in Example 3.3. However, the latter has three attributes, two of which — street and city — represent a structured address. The difference is minor. We could have designed our E/R diagram of Fig. 2.8 to have street and city attributes for the Stars entity set, thus making its corresponding relation Stars look exactly like relation Star of Fig. 3.6. □

3.3.2   From E/R Relationships to Relations

Relationships in the E/R model are also represented by relations. The relation for a given relationship R has the following attributes:

1. For each entity set involved in relationship R, we take its key attribute or attributes as part of the schema of the relation for R.

2. If the relationship has attributes, then these are also attributes of relation R.

If one entity set is involved several times in a relationship, then we must rename the attributes to avoid name duplication. Similarly, should the same attribute name appear twice or more among the attributes of R itself and the entity sets involved in relationship R, then we need to rename to avoid duplication.

Example 3.12: Consider the relationship `Owns` of Fig. 3.15. This relationship connects entity sets `Movies` and `Studios`. Thus, for the relation schema of relation `Owns` we use the key for `Movies`, which is `title` and `year`, and the key of `Studios`, which is `name`. A sample of this relation is

title	*year*	*studioName*
Star Wars	1977	Fox
Mighty Ducks	1991	Disney
Wayne's World	1992	Paramount

We have chosen the attribute `studioName` for clarity; it corresponds to the attribute `name` of `Studios`.

Notice how the relation above, plus the relation of Example 3.10 that we constructed for the entity set `Movies` (and which is shown in Fig. 3.1), contains exactly the information in the relation of Fig 3.12 that we constructed in Example 3.6 for the class `Movie`, excluding its `stars` property.   □

Example 3.13: Similarly, the relationship `Stars-In` of Fig. 3.15 can be transformed into a relation with the attributes `title` and `year` (the key for `Movie`) and attribute `starName`, which is the key for entity set `Stars`. Figure 3.16 shows a sample relation `Stars-In`. Notice how this relation plus Fig. 3.1 contains the information of Fig. 3.13, but they do so without the repetition of nonkey attributes of the `Star` class (attributes `length` and `filmType`) that flaws the schema of Fig. 3.13.

It seems that the year is redundant in Fig. 3.16. However, that is only because these movie titles are unique. Had there been several movies of the same title, like "King Kong", we would see that the year was essential to sort out which stars appear in which version of the movie.   □

Observe several advantages to the database schema that we get starting from an E/R diagram, compared to what we get starting with an ODL design.

title	year	starName
Star Wars	1977	Carrie Fisher
Star Wars	1977	Mark Hamill
Star Wars	1977	Harrison Ford
Mighty Ducks	1991	Emilio Estevez
Wayne's World	1992	Dana Carvey
Wayne's World	1992	Mike Meyers

Figure 3.16: A relation for relationship `Stars-In`

- Relations are often "normalized," meaning that they avoid some of the redundancy present in design directly from the ODL description.

- Two-way ODL relationships are replaced by a single relation representing the relationship in both directions.

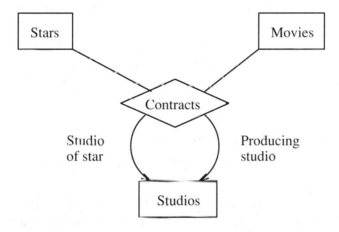

Figure 3.17: The relationship *Contracts*

Example 3.14: Multiway relationships are also easy to convert to relations. Consider the four-way relationship *Contracts* of Fig. 2.12, reproduced here as Fig. 3.17, involving a star, a movie, and two studios — the first holding the star's contract and the second contracting for that star's services in that movie. We represent this relationship by a relation `Contracts` whose schema consists of the attributes from the keys of the following four entity sets:

1. The key `starName` for the star.

2. The key consisting of attributes `title` and `year` for the movie.

ODL-to-Relations Revisited

As we have seen, the result of translating relationships in the E/R model to relations sometimes gives us a more appropriate relational database schema than does the translation of ODL relationships to relations. However, we are free to borrow the E/R technique of separating out a many-one or many-many relationship as a separate relation. That will avoid the redundancy and explosion in the number of tuples that sometimes occurs when we try to implement a multivalued ODL relationship with the class for which it is defined. Let us again remind the reader, however, that Section 3.7 gives us a mechanical way to fix the relation schemas that we get directly from ODL.

---

3. The key `studioOfStar` indicating the name of the first studio; recall we assume the studio name is a key for the entity set `Studio`.

4. The key `producingStudio` indicating the name of the studio that will produce the movie using that star.

Notice that we have been inventive in choosing attribute names for our relation schema, avoiding "name" for any attribute, since it would be unobvious whether that referred to a star's name or studio's name, and in the latter case, which studio. □

3.3.3 Handling Weak Entity Sets

When a weak entity set appears in an E/R diagram, we need to do three things differently.

1. The relation for the weak entity set W itself must include not only the attributes of W but also the key attributes of the other entity sets that help form the key of W. These helping entity sets are easily recognized because they are reached by a double-diamond many-one relationship from W.

2. Any relationships in which the weak entity set W appears must use as a key for W all of its key attributes, including those of other entity sets that contribute to W's key.

3. However, as we shall see, the double-diamond relationships, from the weak entity set W to other entity sets that help provide the key for W, need not be converted to a relation at all. The justification is that the attributes for such a relationship will always be a subset of the attributes for the weak intity set W itself, and thus these relationships provide no additional information, beyond the fact that they help W find its key.

Of course, when introducing these additional attributes to build the key of a weak entity set, we must be careful not to use the same name twice. If necessary, we rename some or all of these attributes.

Example 3.15: Let us consider the weak entity set *Crews* from Fig. 2.27, which we reproduce here as Fig. 3.18. From this diagram we get three relations, whose schemas are:

```
Studios(name, addr)
Crews(number, studioName)
Unit-of(number, studioName, name)
```

The first relation, `Studios`, is constructed in a straightforward manner from the entity set of the same name. The second, `Crews`, comes from the weak entity set *Crews*. The attributes of this relation are the key attributes of *Crews*; if there were any nonkey attributes for *Crews*, they would be included in the relation schema as well. We have chosen `studioName` as the attribute in relation `Crews` that corresponds to the attribute `name` in the entity set *Studios*.

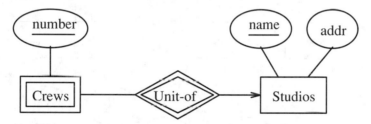

Figure 3.18: The crews example of a weak entity set

The third relation, `Unit-of`, comes from the relationship of the same name. As always, we represent an E/R relationship in the relational model by a relation whose schema has the key attributes of the related entity sets. In this case, `Unit-of` has attributes `number` and `studioName`, the key for weak entity set *Crews*, and attribute `name`, the key for entity set *Studios*. However, notice that since *Unit-of* is a many-one relationship, the studio `studioName` is surely the same as the studio `name`.

For instance, suppose Disney crew #3 is one of the crews of the Disney studio. Then the relationship set for *Unit-of* includes the pair

(Disney crew #3, Disney)

This pair gives rise to the `Unit-of` tuple

(3, Disney, Disney)

As a consequence, we can "merge" the attributes `studioName` and `name` of `Unit-of`, giving us the simpler schema:

```
Unit-of(number, name)
```

However, now we can dispense with the relation `Unit-of` altogether, since its attributes are a subset of the attributes of relation `Crews`. □

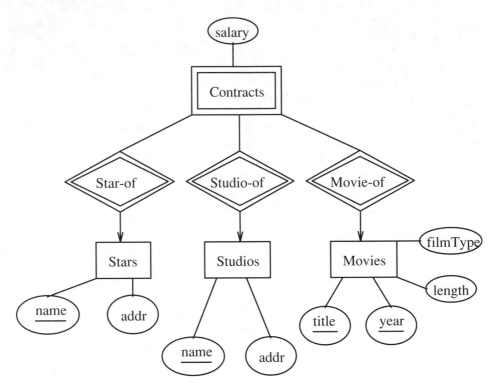

Figure 3.19: The weak entity set *Contracts*

Example 3.16: Now consider the weak entity set *Contracts* from Example 2.31 and Fig. 2.28 in Section 2.6.1. We reproduce this diagram as Fig. 3.19. The schema for relation `Contracts` is

```
Contracts(starName, studioName, title, year, salary)
```

These attributes are the key for *Stars*, suitably renamed, the key for *Studios*, suitably renamed, the two attributes that form the key for *Movies*, and the lone attribute, *salary*, belonging to the entity set *Contracts* itself. There are no relations constructed for the relationships *Star-of*, *Studio-of*, or *Movie-of*. Each would have a schema that is a proper subset of that for `Contracts` above.

Incidentally, notice that the relation we obtain is exactly the same as what we would obtain had we started from the E/R diagram of Fig. 2.13. Recall that figure treats contracts as a three-way relationship among stars, movies, and studios, with a salary attribute attached to *Contracts*. □

The phenomenon observed in Examples 3.15 and 3.16 — that the double-diamond relationship needs no relation — is universal for weak entity sets. The relation for the weak entity set E has a schema that includes the schema of the relations constructed from any of the "double diamond" relationships R that are many-one from E to one of the other entity sets that help form E's key. The reason is that the relation for E includes the key attributes for E, and these include all the key attributes for the two entity sets connected by R. Thus, we can state the following modified rule for weak entity sets.

- If E is a weak entity set, construct for E a relation whose schema consists of all the key attributes for E, including those attributes that are keys of "helping" entity sets related to E by a many-one relationship.

- Do *not* construct a relation for any relationship that is many-one from a weak entity set to another entity set, provided that relationship is a "double-diamond" relationship that helps provide the key for the weak entity set.

3.3.4 Exercises for Section 3.3

* **Exercise 3.3.1:** Convert the E/R diagram of Fig. 3.20 to a relational database schema.

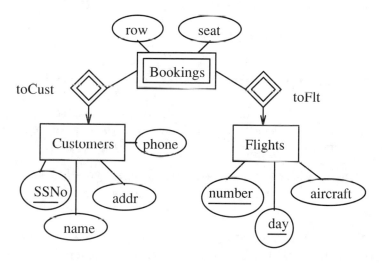

Figure 3.20: An E/R diagram about airlines

* **Exercise 3.3.2:** The E/R diagram of Fig. 3.21 represents ships. Ships are said to be *sisters* if they were designed from the same plans. Convert this diagram to a relational database schema.

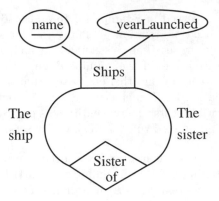

Figure 3.21: An E/R diagram about sister ships

Exercise 3.3.3: Convert the following E/R diagrams to relational database schemas.

a) Figure 2.28.

b) Your answer to Exercise 2.6.1.

c) Your answer to Exercise 2.6.4(a).

d) Your answer to Exercise 2.6.4(b).

3.4   Converting Subclass Structures to Relations

Object-oriented and E/R models treat the notion of subclasses slightly differently. This difference leads to two different ways to organize relations that represent a hierarchy of classes. Recall that the distinction is:

- In ODL, an object belongs to exactly one class. An object inherits properties from all its superclasses but technically is not a member of the superclasses.

- In the E/R model, an "object" can be represented by entities belonging to several entity sets that are related by isa relationships. Thus, the linked entities together represent the object and give that object its properties — attributes and relationships.

Let us see how these two viewpoints encourage different strategies for the design of a relational database schema. It should be borne in mind that neither the ODL nor E/R models force one or the other approach; we can choose an approach tailored to the other model if we prefer.

3.4.1 Relational Representation of ODL Subclasses

First, let us see a technique for turning a hierarchy of ODL subclasses into relation schemas. The principle we shall follow is:

- Every subclass has its own relation.

- In this relation are represented all the properties of that subclass, including all its inherited properties.

Example 3.17: Let us consider the hierarchy of four classes from Fig. 2.22. Recall these classes were:

1. Movie, the broadest class. It is the class discussed in numerous examples of this chapter.

2. Cartoon, a subclass of Movie, with one additional property: a relationship that is a set of stars called voices.

3. MurderMystery, another subclass of Movie, with an additional attribute: weapon.

4. Cartoon-MurderMystery, a subclass of both Cartoon and MurderMystery, with no additional subclasses but (naturally) all the properties of its three superclasses.

The schema for Movie is as before:

```
Movie(title, year, length, filmType, studioName, starName)
```

Some typical tuples appeared in Fig. 3.13. For Cartoon we add to the six attributes of the Movie schema the voice attribute, giving us a seven-attribute schema:

```
Cartoon(title, year, length, filmType,
    studioName, starName, voice)
```

For MurderMystery we have another relation with the six attributes of Movie, plus weapon. That is, the schema for the MurderMystery relation is

```
MurderMystery(title, year, length, filmType,
    studioName, starName, weapon)
```

Finally, the schema for relation Cartoon-MurderMystery involves not only the six Movie attributes but the two attributes voice and weapon from the other superclasses. Thus, the schema for this relation has eight attributes:

```
Cartoon-MurderMystery(title, year, length, filmType,
    studioName, starName, voice, weapon)
```

□

3.4.2   Representing Isa in the Relational Model

The philosophy behind isa hierarchies in the E/R model is that the hierarchy is populated by entities that are related by isa relationships. Therefore, it is natural to create a relation for each entity set and give that relation the attributes of that entity set alone. However, to identify the entities associated with each tuple, we need to include the key attributes for each of the entity sets. As a result, the information for a member of some subclass is scattered around several relations, but that would probably be the case anyway because of the way the E/R-to-relational transformation splits information about E/R attributes and relationships into separate relations.

There is no relation created for an isa relationship. Rather, the isa relationship is implicit in the fact that related entities have the same key values.

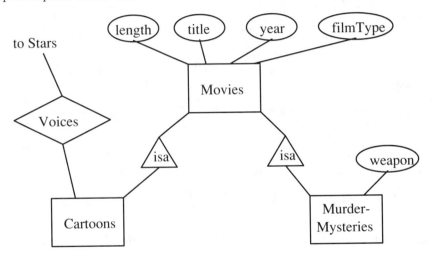

Figure 3.22: The movie hierarchy

Example 3.18: Let us work the hierarchy of Fig. 2.22 in the E/R model. Recall that the relevant part of the E/R diagram was shown in Fig. 2.23, which we reproduce here as Fig. 3.22. The relation schemas needed to represent this part of the diagram are:

1. The relation Movies(title, year, length, filmType). This is the relation discussed in Example 3.10.

2. The relation MurderMysteries(title, year, weapon). The first two attributes are the key for all movies, and the last is the lone attribute for the corresponding entity set.

3. The relation Cartoons(title, year). This relation is the set of cartoons. It has no attributes other than the key for movies, since the extra information about cartoons is contained in the relationship *Voices*.

4. The relation Voices(title, year, name) that corresponds to the relationship *Voices* between *Stars* and *Cartoons*. The last attribute is the key for *Stars* and the first two form the key for *Cartoons*.

Notice that there is no entity set in Fig. 3.22 corresponding to the class Cartoon-MurderMysteries. Hence, unlike the relational design of Example 3.17, there is no special relation for movies that are both cartoons and murder mysteries. For a movie that is both, we obtain its voices from the Voices relation, its weapon from the MurderMysteries relation, and all other information from the Movies relation or from the relation for one of the relationships in which entity sets Movies, Cartoons, and MurderMysteries are involved.

Notice also that the relation Cartoons has a schema that is a subset of the schema for the relation Voices. In many situations, we would be content to eliminate the relation Cartoons, since it appears not to contain any information beyond what is in Voices. However, there may be silent cartoons in our database. Those cartoons would have no voices, and we would therefore lose the fact that these movies were cartoons. In fact, the same problem occurs differently in the relation Cartoons from Example 3.17, where if there are no voices, then there is no mention of the cartoon. This problem can be solved by normalization, as discussed in Section 3.7. □

3.4.3 Comparison of Approaches

Each of the approaches of Sections 3.4.1 and 3.4.2 present their own problems. The ODL translation keeps all properties of an object together in one relation. However, it forces us to search several relations should we want to find an object. For example, using the database schema of Example 3.17, to find the length of a movie we must search four different relations, until we find the relation for the class the movie is in.

On the other hand, the E/R translation repeats the key for an object once for each of the entity sets or relationships to which that object (entity) belongs. That repetition wastes space. Further, we may have to look in several relations to get information about a single object. That would be the case, for example, if in the database schema of Example 3.18 we wanted the length and weapon used for a murder mystery.

3.4.4 Using Null Values to Combine Relations

There is one more approach to representing information about a hierarchy of classes. We may use a special *null value*, denoted NULL. When NULL appears in the component of a tuple for some attribute, it means informally that there is no appropriate value for that attribute of that tuple. While not a part of the traditional relational model, nulls are in fact very useful and play a prominent role in the query language SQL, as we shall see in Section 5.9.

If we are allowed to use NULL as a value in tuples, we can handle a hierarchy of classes with a single relation. This relation has attributes for all the

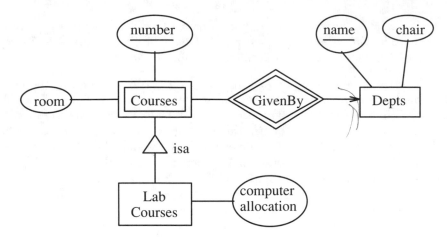

Figure 3.23: E/R diagram for Exercise 3.4.1

properties possessed by objects in any of the classes of the hierarchy. An object
is then represented by a single tuple. This tuple has NULL in each attribute
corresponding to a property that does not belong to the object's class.

Example 3.19: If we applied this approach to the problem of Example 3.17,
we would create a single relation whose schema is:

        Movie(title, year, length, filmType, studioName,
            starName, voice, weapon)

A movie like *Who Framed Roger Rabbit?*, being both a cartoon and a murder
mystery, would be represented by several tuples that had no NULL's; there would
be one tuple for each "voice."[5] On the other hand, *The Little Mermaid*, being a
cartoon but not a murder mystery, would have NULL in the weapon component.
Murder on the Orient Express would have NULL in the voice attribute, while
Gone With the Wind would have NULL's in both voice and weapon attributes.
□

Notice that like the approach of Section 3.4.2, this approach allows us to
find in one relation tuples from all classes in the hierarchy. On the other hand,
like the approach of Section 3.4.1, it also allows us to find all the information
about an object in one relation.

3.4.5 Exercises for Section 3.4

Exercise 3.4.1: Convert the E/R diagram of Fig. 3.23 to a relational database
schema.

---

[5]Actually, *Roger Rabbit*, having both stars and voices, would have tuples for each star-
voice pair. A pure cartoon would need NULL in the starName attribute so voices and other
information could be recorded.

```
interface Course {
    attribute int number;
    attribute string room;
    relationship Dept deptOf inverse Dept::coursesOf;
};

interface LabCourse : Course {
    attribute int computerAlloc;
};

interface Dept {
    unique attribute string name;
    attribute string chair;
    relationship Set<Course> coursesOf
        inverse Course::deptOf;
};
```

Figure 3.24: An ODL description of courses and lab courses

Exercise 3.4.2: In Fig. 3.24 is an ODL description of a schema similar to the E/R diagram of Exercise 3.4.1. Convert it to a relational database schema. Remember that Course objects have an "object identity," and you may invent an attribute representing this OID, e.g., CourseID. You should *not*, in this exercise, mimic the strategy used to convert a weak entity set in Exercise 3.4.1 (although in principle you could do so if you wished).

Exercise 3.4.3: Convert your ODL designs from the following exercises to relational database schemas.

* a) Exercise 2.4.1.

  b) Exercise 2.4.4.

Exercise 3.4.4: Convert your E/R designs from the following exercises to relational database schemas.

* a) Exercise 2.4.3.

  b) Exercise 2.4.4.

! **Exercise 3.4.5:** Convert the E/R diagram of Fig. 3.25 to a relational database schema.

! **Exercise 3.4.6:** How would the relational database schema of Exercise 3.4.5 differ if we had started from the corresponding ODL definition?

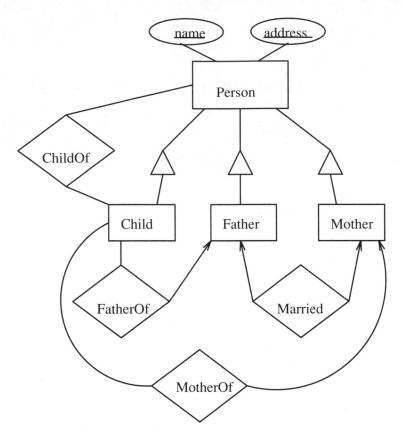

Figure 3.25: E/R diagram for Exercise 3.4.5

3.5   Functional Dependencies

The most important kind of constraint that we deal with in the relational model is a unique-value constraint called a "functional dependency." Knowledge of this type of constraint is vital for the redesign of database schemas to eliminate redundancy, as we shall see in Section 3.7. There are also some other kinds of constraints that help us design good databases schemas: multivalued dependencies, covered in Section 3.8, and existence constraints and independence constraints that we shall take up in Section 4.5.

3.5.1   Definition of Functional Dependency

A *functional dependency* on a relation R is a statement of the form "If two tuples of R agree on attributes $A_1, A_2, \ldots, A_n$ (i.e., the tuples have the same values in their respective components for each of these attributes), then they must also agree in another attribute, B." We write this dependency formally as $A_1 A_2 \cdots A_n \rightarrow B$ and say that "$A_1, A_2, \ldots, A_n$ functionally determine B."

If a set of attributes $A_1, A_2, \ldots, A_n$ functionally determines more than one attribute, say

$$A_1 A_2 \cdots A_n \rightarrow B_1$$
$$A_1 A_2 \cdots A_n \rightarrow B_2$$
$$\cdots$$
$$A_1 A_2 \cdots A_n \rightarrow B_m$$

then we can, as a shorthand, write this set of dependencies as

$$A_1 A_2 \cdots A_n \rightarrow B_1 B_2 \cdots B_m$$

Figure 3.26 suggests what this functional dependency tells us about any two tuples t and u in the relation R.

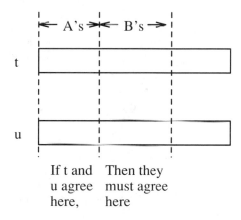

Figure 3.26: The effect of a functional dependency on two tuples.

Example 3.20: Let us consider the relation Movie from Fig. 3.13, an instance of which we reproduce here as Fig. 3.27. There are several functional dependencies that we can reasonably assert about the Movie relation. For instance, we can assert the three dependencies

$$\text{title year} \rightarrow \text{length}$$
$$\text{title year} \rightarrow \text{filmType}$$
$$\text{title year} \rightarrow \text{studioName}$$

Since the three dependencies each have the same left side, title and year, we can summarize them in one line by the shorthand

$$\text{title year} \rightarrow \text{length filmType studioName}$$

Functional Dependencies Tell Us About the Schema

Remember that a functional dependency, like any constraint, is an assertion about the schema of a relation, not about a particular instance. If we look at an instance, we cannot tell for certain that a functional dependency holds. For example, looking at Fig. 3.27 we might suppose that a dependency like `title` → `filmType` holds, because for every tuple in this particular instance of the relation `Movie` it happens that any two tuples agreeing on `title` also agree on `filmType`.

However, we cannot claim this functional dependency for the relation `Movie`. Were our instance to include, for example, tuples for the two versions of *King Kong*, one of which was in color and the other in black-and-white, then the proposed functional dependency would not hold.

Informally, this set of functional dependencies says that if two tuples have the same value in their `title` components, and they also have the same value in their `year` components, then these two tuples must have the same values in their `length` components, the same values in their `filmType` components, and the same values in their `studioName` components. This assertion makes sense if we remember the original design from which the `Movie` relation schema was developed. Attributes `title` and `year` form a key for movie objects. Thus, we expect that given a title and year, there is a unique length for the movie, a unique film type, and a unique owning studio.

title	year	length	filmType	studioName	starName
Star Wars	1977	124	color	Fox	Carrie Fisher
Star Wars	1977	124	color	Fox	Mark Hamill
Star Wars	1977	124	color	Fox	Harrison Ford
Mighty Ducks	1991	104	color	Disney	Emilio Estevez
Wayne's World	1992	95	color	Paramount	Dana Carvey
Wayne's World	1992	95	color	Paramount	Mike Meyers

Figure 3.27: The relation `Movie`

On the other hand, we observe that the statement

$$\texttt{title year} \to \texttt{starName}$$

is false; it is not a functional dependency. We might have expected that dependency to hold, given that `title` and `year` form a key for movies. However, because of how the `Movie` class was defined, it is only true that for each movie there is a uniquely determined *set* of stars. When we converted from ODL to the relational model, we had to create several tuples for each movie, and each tuple had a different star. Thus, even though all these tuples agree in the other properties of the Movie class, they do not agree on the star's name. □

3.5.2 Keys of Relations

We say a set of one or more attributes $\{A_1, A_2, \ldots, A_n\}$ is a *key* for a relation if:

1. Those attributes functionally determine all other attributes of the relation. That is, it is impossible for two distinct tuples of R to agree on all of $A_1, A_2, \ldots, A_n$.

2. No proper subset of $\{A_1, A_2, \ldots, A_n\}$ functionally determines all other attributes of R; i.e., a key must be *minimal*.

When a key consists of a single attribute A, we often say that A (rather than $\{A\}$) is a key.

Example 3.21: Attributes {title, year, starName} form a key for the Movie relation of Fig. 3.27. First, we must show that they functionally determine all the other attributes. That is, suppose two tuples agree on these three attributes: title, year, and starName. Because they agree on title and year, they must agree on the other attributes — length, filmType, and studioName — as we discussed in Example 3.20. Thus, two different tuples cannot agree on all of title, year, and starName; they would in fact be the same tuple.

Now, we must argue that no proper subset of {title, year, starName} functionally determines all other attributes. To see why, begin by observing that title and year do not determine starName, because many movies have more than one star. Thus, {title, year} is not a key.

{year, starName} is not a key because we could have a star in two movies in the same year; thus

$$\text{year starName} \rightarrow \text{title}$$

is not a functional dependency. Also, we claim that {title, starName} is not a key, because we could have two movies with the same title made in different years. Conceivably, these two movies could have a star in common, although frankly we cannot think of an example.[6] □

Sometimes a relation has more than one key. If so, it is common to designate one of the keys as the *primary key*. In commercial database systems, the choice of primary key can influence some implementation issues such as how the relation is stored on disk.

---

[6]Remember that functional dependencies are assumptions or assertions we make about the data. There is no external authority we can appeal to for an absolute decision as to whether a dependency holds or not. Thus, we are free to make any plausible assumptions we wish about which dependencies hold.

What Is "Functional" About Functional Dependencies?

$A_1 A_2 \cdots A_n \rightarrow B$ is called a "functional" dependency because in principle there is a function that takes a list of values, one for each of attributes $A_1, A_2, \ldots, A_n$ and produces a unique value (or no value at all) for B. For example, in the `Movie` relation, we can imagine a function that takes a string like `"Star Wars"` and an integer like 1977 and produces the unique value of `length`, namely 124, that appears in the relation `Movie`. However, this function is not the usual sort of function that we meet in mathematics, because there is no way to compute it from first principles. That is, we cannot perform some operations on strings like `"Star Wars"` and integers like 1977 and come up with the correct length. Rather, the function is only computed by lookup in the relation. We look for a tuple with the given `title` and `year` values and see what value that tuple has for `length`.

3.5.3 Superkeys

A set of attributes that contains a key is called a *superkey*, short for "superset of a key." Thus, every key is a superkey. However, some superkeys are not (minimal) keys. Note that every superkey satisfies the first condition of a key: it functionally determines all other attributes of the relation. However, a superkey need not satisfy the second condition: minimality.

Example 3.22: In the relation of Example 3.21, there are many superkeys. Not only is the key

$$\{\texttt{title}, \texttt{year}, \texttt{starName}\}$$

a superkey, but any superset of this set of attributes, such as

$$\{\texttt{title}, \texttt{year}, \texttt{starName}, \texttt{length}\}$$

is a superkey. $\Box$

3.5.4 Discovering Keys for Relations

When a relation schema was developed by converting an ODL or E/R design to relations, we can often predict the key of the relation. In this section, we shall consider the relations that come from E/R diagrams; Section 3.5.5 discusses the situation when the relations come from ODL designs.

When the relation comes from either an ODL or E/R design, it is quite common (although not certain) that there is only one key for each relation. When there is one key for a relation, a useful convention is to underline the attributes of the key when displaying its relation schema.

Our first rule about inferring keys is:

Other Key Terminology

In some books and articles one finds different terminology regarding keys. One can find the term "key" used the way we have used the term "superkey," that is, a set of attributes that functionally determine all the attributes, with no requirement of minimality. These sources typically use the term "candidate key" for a key that is minimal — that is, a "key" in the sense we use the term.

- If the relation comes from an entity set then the key for the relation is the key attributes of this entity set or class.

Example 3.23: In Examples 3.10 and 3.11 we described how the entity sets *Movies* and *Stars* could be converted to relations. The keys for these entity sets were {*title*, *year*} and {*name*}, respectively. Thus, these are the keys for the corresponding relations, and

```
Movies(title, year, length, filmType)
Stars(name, address)
```

are the schemas of the relations, with keys indicated by underline.   □

Our second rule concerns binary relationships. If a relation R is constructed from a relationship, then the multiplicity of the relationship affects the key for R. There are three cases:

- If the relationship is many-many, then the keys of both connected entity sets are the key attributes for R.

- If the relationship is many-one from entity set E_1 to entity set E_2, then the key attributes of E_1 are key attributes of R, but those of E_2 are not.

- If the relationship is one-one, then the key attributes for either of the connected entity sets are key attributes of R. Thus, there is not a unique key for R.

Example 3.24: Example 3.12 discussed the relationship *Owns*, which is many-one from entity set *Movies* to entity set *Studios*. Thus, the key for the relation Owns is the key attributes title and year, which come from the key for *Movies*. The schema for Owns, with key attributes underlined, is thus

```
Owns(title, year, studioName)
```

In contrast, Example 3.13 discussed the many-many relationship *Stars-in* between *Movies* and *Stars*. Now, all attributes of the resulting relation

---

Other Notions of Functional Dependencies

We take the position that a functional dependency can have several attributes on the left but only a single attribute on the right. Moreover, the attribute on the right may not appear also on the left. However, we allow several dependencies with a common left side to be combined as a shorthand, giving us a set of attributes on the right. We shall also find it occasionally convenient to allow a "trivial" dependency whose right side is one of the attributes on the left.

Other works on the subject often start from the point of view that both left and right side are arbitrary sets of attributes, and attributes may appear on both left and right. There is no important difference between the two approaches, but we shall maintain the position that, unless stated otherwise, there is no attribute on both left and right of a functional dependency.

$$\text{Stars-in}(\underline{\text{title}}, \underline{\text{year}}, \underline{\text{starName}})$$

are key attributes. In fact, the only way the relation from a many-many relationship could not have all its attributes be part of the key is if the relationship itself has an attribute. Then, those attributes are omitted from the key. □

Finally, let us consider multiway relationships. Since we cannot describe all possible dependencies by the arrows coming out of the relationship, there are situations where the key or keys will not be obvious without thinking in detail about which sets of entity sets functionally determine which other sets. One guarantee we can make, however, is

- If a multiway relationship R has an arrow to entity set E, then there is at least one key for the corresponding relation that excludes the key of E.

3.5.5 Keys for Relations Derived from ODL

Matters are somewhat more complex when we convert an ODL design to relations. First, there may be one or more declared keys for an ODL class, but there also may be no key at all among the attributes. In that case, we must introduce into the relation an attribute that is a surrogate for the object identifier of objects in the class, as we discussed in Section 3.2.6.

However, whether the ODL class has a key formed from its own attributes, or we must use the surrogate object ID as a key, there are certain circumstances under which the key attributes for the class are *not* a key for the relation. The reason is that using the approach to translation from ODL to relations that we have adopted, we sometimes put too much into a single relation. The problem arises when the class has relations as part of its definition.

First, suppose a class C has a single-valued relationship R to some class D. Then as suggested in Section 3.2.4, we include the key for D in the relation for C. The key for C is still a key for the corresponding relation.

The problem case is when C has a multivalued relationship R to some class D. If the inverse of R is single-valued in the opposite direction (i.e., R is a one-many relationship) then, as suggested in the box "Representing Relationships in One Direction" in Section 3.2.7, we may represent (the inverse of) R in the relation for D only. The inverse of R presents no problem for D, because in D it is single-valued.

However, suppose that R is many-many, i.e., it and its inverse are multivalued in both C and D. Then the relation constructed for C may have several tuples representing one object of class C. As a result, the key for C is not a key for the corresponding relation. Rather, we have to add the key for D to the key for C to make the key for the relation.

Example 3.25 : In Example 3.7 we constructed the relation for ODL class `Movie` by adding to the attributes for `Movie`

1. The key `studioName` for class `Studio`, to which `Movie` is connected by single-valued relationship `ownedBy` and

2. The key `starName` for class `Star` (to which `Movie` is related by multivalued relationship `stars`).

The first of these, being from a single-valued relationship, does not affect the key for the relation `Movie`. However, the second, being from a multivalued relationship, must be added to the key for relation `Movie`, which therefore becomes

$$\{\texttt{title, year, starName}\}$$

An examination of the sample `Movie` relation in Fig. 3.13 reveals that `title` and `year` by themselves are not a key, but suggests that the addition of `starName` is sufficient to form a key.   □

In general, if the relation for C represents several multivalued relationships from C, then the keys for all the classes that these relationships connect C to must be added to the key for C; the result is the key for C's relation. Of course, if several relationships connect C to the same class D, then the relation for C has distinct attributes representing the key of D for each relationship from C to D.

Because of this paradox, that a key for an ODL class might not suffice as a key for the corresponding relation if we follow the recipe for constructing relations given in Section 3.2, we often need to repair the relations designed by this simple approach. The improvement of these relations will be taken up in Section 3.7. There, we shall see that it is possible to split out the many-many relationships from the relation for either of the connected classes. The resulting collection of relation schemas will look more like those we get directly from many E/R designs.[7]

3.5.6   Exercises for Section 3.5

Exercise 3.5.1: Consider a relation about people in the United States, including their name, Social Security number, street address, city, state, ZIP code, area code, and phone number (7 digits). What functional dependencies would you expect to hold? What are the keys for the relation? To answer this question, you need to know something about the way these numbers are assigned. For instance, can an area code straddle two states? Can a ZIP code straddle two area codes? Can two people have the same Social Security number? Can they have the same address or phone number?

* **Exercise 3.5.2:** Consider a relation representing the present position of molecules in a closed container. The attributes are an ID for the molecule, the x, y, and z coordinates of the molecule, and its velocity in the x, y, and z dimensions. What functional dependencies would you expect to hold? What are the keys?

! **Exercise 3.5.3:** In Exercise 2.3.2 we discussed four different assumptions about the relationship *Births*. For each of these, indicate the key or keys of the relation constructed from this relationship.

!! **Exercise 3.5.4:** Suppose R is a relation with attributes $A_1, A_2, \ldots, A_n$. As a function of n, tell how many superkeys R has, if:

* a) The only key is A_1.

  b) The only keys are A_1 and A_2.

  c) The only keys are $\{A_1, A_2\}$ and $\{A_3, A_4\}$.

  d) The only keys are $\{A_1, A_2\}$ and $\{A_1, A_3\}$.

3.6   Rules About Functional Dependencies

In this section, we shall learn how to *reason* about functional dependencies. That is, suppose we are told of a set of dependencies that a relation satisfies. Often, without knowing exactly what tuples are in the relation, we can deduce that the relation must satisfy certain other dependencies. This ability to discover additional dependencies is essential when we discuss the design of good relation schemas in Section 3.7.

---

[7] Of course, we could alternatively convert ODL designs first to equivalent E/R designs and convert those to relational designs. While this approach would finesse some of the problems inherent in the direct approach of Section 3.2, it is not essential. The relational design techniques of Section 3.7, which we need to know anyway, do the job at least as well.

Example 3.26 : If we are told that a relation R with attributes A, B, and C, satisfies the functional dependencies $A \to B$ and $B \to C$, then we can deduce that R also satisfies the dependency $A \to C$. How does that reasoning go? To prove that $A \to C$, we must consider two tuples of R that agree on A and prove they also agree on C.

Let the tuples agreeing on attribute A be (a, b_1, c_1) and (a, b_2, c_2). We assume the order of attributes in tuples is A, B, C. Since R satisfies $A \to B$, and these tuples agree on A, they must also agree on B. That is, $b_1 = b_2$, and the tuples are really (a, b, c_1) and (a, b, c_2), where b is both b_1 and b_2. Similarly, since R satisfies $B \to C$, and the tuples agree on B, they agree on C. Thus, $c_1 = c_2$; i.e., the tuples *do* agree on C. We have proved that any two tuples of R that agree on A also agree on C, and that is the functional dependency $A \to C$. $\square$

Functional dependencies often can be presented in several different ways, without changing the set of legal instances of the relation; we say the two sets of dependencies are *equivalent*, if so. More generally, we say that a set of functional dependencies S *follows* from a set of functional dependencies T if every relation instance that satisfies all the dependencies in T also satisfies all the dependencies in S. Note then that two sets of dependencies S and T are equivalent if S follows from T and T follows from S.

In this section we shall see several useful rules about functional dependencies. In general, these rules let us replace one set of dependencies by an equivalent set, or to add to a set of dependencies others that follow from the original set. An example is the *transitive rule* that lets us follow chains of functional dependencies, as in Example 3.26. We shall also give an algorithm for answering the general question of whether one functional dependency follows from one or more other dependencies.

3.6.1 The Splitting/Combining Rule

Recall that in Section 3.5.1 we defined the functional dependency

$$A_1 A_2 \cdots A_n \; \to \; B_1 B_2 \cdots B_m$$

to be a shorthand for the set of dependencies

$$A_1 A_2 \cdots A_n \to B_1$$
$$A_1 A_2 \cdots A_n \to B_2$$
$$\cdots$$
$$A_1 A_2 \cdots A_n \to B_m$$

That is, we may split attributes on the right side so that only one attribute appears on the right of each functional dependency. Likewise, we can replace a collection of dependencies with a common left side by a single dependency with the same left side and all the right sides combined into one set of attributes. In either event, the new set of dependencies is equivalent to the old. The equivalence noted above can be used in two ways.

- We can replace a functional dependency $A_1 A_2 \cdots A_n \rightarrow B_1 B_2 \cdots B_m$ by a set of functional dependencies $A_1 A_2 \cdots A_n \rightarrow B_i$ for $i = 1, 2, \ldots, B_m$. This transformation we call the *splitting rule*.

- We can replace a set of functional dependencies $A_1 A_2 \cdots A_n \rightarrow B_i$ for $i = 1, 2, \ldots, m$ by the single dependency $A_1 A_2 \cdots A_n \rightarrow B_1 B_2 \cdots B_m$. We call this transformation the *combining rule*.

For instance, we mentioned in Example 3.20 how the set of dependencies

$$\texttt{title year} \rightarrow \texttt{length}$$
$$\texttt{title year} \rightarrow \texttt{filmType}$$
$$\texttt{title year} \rightarrow \texttt{studioName}$$

is equivalent to the single dependency

$$\texttt{title year} \rightarrow \texttt{length filmType studioName}$$

One might imagine that splitting could be applied to the left sides of functional dependencies as well as to right sides. However, there is no splitting rule for left sides, as the following example shows.

Example 3.27 : Consider one of the dependencies such as

$$\texttt{title year} \rightarrow \texttt{length}$$

for the relation `Movie` in Example 3.20. If we try to split the left side into

$$\texttt{title} \rightarrow \texttt{length}$$
$$\texttt{year} \rightarrow \texttt{length}$$

then we get two false dependencies. That is, `title` does not functionally determine `length`, since there can be two movies with the same title (e.g., *King Kong*) but of different lengths. Similarly, `year` does not functionally determine `length`, because there are certainly movies of different lengths made in any one year. $\Box$

3.6.2   Trivial Dependencies

A functional dependency $A_1 A_2 \cdots A_n \rightarrow B$ is said to be *trivial* if B is one of the A's. For example,

$$\texttt{title year} \rightarrow \texttt{title}$$

is a trivial dependency.

Every trivial dependency holds in every relation, since it says that "two tuples that agree in all of $A_1, A_2, \ldots, A_n$ agree in one of them." Thus, we may assume any trivial dependency, without having to justify it on the basis of beliefs about the data.

In our original definition of functional dependencies, we did not allow a dependency to be trivial. However, there is no harm in including them, since they are always true, and they sometimes simplify the statement of rules.

When we allow trivial dependencies, then we also allow (as shorthands) dependencies in which some of the attributes on the right are also on the left. We say that a dependency $A_1 A_2 \cdots A_n \rightarrow B_1 B_2 \cdots B_m$ is

- *Trivial* if the B's are a subset of the A's.

- *Nontrivial* if at least one of the B's is not among the A's.

- *Completely nontrivial* if none of the B's is also one of the A's.

Thus

$$\texttt{title year} \rightarrow \texttt{year length}$$

is nontrivial, but not completely nontrivial. By eliminating **year** from the right side we would get a completely nontrivial dependency.

We can always remove from the right side of a functional dependency those attributes that appear on the left. That is:

- The functional dependency $A_1 A_2 \cdots A_n \rightarrow B_1 B_2 \cdots B_m$ is equivalent to $A_1 A_2 \cdots A_n \rightarrow C_1 C_2 \cdots C_k$, where the C's are all those B's that are not also A's.

We call this rule, illustrated in Fig. 3.28, the *trivial-dependency rule*.

3.6.3 Computing the Closure of Attributes

Before proceeding to other rules, we shall give a general principle from which all rules follow. Suppose $\{A_1, A_2, \ldots, A_n\}$ is a set of attributes and S is a set of functional dependencies. The *closure* of $\{A_1, A_2, \ldots, A_n\}$ under the dependencies in S is the set of attributes B such that every relation that satisfies all the dependencies in set S also satisfies $A_1 A_2 \cdots A_n \rightarrow B$. That is, $A_1 A_2 \cdots A_n \rightarrow B$ follows from the dependencies of S. We denote the closure of a set of attributes $A_1 A_2 \cdots A_n$ by $\{A_1, A_2, \ldots, A_n\}^+$. To simplify the discussion of computing closures, we shall allow trivial dependencies, so $A_1, A_2, \ldots, A_n$ are always in $\{A_1, A_2, \ldots, A_n\}^+$.

Figure 3.29 illustrates the closure process. Starting with the given set of attributes, we repeatedly expand the set by adding the right sides of functional dependencies as soon as we have included their left sides. Eventually, we cannot expand the set any more, and the resulting set is the closure. The following steps are a more detailed rendition of the algorithm for computing the closure of a set of attributes $\{A_1, A_2, \ldots, A_n\}$ with respect to a set of functional dependencies.

1. Let X be a set of attributes that eventually will become the closure. First, we initialize X to be $\{A_1, A_2, \ldots, A_n\}$.

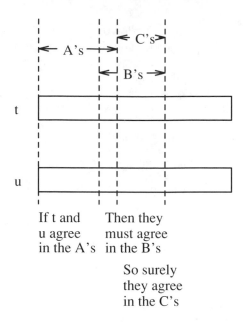

Figure 3.28: The trivial dependency rule

2. Now, we repeatedly search for some functional dependency

$$B_1 B_2 \cdots B_m \; \rightarrow \; C$$

such that all of $B_1, B_2, \ldots, B_m$ are in the set of attributes X, but C is not. We then add C to the set X.

3. Repeat step 2 as many times as necessary until no more attributes can be added to X. Since X can only grow, and the number of attributes of any relation must be finite, eventually nothing more can be added to X.

4. The set X after no more attributes can be added to it is the correct value of $\{A_1, A_2, \ldots, A_n\}^+$.

Example 3.28: Let us consider a relation with attributes A, B, C, D, E, and F. Suppose that this relation has the functional dependencies $AB \rightarrow C$, $BC \rightarrow AD$, $D \rightarrow E$, and $CF \rightarrow B$. What is the closure of $\{A, B\}$, that is, $\{A, B\}^+$?

We start with $X = \{A, B\}$. First, we notice that all the attributes on the left side of functional dependency $AB \rightarrow C$ are in X, so we may add the attribute C, which is on the right side of that dependency. Thus, after one iteration of step 2, X becomes $\{A, B, C\}$.

Next, we see that the left side of $BC \rightarrow AD$ is now contained in X, so

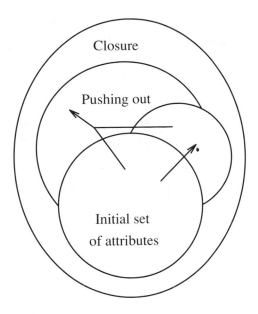

Figure 3.29: Computing the closure of a set of attributes

we may add to X the attributes A and D.[8] A is already there, but D is not, so X next becomes $\{A, B, C, D\}$. At this point, we may use the dependency $D \rightarrow E$ to add E to X, which is now $\{A, B, C, D, E\}$. No more changes to X are possible. In particular, the functional dependency $CF \rightarrow B$ can not be used, because its left side never becomes contained in X. Thus, $\{A, B\}^+ = \{A, B, C, D, E\}$. $\square$

If we know how to compute the closure of any set of attributes, then we can test whether any given functional dependency $A_1 A_2 \cdots A_n \rightarrow B$ follows from a set of dependencies S. First compute $\{A_1, A_2, \ldots, A_n\}^+$ using the set of dependencies S. If B is in $\{A_1, A_2, \ldots, A_n\}^+$, then

$$A_1 A_2 \cdots A_n \rightarrow B$$

does follow from S, and if B is not in $\{A_1, A_2, \ldots, A_n\}^+$, then this dependency does not follow from S. More generally, a dependency with a set of attributes on the right can be tested if we remember that this dependency is a shorthand for a set of dependencies. Thus, $A_1 A_2 \cdots A_n \rightarrow B_1 B_2 \cdots B_m$ follows from set of dependencies S if and only if all of $B_1, B_2, \ldots, B_m$ are in $\{A_1, A_2, \ldots, A_n\}^+$.

Example 3.29: Consider the relation and functional dependencies of Example 3.28. Suppose we wish to test whether $AB \rightarrow D$ follows from these dependencies. We compute $\{A, B\}^+$, which is $\{A, B, C, D, E\}$, as we saw in that

---

[8]Recall that $BC \rightarrow AD$ is shorthand for the pair of dependencies $BC \rightarrow A$ and $BC \rightarrow D$. We could treat each of these dependencies separately if we wished.

Why the Closure Algorithm Works

There is a simple reason that the algorithm for computing closure makes sense. We can prove by induction on the number of times that we apply the growing operation of step 2 that for every attribute D in X, the functional dependency $A_1 A_2 \cdots A_n \to D$ holds (in the special case where D is among the A's, this dependency is trivial). That is, every relation R that satisfies all of the dependencies in S also satisfies $A_1 A_2 \cdots A_n \to D$.

The basis is 0 steps. Then D must be one of $A_1, A_2, \ldots, A_n$, and surely $A_1 A_2 \cdots A_n \to D$ holds in any relation, because it is a trivial dependency.

For the induction, suppose D was added when we used the dependency $B_1 B_2 \cdots B_m \to D$. We know by the inductive hypothesis that R satisfies $A_1 A_2 \cdots A_n \to B_i$ for all $i = 1, 2, \ldots, m$. Put another way, any two tuples of R that agree on all of $A_1, A_2, \ldots, A_n$ also agree on all of $B_1, B_2, \ldots, B_m$. Since R satisfies $B_1 B_2 \cdots B_m \to D$, we also know that these two tuples agree on D. Thus, R satisfies $A_1 A_2 \cdots A_n \to D$.

The proof above shows that the closure algorithm is *sound*; that is, when it places D in $\{A_1, A_2, \ldots, A_n\}^+$, then $A_1 A_2 \cdots A_n \to D$ is a true dependency. What we have not shown is the converse, *completeness*: that whenever $A_1 A_2 \cdots A_n \to D$ holds, D will be placed in $\{A_1, A_2, \ldots, A_n\}^+$. That proof is beyond the scope of this book.

---

example. Since D is a member of the latter set, we conclude that $AB \to D$ does follow.

On the other hand, consider the functional dependency $D \to A$. To test whether this dependency follows from the given dependencies, first compute $\{D\}^+$. To do so, we start with $X = \{D\}$. We can use the dependency $D \to E$ to add E to the set X. However, then we are stuck. We cannot find any other dependency whose left side is contained in X, so $\{D\}^+ = \{D, E\}$. Since A is not a member of $\{D, E\}$, we conclude that $D \to A$ does not follow. $\square$

3.6.4   The Transitive Rule

The transitive rule lets us cascade two functional dependencies.

- If $A_1 A_2 \cdots A_n \to B_1 B_2 \cdots B_m$ and $B_1 B_2 \cdots B_m \to C_1 C_2 \cdots C_k$ hold in relation R, then $A_1 A_2 \cdots A_n \to C_1 C_2 \cdots C_k$ also holds in R.

If some of the C's are among the A's, we may eliminate them from the right side by the trivial-dependencies rule.

To see why the transitive rule holds, apply the test of Section 3.6.3. To test whether $A_1 A_2 \cdots A_n \to C_1 C_2 \cdots C_k$ holds, we need to compute the closure $\{A_1, A_2, \ldots, A_n\}^+$.

Closures and Keys

Notice that $\{A_1, A_2, \ldots, A_n\}^+$ is the set of all attributes if and only if $A_1, A_2, \ldots, A_n$ is a superkey for the relation in question. For only then does $A_1, A_2, \ldots, A_n$ functionally determine all the other attributes. We can test if $A_1, A_2, \ldots, A_n$ is a key for a relation by checking first that $\{A_1, A_2, \ldots, A_n\}^+$ is all attributes, and then checking that for no set S formed by removing one attribute from $\{A_1, A_2, \ldots, A_n\}$ is S^+ the set of all attributes.

The functional dependency $A_1 A_2 \cdots A_n \rightarrow B_1 B_2 \cdots B_m$ tells us that all of $B_1, B_2, \ldots, B_m$ are in $\{A_1, A_2, \ldots, A_n\}^+$. Then, we can use the dependency $B_1 B_2 \cdots B_m \rightarrow C_1 C_2 \cdots C_k$ to add $C_1, C_2, \ldots, C_k$ to $\{A_1, A_2, \ldots, A_n\}^+$. Since all the C's are in $\{A_1, A_2, \ldots, A_n\}^+$, we conclude that

$$A_1 A_2 \cdots A_n \rightarrow C_1 C_2 \cdots C_k$$

holds for any relation that satisfies both $A_1 A_2 \cdots A_n \rightarrow B_1 B_2 \cdots B_m$ and $B_1 B_2 \cdots B_m \rightarrow C_1 C_2 \cdots C_k$.

Example 3.30: Let us begin with the relation Movie of Fig. 3.12 that was constructed in Section 3.2.4 to represent the four attributes of class Movie plus its relationship ownedBy with the Studio class. The relation and some sample data is:

title	*year*	*length*	*filmType*	*studioName*
Star Wars	1977	124	color	Fox
Mighty Ducks	1991	104	color	Disney
Wayne's World	1992	95	color	Paramount

Suppose we decided to represent some data about the owning studio in this same relation. For simplicity, we shall add only a city for the studio, representing its address. The relation might then look like

title	*year*	*length*	*filmType*	*studioName*	*studioAddr*
Star Wars	1977	124	color	Fox	Hollywood
Mighty Ducks	1991	104	color	Disney	Buena Vista
Wayne's World	1992	95	color	Paramount	Hollywood

Two of the dependencies that we might reasonably claim to hold are:

$$\text{title year} \rightarrow \text{studioName}$$
$$\text{studioName} \rightarrow \text{studioAddr}$$

The first is justified because the `ownedBy` relationship of class `Movie` is single-valued; a movie is owned by only one studio. The second is justified because in the class `Studio`, attribute `address` is single-valued; it is of type `string` (see Fig. 2.6).

The transitive rule allows us to combine the two dependencies above to get a new dependency:

$$\text{title year} \rightarrow \text{studioAddr}$$

This dependency says that a title and year (i.e., a movie) determines an address — the address of the studio owning the movie. □

3.6.5   Closing Sets of Functional Dependencies

As we have seen, given a set of dependencies, we can often infer some other dependencies, including both trivial and nontrivial dependencies. We shall, in later sections, want to distinguish between *given* dependencies that are stated initially for a relation and *derived* dependencies that are inferred using one of the rules of this section or by using the algorithm for closing a set of attributes.

Moreover, we sometimes have a choice of which dependencies we use to represent the full set of dependencies for a relation. Any set of given dependencies from which we can infer all the dependencies for a relation will be called a *basis* for that relation. If no proper subset of the dependencies in a basis can also derive the complete set of dependencies, then we say the basis is *minimal.*

Example 3.31 : Consider a relation $R(A, B, C)$ such that each attribute functionally determines the other two attributes. The full set of derived dependencies thus includes six dependencies with one attribute on the left and one on the right; $A \rightarrow B, A \rightarrow C, B \rightarrow A, B \rightarrow C, C \rightarrow A$, and $C \rightarrow B$. It also includes the three nontrivial dependencies with two attributes on the left: $AB \rightarrow C, AC \rightarrow B$, and $BC \rightarrow A$. There are also the shorthands for pairs of dependencies such as $A \rightarrow BC$, and we might also include the trivial dependencies such as $A \rightarrow A$ or dependencies like $AB \rightarrow BC$ that are not completely nontrivial (although in our strict definition of what is a functional dependency we are not required to list trivial or partially trivial dependencies or dependencies that have several attributes on the right).

This relation and its dependencies have several minimal bases. One is

$$\{A \rightarrow B, \ B \rightarrow A, \ B \rightarrow C, \ C \rightarrow B\}$$

Another is

$$\{A \rightarrow B, \ B \rightarrow C, \ C \rightarrow A\}$$

There are many other bases, even minimal bases, for this example relation, and we leave their discovery as an exercise. □

A Complete Set of Inference Rules

If we want to know whether one functional dependency follows from some given dependencies, the closure computation of Section 3.6.3 will always serve. However, it is interesting to know that there is a set of rules, called *Armstrong's axioms*, from which it is possible to derive any functional dependency that follows from a given set. These axioms are:

1. *Reflexivity.* If $\{B_1, B_2, \ldots, B_m\} \subseteq \{A_1, A_2, \ldots, A_n\}$, then $A_1 A_2 \cdots A_n \to B_1 B_2 \cdots B_m$. These are what we have called trivial dependencies.

2. *Augmentation.* If $A_1 A_2 \cdots A_n \to B_1 B_2 \cdots B_m$, then $A_1 A_2 \cdots A_n C_1 C_2 \cdots C_k \to B_1 B_2 \cdots B_m C_1 C_2 \cdots C_k$ for any set of attributes $C_1, C_2, \ldots, C_k$.

3. *Transitivity.* If

$$A_1 A_2 \cdots A_n \to B_1 B_2 \cdots B_m \text{ and } B_1 B_2 \cdots B_m \to C_1 C_2 \cdots C_k$$

then $A_1 A_2 \cdots A_n \to C_1 C_2 \cdots C_k$.

3.6.6 Exercises for Section 3.6

* Exercise 3.6.1: Consider a relation with schema $R(A, B, C, D)$ and functional dependencies $AB \to C$, $C \to D$, and $D \to A$.

a) What are all the nontrivial functional dependencies that follow from the given dependencies?

b) What are all the keys of R?

c) What are all the superkeys for R that are not keys?

Exercise 3.6.2: Repeat Exercise 3.6.1 for the following schemas and dependencies:

i) $S(A, B, C, D)$ with functional dependencies $A \to B$, $B \to C$, and $B \to D$.

ii) $T(A, B, C, D)$ with functional dependencies $AB \to C$, $BC \to D$, $CD \to A$, and $AD \to B$.

iii) $U(A, B, C, D)$ with functional dependencies $A \to B$, $B \to C$, $C \to D$, and $D \to A$.

Exercise 3.6.3: Show that the following rules hold, by using the closure test of Section 3.6.3.

* a) *Augmenting left sides.* If $A_1 A_2 \cdots A_n \rightarrow B$ is a functional dependency, and C is another attribute, then $A_1 A_2 \cdots A_n C \rightarrow B$ follows.

  b) *Full augmentation.* If $A_1 A_2 \cdots A_n \rightarrow B$ is a functional dependency, and C is another attribute, then $A_1 A_2 \cdots A_n C \rightarrow BC$ follows. Note: from this rule, the "augmentation" rule mentioned in the box of Section 3.6.5 on Armstrong's axioms can easily be proved.

  c) *Pseudotransitivity.* Suppose dependencies $A_1 A_2 \cdots A_n \rightarrow B_1 B_2 \cdots B_m$ and $C_1 C_2 \cdots C_k \rightarrow D$ hold, and the B's are each among the C's. Then $A_1 A_2 \cdots A_n E_1 E_2 \cdots E_j \rightarrow D$ holds, where the E's are all those of the C's that are not found among the B's.

  d) *Addition.* If functional dependencies $A_1 A_2 \cdots A_n \rightarrow B_1 B_2 \cdots B_m$ and $C_1 C_2 \cdots C_k \rightarrow D_1 D_2 \cdots D_j$ hold, then functional dependency

$$A_1 A_2 \cdots A_n C_1 C_2 \cdots C_k \rightarrow B_1 B_2 \cdots B_m D_1 D_2 \cdots D_j$$

  also holds. In the above, we should remove one copy of any attribute that appears among both the A's and C's or among both the B's and D's.

! **Exercise 3.6.4:** Show that each of the following are *not* valid rules about functional dependencies by giving example relations that satisfy the given dependencies but not the one that allegedly follows.

* a) If $A \rightarrow B$ then $B \rightarrow A$.

  b) If $AB \rightarrow C$ and $A \rightarrow C$, then $B \rightarrow C$.

  c) If $AB \rightarrow C$, then $A \rightarrow C$ or $B \rightarrow C$.

! **Exercise 3.6.5:** Show that if a relation has no attribute that is functionally determined by all the other attributes, then the relation has no nontrivial functional dependencies at all.

! **Exercise 3.6.6:** Let X and Y be sets of attributes. Show that if $X \subseteq Y$, then $X^+ \subseteq Y^+$, where the closures are taken with respect to the same set of functional dependencies.

! **Exercise 3.6.7:** Prove that $(X^+)^+ = X^+$.

!! **Exercise 3.6.8:** We say a set of attributes X is *closed* (with respect to a given set of functional dependencies) if $X^+ = X$. Consider a relation with schema $R(A, B, C, D)$ and an unknown set of functional dependencies. If we are told which sets of attributes are closed, we can discover the functional dependencies. What are the dependencies if:

* a) All sets of the four attributes are closed.

b) The only closed sets are $\emptyset$ and $\{A, B, C, D\}$.

c) The closed sets are $\emptyset$, {A,B}, and $\{A, B, C, D\}$.

! **Exercise 3.6.9:** Find all the minimal bases for the dependencies and relation of Example 3.31.

!! **Exercise 3.6.10:** Show that if a functional dependency F follows from some given dependencies, then we can prove F from the given dependencies using Armstrong's axioms (defined in the box in Section 3.6.5). *Hint*: Examine the algorithm for computing the closure of a set of attributes and show how each step of that algorithm can be mimicked by inferring some functional dependencies by Armstrong's axioms.

3.7 Design of Relational Database Schemas

We have several times noticed that converting directly from object-oriented ODL designs (and to a lesser extent from E/R designs) leads to problems with the relational database schema. The principal problem we have identified is redundancy, where a fact is repeated in more than one tuple. Moreover, we have identified the most common cause for this redundancy: attempts to group into one relation both single-valued and multivalued properties of an object. For instance, we saw in Section 3.2.2 the redundancy that results when we tried to store single-valued information about movies, such as their length, with multivalued properties such as the set of stars for a movie. The problems are seen in Fig. 3.27, which we reproduce here as Fig. 3.30. We found similar redundancy in that section when we tried to store single-valued birthdate information for a star with a set of addresses for a star.

In this section, we shall tackle the problem of design of good relation schemas in the following stages:

1. We first explore in more detail the problems that arise when our schema is flawed.

2. Then, we introduce the idea of "decomposition," breaking a relation schema (set of attributes) into two smaller schemas.

3. Next, we introduce "Boyce-Codd normal form," or "BCNF." a condition on a relation schema that eliminates these problems.

4. These points are tied together when we explain how to assure the BCNF condition by decomposing relation schemas.

title	year	length	filmType	studioName	starName
Star Wars	1977	124	color	Fox	Carrie Fisher
Star Wars	1977	124	color	Fox	Mark Hamill
Star Wars	1977	124	color	Fox	Harrison Ford
Mighty Ducks	1991	104	color	Disney	Emilio Estevez
Wayne's World	1992	95	color	Paramount	Dana Carvey
Wayne's World	1992	95	color	Paramount	Mike Meyers

Figure 3.30: The relation `Movie` exhibiting anomalies

3.7.1   Anomalies

Problems such as redundancy that occur when we try to cram too much into a single relation are called *anomalies*. The principal kinds of anomalies that we encounter are:

1. *Redundancy.* Information may be repeated unnecessarily in several tuples. Examples are the length and film type for movies as in Fig. 3.30.

2. *Update Anomalies.* We may change information in one tuple but leave the same information unchanged in another. For example, if we found that *Star Wars* was really 125 minutes long, we might carelessly change the length in the first tuple of Fig. 3.30 but not in the second or third tuples. True, we might argue that one should never be so careless. But we shall see that it is possible to redesign relation `Movie` so that the risk of such mistakes does not exist.

3. *Deletion Anomalies.* If a set of values becomes empty, we may lose other information as a side effect. For example, should we delete Emilio Estevez from the set of stars of *Mighty Ducks*, then we have no more stars for that movie in the database. The last tuple for *Mighty Ducks* in the relation `Movie` would disappear, and with it information that it is 95 minutes long and in color.

3.7.2   Decomposing Relations

The accepted way to eliminate these anomalies is to *decompose* relations. Decomposition of R involves splitting the attributes of R to make the schemas of two new relations. Our decomposition rule also involves a way of populating those relations with tuples by "projecting" the tuples of R. After describing the decomposition process, we shall show how to pick a decomposition that eliminates anomalies.

Given a relation R with schema $\{A_1, A_2, \ldots, A_n\}$, we may *decompose* R into two relations S and T with schemas $\{B_1, B_2, \ldots, B_m\}$ and $\{C_1, C_2, \ldots, C_k\}$, respectively, such that

1. $\{A_1, A_2, \ldots, A_n\} = \{B_1, B_2, \ldots, B_m\} \cup \{C_1, C_2, \ldots, C_k\}.$

2. The tuples in relation S are the the *projections* onto $\{B_1, B_2, \ldots, B_m\}$ of all the tuples in R. That is, for each tuple t in the current instance of R, take the components of t in the attributes $B_1, B_2, \ldots, B_m$. These components form a tuple, and this tuple belongs in the current instance of S. However, relations are sets, and the same tuple of S could result from projecting two different tuples of R. If so, we put into the current instance of S only one copy of each tuple.

3. Similarly, the tuples in relation T are the projections, onto set of attributes $\{C_1, C_2, \ldots, C_k\}$, of the tuples in the current instance of R.

Example 3.32: Let us decompose the `Movie` relation of Fig. 3.30. First, we shall decompose the schema. Our choice, whose merit will be seen in Section 3.7.3, is to use

1. A relation called `Movie1`, whose schema is all the attributes except for `starName`.

2. A relation called `Movie2`, whose schema consists of the attributes `title`, `year`, and `starName`.

Now, let us illustrate the process of decomposing relation instances by decomposing the sample data of Fig. 3.30. First, let us construct the projection onto the `Movie1` schema:

{`title`, `year`, `length`, `filmType`, `studioName`}

The first three tuples of Fig. 3.30 each have the same components in these five attributes:

(`Star Wars`, 1977, 124, `color`, `Fox`)

The fourth tuple yields a different tuple for the first five components, and the fifth and sixth tuple each yield the same five-component tuple. The resulting relation for `Movie1` is shown in Fig. 3.31.

title	year	length	filmType	studioName
Star Wars	1977	124	color	Fox
Mighty Ducks	1991	104	color	Disney
Wayne's World	1992	95	color	Paramount

Figure 3.31: The relation `Movie1`

Next, consider the projection of Fig. 3.30 onto the schema of `Movie2`. Each of the six tuples of that figure differ in at least one of the attributes `title`, `year`, and `starName`, so the result is the relation shown in Fig. 3.32. □

title	year	starName
Star Wars	1977	Carrie Fisher
Star Wars	1977	Mark Hamill
Star Wars	1977	Harrison Ford
Mighty Ducks	1991	Emilio Estevez
Wayne's World	1992	Dana Carvey
Wayne's World	1992	Mike Meyers

Figure 3.32: The relation Movie2

Notice how this decomposition eliminates the anomalies we mentioned in Section 3.7.1. The redundancy has been eliminated; for example, the length of each film appears only once, in relation Movie1. The risk of an update anomaly is gone. For instance, since we only have to change the length of *Star Wars* in one tuple of Movie1, we cannot wind up with two different lengths for that movie.

Finally, the risk of a deletion anomaly is gone. If we delete all the stars for *Mighty Ducks*, say, that deletion makes the movie disappear from Movie2. But all the other information about the movie can still be found in Movie1.

It might appear that Movie2 still has redundancy, since the title and year of a movie can appear several times. However, these two attributes form a key for movies, and there is no more succinct way to represent a movie. Moreover, Movie2 does not offer an opportunity for an update anomaly. We might suppose that if we changed the year in, say, the Carrie Fisher tuple but not the other two tuples for *Star Wars*, then there would be an update anomaly. However, there is nothing in our assumed functional dependencies that prevents there from being a different movie named *Star Wars* in 1997, and Carrie Fisher may have starred in that one. Thus, we do not want to prevent changing the year in one *Star Wars* tuple, nor is such a change necessarily incorrect.

3.7.3 Boyce-Codd Normal Form

The goal of decomposition is to replace a relation by several that do not exhibit anomalies. There is, it turns out, a simple condition under which the anomalies discussed above can be guaranteed not to exist. This condition is called *Boyce-Codd normal form*, or *BCNF*.

- A relation R is in BCNF if and only if: whenever there is a nontrivial dependency $A_1 A_2 \cdots A_n \rightarrow B$ for R, it is the case that $\{A_1, A_2, \ldots, A_n\}$ is a superkey for R.

That is, the left side of every nontrivial functional dependency must be a superkey. Recall that a superkey need not be minimal. Thus, an equivalent statement of the BCNF condition is that the left side of every nontrivial functional dependency must contain a key.

When we find a BCNF-violating dependency, it is sometimes useful to find all the other dependencies that have the same left side, whether or not they are BCNF violations. The following is an alternative definition of BCNF in which we look for a set of dependencies with common left side, at least one of which is nontrivial and violates the BCNF condition.

- Relation R is in BCNF if and only if: whenever nontrivial dependency $A_1A_2\cdots A_n \rightarrow B_1B_2\cdots B_m$ holds for R, it must be the case that $\{A_1, A_2, \ldots, A_n\}$ is a superkey for R.

This requirement is equivalent to the original BCNF condition. Recall that the dependency $A_1A_2\cdots A_n \rightarrow B_1B_2\cdots B_m$ is shorthand for the set of dependencies $A_1A_2\cdots A_n \rightarrow B_i$ for $i = 1, 2, \ldots, m$. Since there must be at least one B_i that is not among the A's (or else $A_1A_2\cdots A_n \rightarrow B_1B_2\cdots B_m$ would be trivial), $A_1A_2\cdots A_n \rightarrow B_i$ is a BCNF violation according to our original definition.

Example 3.33: Relation `Movie`, as in Fig. 3.30, is not in BCNF. To see why, we first need to determine what sets of attributes are keys. We argued in Example 3.21 why {`title`, `year`, `starName`} is a key. Thus, any set of attributes containing these three is a superkey. The same arguments we followed in Example 3.21 can be used to explain why no set of attributes that does not include all three of `title`, `year`, and `starName` could be a superkey. Thus, we assert that {`title`, `year`, `starName`} is the only key for `Movie`.

However, consider the functional dependency

```
title year → length filmType studioName
```

which we know holds in `Movie`. Recall the reason we can assert this dependency: the original ODL design has key {`title`, `year`}, single-valued attributes `length` and `filmType`, and single-valued relationship `ownedBy` leading to the owning studio.

Unfortunately, the left side of the above dependency is not a superkey. In particular, we know that `title` and `year` do not functionally determine the sixth attribute, `starName`. Thus, the existence of this dependency violates the BCNF condition and tells us `Movie` is not in BCNF. Moreover, according to the original definition of BCNF, where a single attribute on the right side was required, we can offer any of the three functional dependencies, such as `title year → length`, as a BCNF violation. □

Example 3.34: On the other hand, `Movie1` of Fig. 3.31 is in BCNF. Since

```
title year → length filmType studioName
```

holds in this relation, and we have argued that neither `title` nor `year` by itself functionally determines any of the other attributes, the only key for `Movie1` is {`title, year`}. Moreover, the only nontrivial functional dependencies must have at least `title` and `year` on the left side, and therefore their left sides must be superkeys. Thus, `Movie1` is in BCNF.   □

Example 3.35 : We claim that any two-attribute relation is in BCNF. We need to examine the possible nontrivial dependencies with a single attribute on the right. There are not too many cases to consider, so let us consider them in turn. In what follows, suppose that the attributes are A and B.

1. There are no nontrivial functional dependencies. Then surely the BCNF condition must hold, because only a nontrivial dependency can violate this condition. Incidentally, note that $\{A, B\}$ is the only key in this case.

2. $A \rightarrow B$ holds, but $B \rightarrow A$ does not hold. In this case, A is the only key, and each nontrivial dependency contains A on the left (in fact the left can only be A). Thus there is no violation of the BCNF condition.

3. $B \rightarrow A$ holds, but $A \rightarrow B$ does not hold. This case is symmetric to case (2).

4. Both $A \rightarrow B$ and $B \rightarrow A$ hold. Then both A and B are keys. Surely any dependency has at least one of these on the left, so there can be no BCNF violation.

It is worth noticing from case (4) above that there may be more than one key for a relation. Further, the BCNF condition only requires that *some* key be contained in the left side of any nontrivial dependency, not that all keys are contained in the left side. Also observe that a relation with two attributes, each functionally determining the other, is not completely implausible. For example, a company may assign its employees unique employee ID's and also record their Social Security numbers. A relation with attributes `empID` and `ssNo` would have each attribute functionally determining the other. Put another way, each attribute is a key, since we don't expect to find two tuples that agree on either attribute.   □

3.7.4   Decomposition into BCNF

By repeatedly choosing suitable decompositions, we can break any relation schema into a collection of subsets of its attributes with the following important properties:

1. These subsets are the schemas of relations in BCNF.

2. The data in the original relation is represented faithfully by the data in the relations that are the result of the decomposition, in a sense to be made precise in Section 3.7.6. Roughly, we need to be able to reconstruct the original relation exactly from the decomposed relations.

Example 3.35 suggests that perhaps all we have to do is break a relation schema into two-attribute subsets, and the result is surely in BCNF. However, such an arbitrary decomposition will not satisfy condition (2), as we shall see in Section 3.7.6. In fact, we must be more careful and use the violating functional dependencies to guide our decomposition.

The decomposition strategy we shall follow is to look for a nontrivial functional dependency $A_1 A_2 \cdots A_n \rightarrow B_1 B_2 \cdots B_m$ that violates BCNF; i.e., $\{A_1, A_2, \ldots, A_n\}$ is not a superkey. As a heuristic, we shall generally add to the right side as many attributes as are functionally determined by

$$\{A_1, A_2, \ldots, A_n\}$$

Figure 3.33 illustrates how the attributes are broken into two overlapping relation schemas. One is all the attributes involved in the violating dependency, and the other is the left side plus all the attributes *not* involved in the dependency, i.e., all the attributes except those B's that are not A's.

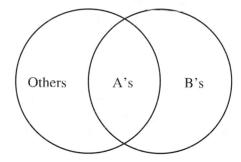

Figure 3.33: Relation schema decomposition based on a BCNF violation

Example 3.36: Consider our running example, the Movie relation of Fig. 3.30. We saw in Example 3.33 that

    title year → length filmType studioName

is a BCNF violation. In this case, the right side already includes all the attributes functionally determined by title and year, so we shall use this BCNF violation to decompose Movie into:

1. The schema with all the attributes of the dependency, that is:

    {title, year, length, filmType, studioName}

2. The schema with all of Movie's attributes except the three that appear on the right of the dependency. Thus, we remove length, filmType, and studioName, leaving the second schema:

{title, year, starName}

Notice that these schemas are the ones selected for relations `Movie1` and `Movie2` in Example 3.32. We observed that these are each in BCNF in Example 3.34. □

Example 3.37 : Let us consider the relation `MovieStudio` that was introduced in Example 3.30. This relation stores information about movies, their owning studios, and the addresses of those studios. The schema and some typical tuples for this relation are shown in Fig. 3.34.

title	*year*	*length*	*filmType*	*studioName*	*studioAddr*
Star Wars	1977	124	color	Fox	Hollywood
Mighty Ducks	1991	104	color	Disney	Buena Vista
Wayne's World	1992	95	color	Paramount	Hollywood
Addams Family	1991	102	color	Paramount	Hollywood

Figure 3.34: The relation `MovieStudio`

Note that `MovieStudio` contains redundant information. Because we added to our usual sample data a second movie owned by Paramount, the address of Paramount is stated twice. However, the source of this problem is not the same as in Example 3.36. In the latter example, the problem was that a multivalued relationship (the stars of a given movie) was being stored with other information about the movie. Here, everything is single-valued: the attribute `length` for a movie, the relationship `ownedBy` that relates a movie to its unique owning studio, and the attribute `address` for studios.

In this case, the problem is that there is a "transitive dependency." That is, as mentioned in Example 3.30, relation `movieStudio` has the dependencies

$$\text{title year} \rightarrow \text{studioName}$$
$$\text{studioName} \rightarrow \text{studioAddr}$$

We may apply the transitive rule to these to get a new dependency

$$\text{title year} \rightarrow \text{studioAddr}$$

That is, a title and year (i.e., the key for movies) functionally determine a studio address — the address of the studio that owns the movie. Since

$$\text{title year} \rightarrow \text{length filmType}$$

is another obvious dependency, we conclude that {title, year} is a key for `MovieStudio`; in fact it is the only key.

On the other hand, dependency

$$\text{studioName} \rightarrow \text{studioAddr}$$

which is one of those used in the application of the transitive rule above, is non-trivial but its left side is not a superkey. This observation tells us `MovieStudio` is not in BCNF. We can fix the problem by following the decomposition rule, using the above dependency. The first schema of the decomposition is the attributes of the dependency itself, that is:

$$\{\text{studioName, studioAddr}\}$$

The second schema is all the attributes of `MovieStudio` except for `studioAddr`, because the latter attribute is on the right of the dependency used in the decomposition. Thus, the other schema is:

$$\{\text{title, year, length, filmType, studioName}\}$$

The projection of Fig. 3.34 onto these schemas gives us the two relations `MovieStudio1` and `MovieStudio2` shown in Figs. 3.35 and 3.36. Each of these is in BCNF. The sole key for `MovieStudio1` is {`title, year`}, and the sole key for `MovieStudio2` is {`studioName`}. In each case, there are no nontrivial dependencies that do not contain these keys on the left. □

title	year	length	filmType	studioName
Star Wars	1977	124	color	Fox
Mighty Ducks	1991	104	color	Disney
Wayne's World	1992	95	color	Paramount
Addams Family	1991	102	color	Paramount

Figure 3.35: The relation MovieStudio1

studioName	studioAddr
Fox	Hollywood
Disney	Buena Vista
Paramount	Hollywood

Figure 3.36: The relation MovieStudio2

In each of the previous examples, one judicious application of the decomposition rule is enough to produce a collection of relations that are in BCNF. In general, that is not the case.

Example 3.38 : We could generalize Example 3.37 to have a chain of functional dependencies longer than two. Consider a relation with schema

{title, year, studioName, president, presAddr}

That is, each tuple of this relation tells about a movie, its studio, the president of the studio, and the address of the president of the studio. Three functional dependencies that we would assume in this relation are

$$title\ year \rightarrow studioName$$
$$studioName \rightarrow president$$
$$president \rightarrow presAddr$$

The sole key for this relation is {title, year}. Thus the last two dependencies above violate BCNF. We could decompose starting with

$$studioName \rightarrow president$$

for example. First, we should add to the right side of this functional dependency any other attributes in the closure of studioName. By the transitive rule applied to studioName → president and president → presAddr, we know

$$studioName \rightarrow presAddr$$

Combining the two dependencies with studioName on the left, we get:

$$studioName \rightarrow president\ presAddr$$

This functional dependency has a maximally expanded right side, so we shall now decompose into the following two relation schemas.

{title, year, studioName}
{studioName, president, presAddr}

The first of these is in BCNF. However, the second has {studioName} for its only key but also has the dependency

$$president \rightarrow presAddr$$

which is a BCNF violation. Thus, we must decompose again, using the expanded dependency in which president is added to the above right side. The resulting three relation schemas, all in BCNF, are:

{title, year, studioName}
{studioName, president}
{president, presAddr}

□

In general, we must keep applying the decomposition rule as many times as needed, until all our relations are in BCNF. We can be sure of ultimate success, because every time we apply the decomposition rule to a relation R, the two resulting schemas each have fewer attributes than that of R. As we saw in Example 3.35, when we get down to two attributes, the relation is sure to be in BCNF.

To see why decomposition always yields smaller schemas, suppose we have a BCNF violation $A_1 A_2 \cdots A_n \rightarrow B_1 B_2 \cdots B_m$. We may assume this dependency has already been expanded to include among the B's any other attribute functionally determined by the A's and that any of the B's that are also among the A's have been removed from the B's.

One of the schemas of the decomposition is all the attributes of R except for the B's. There must be at least one B, so this schema does not include all attributes.

The other schema is all the A's and B's. This set cannot be all the attributes of R, because if it were, then $\{A_1, A_2, \ldots, A_n\}$ would be a superkey for R (i.e., the A's would functionally determine all the other attributes of R). No dependency with a superkey on the left is a BCNF violation.

We conclude that both schemas of the decomposition are smaller than the schema of R. Thus, the repeated decomposition process must eventually reach a collection of BCNF relations.

3.7.5 Projecting Functional Dependencies

When we decompose a relation schema, we need to check that the resulting schemas are in BCNF. As we saw in Example 3.38 it is possible that one or both of the new schemas themselves have BCNF violations. However, how can we tell whether a relation is in BCNF unless we can determine the functional dependencies that hold for that relation? In Example 3.38 we reasoned about the dependencies that hold for the new relations in an ad hoc way. Fortunately, there is a methodical way to find the functional dependencies for the results of a decomposition.

Suppose we have a relation R, which is decomposed into relation S and some other relation. Let F be the set of functional dependencies known to hold for R. To compute the functional dependencies that hold in S do the following:

Consider each set of attributes X that is contained in the set of attributes of S. Compute X^+. Then for each attribute B such that

1. B is an attribute of S,

2. B is in X^+, and

3. B is not in X,

the functional dependency $X \rightarrow B$ holds in S.

Example 3.39: Let R have schema $R(A, B, C, D)$, and suppose the functional dependencies $A \rightarrow B$ and $B \rightarrow C$ are given for R. Let $S(A, C)$ be one of the relations in a decomposition of R. We shall compute the dependencies that hold in S.

In principle, we must compute the closure of each subset of $\{A, C\}$, which is the set of attributes of S. Let us begin with $\{A\}^+$. This set is easily seen to be $\{A, B, C\}$. Since B is not in the schema of S, we do not claim that $A \rightarrow B$ is a dependency for S. However, C is in the schema for S, so we assert dependency $A \rightarrow C$ for S.

Now, we must consider $\{C\}^+$. Since C is not a left side of a given dependency, we get nothing new in the closure, so $\{C\}^+ = \{C\}$. In general, a set that does not contain at least one left side of a given dependency cannot yield any dependencies for S.

We must also consider $\{A, C\}^+$, which is $\{A, B, C\}$. We therefore get no new dependency not already found when we considered $\{A\}^+$. The conclusion is that $A \rightarrow C$ is the only dependency we need assert for S. Of course there are other dependencies for S that are derived from this one, such as $AD \rightarrow C$ or the trivial dependency $A \rightarrow A$. However, they can be obtained by the rules given in Section 3.6 and need not be stated specifically when we give the functional dependencies for S. □

Example 3.40: Now consider $R(A, B, C, D, E)$ decomposed into $S(A, B, C)$ and another relation. Let the functional dependencies of R be $A \rightarrow D$, $B \rightarrow E$, and $DE \rightarrow C$.

First, consider $\{A\}^+ = \{A, D\}$. Since D is not in the schema of S, we get no dependencies here. Similarly, $\{B\}^+ = \{B, E\}$ and $\{C\}^+ = \{C\}$, yielding no dependencies for S.

Now consider pairs. $\{A, B\}^+ = \{A, B, C, D, E\}$. Thus, we get the dependency $AB \rightarrow C$ for S. Neither of the other pairs give us any dependencies for S. Of course the set of all three attributes of S, $\{A, B, C\}$, cannot yield any nontrivial dependencies for S. Thus, the only dependency we need assert for S is $AB \rightarrow C$. □

3.7.6 Recovering Information from a Decomposition

Let us now turn our attention to the question of why the decomposition algorithm of Section 3.7.4 preserves the information that was contained in the original relation. The idea is that if we follow this algorithm, then the projections of the original tuples can be "joined" again to produce all and only the original tuples.

To simplify the situation, let us consider a relation R with schema $\{A, B, C\}$ and a functional dependency $B \rightarrow C$, which we suppose is a BCNF violation. It is possible, for example, that as in Example 3.37, there is a transitive dependency chain, with another functional dependency $A \rightarrow B$. In that case, $\{A\}$ is the only key, and the left side of $B \rightarrow C$ clearly is not a superkey. Another

---

Simplifying the Search for Dependencies

When we derive the functional dependencies for a relation S from those for R using the algorithm of Section 3.7.5, we can sometimes limit the search by not computing the closure of all subsets of the attributes of S. Here are some rules that help reduce the work.

1. It is not necessary to consider the closure of the set of all S's attributes.

2. It is not necessary to consider a set of attributes that does not contain the left side of any dependency.

3. It is not necessary to consider a set that contains an attribute that is in no left side of any functional dependency.

---

possibility is that $B \rightarrow C$ is the only nontrivial dependency, in which case the only key is $\{A, B\}$. Again, the left side of $B \rightarrow C$ is not a superkey. In either case, the required decomposition based on the dependency $B \rightarrow C$ separates the attributes into schemas $\{A, B\}$ and $\{B, C\}$.

Let t be a tuple of R. We may write $t = (a, b, c)$, where a, b, and c are the components of t for attributes A, B, and C, respectively. Tuple t projects as (a, b) for the relation with schema $\{A, B\}$ and as (b, c) for the relation with schema $\{B, C\}$.

It is possible to *join* a tuple from $\{A, B\}$ with a tuple from $\{B, C\}$, provided they agree in the B component. In particular, (a, b) joins with (b, c) to give us the original tuple $t = (a, b, c)$ back again. That happens regardless of what tuple t we started with; we can always join its projections to get t back.

However, getting back those tuples we started with is not enough to assure that the original relation R is truly represented by the decomposition. What might happen if there were two tuples of R, say $t = (a, b, c)$ and $v = (d, b, e)$? When we project t onto $\{A, B\}$ we get $u = (a, b)$, and when we project v onto $\{B, C\}$ we get $w = (b, e)$, as suggested by Fig. 3.37.

Tuples u and w join, since they agree on their B components. The resulting tuple is $x = (a, b, e)$. Is it possible that x is a bogus tuple? That is, could (a, b, e) not be a tuple of R?

Since we assume the functional dependency $B \rightarrow C$ for relation R, the answer is "no." Recall that this dependency says any two tuples of R that agree in their B components must also agree in their C components. Since t and v agree in their B components (they both have b there), they also agree on their C components. That means $c = e$; i.e., the two values we supposed were different are really the same. Thus, (a, b, e) is really (a, b, c); that is, $x = t$.

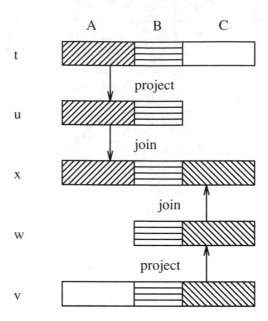

Figure 3.37: Joining two tuples from projected relations

Since t is in R, it must be that x is in R. Put another way, as long as functional dependency $B \rightarrow C$ holds, the joining of two projected tuples cannot produce a bogus tuple. Rather, every tuple produced by joining is guaranteed to be a tuple of R.

This argument works in general. We assumed A, B, and C were each single attributes, but the same argument would apply if they were any sets of attributes. That is, we take any BCNF-violating dependency, let B be the attributes on the left side, C be the attributes on the right but not the left, and A be the attributes on neither side. We may conclude:

- If we decompose a relation according to the method of Section 3.7.4, then the original relation can be recovered exactly by joining the tuples of the new relations in all possible ways.

If we decompose relations in a way that is not based on a functional dependency, then we might not be able to recover the original relation. Here is an example.

Example 3.41 : Suppose we have the relation R with schema $\{A, B, C\}$ as above, but that the dependency $B \rightarrow C$ does not hold. Then R might consist of the two tuples

A	B	C
1	2	3
4	2	5

The projections of R onto the relations with schemas $\{A, B\}$ and $\{B, C\}$ are

A	B
1	2
4	2

and

B	C
2	3
2	5

respectively. Since all four tuples share the same B-value, 2, each tuple of one relation joins with both tuples of the other relation. Thus, when we try to reconstruct R by joining, we get

A	B	C
1	2	3
1	2	5
4	2	3
4	2	5

That is, we get "too much"; we get two bogus tuples, $(1, 2, 5)$ and $(4, 2, 3)$ that were not in the original relation R. □

3.7.7 Third Normal Form

Occasionally, one encounters a relation schema and its dependencies that are not in BCNF but that one doesn't want to decompose further. The following example is typical.

Example 3.42: Suppose we have a relation Bookings with attributes:

1. title, the name of a movie.

2. theater, the name of a theater where the movie is being shown.

3. city, the city where the theater is located.

The intent behind a tuple (m, t, c) is that the movie with title m is currently being shown at theater t in city c.

We might reasonably assert the following functional dependencies:

$$\text{theater} \rightarrow \text{city}$$
$$\text{title city} \rightarrow \text{theater}$$

The first says that a theater is located in one city. The second is not obvious but is based on the normal practice of not booking a movie into two theaters in the same city. We shall assert this dependency if only for the sake of the example.

Let us first find the keys. No single attribute is a key. For example, `title` is not a key because a movie can play in several theaters at once and in several cities at once.[9] Also, `theater` is not a key, because although `theater` functionally determines `city`, there are multiscreen theaters that show many movies at once. Thus, `theater` does not determine `title`. Finally, `city` is not a key because cities usually have more than one theater and more than one movie playing.

On the other hand, two of the three sets of two attributes are keys. Clearly {`title`, `city`} is a key because of the given dependency that says these attributes functionally determine `theater`.

It is also true that {`theater`, `title`} is a key. To see why, start with the given dependency `theater` → `city`. By the augmentation rule of Exercise 3.6.3(a), `theater`, `title` → `city` follows. Intuitively, if `theater` alone functionally determines `city`, then surely `theatre` and `title` together will do so.

The remaining pair of attributes, `city` and `theater`, do not functionally determine `title`, and are therefore not a key. We conclude that the only two keys are

$$\{\texttt{title, city}\}$$
$$\{\texttt{theater, title}\}$$

Now we immediately see a BCNF violation. We were given functional dependency `theater` → `city`, but its left side, `theater`, is not a superkey. We are therefore tempted to decompose, using this BCNF-violating dependency, into the two relation schemas:

$$\{\texttt{theater, city}\}$$
$$\{\texttt{theater, title}\}$$

There is a problem with this decomposition, concerning the functional dependency `title city` → `theater`. There could be current relations for the decomposed schemas that satisfy the dependency `theater` → `city` (which can be checked in the relation {`theater`, `city`}) but that, when joined, yield a relation that does not satisfy `title city` → `theater`. For instance, the two relations

theater	city
Guild	Menlo Park
Park	Menlo Park

---

[9]In this example we assume that there are not two "current" movies with the same title, even though we have previously recognized that there could be two movies with the same title made in different years.

Other Normal Forms

If there is a "third normal form," what happened to the first two "normal forms"? They indeed were defined, but today there is little use for them. *First normal form* is simply the condition that every component of every tuple is an atomic value. *Second normal form* is less restrictive than 3NF. It permits transitive dependencies in a relation but forbids a nontrivial dependency with a left side that is a proper subset of a key. There is also a "fourth normal form" that we shall meet in Section 3.8.

---

and

theater	title
Guild	The Net
Park	The Net

are permissible according to the functional dependencies that apply to each relation, but when we join them we get two tuples

theater	city	title
Guild	Menlo Park	The Net
Park	Menlo Park	The Net

that violate the dependency `title city` $\rightarrow$ `theater`.   □

The solution to the above problem is to relax our BCNF requirement slightly, in order to allow the occasional relation schema, like that of Example 3.42 that cannot be decomposed into BCNF relations without our losing the ability to check each functional dependency within one relation. This relaxed condition is called the *third normal form* condition:

- A relation R is in *third normal form* (3NF) if: whenever $A_1 A_2 \cdots A_n \rightarrow B$ is a nontrivial dependency, either $\{A_1, A_2, \ldots, A_n\}$ is a superkey, or B is a member of some key.

Note that the difference between this 3NF condition and the BCNF condition is the clause "or B is a member of some key." This clause "excuses" a dependency like `theater` $\rightarrow$ `city` in Example 3.42, because the right side, `city`, is a member of a key.

It is beyond the scope of this book to prove that 3NF is in fact adequate for its purposes. That is, we can always decompose a relation schema in a way that does not lose information, into schemas that are in 3NF and allow all functional dependencies to be checked. When these relations are not in BCNF, there will be some redundancy left in the schema, however.

It is interesting to observe that the example we found of a relation schema that is in 3NF but not in BCNF is somewhat different from the non-BCNF examples we have seen earlier. One of the relevant functional dependencies, `theater` → `city`, is of the typical form, based on the fact that a theater is a unique object located in one city. However, the other dependency

<code>title city → theater</code>

comes from an observation about the movie-distribution policies practiced by movie studios. In general, functional dependencies fall into two categories: those based on the fact that we are representing unique objects such as movies and studios, and those based on real-world practices, such as booking movies into at most one theater per city.

3.7.8 Exercises for Section 3.7

Exercise 3.7.1: For each of the following relation schemas and sets of functional dependencies:

* a) $R(A, B, C, D)$ with functional dependencies $AB \to C$, $C \to D$, and $D \to A$.

* b) $R(A, B, C, D)$ with functional dependencies $B \to C$, and $B \to D$.

  c) $R(A, B, C, D)$ with functional dependencies $AB \to C$, $BC \to D$, $CD \to A$, and $AD \to B$.

  d) $R(A, B, C, D)$ with functional dependencies $A \to B$, $B \to C$, $C \to D$, and $D \to A$.

  e) $R(A, B, C, D, E)$ with functional dependencies $AB \to C$, $DE \to C$, and $B \to D$.

  f) $R(A, B, C, D, E)$ with functional dependencies $AB \to C$, $C \to D$, $D \to B$, and $D \to E$.

do the following:

  i) Indicate all the BCNF violations. Do not forget to consider dependencies that are not in the given set, but follow from them. However, it is not necessary to give violations that have more than one attribute on the right side.

  ii) Decompose the relations, as necessary, into collections of relations that are in BCNF.

  iii) Indicate all the 3NF violations.

  iv) Decompose the relations, as necessary, into collections of relations that are in 3NF.

Exercise 3.7.2: We mentioned in Section 3.7.4 that we should expand the right side of a functional dependency that is a BCNF violation if possible. However, it was deemed an optional step. Consider a relation R whose schema is the set of attributes $\{A, B, C, D\}$ with functional dependencies $A \rightarrow B$ and $A \rightarrow C$. Either is a BCNF violation, because the only key for R is $\{A, D\}$. Suppose we begin by decomposing R according to $A \rightarrow B$. Do we ultimately get the same result as if we first expand the BCNF violation to $A \rightarrow BC$? Why or why not?

! Exercise 3.7.3: Let R be as in Exercise 3.7.2, but let the functional dependencies be $A \rightarrow B$ and $B \rightarrow C$. Again compare decomposing using $A \rightarrow B$ first against decomposing by $A \rightarrow BC$ first. *Hint*: When we decompose, we need to think about what functional dependencies hold for the relations that result from the decomposition. Is it sufficient to use only those of the given dependencies that involve only attributes in one of the schemas of the decomposition? What about dependencies that follow from the given dependencies?

! Exercise 3.7.4: Suppose we have a relation schema $R(A, B, C)$ with functional dependency $A \rightarrow B$. Suppose also that we decide to decompose this schema into $S(A, B)$ and $T(B, C)$. Give an example of an instance of relation R whose projection onto S and T and subsequent rejoining as in Section 3.7.6 does not yield the same relation instance.

! Exercise 3.7.5: Suppose we decompose relation $R(A, B, C, D, E)$ into relation $S(A, B, C)$ and other relations. Give the functional dependencies that hold in S if the dependencies for R are:

* a) $AB \rightarrow DE$, $C \rightarrow E$, $D \rightarrow C$, and $E \rightarrow A$.

b) $A \rightarrow D$, $BD \rightarrow E$, $AC \rightarrow E$, and $DE \rightarrow B$.

c) $AB \rightarrow D$, $AC \rightarrow E$, $BC \rightarrow D$, $D \rightarrow A$, and $E \rightarrow B$.

d) $A \rightarrow B$, $B \rightarrow C$, $C \rightarrow D$, $D \rightarrow E$, and $E \rightarrow A$.

In each case, it is sufficient to give a minimal basis for the full set of dependencies of S.

3.8 Multivalued Dependencies

A "multivalued dependency" is an assertion that two attributes or sets of attributes are independent of one another. This condition is, as we shall see, a generalization of the notion of a functional dependency, in the sense that every functional dependency implies a corresponding multivalued dependency. However, there are some situations involving independence of attribute sets that cannot be explained as functional dependencies. In this section we shall explore the cause of multivalued dependencies and see how they can be used in database schema design.

3.8.1 Attribute Independence and Its Consequent Redundancy

There are occasional situations where we design a relation schema and find it is in BCNF, yet the relation has a kind of redundancy that is not related to functional dependencies. The most common source of redundancy in BCNF schemas is the independence of two or more multivalued attributes of some class, when we use the straightforward transformation from ODL to relations that was described in Section 3.2.

Example 3.43 : Suppose the class Star is defined to have a name, a set of addresses, and a set of movies starred in. The definition would be similar to that of Fig. 2.5, but the type of attribute address would differ. The proposed definition of Star is shown in Fig. 3.38.

```
interface Star {
   attribute string name;
   attribute Set<
         Struct Addr {string street, string city}
      > address;
   relationship Set<Movie> starredIn inverse Movie::stars;
   };
```

Figure 3.38: Stars defined to have sets of addresses and movies

In Fig. 3.39 we see some possible tuples in the relation that comes directly from the definition of Fig. 3.38. We have represented sets of addresses exactly as we did in Fig. 3.8. The tuples of that figure have been extended with components corresponding to attributes title and year, the key for the Movie class. These attributes represent the movies related to the star by the relationship starredIn.

name	street	city	title	year
C. Fisher	123 Maple St.	Hollywood	Star Wars	1977
C. Fisher	5 Locust Ln.	Malibu	Star Wars	1977
C. Fisher	123 Maple St.	Hollywood	Empire Strikes Back	1980
C. Fisher	5 Locust Ln.	Malibu	Empire Strikes Back	1980
C. Fisher	123 Maple St.	Hollywood	Return of the Jedi	1983
C. Fisher	5 Locust Ln.	Malibu	Return of the Jedi	1983

Figure 3.39: Sets of addresses independent from movies

We focus in Fig. 3.39 on Carrie Fisher's two hypothetical addresses and three best-known movies. There is no reason to associate an address with one movie and not another. Thus, the only way to express the fact that addresses and movies are independent properties of stars is to have each address appear with each movie. But when we repeat address and movie facts in all combinations, there is obvious redundancy. For instance, Fig. 3.39 repeats each of Carrie Fisher's addresses three times (once for each of her movies) and each movie twice (once for each address).

Yet there is no BCNF violation in the `Star` relation schema suggested by Fig. 3.39. There are, in fact, no nontrivial functional dependencies at all. For example, attribute `city` is not functionally determined by the other four attributes. There might be a star with two homes that had the same street address in different cities. Then there would be two tuples that agreed in all attributes but `city` and disagreed in `city`. Thus,

$$\text{name street title year} \rightarrow \text{city}$$

is not a functional dependency for our `Star` relation. We leave it to the reader to check that none of the five attributes is functionally determined by the other four. That observation is enough to conclude that there are no nontrivial functional dependencies at all (the reader should also consider why this inference is proper). Since there are no nontrivial functional dependencies, it follows that all five attributes form the only key and that there are no BCNF violations. □

3.8.2 Definition of Multivalued Dependencies

A *multivalued dependency* is a statement about some relation R that when you fix the values for one set of attributes, then the values in certain other attributes are independent of the values of all the other attributes in the relation. More precisely, we say the multivalued dependency

$$A_1 A_2 \cdots A_n \twoheadrightarrow B_1 B_2 \cdots B_m$$

holds for a relation R if when we restrict ourselves to the tuples of R that have a certain value for each of the attributes among the A's, then the set of values we find among the B's is independent of the set of values we find among the attributes of R that are not among the A's or B's. Still more precisely, we say this multivalued dependency holds if

> For each pair of tuples t and u of relation R that agree on all the A's, we can find in R is some tuple v that agrees:
>
> 1. With both t and u on the A's,
>
> 2. With t on the B's, and
>
> 3. With u on all attributes of R that are not among the A's or B's.

Note that we can use this rule with t and u interchanged, to infer the existence of a fourth tuple w that agrees with u on the B's and with t on the other attributes. As a consequence, for any fixed values of the A's, the associated values of the B's and the other attributes appear in all possible combinations in different tuples. Figure 3.40 suggests how v relates to t and u when a multivalued dependency holds.

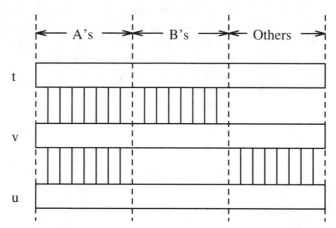

Figure 3.40: A multivalued dependency guarantees that v exists

In general, we may assume that the A's and B's (left side and right side) of a multivalued dependency are disjoint. However, as with functional dependencies, it is permissible to add some of the A's to the right side if we wish. Also note that unlike functional dependencies, where we started with single attributes on the right and allowed sets of attributes on the right as a shorthand, with multivalued dependencies, we must consider sets of attributes on the right immediately. As we shall see in Example 3.45, it is not always possible to break the right sides of multivalued dependencies into single attributes.

Example 3.44: In Example 3.43 we encountered a multivalued dependency that in our notation is expressed:

$$\text{name} \twoheadrightarrow \text{street city}$$

That is, for each star's name, the set of addresses appears in conjunction with each of the star's movies. For an example of how the formal definition of this multivalued dependency applies, consider the first and fourth tuples from Fig. 3.39:

name	street	city	title	year
C. Fisher	123 Maple St.	Hollywood	Star Wars	1977
C. Fisher	5 Locust Ln.	Malibu	Empire Strikes Back	1980

If we let the first tuple be t and the second be u, then the multivalued dependency asserts that we must also find in R the tuple that has name C. Fisher, a street and city that agree with the first tuple, and other attributes (title and year) that agree with the second tuple. There is indeed such a tuple; it is the third tuple of Fig. 3.39.

Similarly, we could let t be the second tuple above and u be the first. Then the multivalued dependency tells us that there is a tuple of R that agrees with the second in attributes name, street, and city and with the first in name, title, and year. This tuple also exists; it is the second tuple of Fig. 3.39. □

3.8.3 Reasoning About Multivalued Dependencies

There are a number of rules about multivalued dependencies that are similar to the rules we learned for functional dependencies in Section 3.6. For example, multivalued dependencies obey

- The *trivial dependencies rule*, which says that if multivalued dependency $A_1 A_2 \cdots A_n \twoheadrightarrow B_1 B_2 \cdots B_m$ holds for some relation, then so does

$$A_1 A_2 \cdots A_n \twoheadrightarrow C_1 C_2 \cdots C_k$$

where the C's are the B's plus one or more of the A's. Conversely, we can also remove attributes from the B's if they are among the A's and infer the multivalued dependency

$$A_1 A_2 \cdots A_n \twoheadrightarrow D_1 D_2 \cdots D_r$$

if the D's are those B's that are not among the A's.

- The *transitive rule*, which says that if $A_1 A_2 \cdots A_n \twoheadrightarrow B_1 B_2 \cdots B_m$ and $B_1 B_2 \cdots B_m \twoheadrightarrow C_1 C_2 \cdots C_k$ hold for some relation, then so does

$$A_1 A_2 \cdots A_n \twoheadrightarrow C_1 C_2 \cdots C_k$$

However, multivalued dependencies do not obey the splitting/combining rule.

Example 3.45 : Consider again Fig. 3.39, where we observed the multivalued dependency

$$\text{name} \twoheadrightarrow \text{street city}$$

If the splitting rule were true for multivalued dependencies, then we would expect

$$\text{name} \twoheadrightarrow \text{street}$$

also to be true. This multivalued dependency says that each star's street addresses are independent of the other attributes, including `city`. However, that statement is false. Consider, for instance, the first two tuples of Fig. 3.39. The hypothetical multivalued dependency would allow us to infer that the tuples with the streets interchanged:

name	street	city	title	year
C. Fisher	5 Locust Ln.	Hollywood	Star Wars	1977
C. Fisher	123 Maple St.	Malibu	Star Wars	1977

were in the relation. But these are not true tuples, because, for instance, the home on 5 Locust Ln. is in Malibu, not Hollywood.   □

However, there are several new rules dealing with multivalued dependencies that we can learn. First,

- Every functional dependency is a multivalued dependency. That is, if $A_1 A_2 \cdots A_n \rightarrow B_1 B_2 \cdots B_m$, then $A_1 A_2 \cdots A_n \twoheadrightarrow B_1 B_2 \cdots B_m$.

To see why, suppose R is some relation for which the functional dependency $A_1 A_2 \cdots A_n \rightarrow B_1 B_2 \cdots B_m$ holds, and suppose t and u are tuples of R that agree on the A's. To show that the multivalued dependency

$$A_1 A_2 \cdots A_n \twoheadrightarrow B_1 B_2 \cdots B_m$$

holds, we have to show that R also contains a tuple v that agrees with t and u on the A's, with t on the B's, and with u on all other attributes. But v can be u. Surely u agrees with t and u on the A's, because we started by assuming that these two tuples agree on the A's. The functional dependency $A_1 A_2 \cdots A_n \rightarrow B_1 B_2 \cdots B_m$ assures us that u agrees with t on the B's. And of course u agrees with itself on the other attributes. Thus, whenever a functional dependency holds, the corresponding multivalued dependency holds.

Another rule that has no counterpart in the world of functional dependencies is the *complementation rule*:

- If $A_1 A_2 \cdots A_n \twoheadrightarrow B_1 B_2 \cdots B_m$ is a multivalued dependency for relation R, then R also satisfies $A_1 A_2 \cdots A_n \twoheadrightarrow C_1 C_2 \cdots C_k$, where the C's are all attributes of R not among the A's and B.

Example 3.46: Again consider the relation of Fig. 3.39, for which we asserted the multivalued dependency

$$\text{name} \twoheadrightarrow \text{street city}$$

The complementation rule says that

$$\text{name} \twoheadrightarrow \text{title year}$$

must also hold in this relation, because `title` and `year` are the attributes not mentioned in the first dependency. The second dependency intuitively means that each star has a set of movies starred in, which are independent of the star's addresses.   □

3.8.4   Fourth Normal Form

The redundancy that we found in Section 3.8.1 to be caused by multivalued dependencies can be eliminated if we use these dependencies in a new decomposition algorithm for relations. In this section we shall introduce a new normal form, called "fourth normal form." In this normal form, all "nontrivial" (in a sense to be defined below) multivalued dependencies are eliminated, as are all functional dependencies that violate BCNF. As a result, the decomposed relations have neither the redundancy from functional dependencies that we discussed in Section 3.7.1 nor the redundancy from multivalued dependencies that we discussed in Section 3.8.1.

A multivalued dependency $A_1 A_2 \cdots A_n \twoheadrightarrow B_1 B_2 \cdots B_m$ for a relation R is *nontrivial* if:

1. None of the B's is among the A's.

2. Not all the attributes of R are among the A's and B's.

The "fourth normal form" condition is essentially the BCNF condition, but applied to multivalued dependencies instead of functional dependencies. Formally:

- A relation R is in *fourth normal form* (4NF) if whenever

$$A_1 A_2 \cdots A_n \twoheadrightarrow B_1 B_2 \cdots B_m$$

  is a nontrivial multivalued dependency, $\{A_1, A_2, \ldots, A_n\}$ is a superkey.

That is, if a relation is in 4NF, then every nontrivial multivalued dependency is really a functional dependency with a superkey on the left. Note that the notions of keys and superkeys depend on functional dependencies only; adding multivalued dependencies does not change the definition of "key."

Example 3.47: The relation of Fig. 3.39 violates the 4NF condition. For example,

name $\twoheadrightarrow$ street city

is a nontrivial multivalued dependency, yet **name** by itself is not a superkey. In fact, the only key for this relation is all the attributes.   □

Fourth normal form is truly a generalization of BCNF. Recall from Section 3.8.3 that every functional dependency is also a multivalued dependency. Thus, every BCNF violation is also a 4NF violation. Put another way, every relation that is in 4NF is therefore in BCNF.

However, there are some relations that are in BCNF but not 4NF. Figure 3.39 is a good example. The only key for this relation is all five attributes, and there are no nontrivial functional dependencies. Thus it is surely in BCNF. However, as we observed in Example 3.47, it is not in 4NF.

3.8.5   Decomposition into Fourth Normal Form

The 4NF decomposition algorithm is quite analogous to the BCNF decomposition algorithm. We find a 4NF violation, say $A_1 A_2 \cdots A_n \twoheadrightarrow B_1 B_2 \cdots B_m$, where $\{A_1, A_2, \ldots, A_n\}$ is not a superkey. Note this multivalued dependency could be a true multivalued dependency, or it could be derived from the corresponding functional dependency $A_1 A_2 \cdots A_n \to B_1 B_2 \cdots B_m$, since every functional dependency is a multivalued dependency. Then we break the schema for the relation R that has the 4NF violation into two schemas:

1. The A's and the B's.

2. The A's and all attributes of R that are not among the A's or B's.

Example 3.48 : Let us continue Example 3.47. We observed that

$$\text{name} \twoheadrightarrow \text{street city}$$

was a 4NF violation. The decomposition rule above tells us to replace the five-attribute schema by one schema that has only the three attributes in the above multivalued dependency and another schema that consists of the left side, `name`, plus the attributes that do not appear in the dependency. These attributes are `title` and `year`, so the following two schemas

$$\{\text{name, street, city}\}$$
$$\{\text{name, title, year}\}$$

are the result of the decomposition. In each schema there are no nontrivial multivalued (or functional) dependencies, so they are in 4NF. Note that in the relation with schema $\{\text{name, street, city}\}$, the multivalued dependency

$$\text{name} \twoheadrightarrow \text{street city}$$

is trivial since it involves all attributes. Likewise, in the relation with schema $\{\text{name, title, year}\}$, the multivalued dependency

$$\text{name} \twoheadrightarrow \text{title year}$$

is trivial. Should one or both schemas of the decomposition not be in 4NF, we would have had to decompose the non-4NF schema(s). $\Box$

As for the BCNF decomposition, each decomposition step leaves us with schemas that have strictly fewer attributes than we started with, so eventually we get to schemas that need not be decomposed further; that is, they are in 4NF. Moreover, the argument justifying the decomposition that we gave in Section 3.7.6 carries over to multivalued dependencies as well. When we decompose a relation because of a multivalued dependency

$$A_1 A_2 \cdots A_n \twoheadrightarrow B_1 B_2 \cdots B_m$$

this dependency is enough to justify the claim that we can reconstruct the original relation from the relations of the decomposition.

Projecting Multivalued Dependencies

When we decompose into fourth normal form, we need to find the multi-valued dependencies that hold in the relations that are the result of the decomposition. We wish it were easier to find these dependencies. However, there is no simple test analogous to computing the closure of a set of attributes (as in Section 3.6.3) for functional dependencies. In fact, even a complete set of rules for reasoning about collections of functional and multivalued dependencies is quite complex and beyond the scope of this book. The section on further reading mentions some places where the subject is treated.

Fortunately, we can often obtain the relevant multivalued dependencies for one of the products of a decomposition by using the transitive rule, the complementation rule, and the intersection rule [Exercise 3.8.7(b)]. We recommend that the reader try these in examples and exercises.

3.8.6 Relationships Among Normal Forms

As we have mentioned, 4NF implies BCNF, which in turn implies 3NF. Thus, for any relation schema, the sets of relation instances for that schema satisfying the three normal forms are related as in Fig. 3.41. That is, if a set of tuples satisfies the 4NF condition, then it surely satisfies the other two normal-form conditions, and if it satisfies the BNCF condition, then it surely is in 3NF. However, depending on the functional dependencies assumed for the schema, there could be sets of tuples in 3NF but not BCNF. Similarly, for certain sets of assumed functional and multivalued dependencies, there will be some sets of tuples in BCNF but not 4NF.

Another way to compare the normal forms is by the guarantees they make about the set of relations that result from a decomposition into that normal form. These observations are summarized in the table of Fig. 3.42. That is, BCNF (and therefore 4NF) eliminates the redundancy and other anomalies that are caused by functional dependencies, while only 4NF eliminates the additional redundancy that is caused by the presence of nontrivial multivalued dependencies that are not functional dependencies. Often, 3NF is enough to eliminate this redundancy, but there are examples where it is not. A decomposition into 3NF can always be chosen so that the functional dependencies are preserved; that is, they are enforced in the decomposed relations (although we have not discussed the algorithm to do so in this book). BCNF does not guarantee preservation of functional dependencies, and none of the normal forms guarantee preservation of multivalued dependencies, although in typical cases the dependencies are preserved.

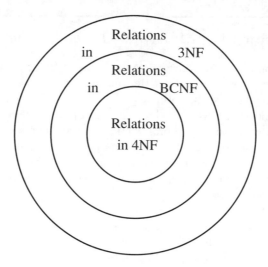

Figure 3.41: 4NF implies BNCF implies 3NF

Property	3NF	BCNF	4NF
Eliminates redundancy due to functional dependencies	Most	Yes	Yes
Eliminates redundancy due to multivalued dependencies	No	No	Yes
Preserves functional dependencies	Yes	Maybe	Maybe
Preserves multivalued dependencies	Maybe	Maybe	Maybe

Figure 3.42: Properties of normal forms and their decompositions

3.8.7   Exercises for Section 3.8

* **Exercise 3.8.1 :** Suppose we have a relation $R(A, B, C)$ with a multivalued dependency $A \twoheadrightarrow B$. If we know that the tuples (a, b_1, c_1), (a, b_2, c_2), and (a, b_3, c_3) are in the current instance of R, what other tuples do we know must also be in R?

* **Exercise 3.8.2 :** Suppose we have a relation in which we want to record for each person their name, Social Security number, and birthdate. Also, for each child of the person, the name, Social Security number, and birthdate of the child, and for each automobile the person owns, its serial number and make. To be more precise, this relation has all tuples

$$(n, s, b, cn, cs, cb, as, am)$$

such that

1. n is the name of the person with Social Security number s.

2. b is n's birthdate.

3. cn is the name of one of n's children.

4. cs is cn's Social Security number.

5. cb is cn's birthdate.

6. as is the serial number of one of n's automobiles.

7. am is the make of the automobile with serial number as.

For this relation:

a) Tell the functional and multivalued dependencies we would expect to hold.

b) Suggest a decomposition of the relation into 4NF.

Exercise 3.8.3: For each of the following relation schemas and dependencies

* a) $R(A, B, C, D)$ with multivalued dependencies $A \twoheadrightarrow B$ and $A \twoheadrightarrow C$.

b) $R(A, B, C, D)$ with multivalued dependencies $A \twoheadrightarrow B$ and $B \twoheadrightarrow CD$.

c) $R(A, B, C, D)$ with multivalued dependency $AB \twoheadrightarrow C$ and functional dependency $B \to D$.

d) $R(A, B, C, D, E)$ with multivalued dependencies $A \twoheadrightarrow B$ and $AB \twoheadrightarrow C$ and functional dependencies $A \to D$ and $AB \to E$.

do the following:

i) Find all the 4NF violations.

ii) Decompose the relations into a collection of relation schemas in 4NF.

! **Exercise 3.8.4:** In Exercise 2.3.2 we discussed four different assumptions about the relationship *Births*. For each of these, indicate the multivalued dependencies (other than functional dependencies) that would be expected to hold in the resulting relation.

Exercise 3.8.5: Give informal arguments why we would not expect any of the five attributes in Example 3.43 to be functionally determined by the other four.

! **Exercise 3.8.6:** Using the definition of multivalued dependency, show why the complementation rule holds.

! Exercise 3.8.7: Show the following rules for multivalued dependencies:

* a) The *union rule.* If X, Y, and Z are sets of attributes, $X \twoheadrightarrow Y$, and $X \twoheadrightarrow Z$, then $X \twoheadrightarrow (Y \cup Z)$.

  b) The *intersection rule.* If X, Y, and Z are sets of attributes, $X \twoheadrightarrow Y$, and $X \twoheadrightarrow Z$, then $X \twoheadrightarrow (Y \cap Z)$.

  c) The *difference rule.* If X, Y, and Z are sets of attributes, $X \twoheadrightarrow Y$, and $X \twoheadrightarrow Z$, then $X \twoheadrightarrow (Y - Z)$.

  d) *Trivial multivalued dependencies.* If $Y \subseteq X$, then $X \twoheadrightarrow Y$ holds in any relation.

  e) *Another source of trivial multivalued dependencies.* If $X \cup Y$ is all the attributes of relation R, then $X \twoheadrightarrow Y$ holds in R.

  f) *Removing attributes shared by left and right side.* If $X \twoheadrightarrow Y$ holds, then $X \twoheadrightarrow (Y - X)$ holds.

! Exercise 3.8.8: Give counterexample relations to show why the following rules for multivalued dependencies do *not* hold.

* a) If $A \twoheadrightarrow BC$, then $A \twoheadrightarrow B$.

  b) If $A \twoheadrightarrow B$, then $A \to B$.

  c) If $AB \twoheadrightarrow C$, then $A \twoheadrightarrow C$.

! Exercise 3.8.9: The conversion from ODL to relations often introduces multivalued dependencies. Give some principles for discovering multivalued dependencies from multivalued attributes and relationships when the relation-schema strategy of Sections 3.2.2 and 3.2.5 are followed.

3.9   An Example Database Schema

Having seen the kinds of problems that can arise when we construct our relations directly from an ODL or E/R design, and having seen what we can do about the anomalies that sometimes occur, let us fix on a single relational database schema that we shall use in examples of the next part of the book — the part devoted to database programming by the user. Our database schema draws upon the running example of movies, stars, and studios, and it uses normalized relations similar to the ones that we developed in the previous sections. However, it includes some attributes that we have not used previously in examples, and it includes one relation — `MovieExec` — that has not appeared before. The purpose of these changes is to give us some opportunities to study different data types and different ways of representing information in examples of Chapters 4 through 8. Figure 3.43 shows the schema.

```
Movie(
    TITLE: string,
    YEAR: integer,
    length: integer,
    inColor: boolean,
    studioName: string,
    producerC#: integer)

StarsIn(
    MOVIETITLE: string,
    MOVIEYEAR: integer,
    STARNAME: string)

MovieStar(
    NAME: string,
    address: string,
    gender: char,
    birthdate: date)

MovieExec(
    name: string,
    address: string,
    CERT#: integer
    netWorth: integer)

Studio(
    NAME: string,
    address: string,
    presC#: integer)
```

Figure 3.43: Example database schema about movies

Our schema has five relations. The attributes of each relation are listed, along with the intended domain for that attribute. The key attributes for a relation are shown in capitals in Fig. 3.43, although when we refer to them in text, they will be lower-case as they have been heretofore. For instance, all three attributes together form the key for relation StarsIn. Relation Movie has six attributes; title and year together constitute the key for Movie, as they have previously. Attribute title is a string, and year is an integer.

The major modifications to the schema compared with what we have seen so far are:

- There is a notion of a *certificate number* for movie executives — studio presidents and movie producers. This certificate is a unique integer that we imagine is maintained by some external authority, perhaps a registry of executives or a "union."

- We use certificate numbers as the key for movie executives, although movie stars do not always have certificates and we shall continue to use name as the key for stars. That decision is probably unrealistic, since two stars could have the same name, but we take this road in order to illustrate some different options.

- We introduced the producer as another property of movies. This information is represented by a new attribute, producerC#, of relation Movie. This attribute is intended to be the certificate number of the producer. Producers are expected to be movie executives, as are studio presidents. There may also be other executives in the MovieExec relation.

- Attribute filmType of Movie has been changed from an enumerated type to a boolean-valued attribute called inColor: true if in color and false if in black and white. The motivation is that not all database languages support enumerated types.

- The attribute gender has been added for movie stars. Its type is "character," either M for male or F for female. Attribute birthdate, of type "date" (a special type supported by many commercial database systems or just a character string if we prefer) has also been added.

- All addresses have been made strings, rather than pairs consisting of a street and city. The purpose is to make addresses in different relations comparable easily and to simplify operations on addresses.

We conclude with a brief commentary on the five relations, their attributes and their derivation from the earlier ODL or E/R designs.

1. Movie is one of the relations in the decomposition of relation Movie in Example 3.36, to which we have added attribute producerC# representing the producer of the movie.

2. `StarsIn` is the other relation in the decomposition of Example 3.36. This same relation is also needed if we create a relation `Star` from the ODL class of the same name and then put that relation into BCNF. That is, starting with the ODL definition of Fig. 2.5, we would get a relation `Star` with attributes `name`, `address`, `title`, and `year`. The last two represent the `starredIn` relationship. We find that {`name`, `title`, `year`} is the key, but `name` → `address` is a functional dependency. Thus, the relation would have to be decomposed into schemas {`name`, `address`} (which has been expanded into our relation `MovieStar`) and {`name`, `title`, `year`} (which is essentially our relation `StarsIn`). Our relation `StarsIn` also represents the relationship *Stars-in* of the E/R diagram of Fig. 2.8.

3.10 Summary of Chapter 3

+ *Relational Model*: Relations are tables representing information. Columns are headed by attributes; each attribute has an associated domain, or data type. Rows are called tuples, and a tuple has one component for each attribute of the relation.

+ *Schemas*: A relation name, together with the attributes of that relation, form the relation schema. A collection of relation schemas forms a database schema. Particular data for a relation or collection of relations is called an instance of that relation schema or database schema.

+ *Converting Entity Sets to Relations*: The relation for an entity set has one attribute for each attribute of the entity set. An exception is a weak entity set E, whose relation must also have attributes for the key attributes of those other entity sets that help identify entities of E.

+ *Converting Relationships to Relations*: The relation for an E/R relationship has attributes corresponding to the key attributes of each entity set that participates in the relationship.

+ *Converting ODL Classes to Relations*: The relation for an ODL class C has one attribute for each attribute of the class. It may also have attributes for the key of a class D to which C is related by a relationship. Since relationships in ODL have inverses, we recommend storing a many-one relationship from C to D with C and not with D.

+ *Converting ODL Many-Many Relationships to Relations*: Many-many relationships can be stored with either class, but they result in an explosion in the number of tuples in the relation. This awkwardness in the relational design can be removed by the process of normalization. Alternatively, many-many relationships in ODL can be represented by a separate relation as they would be in the E/R model.

✦ *Converting Subclasses to Relations*: One approach is to partition entities or objects among the various subclasses and create a relation, with all necessary attribute, for each subclass. A second approach is to represent all entities or objects in a master relation with the only the attributes of the most general class. Entities or objects in subclasses are also in special relations for whatever subclasses they belong to. These relations have only the key attributes for the general class and the attributes special to the subclass.

✦ *Functional Dependencies*: A functional dependency is a statement that two tuples of a relation that agree on some particular set of attributes must also agree on some other particular attribute.

✦ *Keys*: A superkey for a relation is a set of attributes that functionally determine all the attributes of the relation. A key is a superkey such that no proper subset of the key also functionally determines all the attributes.

✦ *Reasoning About Functional Dependencies*: There are many rules that let us infer that one functional dependency $X \to A$ holds in any relation instance that satisfies some other given set of functional dependencies. The simplest approach to verifying that $X \to A$ holds usually is to compute the closure of X, using the given dependencies to expand X until it includes A.

✦ *Decomposing Relations*: We can decompose one relation schema into two without losing information as long as the attributes in both schemas forms a superkey for at least one of the decomposed relations.

✦ *Boyce-Codd Normal Form*: A relation is in BCNF if the only nontrivial functional dependencies say that some superkey functionally determines one of the other attributes. It is possible to decompose any relation into a collection of BCNF relations without losing information. A major benefit of BCNF is that it eliminates redundancy caused by the existence of functional dependencies.

✦ *Third Normal Form*: Sometimes decomposition into BCNF can prevent us from checking certain functional dependencies. A relaxed form of BCNF, called 3NF, allows a functional dependency $X \to A$ even if X is not a superkey, provided A is a member of some key. 3NF does not eliminate all redundancy due to functional dependencies, but often does so.

✦ *Multivalued Dependencies*: A multivalued dependency is a statement that two sets of attributes in a relation have sets of values that appear in all possible combinations. A common cause of multivalued dependencies is designing a relation to represent an ODL class with two or more multivalued attributes or relationships.

✦ *Fourth Normal Form*: Multivalued dependencies can also cause redundancy in a relation. 4NF is like BCNF, but also forbids nontrivial multivalued dependencies (unless they are actually functional dependencies that are allowed by BCNF). It is possible to decompose a relation into 4NF without losing information.

3.11 References for Chapter 3

The classic paper by Codd on the relational model is [4]. This paper introduces the idea of functional dependencies, as well as the basic relational concept. Third normal form was also described there, while Boyce-Codd normal form is described by Codd in a later paper [5].

Multivalued dependencies and fourth normal form were defined by Fagin in [7]. However, the idea of multivalued dependencies also appears independently in [6] and [9].

Armstrong was the first to study rules for inferring functional dependencies [1]. The rules for functional dependencies that we have covered here (including what we call "Armstrong's axioms") and rules for inferring multivalued dependencies as well, come from [2]. The technique for testing a functional dependency by computing the closure for a set of attributes is from [3].

There are a number of algorithms and/or proofs that algorithms work which have not been given in this book. These include explanations of why the closure algorithm for inferring functional dependencies works, how one infers multivalued dependencies, how one projects multivalued dependencies onto decomposed relations, and how one decomposes into 3NF without losing the ability to check functional dependencies. These and other matters concerned with dependencies are explained in [8].

1. Armstrong, W. W., "Dependency structures of database relationships," *Proceedings of the 1974 IFIP Congress*, pp. 580–583.

2. Beeri, C., R. Fagin, and J. H. Howard, "A complete axiomatization for functional and multivalued dependencies," *ACM SIGMOD International Conference on Management of Data*, pp. 47–61, 1977.

3. Bernstein, P. A., "Synthesizing third normal form relations from functional dependencies," *ACM Transactions on Database Systems* **1**:4, pp. 277–298, 1976.

4. Codd, E. F., "A relational model for large shared data banks," *Comm. ACM* **13**:6, pp. 377–387, 1970.

5. Codd, E. F., "Further normalization of the data base relational model," in *Database Systems* (R. Rustin, ed.), Prentice-Hall, Englewood Cliffs, NJ, 1972.

6. Delobel, C., "Normalization and hierarchical dependencies in the relational data model," *ACM Transactions on Database Systems* **3**:3, pp. 201–222, 1978.

7. Fagin, R., "Multivalued dependencies and a new normal form for relational databases," *ACM Transactions on Database Systems* **2**:3, pp. 262–278, 1977.

8. Ullman, J. D., *Principles of Database and Knowledge-Base Systems, Volume I*, Computer Science Press, New York, 1988.

9. Zaniolo, C. and M. A. Melkanoff, "On the design of relational database schemata," *ACM Transactions on Database Systems* **6**:1, pp. 1–47, 1981.

Chapter 4

Operations in the Relational Model

In this chapter we begin the study of databases from the point of view of the user. Often, the principal issue for the user is *querying* the database, that is, writing programs that answer questions about the current instance of the database. In this chapter, we shall study the question of database queries from an abstract point of view, defining the principal query operators.

While ODL uses methods that, in principle, can perform any operation on data, and the E/R model does not embrace a specific way of manipulating data, the relational model has a concrete set of "standard" operations on data. Thus, our study of database operations in the abstract will focus on the relational model and its operations. These operations can be expressed in either an algebra, called "relational algebra," or in a form of logic, called "Datalog." We shall learn each of these notations in this chapter.

Later chapters let us see the languages and features that today's commercial database systems offer the user. The abstract query operators will appear primarily as operations in the SQL query language discussed in Chapters 5 through 7. However, they also appear in the OQL language mentioned in Chapter 8.

4.1 An Algebra of Relational Operations

To begin our study of operations on relations, we shall learn about a special algebra, called *relational algebra*, that consists of some simple but powerful ways to construct new relations from old ones. *Expressions* in relational algebra start from relations as operands; relations can either be represented by their name (e.g., R or Movie) or represented explicitly as a list of their tuples. We can then build progressively more complex expressions by applying any of the operators to be described below, either to relations or to simpler expressions of relational

173

algebra. A *query* is an expression of relational algebra. Thus, relational algebra is our first concrete example of a query language.

The operations of relational algebra fall into four broad classes:

1. The usual set operations — union, intersection, and difference — applied to relations.

2. Operations that remove parts of a relation: "selection" eliminates some rows (tuples), and "projection" eliminates some columns.

3. Operations that combine the tuples of two relations, including "Cartesian product," which pairs the tuples of two relations in all possible ways, and various kinds of "join" operations, which selectively pair tuples from two relations.

4. An operation called "renaming" that does not affect the tuples of a relation, but changes the relation schema, i.e., the names of the attributes and/or the name of the relation itself.

These operations are not enough to do any possible computation about relations; in fact they are quite limited. However, they capture much of what we really want to do with databases, and they form a large part of the standard relational query language SQL, as we shall see in Chapter 5. We shall, however, discuss briefly in Sections 4.6 and 4.7 some of the computational capabilities that are present in real query languages like SQL and yet are not part of relational algebra.

4.1.1 Set Operations on Relations

The three most common operations on sets are union, intersection, and difference. We assume the reader is familiar with these operations, which are defined as follows on arbitrary sets R and S:

- $R \cup S$, the *union* of R and S, is the set of elements that are in R or S or both. An element appears only once in the union even if it is present in both R and S.

- $R \cap S$, the *intersection* of R and S, is the set of elements that are in both R and S.

- $R - S$, the *difference* of R and S, is the set of elements that are in R but not in S. Note that $R - S$ is different from $S - R$; the latter is the set of elements that are in S but not in R.

When we apply these operations to relations, we need to put some conditions on R and S:

1. R and S must have schemas with identical sets of attributes.

2. Before we compute the set-theoretic union, intersection, or difference of sets of tuples, the columns of R and S must be ordered so that the order of attributes is the same for both relations.

Sometimes we would like to take the union, intersection, or difference of relations that have the same number of attributes but use different names for their attributes. If so, we may use the renaming operator discussed in Section 4.1.8 to change the schema of one or both relations and give them the same set of attributes.

name	address	gender	birthdate
Carrie Fisher	123 Maple St., Hollywood	F	9/9/99
Mark Hamill	456 Oak Rd., Brentwood	M	8/8/88

Relation R

name	address	gender	birthdate
Carrie Fisher	123 Maple St., Hollywood	F	9/9/99
Harrison Ford	789 Palm Dr., Beverly Hills	M	7/7/77

Relation S

Figure 4.1: Two relations

Example 4.1: Suppose we have the two relations R and S, instances of the relation MovieStar of Section 3.9. Current instances of R and S are shown in Fig. 4.1. Then the union $R \cup S$ is

name	address	gender	birthdate
Carrie Fisher	123 Maple St., Hollywood	F	9/9/99
Mark Hamill	456 Oak Rd., Brentwood	M	8/8/88
Harrison Ford	789 Palm Dr., Beverly Hills	M	7/7/77

Note that the two tuples for Carrie Fisher from the two relations appear only once in the result.

The intersection $R \cap S$ is

name	address	gender	birthdate
Carrie Fisher	123 Maple St., Hollywood	F	9/9/99

Now, only the Carrie Fisher tuple appears, because only it is in both relations. The difference $R - S$ is

name	address	gender	birthdate
Mark Hamill	456 Oak Rd., Brentwood	M	8/8/88

That is, the Fisher and Hamill tuples appear in R and thus are candidates for $R - S$. However, the Fisher tuple also appears in S and so is not in $R - S$. □

4.1.2 Projection

The *projection* operator is used to produce from a relation R a new relation that has only some of R's columns. The value of expression $\pi_{A_1, A_2, \ldots, A_n}(R)$ is a relation that has only the columns for attributes $A_1, A_2, \ldots, A_n$ of R. The schema for the resulting value is the set of attributes $\{A_1, A_2, \ldots, A_n\}$, which we conventionally show in the order listed.

title	year	length	inColor	studioName	producerC#
Star Wars	1977	124	true	Fox	12345
Mighty Ducks	1991	104	true	Disney	67890
Wayne's World	1992	95	true	Paramount	99999

Figure 4.2: The relation Movie

Example 4.2: Consider the relation Movie with the relation schema described in Section 3.9. An instance of this relation is shown in Fig. 4.2. We can project this relation onto the first three attributes with the expression

$$\pi_{title, year, length}(\text{Movie})$$

The resulting relation is

title	year	length
Star Wars	1977	124
Mighty Ducks	1991	104
Wayne's World	1992	95

As another example, we can project onto the attribute inColor with the expression $\pi_{inColor}(\text{Movie})$. The result is the single-column relation

inColor
true

Notice that there is only one tuple in the resulting relation, since all three tuples of Fig. 4.2 have the same value in their component for attribute inColor. □

4.1.3 Selection

The *selection* operator, applied to a relation R, produces a new relation with a subset of R's tuples. The tuples in the resulting relation are those that satisfy some condition C that involves the attributes of R. We denote this operation $\sigma_C(R)$. The schema for the resulting relation is the same as R's schema, and we conventionally show the attributes in the same order as we use for R.

C is a conditional expression of the type that we are familiar with from conventional programming languages; for example, conditional expressions follow the keyword `if` in programming languages such as C or Pascal. The only difference is that the operands in C are either constants or attributes of R. We apply C to each tuple t of R by substituting, for each attribute A appearing in condition C, the component of t for attribute A. If after substituting for each attribute of C the condition C is true, then t is one of the tuples that appear in the result of $\sigma_C(R)$; otherwise t is not in the result.

Example 4.3: Let the relation `Movie` be as in Fig. 4.2. Then the value of expression $\sigma_{length \geq 100}(\texttt{Movie})$ is

title	year	length	inColor	studioName	producerC#
Star Wars	1977	124	true	Fox	12345
Mighty Ducks	1991	104	true	Disney	67890

The first tuple satisfies the condition $length \geq 100$ because when we substitute for $length$ the value 124 found in the component of the first tuple for attribute `length`, the condition becomes $124 \geq 100$. The latter condition is true, so we accept the first tuple. The same argument explains why the second tuple of Fig. 4.2 is in the result.

The third tuple has a `length` component 95. Thus, when we substitute for $length$ we get the condition $95 \geq 100$, which is false. Hence the last tuple of Fig. 4.2 is not in the result. □

Example 4.4: Suppose we want the set of tuples in the relation

    Movie(title, year, length, inColor, studioName, producerC#)

that represent Fox movies at least 100 minutes long. We can get these with a more complicated condition, involving the AND of two subconditions. The expression is

$$\sigma_{length \geq 100 \text{ AND } studioName='\texttt{Fox}'}(\texttt{Movie})$$

The tuple

title	year	length	inColor	studioName	producerC#
Star Wars	1977	124	true	Fox	12345

is the only one in the resulting relation. □

A	B
1	2
3	4

Relation R

B	C	D
2	5	6
4	7	8
9	10	11

Relation S

A	$R.B$	$S.B$	C	D
1	2	2	5	6
1	2	4	7	8
1	2	9	10	11
3	4	2	5	6
3	4	4	7	8
3	4	9	10	11

Result $R \times S$

Figure 4.3: Two relations and their Cartesian product

4.1.4 Cartesian Product

The *Cartesian product* (or just *product*) of two sets R and S is the set of pairs that can be formed by choosing the first element of the pair to be any element of R and the second an element of S. This product is denoted $R \times S$. When R and S are relations, the product is essentially the same. However, since the members of R and S are tuples, usually consisting of more than one component, the result of pairing a tuple from R with a tuple from S is a longer tuple, with one component for each of the components of the constituent tuples. The components from R precede the components from S in this order.

The relation schema for the resulting relation is the union of the schemas for R and S. However, if R and S should happen to have some attributes in common, then we need to invent new names for at least one of each pair of identical attributes. To disambiguate an attribute A that is in the schemas of both R and S, we use $R.A$ for the attribute from R and $S.A$ for the attribute from S.

Example 4.5: For conciseness, let us use an abstract example that illustrates the product operation. Let relations R and S have the schemas and tuples shown in Fig. 4.3. Then the product $R \times S$ consists of the six tuples shown in that figure. Note how we have paired each of the two tuples of R with each of the three tuples of S. Since B is an attribute of both schemas, we have used $R.B$ and $S.B$ in the schema for $R \times S$. The other attributes are unambiguous, and their names appear in the resulting schema unchanged. □

4.1.5 Natural Joins

More often than we want to take the product of two relations, we find a need to *join* them by pairing only those tuples that match in some way. The simplest sort of match is the *natural join* of two relations R and S, denoted $R \bowtie S$, in which we pair only those tuples from R and S that agree in whatever attributes are common to the schemas of R and S. More precisely, let $A_1, A_2, \ldots, A_n$ be the attributes in both the schema of R and the schema of S. Then a tuple r from R and a tuple s from S are successfully paired if and only if r and s agree on each of the attributes $A_1, A_2, \ldots, A_n$.

If the tuples r and s are successfully paired in the join $R \bowtie S$, then the result of the pairing is a tuple, called the *joined tuple*, with one component for each of the attributes in the union of the schemas of R and S. The joined tuple agrees with tuple r in each attribute in the schema of R, and it agrees with s in each attribute in the schema of S. Since r and s are successfully paired, we know that r and s agree on attributes that are in the schemas of both R and S. Thus, it is possible for the joined tuple to agree with both r and s on those attributes that are in both schemas. The construction of the joined tuple is suggested by Fig. 4.4.

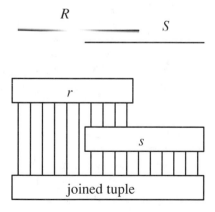

Figure 4.4: Joining tuples

Note also that this join operation is the same one that we used in Section 3.7.6 to recombine relations that had been projected onto two subsets of their attributes. There the motivation was to explain why BCNF decomposition made sense. In Section 4.1.7 we shall see another use for the natural join: combining two relations so that we can write a query that relates attributes of each.

Example 4.6: The natural join of the relations R and S from Fig. 4.3 is

A	B	C	D
1	2	5	6
3	4	7	8

The only attribute common to R and S is B. Thus, to pair successfully, tuples need only to agree in their B components. If so, the resulting tuple has components for attributes A (from R), B (from either R or S), C (from S), and D (from S).

In this example, the first tuple of R successfully pairs with only the first tuple of S; they share the value 2 on their common attribute B. This pairing yields the first tuple of the result: $(1, 2, 5, 6)$. The second tuple of R pairs successfully only with the second tuple of S, and the pairing yields $(3, 4, 7, 8)$. Note that the third tuple of S does not pair with any tuple of R and thus has no effect on the result of $R \bowtie S$. A tuple that fails to pair with any tuple of the other relation in join is sometimes said to be a *dangling tuple*. □

Example 4.7: The previous example does not illustrate all the possibilities inherent in the natural join operator. For example, no tuple paired successfully with more than one tuple, and there was only one attribute in common to the two relation schemas. In Fig. 4.5 we see two other relations, U and V, that share two attributes between their schemas, B and C. We also show an instance in which one tuple joins with several tuples.

For tuples to pair successfully, they must agree in both the B and C components. Thus, the first tuple of U pairs successfully with the first two tuples of V, while the second and third tuples of U pair successfully with the third tuple of V. The result of these four pairings is shown in Fig. 4.5. □

4.1.6   Theta-Joins

The natural join forces us to pair tuples using one specific condition. While this way, equating shared attributes, is the most common basis on which relations are joined, it is sometimes desirable to pair tuples from two relations on some other basis. For that purpose, we have a related notation called the *theta-join*; the "theta" refers to an arbitrary condition, which we shall represent by C rather than θ.

The notation for a theta-join of relations R and S based on condition C is $R \bowtie_C S$. The result of this operation is constructed as follows:

1. Take the product of R and S.

A	B	C
1	2	3
6	7	8
9	7	8

Relation U

B	C	D
2	3	4
2	3	5
7	8	10

Relation V

A	B	C	D
1	2	3	4
1	2	3	5
6	7	8	10
9	7	8	10

Result $U \bowtie V$

Figure 4.5: Natural join of relations

2. Select from the product only those tuples that satisfy the condition C.

As with the product operation, the schema for the result is the union of the schemas of R and S, with "$R.$" or "$S.$" prefixed to attributes if necessary to indicate from which schema the attribute came.

Example 4.8: Consider the operation $U \bowtie_{A<D} V$, where U and V are the relations from Fig. 4.5. We must consider all nine pairs of tuples, one from each relation, and see whether the A component from the U-tuple is less than the D component of the V-tuple. The first tuple of U, with an A component of 1, successfully pairs with each of the tuples from V. However, the second and third tuples from U, with A components of 6 and 9, respectively, pair successfully with only the last tuple of V. Thus, the result has only five tuples, constructed from the five successful pairings. This relation is shown in Fig. 4.6. □

Notice that the schema for the result in Fig. 4.6 consists of all six attributes, with U and V prefixed to their respective occurrences of attributes B and C to distinguish them. Thus, the theta-join contrasts with natural join, since in the

A	$U.B$	$U.C$	$V.B$	$V.C$	D
1	2	3	2	3	4
1	2	3	2	3	5
1	2	3	7	8	10
6	7	8	7	8	10
9	7	8	7	8	10

Figure 4.6: Result of $U \bowtie_{A<D} V$

latter common attributes are merged into one copy. Of course it makes sense to do so in the case of the natural join, since tuples don't pair unless they agree in their common attributes. In the case of a theta-join, there is no guarantee that compared attributes will agree in the result, since the comparison operator might not be $=$.

Example 4.9 : Here is a theta-join on the same relations U and V that has a more complex condition:

$$U \bowtie_{A<D \text{ AND } U.B \neq V.B} V$$

That is, we require for successful pairing not only that the A component of the U-tuple be less than the D component of the V-tuple, but that the two tuples disagree on their respective B components. The tuple

A	$U.B$	$U.C$	$V.B$	$V.C$	D
1	2	3	7	8	10

is the only one to satisfy both conditions, so this relation is the result of the theta-join above. □

4.1.7   Combining Operations to Form Queries

If all we could do was to write single operations on one or two relations as queries, then relational algebra would not be as useful as it is. However, relational algebra, like all algebras, allows us to form expressions of arbitrary complexity by applying operators either to given relations or to relations that are the result of applying one or more relational operators to relations.

One can construct expressions of relational algebra by applying operators to subexpressions, using parentheses when necessary to indicate grouping of operands. It is also possible to represent expressions as expression trees; the latter often are easier for us to read, although they are less convenient as a machine-readable notation.

Example 4.10: Let us reconsider the decomposed `Movie` relation of Example 3.32. Suppose we want to know "What are the titles and years of movies made by Fox that are at least 100 minutes long?" One way to compute the answer to this query is:

1. Select those `Movie` tuples that have $length \geq 100$.

2. Select those `Movie` tuples that have $studioName = $ 'Fox'.

3. Compute the intersection of (1) and (2).

4. Project the relation from (3) onto attributes `title` and `year`.

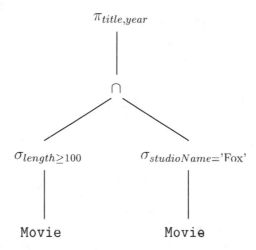

Figure 4.7: Expression tree for a relational algebra expression

In Fig. 4.7 we see the above steps represented as an expression tree. The two selection nodes correspond to steps (1) and (2). The intersection node corresponds to step (3), and the projection node is step (4).

Alternatively, we could represent the same expression in a conventional, linear notation, with parentheses. The formula

$$\pi_{title,year}\left(\sigma_{length \geq 100}(\text{Movie}) \cap \sigma_{studioName=\text{'Fox'}}(\text{Movie})\right)$$

represents the same expression.

Incidentally, there is often more than one relational algebra expression that represents the same computation. For instance, the above query could also be written by replacing the intersection by logical `AND` within a single selection operation. That is,

---

Equivalent Expressions and Query Optimization

All database systems have a query-answering system, and many of them are based on a language that is similar in expressive power to relational algebra. Thus, the query asked by a user may have many *equivalent expressions* (expressions that produce the same answer, whenever they are given the same relations as operands), and some of these may be much more quickly evaluated. An important job of the query "optimizer" discussed briefly in Section 1.2.3 is to replace one expression of relational algebra by an equivalent expression that is more efficiently evaluated.

$$\pi_{title,year}\Big(\sigma_{length \geq 100 \text{ AND } studioName='\text{Fox}'}(\text{Movie})\Big)$$

is an equivalent form of the query.   □

Example 4.11 : One use of the natural join operation is to recombine relations that were decomposed to put them into BCNF. Recall the decomposed relations from Example 3.32:[1]

> Movie1 with schema {title, year, length, filmType, studioName}
> Movie2 with schema {title, year, starName}

Let us write an expression to answer the query "Find the stars of movies that are at least 100 minutes long." This query relates the starName attribute of Movie1 with the length attribute of Movie2. We can connect these attributes by joining the two relations. The natural join successfully pairs only those tuples that agree on title and year; that is, pairs of tuples that refer to the same movie. Thus, Movie1 ⋈ Movie2 is an expression of relational algebra that produces the relation we called Movie in Example 3.32. That relation is the non-BNCF relation whose schema is all six attributes and that contains several tuples for the same movie when that movie has several stars.

To the join of Movie1 and Movie2 we must apply a selection that enforces the condition that the length of the movie is at least 100 minutes. We then project onto the desired set of attributes: title and year. The expression

$$\pi_{title,year}\Big(\sigma_{length \geq 100}(\text{Movie1} \bowtie \text{Movie2})\Big)$$

expresses the desired query in relational algebra.   □

---

[1] Remember that the relation Movie of that example has a somewhat different relation schema from the relation Movie that we introduced in Section 3.9 and used in Examples 4.2, 4.3, and 4.4.

4.1.8 Renaming

In order to control the names of the attributes used for relations that are constructed by one or more applications of the relational algebra operations, it is often convenient to use an operator that explicitly renames operations. We shall use the operator $\rho_{S(A_1,A_2,...,A_n)}(R)$ to rename a relation R. The resulting relation has exactly the same tuples as R, but the name of the relation is S. Moreover, the attributes of the result relation S are named $A_1, A_2, \ldots, A_n$, in order from the left. If we only want to change the name of the relation to S and leave the attributes as they are in R, we can just say $\rho_S(R)$.

Example 4.12 : In Example 4.5 we took the product of two relations R and S from Fig. 4.3 and used the convention that when an attribute appears in both operands, it is renamed by prefixing the relation name to it. These relations R and S are repeated in Fig. 4.8.

Suppose, however, that we do not wish to call the two versions of B by names $R.B$ and $S.B$; rather we want to continue to use the name B for the attribute that comes from R, and we want to use X as the name of the attribute B coming from S. We can rename the attributes of S so the first is called X. The result of the expression $\rho_{S(X,C,D)}(S)$ is a relation named S that looks just like the relation S from Fig. 4.3, but its first column has attribute X instead of S.

When we take the product of R with this new relation, there is no conflict of names among the attributes, so no further renaming is done. That is, the result of the expression $R \times \rho_{S(X,C,D)}(S)$ is the relation $R \times S$ from Fig. 4.3, except that the five columns are labeled A, B, X, C, and D, from the left. This relation is shown in Fig. 4.8.

As an alternative, we could take the product without renaming, as we did in Example 4.5, and then rename the result. The expression $\rho_{RS(A,B,X,C,D)}(R \times S)$ yields the same relation as in Fig. 4.8, with the same set of attributes, but the relation has a name, RS, which the result relation in Fig. 4.8 does not. □

4.1.9 Dependent and Independent Operations

Some of the operations that we have described in Section 4.1 can be expressed in terms of other relational-algebra operations. For example, intersection can be expressed in terms of set difference:

$$R \cap S = R - (R - S)$$

That is, if R and S are any two relations with the same schema, the intersection of R and S can be computed by first subtracting S from R to form a relation T consisting of all those tuples in R but not S. We then subtract T from R, leaving only those tuples of R that are also in S.

The two forms of join are also expressible in terms of other operations. Theta-join can be expressed by product and selection:

A	B
1	2
3	4

Relation R

B	C	D
2	5	6
4	7	8
9	10	11

Relation S

A	B	X	C	D
1	2	2	5	6
1	2	4	7	8
1	2	9	10	11
3	4	2	5	6
3	4	4	7	8
3	4	9	10	11

Result $R \times \rho_{S(X,C,D)}(S)$

Figure 4.8: Two relations and their product

$$R \bowtie_C S = \sigma_C(R \times S)$$

The natural join of R and S can be expressed by starting with the product $R \times S$. We then apply the selection operator with a condition C of the form

$$R.A_1 = S.A_1 \text{ AND } R.A_2 = S.A_2 \text{ AND} \cdots \text{AND } R.A_n = S.A_n$$

where $A_1, A_2, \ldots, A_n$ are all the attributes appearing in the schemas of both R and S. Finally, we must project out one copy of each of the equated attributes. Let L be the list of attributes in the schema of R followed by those attributes in the schema of S that are not also in the schema of R. Then

$$R \bowtie S = \pi_L\Big(\sigma_C(R \times S)\Big)$$

Example 4.13: The natural join of the relations U and V from Fig. 4.5 can be written in terms of product, selection, and projection as:

$$\pi_{A,U.B,U.C,D}\Big(\sigma_{U.B=V.B \text{ AND } U.C=V.C}(U \times V)\Big)$$

That is, we take the product $U \times V$. Then we select for equality between each pair of attributes with the same name — B and C in this example. Finally, we project onto all the attributes except one of the B's and one of the C's; we have chosen to eliminate the attributes of V whose names also appear in the schema of U.

For another example, the theta-join of Example 4.9 can be written

$$\sigma_{A<D \text{ AND } U.B \neq V.B}(U \times V)$$

That is, we take the product of the relations U and V and then apply the condition that appeared in the theta-join. □

The redundancies mentioned in this section are the only "redundancies" among the operations that we have introduced. The six remaining operations — union, difference, selection, projection, product, and renaming — form an independent set, none of which can be written in terms of the other five.

4.1.10 Exercises for Section 4.1

Exercise 4.1.1: In this exercise we introduce one of our running examples of a relational database schema and some sample data. The database schema consists of four relations, whose schemas are:

```
Product(maker, model, type)
PC(model, speed, ram, hd, cd, price)
Laptop(model, speed, ram, hd, screen, price)
Printer(model, color, type, price)
```

The Product relation gives the manufacturer, model number and type (PC, laptop, or printer) of various products. We assume for convenience that model numbers are unique over all manufacturers and product types; that assumption is not realistic, and a real database would include a code for the manufacturer as part of the model number. The PC relation gives for each model number that is a PC the speed (of the processor, in megahertz), the amount of RAM (in megabytes), the size of the hard disk (in gigabytes), the speed of the CD reader (e.g., 4x), and the price. The Laptop relation is similar, except that the screen size (in inches) is recorded in place of the CD speed. The Printer relation records for each printer model whether the printer produces color output (true, if so), the process type (laser, ink-jet, or dry), and the price.

Some sample data for the relation Product is shown in Fig. 4.9. Sample data for the other three relations is shown in Fig. 4.10. Manufacturers and model numbers have been "sanitized," but the data is typical of products on sale at the end of 1996.

Write expressions of relational algebra to answer the following queries. For the data of Figs. 4.9 and 4.10, show the result of your query. However, your answer should work for arbitrary data, not just the data of these figures. *Hint*:

maker	model	type
A	1001	pc
A	1002	pc
A	1003	pc
B	1004	pc
B	1006	pc
B	3002	printer
B	3004	printer
C	1005	pc
C	1007	pc
D	1008	pc
D	1009	pc
D	1010	pc
D	2001	laptop
D	2002	laptop
D	2003	laptop
D	3001	printer
D	3003	printer
E	2004	laptop
E	2008	laptop
F	2005	laptop
G	2006	laptop
G	2007	laptop
H	3005	printer
I	3006	printer

Figure 4.9: Sample data for Product

model	speed	ram	hd	cd	price
1001	133	16	1.6	6x	1595
1002	120	16	1.6	6x	1399
1003	166	24	2.5	6x	1899
1004	166	32	2.5	8x	1999
1005	166	16	2.0	8x	1999
1006	200	32	3.1	8x	2099
1007	200	32	3.2	8x	2349
1008	180	32	2.0	8x	3699
1009	200	32	2.5	8x	2599
1010	160	16	1.2	8x	1495

(a) Sample data for relation PC

model	speed	ram	hd	screen	price
2001	100	20	1.10	9.5	1999
2002	117	12	0.75	11.3	2499
2003	117	32	1.00	10.4	3599
2004	133	16	1.10	11.2	3499
2005	133	16	1.00	11.3	2599
2006	120	8	0.81	12.1	1999
2007	150	16	1.35	12.1	4799
2008	120	16	1.10	12.1	2099

(b) Sample data for relation Laptop

model	color	type	price
3001	true	ink-jet	275
3002	true	ink-jet	269
3003	false	laser	829
3004	false	laser	879
3005	false	ink-jet	180
3006	true	dry	470

(c) Sample data for relation Printer

Figure 4.10: Sample data for relations of Exercise 4.1.1

For the harder expressions, it may be helpful to define one or more intermediate relations in terms of the given relations (Product, etc.) and then use these relations in a final expression. You can then substitute for the intermediate relations in your final expression, to get an expression in terms of the given relations.

* a) What PC models have a speed of at least 150?

b) Which manufacturers make laptops with a hard disk of at least one gigabyte?

c) Find the model number and price of all products (of any type) made by manufacturer B.

d) Find the model numbers of all color laser printers.

e) Find those manufacturers that sell Laptops, but not PC's.

*! f) Find those hard-disk sizes that occur in two or more PC's.

! g) Find those pairs of PC models that have both the same speed and RAM. A pair should be listed only once; e.g., list (i, j) but not (j, i).

*!! h) Find those manufacturers of at least two different computers (PC's or laptops) with speeds of at least 133.

!! i) Find the manufacturer(s) of the computer (PC or laptop) with the highest available speed.

!! j) Find the manufacturers of PC's with at least three different speeds.

!! k) Find the manufacturers who sell exactly three different models of PC.

Exercise 4.1.2: Draw expression trees for each of your expressions of Exercise 4.1.1.

Exercise 4.1.3: This exercise introduces another running example, concerning World War II capital ships. It involves the following relations:

```
Classes(class, type, country, numGuns, bore, displacement)
Ships(name, class, launched)
Battles(name, date)
Outcomes(ship, battle, result)
```

Ships are built in "classes" from the same design, and the class is usually named for the first ship of that class. The relation Classes records the name of the class, the type (bb for battleship or bc for battlecruiser), the country that built the ship, the number of main guns, the bore (diameter of the gun barrel, in inches) of the main guns, and the displacement (weight, in tons). Relation Ships records the name of the ship, the name of its class, and the year in which the ship was launched. Relation `Battles` gives the name and date of battles involving these ships, and relation `Outcomes` gives the result (sunk, damaged, or ok) for each ship in each battle.

Figures 4.11 and 4.12 give some sample data for these four relations.[2] Note that, unlike the data for Exercise 4.1.1, there are some "dangling tuples" in this data, e.g., ships mentioned in `Outcomes` that are not mentioned in `Ships`.

Write expressions of relational algebra to answer the following queries. For the data of Figs. 4.11 and 4.12, show the result of your query. However, your answer should work for arbitrary data, not just the data of these figures.

a) Give the class names and countries of the classes that carried guns of at least 16-inch bore.

b) Find the ships launched prior to 1921.

c) Find the ships sunk in the battle of the North Atlantic.

d) The treaty of Washington in 1921 prohibited capital ships heavier than 35,000 tons. List the ships that violated the treaty of Washington.

e) List the name, displacement, and number of guns of the ships engaged in the battle of Guadalcanal.

f) List all the capital ships mentioned in the database. (Remember that all these ships may not appear in the `Ships` relation.)

! g) Find the classes that had only one ship as a member of that class.

! h) Find those countries that had both battleships and battlecruisers.

! i) Find those ships that "lived to fight another day"; they were damaged in one battle, but later fought in another.

Exercise 4.1.4: Draw expression trees for each of your expressions of Exercise 4.1.3.

* **Exercise 4.1.5:** What is the difference between the natural join $R \bowtie S$ and the theta-join $R \bowtie_C S$ where the condition C is that $R.A = S.A$ for each attribute A appearing in the schemas of both R and S?

! **Exercise 4.1.6:** An operator on relations is said to be *monotone* if whenever we add a tuple to one of its arguments, the result contains all the tuples that it contained before adding the tuple, plus perhaps more tuples. Which of the operators described in this section are monotone? For each, either explain why it is monotone or give an example showing it is not.

---

[2]Source: J. N. Westwood, *Fighting Ships of World War II*, Follett Publishing, Chicago, 1975 and R. C. Stern, *US Battleships in Action*, Squadron/Signal Publications, Carrollton, TX, 1980.

class	type	country	numGuns	bore	displacement
Bismarck	bb	Germany	8	15	42000
Iowa	bb	USA	9	16	46000
Kongo	bc	Japan	8	14	32000
North Carolina	bb	USA	9	16	37000
Renown	bc	Gt. Britain	6	15	32000
Revenge	bb	Gt. Britain	8	15	29000
Tennessee	bb	USA	12	14	32000
Yamato	bb	Japan	9	18	65000

(a) Sample data for relation Classes

name	date
North Atlantic	5/24-27/41
Guadalcanal	11/15/42
North Cape	12/26/43
Surigao Strait	10/25/44

(b) Sample data for relation Battles

ship	battle	result
Bismarck	North Atlantic	sunk
California	Surigao Strait	ok
Duke of York	North Cape	ok
Fuso	Surigao Strait	sunk
Hood	North Atlantic	sunk
King George V	North Atlantic	ok
Kirishima	Guadalcanal	sunk
Prince of Wales	North Atlantic	damaged
Rodney	North Atlantic	ok
Scharnhorst	North Cape	sunk
South Dakota	Guadalcanal	damaged
Tennessee	Surigao Strait	ok
Washington	Guadalcanal	ok
West Virginia	Surigao Strait	ok
Yamashiro	Surigao Strait	sunk

(c) Sample data for relation Outcomes

Figure 4.11: Data for Exercise 4.1.3

name	class	launched
California	Tennessee	1921
Haruna	Kongo	1915
Hiei	Kongo	1914
Iowa	Iowa	1943
Kirishima	Kongo	1915
Kongo	Kongo	1913
Missouri	Iowa	1944
Musashi	Yamato	1942
New Jersey	Iowa	1943
North Carolina	North Carolina	1941
Ramillies	Revenge	1917
Renown	Renown	1916
Repulse	Renown	1916
Resolution	Revenge	1916
Revenge	Revenge	1916
Royal Oak	Revenge	1916
Royal Sovereign	Revenge	1916
Tennessee	Tennessee	1920
Washington	North Carolina	1941
Wisconsin	Iowa	1944
Yamato	Yamato	1941

Figure 4.12: Sample data for relation Ships

! **Exercise 4.1.7 :** Suppose relations R and S have n tuples and m tuples, respectively. Give the minimum and maximum numbers of tuples that the results of the following expressions can have.

* a) $R \cup S$.

 b) $R \bowtie S$.

 c) $\sigma_C(R) \times S$, for some condition C.

 d) $\pi_L(R) - S$, for some list of attributes L.

! **Exercise 4.1.8 :** The *semijoin* of relations R and S, denoted $R \ltimes S$, is the set of tuples of R that agree with at least one tuple of S on all attributes that are common to the schemas of R and S. Give three different expressions of relational algebra that are equivalent to $R \ltimes S$.

!! **Exercise 4.1.9 :** Let R be a relation with schema

$$(A_1, A_2, \ldots, A_n, B_1, B_2, \ldots, B_m)$$

and let S be a relation with schema $(B_1, B_2, \ldots, B_m)$; that is, the attributes of S are a subset of the attributes of R. The *quotient* of R and S, denoted $R \div S$, is the set of tuples t over attributes $A_1, A_2, \ldots, A_n$ (i.e., the attributes of R that are not attributes of S) such that for every tuple s in S, the tuple ts, consisting of the components of t for $A_1, A_2, \ldots, A_n$ and the components of s for $B_1, B_2, \ldots, B_m$, is a member of R. Give an expression of relational algebra, using the operators we have defined previously in this section, that is equivalent to $R \div S$.

4.2   A Logic for Relations

There is another approach to expressing queries about relations that is based on logic rather than algebra. Interestingly, the two approaches (logical and algebraic) lead to the same class of queries that can be expressed. The logical query language introduced in this section is called *Datalog* ("database logic"); it consists of if-then rules. In one of these rules, we express the idea that from certain combinations of tuples in certain relations we may infer that some other tuple is in some other relation, or in the answer to a query.

4.2.1   Predicates and Atoms

Relations are represented in Datalog by symbols called *predicates*. Each predicate takes a fixed number of arguments, and a predicate followed by its arguments is called an *atom*. The syntax of atoms is just like that of function calls in conventional programming languages; for example $P(x_1, x_2, \ldots, x_n)$ is an atom consisting of the predicate P with arguments $x_1, x_2, \ldots, x_n$.

In essence, a predicate is the name of a function that returns a boolean value. If R is a relation with n attributes in some fixed order, then we shall also use R as the name of a predicate corresponding to this relation. The atom $R(a_1, a_2, \ldots, a_n)$ has value TRUE if $(a_1, a_2, \ldots, a_n)$ is a tuple of R; the atom has value FALSE otherwise.

Example 4.14: Let R be the relation

A	B
1	2
3	4

from Fig. 4.3. Then $R(1,2)$ is true and so is $R(3,4)$. However, for any other values x and y, $R(x,y)$ is false. □

A predicate can take variables as well as constants as arguments. If an atom has variables for more than one of its arguments, then it is a boolean-valued function that takes values for these variables and returns TRUE or FALSE.

Example 4.15: If R is the predicate from Example 4.14, then $R(x,y)$ is the function that tells, for any x and y, whether the tuple (x,y) is in relation R. For the particular instance of R mentioned in Example 4.14, $R(x,y)$ returns TRUE when either

1. $x = 1$ and $y = 2$, or

2. $x = 3$ and $y = 4$

and FALSE otherwise. As another example, the atom $R(1, z)$ returns TRUE if $z = 2$ and returns FALSE otherwise. □

4.2.2 Arithmetic Atoms

There is another kind of atom that is important in Datalog: an *arithmetic atom*. This kind of atom is a comparison between two arithmetic expressions, for example $x < y$ or $x + 1 \geq y + 4 \times z$. For contrast, we shall call the atoms introduced in Section 4.2.1 *relational atoms*; both are "atoms."

Note that arithmetic and relational atoms each take as arguments the values of any variables and return a boolean value. In effect, arithmetic comparisons like $<$ or $\geq$ are like the names of relations that contain all the true pairs. Thus, we can visualize the relation "$<$" as containing all the tuples, such as $(1,2)$ or $(-1.5, 65.4)$, that have a first component less than their second component. Remember, however, that database relations are always finite, and usually change from time to time. In contrast, arithmetic-comparison relations such as $<$ are both infinite and unchanging.

4.2.3   Datalog Rules and Queries

Operations similar to those of relational algebra are described in Datalog by *rules*, which consist of

1. A relational atom called the *head*, followed by

2. The symbol ←, which we often read "if," followed by

3. A *body* consisting of one or more atoms, called *subgoals*, which may be either relational or arithmetic. Subgoals are connected by AND, and any subgoal may optionally be preceded by the logical operator NOT.

Example 4.16 : The Datalog rule

$$\text{LongMovie(t,y)} \leftarrow \text{Movie(t,y,l,c,s,p)} \text{ AND } l \geq 100$$

can be used to compute the "long movies," those at least 100 minutes long. It refers to our standard relation Movie defined in Section 3.9, with schema

    Movie(title, year, length, inColor, studioName, producerC#)

The head of the rule is the atom $LongMovie(t, y)$. The body of the rule consists of two subgoals:

1. The first subgoal has predicate $Movie$ and six arguments, corresponding to the six attributes of the Movie relation. Each of these arguments has a different variable: t for the title component, y for the year component, l for the length component, and so on. We can see this subgoal as saying: "Let (t, y, l, c, s, p) be a tuple in the current instance of relation Movie." More precisely, $Movie(t, y, l, c, s, p)$ is true whenever the six variables have values that are the six components of some one Movie tuple.

2. The second subgoal, $l \geq 100$, is true whenever the length component of a Movie tuple is at least 100.

The rule as a whole can be thought of as saying: $LongMovie(t, y)$ is true whenever we can find a tuple in Movie with:

a) t and y as the first two components (for title and year),

b) A third component l (for length) that is at least 100, and

c) Any values in components 4 through 6.

Notice that this rule is thus equivalent to the "assignment statement" in relational algebra:

$$\text{LongMovie} = \pi_{title,year}\Big(\sigma_{length \geq 100}(\text{Movie})\Big)$$

Anonymous Variables

Frequently, Datalog rules have some variables that appear only once. The names used for these variables are thus irrelevant; it is only when a variable appears more than once that we care about its name so we can see it is the same variable in its second and subsequent appearances. Thus, we shall allow the common convention that an underscore, _, as an argument of an atom, stands for a variable that appears only there. Multiple occurrences of _ stand for different variables, never the same variable. For instance, the rule of Example 4.16 could be written

LongMovie(t,y) ← Movie(t,y,l,_,_,_) AND l ≥ 100

The three variables c, s, and p that appear only once have each been replaced by underscores. We cannot replace any of the other variables, since each appears twice in the rule.

---

whose right side is a relational-algebra expression. □

A *query* in Datalog is a collection of one or more rules. If there is only one relation that appears in the rule heads, then the value of this relation is taken to be the answer to the query. Thus, in Example 4.16, LongMovie is the answer to the query. If there is more than one relation among the rule heads, then one of these relations is the answer to the query, while the others assist in the definition of the answer. We must designate which of relation is the intended answer to the query, perhaps by giving it a name such as Answer.

4.2.4 Meaning of Datalog Rules

Example 4.16 gave us a hint of the meaning of a Datalog rule. More precisely, imagine the variables of the rule ranging over all possible values. Whenever these variables all have values that make all the subgoals true, then we see what the value of the head is for those variables, and we add the resulting tuple to the relation whose predicate is in the head.

For instance, we can imagine the six variables of Example 4.16 ranging over all possible values. The only combinations of values that can make all the subgoals true are when the values of (t, y, l, c, s, p) in that order form a tuple of Movie. Moreover, since the $l \geq 100$ subgoal must also be true, this tuple must be one where l, the value of the length component, is at least 100. When we find such a combination of values, we put the tuple (t, y) in the head's relation LongMovie.

There are, however, restrictions that we must place on the way variables are used in rules, so that the result of a rule is a finite relation and so that rules with arithmetic subgoals or with *negated* subgoals (those with NOT in front of them) make intuitive sense. This condition, which we call the *safety* condition, is:

- Every variable that appears anywhere in the rule must appear in some nonnegated, relational subgoal.

In particular, any variable that appears in the head, in a negated relational subgoal, or in any arithmetic subgoal, must also appear in a nonnegated, relational subgoal.

Example 4.17: Consider the rule

$$\texttt{LongMovie(t,y)} \leftarrow \texttt{Movie(t,y,l,\_,\_,\_)} \text{ AND } l \geq 100$$

from Example 4.16. The first subgoal is a nonnegated, relational subgoal, and it contains all the variables that appear anywhere in the rule. In particular, the two variables t and y that appear in the head also appear in the first subgoal of the body. Likewise, variable l appears in an arithmetic subgoal, but it also appears in the first subgoal.   □

Example 4.18: The following rule has three safety violations:

$$\texttt{P(x,y)} \leftarrow \texttt{Q(x,z)} \text{ AND NOT } \texttt{R(w,x,z)} \text{ AND } x<y$$

1. The variable y appears in the head but not in any nonnegated, relational subgoal. Notice the fact that y appears in the arithmetic subgoal $x < y$ does not help to limit the possible values of y to a finite set. As soon as we find values a, b, and c for w, x, and z respectively that satisfy the first two subgoals, the infinite number of tuples (a, d) where $d > a$ wind up in the head's relation P.

2. Variable w appears in a negated, relational subgoal but not in a nonnegated, relational subgoal.

3. Variable y appears in an arithmetic subgoal, but not in a nonnegated, relational subgoal.

Thus, it is not a safe rule and cannot be used in Datalog.   □

There is another way to define the meaning of safe rules. Instead of considering all of the possible assignments of values to variables, we consider the set of tuples in the relation corresponding to each nonnegated, relational subgoal. If some assignment of tuples for each nonnegated, relational subgoal is *consistent*, in the sense that it assigns the same value to each occurrence of a variable, then consider the resulting assignment of values to all the variables of the rule. Notice that because the rule is safe, every variable is assigned a value.

For each consistent assignment, we consider the negated, relational subgoals and the arithmetic subgoals, to see if the assignment of values to variables makes them all true. Remember that a negated subgoal is true if its atom is false. If all the subgoals are true, then we see what tuple the head becomes under this assignment of values to variables. This tuple is added to the relation whose predicate is the head.

Example 4.19: Consider the Datalog rule

$$P(x,y) \leftarrow Q(x,z) \text{ AND } R(z,y) \text{ AND NOT } Q(x,y)$$

Let relation Q contain the two tuples $(1,2)$ and $(1,3)$. Let relation R contain tuples $(2,3)$ and $(3,1)$. There are two nonnegated, relational subgoals, $Q(x,z)$ and $R(z,y)$, so we must consider all combinations of assignments of tuples from relations Q and R, respectively, to these subgoals. The table of Fig. 4.13 considers all four combinations.

	Tuple for $Q(x,z)$	Tuple for $R(z,y)$	Consistent Assignment?	NOT $Q(x,y)$ True?	Resulting Head
1)	$(1,2)$	$(2,3)$	Yes	No	—
2)	$(1,2)$	$(3,1)$	No; $z = 2,3$	Irrelevant	—
3)	$(1,3)$	$(2,3)$	No; $z = 3,2$	Irrelevant	—
4)	$(1,3)$	$(3,1)$	Yes	Yes	$P(1,1)$

Figure 4.13: All possible assignments of tuples to $Q(x,z)$ and $R(z,y)$

The second and third options in Fig. 4.13 are not consistent. Each assigns two different values to the variable z. Thus, we do not consider these tuple-assignments further.

The first option, where subgoal $Q(x,z)$ is assigned the tuple $(1,2)$ and subgoal $R(z,y)$ is assigned tuple $(2,3)$, yields a consistent assignment, with x, y, and z given the values 1, 3, and 2, respectively. We thus proceed to the test of of the other subgoals, those that are not nonnegated, relational subgoals. There is only one: NOT $Q(x,y)$. For this assignment of values to the variables, this subgoal becomes NOT $Q(1,3)$. Since $(1,3)$ is a tuple of Q, this subgoal is false, and no head tuple is produced for the tuple-assignment (1).

The final option is (4). Here, the assignment is consistent; x, y, and z are assigned the values 1, 1, and 3, respectively. The subgoal NOT $Q(x,y)$ takes on the value NOT $Q(1,1)$. Since $(1,1)$ is not a tuple of Q, this subgoal is true. We thus evaluate the head $P(x,y)$ for this assignment of values to variables and find it is $P(1,1)$. Thus the tuple $(1,1)$ is in the relation P. Since we have exhausted all tuple-assignments, this is the only tuple in P. □

4.2.5   Extensional and Intensional Predicates

It is useful to make the distinction between

- *Extensional* predicates, which are predicates whose relations are stored in a database, and

- *Intensional* predicates, whose relations are computed by applying one or more Datalog rules.

The difference is the same as that between the operands of a relational-algebra expression, which are "extensional" (i.e., defined by their *extension*, which is another name for the "current instance of a relation) and the relations computed by a relational-algebra expression, either as the final result or as an intermediate result corresponding to some subexpression; these relations are "intensional" (i.e., defined by the programmer's "intent").

When talking of Datalog rules, we shall refer to the relation corresponding to a predicate as "intensional" or "extensional," if the predicate is intensional or extensional, respectively. We shall also use the abbreviation *IDB* for "intensional database" to refer to either an intensional predicate or its corresponding relation. Similarly, we use abbreviation *EDB* for "extensional database" for extensional predicates or their relation.

Thus, in Example 4.16, `Movie` is an EDB relation, defined by its extension. The predicate *Movie* is likewise an EDB predicate. Relation and predicate `LongMovie` are both intensional.

An EDB predicate can never appear in the head of a rule, although it can appear in the body of a rule. IDB predicates can appear in either the head or the body of rules, or both. It is also common to construct a single relation by using several rules with the same predicate in the head. We shall see an illustration of this idea in Example 4.21, regarding the union of two relations.

By using a series of intensional predicates, we can build progressively more complicated functions of the EDB relations. The process is similar to the building of relational-algebra expressions using several operators. We shall see examples of using several intensional predicates in the following section as well.

4.2.6   Exercises for Section 4.2

Exercise 4.2.1: Write each of the queries of Exercise 4.1.1 in Datalog. You should use only safe rules, but you may wish to use several IDB predicates corresponding to subexpressions of complicated relational-algebra expressions.

Exercise 4.2.2: Write each of the queries of Exercise 4.1.3 in Datalog. Again, use only safe rules, but you may use several IDB predicates if you like.

!! **Exercise 4.2.3:** The requirement we gave for safety of Datalog rules is sufficient to guarantee that the head predicate has a finite relation if the predicates of the relational subgoals have finite relations. However, this requirement is too strong. Give an example of a Datalog rule that violates the condition, yet whatever finite relations we assign to the relational predicates, the head relation will be finite.

4.3 From Relational Algebra to Datalog

Each of the relational-algebra operators can be mimicked by one or several Datalog rules. In this section we shall consider each operator in turn. We shall then consider how to combine Datalog rules to mimic complex algebraic expressions.

4.3.1 Intersection

The intersection of two relations is expressed by a rule that has subgoals for both relations, with the same variables in corresponding arguments.

Example 4.20 : Let us use the relations R and S from Fig. 4.1 as an example. Recall these relations each had a schema with four attributes: name, address, gender, and birthdate. Thus, their intersection is computed by the Datalog rule

$$\texttt{I(n,a,g,b)} \leftarrow \texttt{R(n,a,g,b) AND S(n,a,g,b)}$$

Here, I is an IDB predicate, whose relation becomes $R \cap S$ when we apply this rule. That is, in order for a tuple (n, a, g, b) to make both subgoals true, that tuple must be in both R and S. $\Box$

4.3.2 Union

The union of two relations is constructed by two rules. Each has an atom corresponding to one of the relations as its sole subgoal, and the heads of both rules have the same IDB predicate in the head. The arguments in the heads are exactly the same as in the subgoal of their rule.

Example 4.21 : To take the union of the relations R and S from Example 4.20 we use two rules

$$\begin{aligned} &1. \ \texttt{U(n,a,g,b)} \leftarrow \texttt{R(n,a,g,b)} \\ &2. \ \texttt{U(n,a,g,b)} \leftarrow \texttt{S(n,a,g,b)} \end{aligned}$$

Rule (1) says that every tuple in R is a tuple in the IDB relation U. Rule (2) similarly says that every tuple in S is in U. Thus, the two rules together imply that every tuple in $R \cup S$ is in U. If we write no more rules with U in the head, then there is no way any other tuples can get into the relation U, in which case

---

Variables Are Local to a Rule

Notice that the names we choose for variables in a rule are arbitrary and have no connection to the variables used in any other rule. The reason there is no connection is that each rule is evaluated alone and contributes tuples to its head's relation independent of other rules. Thus, for instance, we could replace the second rule of Example 4.21 by

$$U(w,x,y,z) \leftarrow S(w,x,y,z)$$

while leaving the first rule unchanged, and the two rules would still compute the union of R and S. Note, however, that when substituting one variable a for another variable b within a rule, we must substitute a for all occurrences of b within the rule. Moreover, the substituting variable a that we choose must not be a variable that already appears in the rule.

---

we can conclude that U is exactly $R \cup S$.[3] Recall that, since relations are sets, a tuple appears only once in relation U, even if it appears in both R and S.   □

4.3.3   Difference

The difference of relations R and S is computed by a single rule with a negated subgoal. That is, the nonnegated subgoal has predicate R and the negated subgoal has predicate S. These subgoals and the head all have the same variables for corresponding arguments.

Example 4.22 : If R and S are the relations from Example 4.20 then the rule

$$D(n,a,g,b) \leftarrow R(n,a,g,b) \text{ AND NOT } S(n,a,g,b)$$

defines D to be the relation $R - S$.   □

4.3.4   Projection

To compute a projection of a relation R, we use one rule with a single subgoal with predicate R. The arguments of this subgoal are distinct variables, one for each attribute of the relation. The head has an atom with arguments that are the variables corresponding to the attributes in the projection list, in the desired order.

Example 4.23 : Suppose we want to project the relation

---

[3]In fact, we should assume in each of the examples of this section that there are no other rules for an IDB predicate besides those that we show explicitly. If there are other rules, then we cannot rule out the existence of other tuples in the relation for that predicate.

```
Movie(title, year, length, inColor, studioName, producerC#)
```

onto its first three attributes — `title`, `year`, and `length`, as in Example 4.2. The rule

$$P(t,y,l) \leftarrow Movie(t,y,l,c,s,p)$$

serves, defining a relation called P to be the result of the projection. □

4.3.5 Selection

Selections can be somewhat more difficult to express in Datalog. The simple case is when the selection condition is the AND of one or more arithmetic comparisons. In that case, we create a rule with

1. One relational subgoal for the relation upon which we are performing the selection. This atom has distinct variables for each component, one for each attribute of the relation.

2. For each comparison in the selection condition, an arithmetic subgoal that is identical to this comparison. However, while in the selection condition an attribute name was used, in the arithmetic subgoal we use the corresponding variable, following the correspondence established by the relational subgoal.

Example 4.24 : The selection

$$\sigma_{length \geq 100 \text{ AND } studioName=\text{'Fox'}}(Movie)$$

from Example 4.4 can be written as a Datalog rule

$$S(t,y,l,c,s,p) \leftarrow Movie(t,y,l,c,s,p) \text{ AND } l \geq 100 \text{ AND } s = \text{'Fox'}$$

The result is the relation S. Note that l and s are the variables corresponding to attributes `length` and `studioName` in the standard order we have used for the attributes of `Movie`. □

Now, let us consider selections that involve the OR of conditions. We cannot necessarily replace such selections by single Datalog rules. However, selection for the OR of two conditions is equivalent to selecting for each condition separately and then taking the union of the results. Thus, the OR of n conditions can be expressed by n rules, each of which defines the same head predicate. The ith rule performs the selection for the ith of the n conditions.

Example 4.25 : Let us modify the selection of Example 4.24 by replacing the AND by an OR to get the selection:

$$\sigma_{length \geq 100 \text{ OR } studioName=\text{'Fox'}}(Movie)$$

That is, find all those movies that are either long or by Fox. We can write two
rules, one for each of the two conditions:

1. `S(t,y,l,c,s,p) ← Movie(t,y,l,c,s,p) AND l ≥ 100`
2. `S(t,y,l,c,s,p) ← Movie(t,y,l,c,s,p) AND s = 'Fox'`

Rule (1) produces movies at least 100 minutes long, and rule (2) produces
movies by Fox. □

Even more complex selection conditions can be formed by several applications, in any order, of the logical operators AND, OR, and NOT. However, there is
a widely known technique, which we shall not present here, for rearranging any
such logical expression into "conjunctive normal form," where the expression is
the OR of "conjuncts." A *conjunct*, in turn, is the AND of "literals," and a *literal*
is either a comparison or a negated comparison.[4]

We can represent any literal by a subgoal, perhaps with a NOT in front of it.
If the subgoal is arithmetic, the NOT can be incorporated into the comparison
operator. For example, NOT x ≥ 100 can be written as x < 100. Then, any
conjunct can be represented by a single Datalog rule, with one subgoal for each
comparison. Finally, every conjunctive-normal-form expression can be written
by several Datalog rules, one rule for each conjunct. These rules take the union,
or OR, of the results from each of the conjuncts.

Example 4.26 : We gave a simple example of this algorithm in Example 4.25.
A more difficult example can be formed by negating the condition of that example. We then have the expression:

$$\sigma_{\texttt{NOT } (length \geq 100 \texttt{ OR } studioName = \texttt{'Fox'})}(\texttt{Movie})$$

That is, find all those movies that are neither long nor by Fox.

Here, a NOT is applied to an expression that is itself not a simple comparison.
Thus, we must push the NOT down the expression, using one form of *DeMorgan's
law*, which says that the negation of an OR is the AND of the negations. That is,
the selection can be rewritten:

$$\sigma_{(\texttt{NOT } (length \geq 100)) \texttt{ AND } (\texttt{NOT } (studioName = \texttt{'Fox'}))}(\texttt{Movie})$$

Now, we can take the NOT's inside the comparisons to get the expression:

$$\sigma_{length < 100 \texttt{ AND } studioName \neq \texttt{'Fox'}}(\texttt{Movie})$$

This expression can be converted into the Datalog rule

`S(t,y,l,c,s,p) ← Movie(t,y,l,c,s,p) AND l < 100 AND s ≠ 'Fox'`

□

---

[4]See, e.g., A. V. Aho and J. D. Ullman, *Foundations of Computer Science*, Computer
Science Press, New York, 1992.

Example 4.27 : Let us consider a similar example where we have the negation of an AND in the selection. Now, we use the second form of DeMorgan's law, which says that the negation of an AND is the OR of the negations. We begin with the algebraic expression

$$\sigma_{\text{NOT } (length \geq 100 \text{ AND } studioName=\text{'Fox'})}(\text{Movie})$$

That is, find all those movies that are not both long and by Fox.

We apply DeMorgan's law to push the NOT below the AND, to get:

$$\sigma_{(\text{NOT } (length \geq 100)) \text{ OR } (\text{NOT } (studioName=\text{'Fox'}))}(\text{Movie})$$

Again we take the NOT's inside the comparisons to get:

$$\sigma_{length < 100 \text{ OR } studioName \neq \text{'Fox'}}(\text{Movie})$$

Finally, we write two rules, one for each part of the OR. The resulting Datalog rules are:

1. S(t,y,l,c,s,p) ← Movie(t,y,l,c,s,p) AND l < 100
2. S(t,y,l,c,s,p) ← Movie(t,y,l,c,s,p) AND s ≠ 'Fox'

□

4.3.6 Product

The product of two relations $R \times S$ can be expressed by a single Datalog rule. This rule has two subgoals, one for R and one for S. Each of these subgoals has distinct variables, one for each attribute of R or S. The IDB predicate in the head has as arguments all the variables that appear in either subgoal, with the variables appearing in the R-subgoal listed before those of the S-subgoal.

Example 4.28 : Let us consider the two four-attribute relations R and S from Example 4.20. The rule

$$P(a,b,c,d,w,x,y,z) \leftarrow R(a,b,c,d) \text{ AND } S(w,x,y,z)$$

defines P to be $R \times S$. We have arbitrarily used variables at the beginning of the alphabet for the arguments of R and variables at the end of the alphabet for S. These variables all appear in the rule head.   □

4.3.7 Joins

We can take the natural join of two relations by a Datalog rule that looks much like the rule for a product. The difference is that if we want $R \bowtie S$, then we must be careful to use the same variable for attributes of R and S that have the same name and to use different variables otherwise. For instance, we can use the attribute names themselves as the variables. The head is an IDB predicate that has each variable appearing once.

Example 4.29 : Consider relations with schemas $R(A, B)$ and $S(B, C, D)$. Their natural join may be defined by the rule

```
J(a,b,c,d) ← R(a,b) AND S(b,c,d)
```

Notice how the variables used in the subgoals correspond in an obvious way to the attributes of the relations R and S.   □

We can also convert theta-joins to Datalog in a straightforward way. Recall from Section 4.1.9 how a theta-join can be expressed as a product followed by a selection. If the selection condition is a conjunct, that is, the AND of comparisons, then we may simply start with the Datalog rule for the product and add additional, arithmetic subgoals, one for each of the comparisons.

Example 4.30 : Let us consider the relations $U(A, B, C)$ and $V(B, C, D)$ from Example 4.9, where we applied the theta-join

$$U \bowtie_{A<D \text{ AND } U.B \neq V.B} V$$

We can construct the Datalog rule

```
J(a,ub,uc,vb,vc,d) ← U(a,ub,uc) AND V(vb,vc,d) AND
                     a < d AND ub ≠ vb
```

to perform the same operation. We have used ub as the variable corresponding to attribute B of U, and similarly used vb, uc, and vc, although any six distinct variables for the six attributes of the two relations would be fine. The first two subgoals introduce the two relations, and the second two subgoals enforce the two comparisons that appear in the condition of the theta-join.   □

If the condition of the theta-join is not a conjunction, then we convert it to conjunctive normal form, as discussed in Section 4.3.5. We then create one rule for each conjunct. In this rule, we begin with the subgoals for the product and then add subgoals for each literal in the conjunct. The heads of all the rules are identical and have one argument for each attribute of the two relations being theta-joined.

Example 4.31 : In this example, we shall make a simple modification to the algebraic expression of Example 4.30. The AND will be replaced by an OR. There are no negations in this expression, so it is already in conjunctive normal form. There are two conjuncts, each with a single literal. The expression is:

$$U \bowtie_{A<D \text{ OR } U.B \neq V.B} V$$

Using the same variable-naming scheme as in Example 4.30, we obtain the two rules

1. `J(a,ub,uc,vb,vc,d ← U(a,ub,uc) AND V(vb,vc,d) AND a < d`
2. `J(a,ub,uc,vb,vc,d ← U(a,ub,uc) AND V(vb,vc,d) AND ub ≠ vb`

Each rule has subgoals for the two relations involved plus a subgoal for one of the two conditions $A < D$ or $U.B \neq V.B$.   □

4.3.8 Simulating Multiple Operations with Datalog

Datalog rules are not only capable of mimicking a single operation of relational algebra. We can in fact mimic any algebraic expression. The trick is to look at the expression tree for the relational-algebra expression and create one IDB predicate for each interior node of the tree. The rule or rules for each IDB predicate is whatever we need to apply the operator at the corresponding node of the tree. Those operands of the tree that are extensional (i.e., they are relations of the database) are represented by the corresponding predicate. Operands that are themselves interior nodes, are represented by the corresponding IDB predicate.

Example 4.32: Consider the algebraic expression

$$\pi_{title,year}\Big(\sigma_{length \geq 100}(\texttt{Movie}) \cap \sigma_{studioName='\texttt{Fox}'}(\texttt{Movie})\Big)$$

from Example 4.10, whose expression tree appeared in Fig. 4.7. We repeat this tree as Fig. 4.14. There are four interior nodes, so we need to create four IDB predicates. Each of these predicates has a single Datalog rule, and we summarize all the rules in Fig. 4.15.

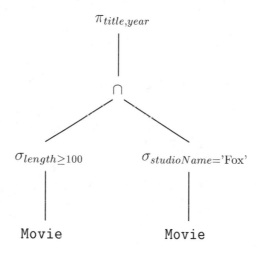

Figure 4.14: Expression tree

The lowest two interior nodes perform simple selections on the EDB relation `Movie`, so we can create the IDB predicates W and X to represent these selections. Rules (1) and (2) of Fig. 4.15 describe these selections. For example, rule (1) defines W to be those tuples of `Movie` that have a length at least 100.

Then rule (3) defines predicate Y to be the intersection of W and X, using the form of rule we learned for an intersection in Section 4.3.1. Finally, rule (4)

```
1. W(t,y,l,c,s,p) ← Movie(t,y,l,c,s,p) AND l ≥ 100
2. X(t,y,l,c,s,p) ← Movie(t,y,l,c,s,p) AND s = 'Fox'
3. Y(t,y,l,c,s,p) ← W(t,y,l,c,s,p) AND X(t,y,l,c,s,p)
4. Z(t,y) ← Y(t,y,l,c,s,p)
```

Figure 4.15: Datalog rules to perform several algebraic operations

defines predicate Z to be the projection of Y onto the title and year attributes. We here use the technique for simulating a projection that we learned in Section 4.3.4. The predicate Z is the "answer" predicate; that is, regardless of the value of relation Movie, the relation defined by Z is the same as the result of the algebraic expression with which we began this example.

Note that in this example, we can substitute for the Y subgoal in rule (4) of Fig. 4.15, replacing it with the body of rule (3). Then, we can substitute for the W and X subgoals, using the bodies of rules (1) and (2). Since the Movie subgoal appears in both of these bodies, we can eliminate one copy. As a result, Z can be defined by the single rule:

```
Z(t,y) ← Movie(t,y,l,c,s,p) AND l ≥ 100 AND s = 'Fox'
```

However, it is not common that a complex expression of relational algebra is equivalent to a single Datalog rule.   □

4.3.9   Exercises for Section 4.3

Exercise 4.3.1 : Let $R(a, b, c)$, $S(a, b, c)$, and $T(a, b, c)$ be three relations. Write one or more Datalog rules that define the result of each of the following expressions of relational algebra:

  a) $R \cup S$.

  b) $R \cap S$.

  c) $R - S$.

* d) $(R \cup S) - T$.

! e) $(R - S) \cap (R - T)$.

  f) $\pi_{a,b}(R)$.

*! g) $\pi_{a,b}(R) \cap \rho_{U(a,b)}\big(\pi_{b,c}(S)\big)$.

Exercise 4.3.2 : Let $R(x, y, z)$ be a relation. Write one or more Datalog rules that define $\sigma_C(R)$, where C is the following conditions:

  a) $x = y$.

* b) $x < y$ AND $y < z$.

  c) $x < y$ OR $y < z$.

  d) NOT $(x < y$ OR $x > y)$.

*! e) NOT $\big((x < y$ OR $x > y)$ AND $y < z\big)$.

 ! f) NOT $\big((x < y$ OR $x < z)$ AND $y < z\big)$.

Exercise 4.3.3: Let $R(a, b, c)$, $S(b, c, d)$, and $T(d, e)$ be three relations. Write single Datalog rules for each of the natural joins:

  a) $R \bowtie S$.

  b) $S \bowtie T$.

 ! c) $(R \bowtie S) \bowtie T$. (*Note*: since the natural join is associative and commutative, the order of the join of these three relations is irrelevant.)

Exercise 4.3.4: Let $R(x, y, z)$ and $S(x, y, z)$ be two relations. Write one or more Datalog rules to define each of the theta-joins $R \bowtie_C S$, where C is one of the conditions of Exercise 4.3.2. For each of these conditions, interpret each arithmetic comparison as comparing an attribute of R on the left with an attribute of S on the right. For instance, $x < y$ stands for $R.x < S.y$.

! **Exercise 4.3.5:** It is also possible to convert Datalog rules into equivalent relational-algebra expressions. While we have not discussed the method of doing so in general, it is possible to work out many simple examples. For each of the Datalog rules below, write an expression of relational algebra that defines the same relation as the head of the rule.

* a) P(x,y) ← Q(x,z) AND R(z,y)

  b) P(x,y) ← Q(x,z) AND Q(z,y)

  c) P(x,y) ← Q(x,z) AND R(z,y) AND x < y

4.4 Recursive Programming in Datalog

While relational algebra can express many useful operations on relations, there are some computations that cannot be written as an expression of relational algebra. A common kind of operation on data that we cannot express in relational algebra involves an infinite sequence of similar but growing expressions of that algebra, which is called a *recursion*.

Example 4.33: An example of a recursive operation taken from the movie industry is the matter of sequels. Often, a successful movie is followed by a sequel; if the sequel does well then the sequel has a sequel, and so on. Thus, a movie may be ancestral to a long sequence of other movies. Suppose we have a relation SequelOf(movie, sequel) containing pairs consisting of a movie and its immediate sequel. Examples of tuples in this relation are:

movie	sequel
Naked Gun	Naked Gun $2_{1/2}$
Naked Gun $2_{1/2}$	Naked Gun $33_{1/3}$

We might also have a more general notion of a *follow-on* to a movie, which is a sequel, a sequel of a sequel, and so on. In the relation above, *Naked Gun $33_{1/3}$* is a follow-on to *Naked Gun*, but not a sequel in the strict sense we are using the term "sequel" here. It saves space if we store only the immediate sequels in the relation and construct the follow-ons if we need them. In the above example, we store only one fewer pair, but for the five *Rocky* movies we store six fewer pairs, and for the 18 *Friday the 13th* movies we store 136 fewer pairs.

However, it is not immediately obvious how we construct the relation of follow-ons from the relation SequelOf. We can construct the sequels of sequels by joining SequelOf with itself once. An example of such an expression, using renaming so that the join becomes a natural join, is:

$$\pi_{first,third}\big(\rho_{R(first,second)}(\texttt{SequelOf}) \bowtie \rho_{S(second,third)}(\texttt{SequelOf})\big)$$

In this expression, SequelOf is renamed twice, once so its attributes are called **first** and **second**, and again so its attributes are called **second** and **third**. Thus, the natural join asks for tuples (m_1, m_2) and (m_3, m_4) in SequelOf such that $m_2 = m_3$. We then produce the pair (m_1, m_4). Note that m_4 is the sequel of the sequel of m_1.

Similarly, we could join three copies of SequelOf to get the sequels of sequels of sequels (e.g., *Rocky* and *Rocky IV*). We could in fact produce the ith sequels for any fixed value of i by joining SequelOf with itself $i - 1$ times. We could then take the union of SequelOf and any finite number of these joins to get all the sequels up to some fixed limit.

What we cannot do in relational algebra is ask for the "infinite union" of the infinite sequence of expressions that give the ith sequels for each i. Note that relational algebra's union allows us only to take the union of two relations, not an infinite number. By applying the union operator any finite number of times in an algebraic expression, we can take the union of any finite number of relations, but we cannot ever take the union of an infinite number of relations in an algebraic expression. □

4.4.1 The Fixedpoint Operator

Fortunately, we do not have to add to relational algebra a messy convention for expressing infinite unions of "similar" expressions. There is a common way to express relations such as `FollowOn(x,y)` (i.e., movie y is a follow-on to movie x in the sense of Example 4.33) that are built by an infinite, yet regular, process from other relations, such as `SequelOf`. We write an equation in which `FollowOn` is described in terms of itself and `SequelOf` and then say that the value of `FollowOn` is the smallest relation (*least fixedpoint*) that satisfies the equation. We shall use the symbol ϕ to indicate that the least fixedpoint of an equation is to be taken.

Example 4.34: Here is the least fixedpoint operator applied to an equation that describes the relation `FollowOn(x,y)`:

$$\phi\Big(\texttt{FollowOn} = \rho_{SequelOf(x,y)}(\texttt{SequelOf}) \cup$$
$$\rho_{R(x,y)}\big(\pi_{movie,y}(\texttt{SequelOf} \bowtie_{sequel=x} \texttt{FollowOn})\big)\Big)$$

An intuitive statement of this equation is "Movie y is a follow-on to movie x if either it is a sequel of x or it is a follow-on to a sequel of x.

To understand the equation, we should first note that the attributes of `FollowOn` are x and y. Relation `FollowOn` is equated to the union of two terms. The first term, $\rho_{SequelOf(x,y)}(\texttt{SequelOf})$, is a copy of `SequelOf`, renamed so its attributes match those of `FollowOn`. The second term is a theta-join `SequelOf` $\bowtie_{sequel=x}$ `FollowOn`, which joins all pairs (a, b) from `SequelOf` with pairs (b, c) from `FollowOn`. The result is tuples (a, b, b, c) whose attributes are `movie`, `sequel`, `x`, and `y`, respectively. The second term of the union continues by projecting onto the first and fourth components, `movie` and `y`, and then renaming the attributes `x` and `y`.

In the fixedpoint equation, `FollowOn` is thus equated to the union of relation `SequelOf` and the result of this second term, which computes follow-ons of sequels. That is, `FollowOn` consists of all those pairs (x, y) that either are in `SequelOf`, or are such that y is a follow-on of a sequel of x. Put another way, y is a sequel of a sequel of $\cdots$ of a sequel of x, for some number of uses of the term "sequel of." $\square$

4.4.2 Computing the Least Fixedpoint

However, it may not be clear from the equation of Example 4.34 why the least solution for `FollowOn` is exactly what we think of as the set of follow-on pairs of movies. To understand the meaning of the fixedpoint operator, we have to understand how the least fixedpoint can be computed. In Section 4.4.4 we shall discuss problems that come up when the difference operator appears in the equation, but for equations without difference, the following method works.

1. Begin by assuming that the relation R on the left side of the equation is empty.

2. Repeatedly compute a new value of the relation R by evaluating the right side using the old value of R.

3. Stop when after one iteration the old and new values are the same.

Example 4.35 : Let us show the computation of `FollowOn` when the relation `SequelOf` consists of the following three tuples:

movie	sequel
Rocky	Rocky II
Rocky II	Rocky III
Rocky III	Rocky IV

At the first round of computation, `FollowOn` is assumed empty. Thus, the join of `SequelOf` and `FollowOn` in the fixedpoint equation is empty, and the only tuples come from the first term of the union, `SequelOf`. Thus, after the first round, the value of `FollowOn` is identical to the `SequelOf` relation above. The situation after round 1 is shown in Fig. 4.16.

x	y
Rocky	Rocky II
Rocky II	Rocky III
Rocky III	Rocky IV

Figure 4.16: Relation `FollowOn` after round 1

In the second round, we use the relation from Fig. 4.16 as `FollowOn` and again compute the right side of the fixedpoint equation. The first term of the union, `SequelOf`, gives us the three tuples that we already have. For the second term, we must join the relation `SequelOf`, which has the three tuples shown in Fig. 4.16, with the current relation `FollowOn`, which is the same relation. To do so, we look for pairs of tuples such that the second component of the one from `SequelOf` equals the first component of the one from `FollowOn`.

Thus, we can take the tuple (Rocky, Rocky II) from `SequelOf` and pair it with the tuple (Rocky II, Rocky III) from `FollowOn` to get the new tuple (Rocky, Rocky III) for `FollowOn`. Similarly, we can take the tuple

(Rocky II, Rocky III)

from `SequelOf` and tuple (Rocky III, Rocky IV) from `FollowOn` to get new tuple (Rocky II, Rocky IV) for `FollowOn`. However, no other pairs of tuples — one from `SequelOf` and the other from the old value of `FollowOn` — join.

Thus, after the second round, FollowOn has the five tuples shown in Fig. 4.17. Intuitively, just as Fig. 4.16 contained only those follow-on facts that are based on a single sequel, Fig. 4.17 contains those follow-on facts based on one or two sequels.

x	y
Rocky	Rocky II
Rocky II	Rocky III
Rocky III	Rocky IV
Rocky	Rocky III
Rocky II	Rocky IV

Figure 4.17: Relation FollowOn after round 2

In the third round, we use the relation from Fig. 4.17 for FollowOn and again evaluate the right side of the fixedpoint equation. We get all the tuples we already had, of course, and one more tuple. When we join the tuple (Rocky, Rocky II) from SequelOf with the tuple (Rocky II, Rocky IV) from the current value of FollowOn, we get the new tuple (Rocky, Rocky IV). Thus, after round 3, the value of FollowOn is as shown in Fig. 4.18.

x	y
Rocky	Rocky II
Rocky II	Rocky III
Rocky III	Rocky IV
Rocky	Rocky III
Rocky II	Rocky IV
Rocky	Rocky IV

Figure 4.18: Relation FollowOn after round 3

When we proceed to round 4, we get no new tuples, so we stop. The true relation FollowOn defined by this fixedpoint computation is the one shown in Fig. 4.18. □

4.4.3 Fixedpoint Equations in Datalog

The relational algebra expressions needed for useful fixedpoint equations tend to be quite complicated. It is often easier to express them by a collection of Datalog rules, and this notation will be used from here on in this section. As we shall see in Section 5.10, the implementation of these ideas in SQL3 uses a fixedpoint notation that is more algebraic than logical, because that style is more in keeping with the dictions of SQL.

The general idea behind logical fixedpoint equations is to start with one or more relations whose values are assumed known; these are the extensional database relations or EDB relations. Other relations are defined by appearing in the heads of rules. These relations are the intensional database relations, or IDB relations. The bodies of these rules may contain subgoals whose predicates are either EDB or IDB relations, as well as arithmetic atoms. If one or more IDB relations are defined by rules that use the same relations in the bodies, then the rules effectively define these IDB relations by a fixedpoint equation, just as in the relational-algebra equation of Example 4.34.

Example 4.36: We can define the IDB relation `FollowOn` by the following two Datalog rules:

1. `FollowOn(x,y) ← SequelOf(x,y)`
2. `FollowOn(x,y) ← SequelOf(x,z) AND FollowOn(z,y)`

The first rule is the basis; it tells us that every sequel is a follow-on. This rule corresponds to the first term of the union in the equation of Example 4.34.

The second rule says that every follow-on of a sequel of movie x is also a follow-on of x. More precisely: if z is a sequel of x, and we have found that y is a follow-on of z, then y is a follow-on of x. $\square$

The rules of Example 4.36 say exactly the same thing as the fixedpoint equation of Example 4.35. Thus, the computation of the value of `FollowOn` for these rules is identical to the computation in Example 4.35. In general, we can compute the values of the IDB relations defined by any collection of Datalog rules without negated subgoals by starting with all IDB relations empty, and iteratively computing new values for the IDB relations by applying the rules to the EDB relations and the previous values of the IDB relations, until the IDB relations no longer change.

Example 4.37: More complex examples of the use of recursion can be found in a study of paths in a graph. Figure 4.19 shows a graph representing some flights of two hypothetical airlines — *Untried Airlines* (UA), and *Arcane Airlines* (AA) — among the cities San Francisco, Denver, Dallas, Chicago, and New York.

We may imagine that the flights are represented by an EDB relation:

Flights(airline, from, to, departs, arrives)

The tuples in this relation for the data of Fig. 4.19 are shown in Fig. 4.20.

The simplest recursive question we can ask is "For what pairs of cities (x,y) is it possible to get from city x to city y by taking one or more flights?" The following two rules describe a relation `Reaches(x,y)` that contains exactly these pairs of cities.

1. `Reaches(x,y) ← Flights(a,x,y,d,r)`
2. `Reaches(x,y) ← Reaches(x,z) AND Reaches(z,y)`

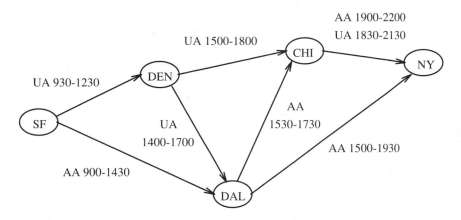

Figure 4.19: A map of some airline flights

airline	from	to	departs	arrives
UA	SF	DEN	930	1230
AA	SF	DAL	900	1430
UA	DEN	CHI	1500	1800
UA	DEN	DAL	1400	1700
AA	DAL	CHI	1530	1730
AA	DAL	NY	1500	1930
AA	CHI	NY	1900	2200
UA	CHI	NY	1830	2130

Figure 4.20: Tuples in the relation `Flights`

The first rule says that `Reaches` contains those pairs of cities for which there is a direct flight from the first to the second; the airline a, departure time d, and arrival time r are arbitrary in this rule. The second rule says that if you can reach from city x to city z and you can reach from z to y, then you can reach from x to y. Notice that we have used the nonlinear form of recursion here, as was described in the box on "Other Forms of Recursion." This form is slightly more convenient here, because another use of `Flights` in the recursive rule would involve three more variables for the unused components of `Flights`.

To evaluate the relation `Reaches`, we follow the same iterative process introduced in Section 4.4.2. We begin by using Rule (1) to get the following pairs in `Reaches`: (SF, DEN), (SF, DAL), (DEN, CHI), (DEN, CHI), (DAL, CHI), (DAL, NY), and (CHI, NY). These are the seven pairs represented by arcs in Fig. 4.19.

In the next round, we apply the recursive Rule (2) to put together pairs of arcs such that the head of one is the tail of the next. That gives us the additional pairs (SF, CHI), (DEN, NY), and (SF, NY). The next round combines

---

Other Forms of Recursion

In Examples 4.34 and 4.36 we used a *right-recursive* form for the recursion, where the use of the recursive relation FollowOn appears after the EDB relation SequelOf. We could also write similar *left-recursive* rules by putting the recursive relation first. These rules are:

1. FollowOn(x,y) ← SequelOf(x,y)
2. FollowOn(x,y) ← FollowOn(x,z) AND SequelOf(z,y)

Informally, y is a follow-on of x if it is either a sequel of x or a sequel of a follow-on of x.

We could even use the recursive relation twice, as in the *nonlinear* recursion:

1. FollowOn(x,y) ← SequelOf(x,y)
2. FollowOn(x,y) ← FollowOn(x,z) AND FollowOn(z,y)

Informally, y is a follow-on of x if it is either a sequel of x or a follow-on of a follow-on of x. All three of these forms give the same value for relation FollowOn: the set of pairs (x, y) such that y is a sequel of a sequel of $\cdots$ (some number of times) of x.

---

these two-arc pairs and all the single-arc pairs together to form paths of length up to four arcs. In this particular diagram, we get no new pairs. The relation Reaches thus consists of the ten pairs (x, y) such that y is reachable from x in the diagram of Fig. 4.19. Because of the way we drew the diagram, these pairs happen to be exactly those (x, y) such that y is to the right of x in Fig 4.19. □

Example 4.38: A more complicated definition of when two flights can be combined into a longer sequence of flights is to require that the second leaves an airport at least an hour after the first arrives at that airport. Now, we use an IDB predicate, which we shall call Connects(x,y,d,r), that says we can take one or more flights, starting at city x at time d and arriving at city y at time r. If there are any connections, then there is at least an hour to make the connection.

The rules for Connects are:[5]

1. Connects(x,y,d,r) ← Flights(a,x,y,d,r)
2. Connects(x,y,d,r) ← Connects(x,z,d,t1) AND
                        Connects(z,y,t2,r) AND t1 <= t2 + 100

---

[5]These rules only work on the assumption that there are no flights operating at midnight.

In the first round, rule (1) gives us the eight `Connects` facts shown in Fig. 4.21. Each corresponds to one of the flights indicated in the diagram of Fig. 4.19; note that one of the seven arcs of that figure represents two flights at different times.

x	y	d	r
SF	DEN	930	1230
SF	DAL	900	1430
DEN	CHI	1500	1800
DEN	DAL	1400	1700
DAL	CHI	1530	1730
DAL	NY	1500	1930
CHI	NY	1900	2200
CHI	NY	1830	2130

Figure 4.21: Basis tuples for relation `Connects`

We now try to combine these tuples using Rule (2). For example, the second and fifth of these tuples combine to give the tuple (SF, CHI, 900, 1730). However, the second and sixth tuples do not combine because the arrival time in Dallas is 1430, and the departure time from Dallas, 1500, is only half an hour later. Figure 4.22 shows the `Connects` tuples after the second round. Above the line are the original tuples from round 1, and the six tuples added on round 2 are shown below the line. The line is not part of the relation.

x	y	d	r
SF	DEN	930	1230
SF	DAL	900	1430
DEN	CHI	1500	1800
DEN	DAL	1400	1700
DAL	CHI	1530	1730
DAL	NY	1500	1930
CHI	NY	1900	2200
CHI	NY	1830	2130
SF	CHI	900	1730
SF	CHI	930	1800
SF	DAL	930	1700
DEN	NY	1500	2200
DAL	NY	1530	2130
DAL	NY	1530	2200

Figure 4.22: Relation `Connects` after second round

In the third round, we must in principle consider all pairs of tuples in Fig. 4.22 as candidates for the two `Connects` tuples in the body of rule (2). However, if both tuples are above the line, then they would have been considered during round 2 and therefore will not yield a `Connects` tuple we have not seen before. The only way to get a new tuple is if at least one of the two `Connects` tuple used in the body of rule (2) were added at the previous round; i.e., they are below the line in Fig. 4.22.

The third round only gives us three new tuples. These are shown at the bottom of Fig. 4.23. The two lines in this figure separate the eight tuples of round 1, the six additional tuples of round 2, and the three new tuples from round 3. There are no new tuples in the fourth round, so our computation is complete. Thus, the entire relation `Connects` is Fig. 4.23. □

x	y	d	r
SF	DEN	930	1230
SF	DAL	900	1430
DEN	CHI	1500	1800
DEN	DAL	1400	1700
DAL	CHI	1530	1730
DAL	NY	1500	1930
CHI	NY	1900	2200
CHI	NY	1830	2130
SF	CHI	900	1730
SF	CHI	930	1800
SF	DAL	930	1700
DEN	NY	1500	2200
DAL	NY	1530	2130
DAL	NY	1530	2200
SF	NY	900	2130
SF	NY	900	2200
SF	NY	930	2200

Figure 4.23: Relation `Connects` after third round

4.4.4 Negation in Recursive Rules

Sometimes it is necessary to use negation in rules that also involve recursion. There is a safe way and an unsafe way to mix recursion and negation. Generally, it is considered appropriate to use negation only in situations where the negation does not appear inside the fixedpoint operation. To see the difference, we shall consider two examples of recursion and negation, one appropriate and the other paradoxical. We shall see that only "stratified" negation is useful when there is recursion; the term "stratified" will be defined precisely after the examples.

Example 4.39: Suppose we want to find those pairs of cities (x, y) in the map of Fig. 4.19 such that UA flies from x to y (perhaps through several other cities), but AA does not. We can recursively define a predicate UAreaches as we defined Reaches in Example 4.37, but restricting ourselves only to UA flights, as follows:

  1. UAreaches(x,y) ← Flights(UA,x,y,d,r)
  2. UAreaches(x,y) ← UAreaches(x,z) AND UAreaches(z,y)

Similarly, we can recursively define the predicate AAreaches to be those pairs of cities (x, y) such that one can travel from x to y using only AA flights, by:

  1. AAreaches(x,y) ← Flights(AA,x,y,d,r)
  2. AAreaches(x,y) ← AAreaches(x,z) AND AAreaches(z,y)

Now, it is a simple matter to compute the UAonly predicate consisting of those pairs of cities (x, y) such that one can get from x to y on UA flights but not on AA flights, with the nonrecursive rule:

  UAonly(x,y) ← UAreaches(x,y) AND NOT AAreaches(x,y)

This rule computes the set difference of UAreaches and AAreaches.

For the data of Fig. 4.19, UAreaches is seen to consist of the following pairs: (SF, DEN), (SF, DAL), (SF, CHI), (SF, NY), (DEN, DAL), (DEN, CHI), (DEN, NY), and (CHI, NY). This set is computed by the iterative fixedpoint process outlined in Section 4.4.2. Similarly, we can compute the value of AAreaches for this data; it is: (SF, DAL), (SF, CHI), (SF, NY), (DAL, CHI), (DAL, NY), and (CHI, NY). When we take the difference of these sets of pairs we get: (SF, DEN), (DEN, DAL), (DEN, CHI), and (DEN, NY). This set of four pairs is the value of predicate UAonly. □

Example 4.40: Now, let us consider an abstract example where things don't work as well. Suppose we have a single EDB predicate R. This predicate is unary (one-argument), and it has a single tuple, (0). There are two IDB predicates, P and Q, also unary. They are defined by the two rules

  1. P(x) ← R(x) AND NOT Q(x)
  2. Q(x) ← R(x) AND NOT P(x)

Informally, the two rules tell us that an element x in R is either in P or in Q but not both. Notice that P and Q are defined recursively in terms of each other.

When we defined what recursive rules meant in Section 4.4.1, we said we want the least fixedpoint, that is, the smallest relations that made the rules true as algebraic equations. Rule 1 says that as relations, $P = R - Q$, and rule 2 says that $Q = R - P$. Since R contains only the tuple (0), we know that only (0) can be in either P or Q. But where is (0)? It cannot be in neither, since then the equations are not satisfied; for instance $P = R - Q$ would imply that $\emptyset = \{(0)\} - \emptyset$, which is false.

If we let $P = \{(0)\}$ while $Q = \emptyset$, then we do get a solution to both equations. $P = R - Q$ becomes $\{(0)\} = \{(0)\} - \emptyset$, which is true, and $Q = R - P$ becomes $\emptyset = \{(0)\} - \{(0)\}$, which is also true.

However, we can also let $P = \emptyset$ and $Q = \{(0)\}$. This choice too satisfies both rules. We thus have two solutions:

$$a) \quad P = \{(0)\} \quad Q = \emptyset$$
$$b) \quad P = \emptyset \quad\quad Q = \{(0)\}$$

Both are minimal, in the sense that if we throw any tuple out of any relation, the resulting relations no longer satisfy the rules. We cannot, therefore, decide between the two minimal fixedpoints (a) and (b). Thus, we cannot answer a simple question such as "Is $P(0)$ true?" □

In Example 4.40, we saw that our idea of defining the meaning of recursive rules or of fixedpoint equations by finding the minimal fixedpoint no longer works when recursion and negation are tangled up too intimately. There can be more than one minimal fixedpoint, and these fixedpoints can contradict each other. It would be good if some other approach to defining the meaning of recursive negation would work better, but unfortunately, there is no general agreement about what such rules or equations should mean.

Thus, it is conventional to restrict ourselves to recursions in which negation is *stratified*. For instance, the SQL3 standard for recursion discussed in Section 5.10 makes this restriction. As we shall see, when negation is stratified there is an algorithm to compute one particular minimal fixedpoint (perhaps out of many such fixedpoints) that matches our intuition about what the rules mean. We define the property of being stratified as follows.

1. Draw a graph whose nodes correspond to the IDB predicates.

2. Draw an arc from node A to node B if a rule with predicate A in the head has a negated subgoal with predicate B. Label this arc with a $-$ sign to indicate it is a *negative* arc.

3. Draw an arc from node A to node B if a rule with head predicate A has a non-negated subgoal with predicate B. This arc does not have a minus-sign as label.

If this graph has a cycle containing one or more negative arcs, then the recursion is not stratified. Otherwise, the graph is stratified. We can group the IDB predicates into *strata*. The stratum of a predicate A is the largest number of negative arcs on a path beginning from A.

If the recursion it stratified, then we may evaluate the IDB predicates in the order of their strata, lowest first. This strategy produces one of the minimal fixedpoints of the rules. More importantly, computing the IDB predicates in the order implied by their strata appears always to make sense and give us the "right" fixedpoint. In contrast, as we have seen in Example 4.40, unstratified recursions may leave us with no "right" fixedpoint at all, even if there are many to choose from.

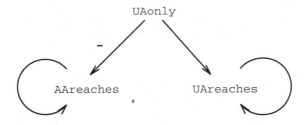

Figure 4.24: Graph constructed from a stratified recursion

Example 4.41: The graph for the predicates of Example 4.39 is shown in Fig. 4.24. `AAreaches` and `UAreaches` are in stratum 0, because none of the paths beginning at their nodes involves a negative arc. `UAonly` has stratum 1, because there are paths with one negative arc leading from that node, but no paths with more than one negative arc. Thus, we must completely evaluate `AAreaches` and `UAreaches` before we start evaluating `UAonly`.

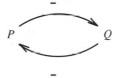

Figure 4.25: Graph constructed from an unstratified recursion

Compare the situation when we construct the graph for the IDB predicates of Example 4.40. This graph is shown in Fig. 4.25. Since rule 1 has head P with negated subgoal Q, there is a negative arc from P to Q. Since rule 2 has head Q with negated subgoal P, there is also a negative arc in the opposite direction. There is thus a negative cycle, and the rules are not stratified. □

4.4.5 Exercises for Section 4.4

Exercise 4.4.1: If we add or delete arcs to the diagram of Fig. 4.19, we may change the value of the relation `Reaches` of Example 4.37, the relation `Connects` of Example 4.38, or the relations `UAreaches` and `AAreaches` of Example 4.39. Give the new values of these relations if we:

* a) Add an arc from `CHI` to `SF` labeled AA, 1900-2100.

b) Add an arc from `NY` to `DEN` labeled UA, 900-1100.

c) Add both arcs from (a) and (b).

d) Delete the arc from `DEN` to `DAL`.

Exercise 4.4.2: Write Datalog rules (using stratified negation, if negation is necessary) to describe the following modifications to the notion of "follow-on" from Example 4.33. You may use EDB relation `SequelOf` and the IDB relation `FollowOn` defined in Example 4.36.

* a) `P(x,y)` meaning that movie y is a follow-on to movie x, but not a sequel of x (as defined by the EDB relation `SequelOf`).

b) `Q(x,y)` meaning that y is a follow-on of x, but neither a sequel nor a sequel of a sequel.

! c) `R(x)` meaning that movie x has at least two follow-ons. Note that both could be sequels, rather than one being a sequel and the other a sequel of a sequel.

! d) `S(x,y)`, meaning that y is a follow-on of x but y has at most one follow-on.

Exercise 4.4.3: ODL classes and their relationships can be described by a relation `Rel(class, rclass, mult)`. Here, `mult` gives the multiplicity of a relationship, either `multi` for a multivalued relationship, or `single` for a single-valued relationship. The first two attributes are the related classes; the relationship goes from `class` to `rclass` (related class). For example, the relation `Rel` representing the three ODL classes of our running movie example from Fig. 2.6 is shown in Fig. 4.26.

class	rclass	mult
Star	Movie	multi
Movie	Star	multi
Movie	Studio	single
Studio	Movie	multi

Figure 4.26: Representing ODL relationships by relational data

We can also see this data as a graph, in which the nodes are classes and the arcs go from a class to a related class, with label `multi` or `single`, as appropriate. Figure 4.27 illustrates this graph for the data of Fig. 4.26.

For each of the following, write Datalog rules, using stratified negation if negation is necessary, to express the described predicate(s). You may use `Rel` as an EDB relation. Show the result evaluating your rules, round-by-round, on the data from Fig. 4.26.

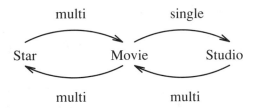

Figure 4.27: Representing relationships by a graph

a) Predicate P(class, eclass), meaning that there is a path[6] in the graph of classes that goes from class to eclass. The latter class can be thought of as "embedded" in class, since it is in a sense part of a part of an $\cdots$ object of the first class.

*! b) Predicates S(class, eclass) and M(class, eclass). The first means that there is a "single-valued embedding" of eclass in class, that is, a path from class to eclass along which every arc is labeled single. The second, M, means that there is a "multivalued embedding" of eclass in class, i.e., a path from class to eclass with at least one arc labeled multi.

c) Predicate Q(class, eclass) that says there is a path from class to eclass but no single-valued path. You may use IDB predicates defined previously in this exercise.

4.5 Constraints on Relations

The relational model provides a means to express common constraints, such as the referential integrity constraints introduced in Section 2.5. In fact, we shall see that relational algebra offers us convenient ways to express a wide variety of other constraints. Even functional dependencies can be expressed in relational algebra, as we shall see in Example 4.44. Constraints are quite important in database programming, and we shall cover in Chapter 6 how SQL database systems can enforce the same sorts of constraints as we can express in relational algebra.

4.5.1 Relational Algebra as a Constraint Language

There are two ways in which we can use expressions of relational algebra to express constraints.

1. If R is an expression of relational algebra, then $R = \emptyset$ is a constraint that says "The value of R must be empty," or equivalently "There are no tuples in the result of R."

---

[6]We shall not consider empty paths to be "paths" in this exercise.

2. If R and S are expressions of relational algebra, then $R \subseteq S$ is a constraint. It says "Every tuple in the result of R must also be in the result of S." Of course the result of S may contain additional tuples not produced by R.

These ways of expressing constraints are actually equivalent in what they can express, but sometimes one or the other is clearer or more succinct. That is, the constraint $R \subseteq S$ could just as well have been written $R - S = \emptyset$. To see why, notice that if every tuple in R is also in S, then surely $R - S$ is empty. Conversely, if $R - S$ contains no tuples, then every tuple in R must be in S (or else it would be in $R - S$).

On the other hand, a constraint of the first form, $R = \emptyset$, could just as well have been written $R \subseteq \emptyset$. Technically, $\emptyset$ is not an expression of relational algebra, but since there are expressions that evaluate to $\emptyset$, such as $R - R$, there is no harm in using $\emptyset$ as a relational-algebra expression.

In the following sections, we shall see how to express significant constraints in one of these two styles. As we shall see in Chapter 6, it is the first style — equal-to-the-emptyset — that is most commonly used in SQL programming. However, as shown above, we are free to think in terms of set-containment if we wish and later convert our constraint to the equal-to-the-emptyset style.

4.5.2 Referential Integrity Constraints

A common kind of constraint, called "referential integrity" in Section 2.5, asserts that a value appearing in one context also appears in another, related context. We saw referential integrity as a matter of relationships "making sense." That is, if an object or entity A is related to object or entity B, then B must really exist. For example, in ODL terms, if a relationship in object A is represented physically by a pointer, then the pointer must not be null and must point to a genuine object.

In the relational model, referential integrity constraints look somewhat different. If we have a value v in a tuple of one relation R, then because of our design intentions we may expect that v will appear in a particular component of some tuple of another relation S. An example will illustrate how referential integrity in the relational model can be expressed in relational algebra.

Example 4.42: Let us think of our running movie database schema, particularly the two relations

```
Movie(title, year, length, inColor, studioName, producerC#)
MovieExec(name, address, cert#, netWorth)
```

We might reasonably assume that the producer of every movie would have to appear in the MovieExec relation. If not, there is something wrong, and we would at least want a system implementing a relational database to inform us that we had a movie with a producer of which the system had no knowledge.

To be more precise, the `producerC#` component of each `Movie` tuple must also appear in the `cert#` component of some `MovieExec` tuple. Since executives are uniquely identified by their certificate numbers, we would thus be assured that the movie's producer is found among the movie executives. We can express this constraint by the set-containment

$$\pi_{\texttt{producerC\#}}(\texttt{Movie}) \subseteq \pi_{\texttt{cert\#}}(\texttt{MovieExec})$$

The value of the expression on the left is the set of all certificate numbers appearing in `producerC#` components of `Movie` tuples. Likewise, the expression on the right's value is the set of all certificates in the `cert#` component of `MovieExec` tuples. Our constraint says that every certificate in the former set must also be in the latter set.

Incidentally, we could express the same constraint as an equality to the emptyset:

$$\pi_{\texttt{producerC\#}}(\texttt{Movie}) - \pi_{\texttt{cert\#}}(\texttt{MovieExec}) = \emptyset$$

□

Example 4.43 : We can similarly express a referential integrity constraint where the "value" involved is represented by more than one attribute. For instance, we may want to assert that any movie mentioned in the relation

        StarsIn(movieTitle, movieYear, starName)

also appears in the relation

        Movie(title, year, length, inColor, studioName, producerC#)

Movies are represented in both relations by title-year pairs, because we agreed that one of these attributes alone was not sufficient to identify a movie. The constraint

$$\pi_{\texttt{movieTitle, movieYear}}(\texttt{StarsIn}) \subseteq \pi_{\texttt{title, year}}(\texttt{Movie})$$

expresses this referential integrity constraint by comparing the title-year pairs produced by projecting both relations onto the appropriate lists of components.
□

4.5.3 Additional Constraint Examples

The same constraint notation allows us to express far more than referential integrity. For example, we can express any functional dependency as an algebraic constraint, although the notation is more cumbersome than the functional-dependency notation we have been using.

Example 4.44 : Let us express the functional dependency

$$\text{name} \rightarrow \text{address}$$

for the relation

    MovieStar(name, address, gender, birthdate)

as an algebraic constraint. The idea is that if we construct all pairs of MovieStar tuples (t_1, t_2), we must not find a pair that agree in the name component and disagree in the address component. To construct the pairs, we use a Cartesian product, and to search for pairs that violate the functional dependency we use a selection. We then assert the constraint by equating the result to $\emptyset$.

To begin, since we are taking the product of a relation with itself, we need to rename at least one copy, in order to have names for the attributes of the product. For succinctness, let us use two new names, MS1 and MS2, to refer to the MovieStar relation. Then the functional dependency can be expressed by the algebraic constraint

$$\sigma_{\text{MS1.name=MS2.name AND MS1.address}\neq\text{MS2.address}}(\text{MS1} \times \text{MS2}) = \emptyset$$

In the above, MS1 in the product MS1 × MS2 is shorthand for the renaming:

$$\rho_{MS1(name,address,gender,birthdate)}(\text{MovieStar})$$

and MS2 is a similar renaming of MovieStar. □

Another kind of constraint that we sometimes need is a domain constraint. Often, a domain constraint simply requires that values for an attribute have a specific data type, such as integer or character string of length 30. These constraints cannot be addressed in relational algebra, because types like integer are not part of this algebra. However, often a domain constraint involves specific values that we require for an attribute. If the set of acceptable values can be expressed in the language of selection conditions, then this domain constraint can be expressed in the algebraic constraint language.

Example 4.45: Suppose we wish to specify that the only legal values for the gender attribute of MovieStar are 'F' and 'M'. We can express this constraint algebraically by:

$$\sigma_{\text{gender}\neq'\text{F}' \text{ AND gender}\neq'\text{M}'}(\text{MovieStar}) = \emptyset$$

That is, the set of tuples in MovieStar whose gender component is equal to neither 'F' nor 'M' is empty. □

Finally, there are some constraints that fall into none of the categories outlined in Section 2.5. The algebraic constraint language lets us express many new kinds of constraints. We offer one example here.

Example 4.46: Suppose we wish to require that one must have a net worth of at least $10,000,000 to be the president of a movie studio. This constraint cannot be classified as a domain, single-value, or referential integrity constraint. Yet we can express it algebraically as follows. First, we need to theta-join the two relations

> MovieExec(name, address, cert#, netWorth)
> Studio(name, address, presC#)

using the condition that `presC#` from `Studio` and `cert#` from `MovieExec` are equal. That join combines pairs of tuples consisting of a studio and an executive, such that the executive is the president of the studio. If we select from this relation those tuples where the net worth is less than ten million, we have a set that, according to our constraint, must be empty. Thus, we may express the constraint as:

$$\sigma_{\text{netWorth}<10000000}(\text{Studio} \bowtie_{\text{presC\#}=\text{cert\#}} \text{MovieExec}) = \emptyset$$

An alternative way to express the same constraint is to compare the set of certificates that represent studio presidents with the set of certificates that represent executives with a net worth of at least $10,000,000; the former must be a subset of the latter. The containment

$$\pi_{\text{presC\#}}(\text{Studio}) \subseteq \pi_{\text{cert\#}}\Big(\sigma_{\text{netWorth}\geq10000000}(\text{MovieExec})\Big)$$

expresses the above idea.   □

4.5.4   Exercises for Section 4.5

Exercise 4.5.1: Express the following constraints about the relations of Exercise 4.1.1, reproduced here:

> Product(maker, model, type)
> PC(model, speed, ram, hd, cd, price)
> Laptop(model, speed, ram, hd, screen, price)
> Printer(model, color, type, price)

You may write your constraints either as containments or by equating an expression to the empty set. For the data of Exercise 4.1.1, indicate any violations to your constraints.

* a) A PC with a processor speed less than 150 must not sell for more than $1500.

  b) A laptop with a screen size less than 11 inches must have at least a 1 gigabyte hard disk or sell for less than $2000.

! c) No manufacturer of PC's may also make laptops.

*!! d) A manufacturer of a PC must also make a laptop with at least as great a processor speed.

! e) If a laptop has a larger main memory than a PC, then the laptop must also have a higher price than the PC.

Exercise 4.5.2 : Express the following constraints in relational algebra. The constraints are based on the relations of Exercise 4.1.3:

```
Classes(class, type, country, numGuns, bore)
Ships(name, class, launched)
Battles(name, date)
Outcomes(ship, battle, result)
```

You may write your constraints either as containments or by equating an expression to the empty set. For the data of Exercise 4.1.3, indicate any violations to your constraints.

a) No class of ships may have guns with larger than 16-inch bore.

b) If a class of ships has more than 9 guns, then their bore must be no larger than 14 inches.

! c) No class may have more than 2 ships.

! d) No country may have both battleships and battlecruisers.

!! e) No ship with more than 9 guns may be in a battle with a ship having fewer than 9 guns that was sunk.

Exercise 4.5.3 : It is possible to express constraints in Datalog as well as relational algebra. We write a Datalog rule or rules defining one particular IDB predicate whose value is constrained to be empty. Write each of the following constraints in Datalog.

* a) The constraint of Example 4.42.

b) The constraint of Example 4.43.

c) The constraint of Example 4.44.

d) The constraint of Example 4.45.

e) The constraint of Example 4.46.

! **Exercise 4.5.4 :** Suppose R and S are two relations. Let C be the referential integrity constraint that says: whenever R has a tuple with some values $v_1, v_2, \ldots, v_n$ in particular attributes $A_1, A_2, \ldots, A_n$, there must be a tuple of S that has the same values $v_1, v_2, \ldots, v_n$ in particular attributes $B_1, B_2, \ldots, B_n$. Show how to express constraint C in relational algebra.

‼ **Exercise 4.5.5 :** Let R be a relation, and suppose functional dependency $A_1 A_2 \cdots A_n \rightarrow B$ is a functional dependency involving the attributes of R. Write in relational algebra the constraint that says this functional dependency must hold in R.

4.6 Relational Operations on Bags

While a set of tuples (i.e., a relation) is a simple, natural model of data as it might appear in a database, commercial database systems are rarely if ever based purely on sets. In some situations, relations as they appear in database systems are permitted to have duplicate tuples. Recall that if a "set" is allowed to have multiple occurrences of a member, then that set is called a *bag* or *multiset*. In this section, we shall consider relations that are bags rather than sets; that is, we shall allow the same tuple to appear more than once in a relation. When we refer to a "set," we mean a relation without duplicate tuples; a "bag" means a relation that may (or may not) have duplicate tuples.

Example 4.47 : The relation in Fig. 4.28 is a bag of tuples. In it, the tuple $(1, 2)$ appears three times and the tuple $(3, 4)$ appears once. If Fig. 4.28 were a set-valued relation, we would have to eliminate two occurrences of the tuple $(1, 2)$. In a bag-valued relation, we *do* allow multiple occurrences of the same tuple, but like sets, the order of tuples does not matter. □

A	B
1	2
3	4
1	2
1	2

Figure 4.28: A bag

4.6.1 Why Bags?

When we think about implementing relations efficiently, we can see several ways that allowing relations to be bags rather than sets can speed up operations on relations. For example, when we do a projection, allowing the resulting relation to be a bag lets us work with each tuple independently. If we want a set as the result, we need to compare the result of projecting out the undesired components from each tuple with the result of all the other projected tuples, to make sure that we have not seen this projection before. However, if we can accept a bag as the result, then we simply project each tuple and add it to the result; no comparison with other projected tuples is necessary.

A	B	C
1	2	5
3	4	6
1	2	7
1	2	8

Figure 4.29: Bag for Example 4.48

Example 4.48: The bag of Fig. 4.28 could be the result of projecting the relation shown in Fig. 4.29 onto attributes A and B, provided we allow the result to be a bag and do not eliminate the duplicate occurrences of $(1, 2)$. Had we used the ordinary projection operator of relational algebra, and therefore eliminated duplicates, the result would be only

A	B
1	2
3	4

Note that the bag result, although larger, can be computed more quickly, since there is no need to compare each tuple $(1, 2)$ or $(3, 4)$ with previously generated tuples.

Moreover, if we are projecting a relation in order to take an aggregate (as discussed in Section 5.5), such as "Find the average value of A in Fig. 4.29," we could not use the set model to think of the projected relation. As a set, the average value of A is 2, because there are only two values of A — 1 and 3 — in Fig. 4.29, and their average is 2. However, if we treat the A column in Fig. 4.29 as a bag $\{1, 3, 1, 1\}$, we get the correct average of A, which is 1.5, among the four tuples of Fig. 4.29. □

Another way that allowing bags as results saves time is if we take the union of two relations. If we compute the union $R \cup S$ and insist on a set as the result, then each tuple in S must be checked for membership in R. If found to be in R, then this tuple of S is not added to the union; otherwise it is added to the union. However, if we accept a bag as the result, then we just copy all the tuples of R and S into the answer, regardless of whether or not they appear in both relations.

4.6.2 Union, Intersection, and Difference of Bags

When we take the union of two bags, we add the number of occurrences of each tuple. That is, if R is a bag in which the tuple t appears n times, and S is a bag in which the tuple t appears m times, then in the bag $R \cup S$ tuple t appears $n + m$ times. Note that either n or m (or both) can be 0.

When we intersect two bags R and S, in which tuple t appears n and m times, respectively, in $R \cap S$ tuple t appears $\min(n, m)$ times. When we compute $R - S$, the difference of bags R and S, tuple t appears in $R - S$ $\max(0, n - m)$ times. That is, if t appears in R more times than it appears in S, then in $R - S$ tuple t appears the number of times it appears in R, minus the number of times it appears in S. However, if t appears at least as many times in S as it appears in R, then t does not appear at all in $R - S$. Intuitively, occurrences of t in S each "cancel" one occurrence in R.

Example 4.49: Let R be the relation of Fig. 4.28, that is, a bag in which tuple $(1, 2)$ appears three times and $(3, 4)$ appears once. Let S be the bag

A	B
1	2
3	4
3	4
5	6

Then the bag union $R \cup S$ is the bag in which $(1, 2)$ appears four times (three times for its occurrences in R and once for its occurrence in S); $(3, 4)$ appears three times, and $(5, 6)$ appears once.

The bag intersection $R \cap S$ is the bag

A	B
1	2
3	4

with one occurrence each of $(1, 2)$ and $(3, 4)$. That is, $(1, 2)$ appears three times in R and once in S, and $\min(3, 1) = 1$, so $(1, 2)$ appears once in $R \cap S$. Similarly, $(3, 4)$ appears $\min(1, 2) = 1$ time in $R \cap S$. Tuple $(5, 6)$, which appears once in S but zero times in R appears $\min(0, 1) = 0$ times in $R \cap S$.

The bag difference $R - S$ is the bag

A	B
1	2
1	2

To see why, notice that $(1, 2)$ appears three times in R and once in S, so in $R - S$ it appears $\max(0, 3 - 1) = 2$ times. Tuple $(3, 4)$ appears once in R and twice in S, so in $R - S$ it appears $\max(0, 1 - 2) = 0$ times. No other tuple appears in R, so there can be no other tuples in $R - S$.

As another example, the bag difference $S - R$ is the bag

A	B
3	4
5	6

Bag Operations on Sets

Imagine we have two sets R and S. Every set may be thought of as a bag; the bag just happens to have at most one occurrence of any tuple. Suppose we intersect $R \cap S$, but we think of R and S as bags and use the bag intersection rule. Then we get the same result as we would get if we thought of R and S as sets. That is, thinking of R and S as bags, a tuple t is in $R \cap S$ the minimum of the number of times it is in R and S. Since R and S are sets, t can be in each only 0 or 1 times. Whether we use the bag or set intersection rules, we find that t can appear at most once in $R \cap S$, and it appears once exactly when it is in both R and S. Similarly, if we use the bag difference rule to compute $R - S$ or $S - R$ we get exactly the same result as if we used the set rule.

However, union behaves differently, depending on whether we think of R and S as sets or bags. If we use the bag rule to compute $R \cup S$, then the result may not be a set, even if R and S are sets. In particular, if tuple t appears in both R and S, then t appears twice in $R \cup S$ if we use the bag rule for union, but if we use the set rule then t appears only once in $R \cup S$. Thus, when taking unions, we must be especially careful to specify whether we are using the bag or set definition of union.

Tuple $(3, 4)$ appears once because that is the difference in the number of times it appears in S minus the number of times it appears in R. Tuple $(5, 6)$ appears once in $S - R$ for the same reason. The resulting bag happens to be a set in this case. □

4.6.3 Projection of Bags

We have already illustrated the projection of bags. As we saw in Example 4.48, each tuple is processed independently during the projection. If R is the bag of Fig. 4.29 and we compute the bag-projection $\pi_{A,B}(R)$, then we get the bag of Fig. 4.28.

If the elimination of one or more attributes during the projection causes the same tuple to be created from several tuples, these duplicate tuples are not eliminated from the result of a bag-projection. Thus, the three tuples $(1, 2, 5)$, $(1, 2, 7)$, and $(1, 2, 8)$ of the relation R from Fig. 4.29 each gave rise to the same tuple $(1, 2)$ after projection onto attributes A and B. In the bag result, there are three occurrences of tuple $(1, 2)$, while in the set-projection, this tuple appears only once.

Algebraic Laws for Bags

An algebraic law is an equivalence between two expressions of relational algebra whose arguments are variables standing for relations. The equivalence asserts that no matter what relations we substitute for these variables, the two expressions define the same relation. An example of a well-known law is the commutative law for union: $R \cup S \equiv S \cup R$. This law happens to hold whether we regard relation-variables R and S as standing for sets or bags. However, there are a number of other laws that hold when relational algebra is interpreted in the conventional manner — with relations as sets — but that do not hold when relations are interpreted as bags. A simple example of such a law is the distributive law of set difference over union, $(R \cup S) - T \equiv (R - T) \cup (S - T)$. This law holds for sets but not for bags. To see why it fails for bags, suppose R, S, and T each have one copy of tuple t. Then the expression on the left has one t, while the expression on the right has none. As sets, neither would have t. Some exploration of algebraic laws for bags appears in Exercises 4.6.4 and 4.6.5.

4.6.4 Selection on Bags

To apply a selection to a bag, we apply the selection condition to each tuple independently. As always with bags, we do not eliminate duplicate tuples in the result.

Example 4.50: If R is the bag

A	B	C
1	2	5
3	4	6
1	2	7
1	2	7

then the result of the bag-selection $\sigma_{C \geq 6}(R)$ is

A	B	C
3	4	6
1	2	7
1	2	7

That is, all but the first tuple meets the selection condition. The last two tuples, which are duplicates in R, are each included in the result. □

4.6.5 Product of Bags

The rule for the Cartesian product of bags is the expected one. Each tuple of one relation is paired with each tuple of the other, regardless of whether it is a duplicate or not. As a result, if a tuple r appears in a relation R m times, and tuple s appears n times in relation S, then in the product $R \times S$, the tuple rs will appear mn times.

Example 4.51: Let R and S be the bags shown in Fig. 4.30. Then the product $R \times S$ consists of six tuples, as shown in Fig. 4.30(c). Note that the usual convention regarding attribute names that we developed for set-relations applies equally well to bags. Thus, the attribute B, which belongs to both relations R and S, appears twice in the product, each time prefixed by one of the relation names. □

A	B
1	2
1	2

(a) The relation R

B	C
2	3
4	5
4	5

(b) The relation S

A	$R.B$	$S.B$	C
1	2	2	3
1	2	2	3
1	2	4	5
1	2	4	5
1	2	4	5
1	2	4	5

(c) The product $R \times S$

Figure 4.30: Computing the product of bags

4.6.6 Joins of Bags

Joining bags also presents no surprises. We compare each tuple of one relation with each tuple of the other, decide whether or not this pair of tuples joins successfully, and if so we put the resulting tuple in the answer. When constructing the answer, we do not eliminate duplicate tuples.

Example 4.52: The natural join $R \bowtie S$ of the relations R and S seen in Fig. 4.30 is

A	B	C
1	2	3
1	2	3

That is, tuple $(1, 2)$ of R joins with $(2, 3)$ of S. Since there are two copies of $(1, 2)$ in R and one copy of $(2, 3)$ in S, there are two pairs of tuples that join to give the tuple $(1, 2, 3)$. No other tuples from R and S join successfully.

As another example on the same relations R and S, the theta-join

$$R \bowtie_{R.B < S.B} S$$

produces the bag

A	R.B	S.B	C
1	2	4	5
1	2	4	5
1	2	4	5
1	2	4	5

The computation of the join is as follows. Tuple $(1, 2)$ from R and $(4, 5)$ from S meet the join condition. Since each appears twice in its relation, the number of times the joined tuple appears in the result is 2×2 or 4. The other possible join of tuples — $(1, 2)$ from R with $(2, 3)$ from S — fails to meet the join condition, so this combination does not appear in the result. □

4.6.7 Datalog Rules Applied to Bags

The techniques for computing selections, projections, and joins of bags can also be applied to Datalog rules, provided there are no negated, relational subgoals. Roughly, we take the join of the relations represented by the various subgoals, apply to the result any selections implied by arithmetic subgoals, and project the result onto the head. At each step, we use the algorithm appropriate to bags.

It is conceptually simpler to generalize the second approach for evaluating Datalog rules that we gave in Section 4.2.4. Recall this technique involves looking at each of the nonnegated, relational subgoals and substituting for it all tuples of the relation for the predicate of that subgoal. If a selection of tuples for each subgoal gives a consistent value to each variable, and the arithmetic subgoals all become true,[7] then we see what the head becomes with this assignment of values to variables. The resulting tuple is put in the head relation.

Since we are now dealing with bags, we do not eliminate duplicates from the head. Moreover, as we consider all combinations of tuples for the subgoals, a tuple appearing n times in the relation for a subgoal gets considered n times as the tuple for that subgoal, in conjunction with all combinations of tuples for the other subgoals.

Example 4.53: Consider the rule

$$H(x,z) \leftarrow R(x,y) \text{ AND } S(y,z)$$

and let R and S be the relations of Fig. 4.30. The only time we get a consistent assignment of tuples to the subgoals (i.e., an assignment where the value of y from each subgoal is the same) is when the first subgoal is assigned the tuple $(1, 2)$ from R and the second subgoal is assigned tuple $(2, 3)$ from S. Since $(1, 2)$ appears twice in R, and $(2, 3)$ appears once in S, there will be two assignments of tuples that give the variable assignments $x = 1$, $y = 2$, and $z = 3$. The tuple of the head, which is (x, z), is for each of these assignments $(1, 3)$. Thus the tuple (1.3) appears twice in the head relation H, and no other tuple appears there. That is, the relation

H1	H2
1	3
1	3

is the head relation defined by this rule, where we have taken the liberty of naming the attributes of the relation $H1$ and $H2$. More generally, had tuple $(1, 2)$ appeared n times in R and tuple $(2, 3)$ appeared m times in S, then tuple $(1, 3)$ would appear nm times in H.   □

If a relation is defined by several rules, then the result is the bag-union of whatever tuples are produced by each rule.

Example 4.54: Consider a relation H defined by the two rules

$$H(x,y) \leftarrow S(x,y) \text{ AND } x>1$$
$$H(x,y) \leftarrow S(x,y) \text{ AND } y<5$$

Suppose that the relation S has the value from Fig. 4.30(b), which is

B	C
2	3
4	5
4	5

---

[7]Note that there must not be any negated relational subgoals in the rule. There is not a clearly defined meaning of arbitrary Datalog rules with negated, relational subgoals under the bag model.

The first rule puts each of the three tuples of S into H, since they each have a first component greater than 1. The second rule puts only the tuple $(2, 3)$ into H, since $(4, 5)$ does not satisfy the condition $y < 5$. Thus, the resulting relation H has two copies of the tuple $(2, 3)$ and two copies of the tuple $(4, 5)$. $\square$

4.6.8   Exercises for Section 4.6

* **Exercise 4.6.1:** Let PC be the relation of Fig. 4.10(a), and suppose we compute the projection $\pi_{speed}(\text{PC})$. What is the value of this expression as a set? As a bag? What is the average value of tuples in this projection, when treated as a set? As a bag?

Exercise 4.6.2: Repeat Exercise 4.6.1 for the projection $\pi_{hd}(\text{PC})$.

Exercise 4.6.3: This exercise refers to the "battleship" relations of Exercise 4.1.3.

    a) The expression $\pi_{bore}(\text{Classes})$ yields a single-column relation with the bores of the various classes. For the data of Exercise 4.1.3, what is this relation as a set? As a bag?

  ! b) Write an expression of relational algebra to give the bores of the ships (not the classes). Your expression must make sense for bags; that is, the number of times a value b appears must be the number of ships that have bore b.

! **Exercise 4.6.4:** Certain algebraic laws for relations as sets also hold for relations as bags. Explain why each of the laws below hold for bags as well as sets.

  * a) The associative law for union: $(R \cup S) \cup T \equiv R \cup (S \cup T)$.

  b) The associative law for intersection: $(R \cap S) \cap T \equiv R \cap (S \cap T)$.

  c) The associative law for natural join: $(R \bowtie S) \bowtie T \equiv R \bowtie (S \bowtie T)$.

  d) The commutative law for union: $(R \cup S) \equiv (S \cup R)$.

  e) The commutative law for intersection: $(R \cap S) \equiv (S \cap R)$.

  f) The commutative law for natural join: $(R \bowtie S) \equiv (S \bowtie R)$.

  g) $\pi_L(R \cup S) \equiv \pi_L(R) \cup \pi_L(S)$. Here, L is an arbitrary list of attributes.

  * h) The distributive law of union over intersection: $R \cup (S \cap T) \equiv (R \cup S) \cap (R \cup T)$.

  i) $\sigma_{C \text{ AND } D}(R) \equiv \sigma_C(R) \cap \sigma_D(R)$. Here, C and D are arbitrary conditions about the tuples of R.

!! **Exercise 4.6.5:** The following algebraic laws hold for sets but not for bags. Explain why they hold for sets and give counterexamples to show that they do not hold for bags.

* a) $(R \cap S) - T \equiv R \cap (S - T)$.

  b) The distributive law of intersection over union: $R \cap (S \cup T) \equiv (R \cap S) \cup (R \cap T)$.

  c) $\sigma_C \text{ OR } D(R) \equiv \sigma_C(R) \cup \sigma_D(R)$. Here, C and D are arbitrary conditions about the tuples of R.

4.7   Other Extensions to the Relational Model

There are a number of other concepts and operations that are not a part of the formal relational model but appear in real query languages. In this section we mention operations that modify relations, compute "aggregations" such as sums of columns in a relation, and define "views" or named functions of relations. Each of them appears in the database language SQL and will be revisited in Chapter 5. We shall also see some of them in our discussion of the query language OQL in Chapter 8.

4.7.1   Modifications

Relational algebra or Datalog are "query languages," in the sense that they each let us compute a relation or answer that is a function of some given relations. While queries are important, a database that could not be changed would not be interesting. Therefore, all real database languages include both the ability to query the database and the ability to modify the database. At the minimum, we need commands to

1. Insert tuples into a relation.

2. Delete tuples from a relation.

3. Update existing tuples by changing one or more components.

4.7.2   Aggregations

The relational algebra operations work on tuples independently of the other tuples in the same relation. Often, we wish to combine the tuples of a single relation to produce some *aggregate* value, that is, a function of all the tuples blended in some way. For instance, in our running movie example we might want to:

- Count the number of different movies mentioned in the Movie relation.

- Produce a table giving the sum of the lengths of the movies produced by each studio.

- Find the movie executive with the largest net worth.

Thus, real database query languages let us apply *aggregation operators*, principally count, sum, average, minimum, and maximum, to columns of a relation.

4.7.3 Views

We can think of an expression of relational algebra as a "program" that computes a relation R and prints or otherwise produces R as a result. However, there is another interpretation of a relational expression. We can regard it as a formula defining a relation that is not produced until the formula is applied to real relations. Such formulas are called *views* in database terminology. We shall see that it is common for views to be given names and for these names to be used as arguments of other relational expressions, as if the views were real relations.

Datalog rules illustrate the distinction between a query and a view as well. Recall that we regard predicates or relations defined by Datalog rules as "intensional"; that is, they are definitions of a relation that need not exist in "extensional" or stored form. A view is equivalent to an intensional predicate. Just as intensional predicates can be used in bodies of rules, a view can be used as an argument in an algebraic expression. Likewise, just as a collection of Datalog rules can be applied to a database consisting of stored relations, a view can likewise be evaluated when needed.

4.7.4 Null Values

There are many situations in which we must assign a value for a component of a tuple, but we cannot tell what that value is. For example, we may know that Kevin Costner is a movie star, but not know his birthdate. Since all `MovieStar` tuples have a `birthdate` component, what are we to do? The answer is that we can use a special value NULL, called the *null value*, for that component. The value NULL is in some senses just like any other value. However, in other ways it is not a value. In particular, we do not regard two NULL components as equal to each other when we take a join of two relations. For instance, two movie stars with NULL as the values of their `birthdate` components are not presumed to have the same birthdays.

There are many different interpretations that can be put on null values. Here are some of the most common.

1. *Value unknown*: that is, "I know there is some value that belongs here but I don't know what it is." An unknown birthdate, as discussed above, is an example.

2. *Value inapplicable*: "There is no value that makes sense here." For example, if we had a `spouse` attribute for the `MovieStar` relation, then an unmarried star would of necessity have a null value for that attribute, not because we don't know the spouse's name, but because there is none.

3. *Value withheld*: "We are not entitled to know the value that belongs here." For instance, an unlisted phone number might appear as `NULL` in the component for a `phone` attribute.

4.8   Summary of Chapter 4

✦ *Relational Algebra*: This algebra is an important form of query language for the relational model. Its principal operators are union, intersection, difference, selection, projection, Cartesian product, natural join, theta-join, and renaming.

✦ *Datalog*: This form of logic is another important type of query language for the relational model. In Datalog, one writes rules in which a predicate or relation is defined in terms of a body, consisting of subgoals. The head and subgoals are each atoms, and an atom consists of an (optionally negated) predicate applied to some number of arguments. All queries that can be expressed in relational algebra can also be expressed in Datalog.

✦ *Recursive Datalog*: Datalog rules can also be recursive, allowing a relation to be defined in terms of itself. The meaning of recursive Datalog rules is the least fixedpoint, the smallest set of tuples for the defined relations that makes the heads of the rules exactly equal to what their bodies imply.

✦ *Stratified Negation*: When a recursion involves negation, the least fixedpoint may not be unique, and in some cases there is no acceptable meaning to the Datalog rules. Therefore, uses of negation inside a recursion must be forbidden, leading to a requirement for stratified negation. For rules of this type, there is one (of perhaps several) least fixedpoints that is the generally accepted meaning of the rules.

✦ *Relations as Bags*: In commercial database systems, relations are actually bags, in which the same tuple is allowed to appear several times. The operations of relational algebra on sets can be extended to bags, but there are some algebraic laws that fail to hold.

✦ *Relations in Commercial Systems*: In addition to using the bag model of relations, commercial systems offer operations not present in relational algebra or Datalog. These operations include insertion, deletion, and update of tuples in relations, aggregations on relations, and null values in tuples.

4.9 References for Chapter 4

Relational algebra was another contribution of the fundamental paper [4] on the relational model. Logical query languages had a less straightforward origin. Codd introduced a form of first-order logic called *relational calculus* in one of his early papers on the relational model [5]. Relational calculus is an expression language, much like relational algebra, and is in fact equivalent in expressive power to relational algebra, a fact proved in [5].

Datalog, looking more like logical rules, was inspired by the programming language Prolog. Because it allows recursion, it is more expressive than relational calculus. The book [6] originated much of the development of logic as a query language, while [2] placed the ideas in the context of database systems. The original paper on the use of queries to express constraints is [8].

The idea that the stratified approach gives the correct choice of fixedpoint comes from [3], although the idea of using this approach to evaluating Datalog rules was the independent idea of [1], [7], and [10]. More on stratified negation, on the relationship between relational algebra, Datalog, and relational calculus, and on the evaluation of Datalog rules, with or without negation, can be found in [9].

1. Apt, K. R., H. Blair, and A Walker, "Towards a theory of declarative knowledge," in *Foundations of Deductive Databases and Logic Programming* (J. Minker, ed.), pp. 89–148, Morgan-Kaufmann, San Francisco, 1988.

2. Bancilhon, F. and R. Ramakrishnan, "An amateur's introduction to recursive query-processing strategies," *ACM SIGMOD Intl. Conf. on Management of Data*, pp. 16–52, 1986.

3. Chandra, A. K. and D. Harel, "Structure and complexity of relational queries," *J. Computer and System Sciences* **25**:1, pp. 99–128.

4. Codd, E. F., "A relational model for large shared data banks," *Comm. ACM* **13**:6, pp. 377–387, 1970.

5. Codd, E. F., "Relational completeness of database sublanguages," in *Database Systems* (R. Rustin, ed.), Prentice Hall, Engelwood Cliffs, NJ, 1972.

6. Gallaire, H. and J. Minker, *Logic and Databases*, Plenum Press, New York, 1978.

7. Naqvi, S., "Negation as failure for first-order queries," *Proc. Fifth ACM Symp. on Principles of Database Systems*, pp. 114–122, 1986.

8. Nicolas, J.-M., "Logic for improving integrity checking in relational databases," *Acta Informatica* **18**:3, pp. 227–253, 1982.

9. Ullman, J. D., *Principles of Database and Knowledge-Base Systems, Volume I*, Computer Science Press, New York, 1988.

10. Van Gelder, A, "Negation as failure using tight derivations for general logic programs," in *Foundations of Deductive Databases and Logic Programming* (J. Minker, ed.), pp. 149–176, Morgan-Kaufmann, San Francisco, 1988.

Chapter 5

The Database Language SQL

The most commonly used relational database systems query and modify the database through a language called SQL (sometimes pronounced "sequel"). SQL stands for "Structured Query Language." An important core of SQL is equivalent to relational algebra, although there are many important features of SQL that go beyond what is found in relational algebra, for example aggregation (e.g., sums, counts) and database updates.

There are many different dialects of SQL. First, there are two major standards: ANSI (American National Standards Institute) SQL and an updated standard adopted in 1992, called SQL-92 or SQL2. There is also an emerging standard called SQL3 that extends SQL2 with many new features such as recursion, triggers, and objects. Then, there are versions of SQL produced by the principal vendors of database management systems. These all include the capabilities of the original ANSI standard. They also conform to a large extent to the more recent SQL2, although each has its variations and extensions beyond SQL2, including some of the features in the proposed SQL3 standard.

In this and the next two chapters we shall discuss the use of SQL as a query language. This chapter focuses on the generic query interface for SQL. That is, we consider SQL as a stand-alone query language, where we sit at a terminal and ask queries of a database or request database modifications. Query answers are displayed for us at our terminal. In our discussion of SQL ranging over this and the next two chapters, we shall generally conform to the SQL2 standard, emphasizing features found in almost all commercial systems as well as the earlier ANSI standard. In some cases, where the SQL2 standard does not cover a subject adequately, we shall follow the most recent available version of the evolving SQL3 standard.

The intent of this chapter and the following two chapters is to provide the reader with a sense of what SQL is about, more at the level of a "tutorial" than a "manual." Thus, we focus on the most commonly used features only.

The references mention places where more of the details of the language and its dialects can be found.

5.1 Simple Queries in SQL

Perhaps the simplest form of query in SQL asks for those tuples of some one relation that satisfy a condition. Such a query is analogous to a selection in relational algebra. This simple query, like almost all SQL queries, uses the three keywords, SELECT, FROM, and WHERE that characterize SQL.

```
Movie(title, year, length, inColor, studioName, producerC#)
StarsIn(movieTitle, movieYear, starName)
MovieStar(name, address, gender, birthdate)
MovieExec(name, address, cert#, netWorth)
Studio(name, address, presC#)
```

Figure 5.1: Example database schema, repeated

Example 5.1: In this and subsequent examples, we shall use the database schema described in Section 3.9. To review, these relation schemas are the ones shown in Fig. 5.1. We shall see in Section 5.7 how to express schema information in SQL, but for the moment, assume that each of the relations and domains mentioned in Section 3.9 apply to their SQL counterparts.

As our first query, let us ask about the relation

```
Movie(title, year, length, inColor, studioName, producerC#)
```

for all movies produced by Disney Studios in 1990. In SQL, we say

```
SELECT *
FROM Movie
WHERE studioName = 'Disney' AND year = 1990;
```

This query exhibits the characteristic select-from-where form of most SQL queries.

- The FROM clause gives the relation or relations to which the query refers. In our example, the query is about the relation Movie.

- The WHERE clause is a condition, much like a selection-condition in relational algebra, which tuples must satisfy in order to match the query. Here, the condition is that the studioName attribute of the tuple has the value 'Disney' and the year attribute of the tuple has the value 1990. All tuples meeting both stipulations satisfy the condition; other tuples do not.

- The SELECT clause tells which attributes of the tuples matching the condition are produced as part of the answer. The * in this example indicates that the entire tuple is produced. The result of the query is the relation consisting of all tuples produced by this process.

One way to interpret this query is to consider each tuple of the relation mentioned in the FROM clause. The condition in the WHERE clause is applied to the tuple. More precisely, any attributes mentioned in the WHERE clause are replaced by the value in the tuple's component for that attribute. The condition is then evaluated, and if true, the components appearing in the SELECT clause are produced as one tuple of the answer. Thus, the result of the query is the Movie tuples for those movies produced by Disney in 1990, for example, *Pretty Woman.*

In detail, when the SQL query processor encounters the Movie tuple

title	*year*	*length*	*inColor*	*studioName*	*producerC#*
Pretty Woman	1990	119	true	Disney	999

(here, 999 is the imaginary certificate number for the producer of this movie), the value 'Disney' is substituted for attribute studioName and value 1990 is substituted for attribute year in the condition of the WHERE clause, because these are the values for those attributes in the tuple in question. The WHERE clause thus becomes

```
WHERE 'Disney' = 'Disney' AND 1990 = 1990
```

Since this condition is evidently true, the tuple for *Pretty Woman* passes the test of the WHERE clause and the tuple becomes part of the result of the query. □

5.1.1 Projection in SQL

We can, if we wish, eliminate some of the components of the chosen tuples; that is, we can project the relation produced by an SQL query onto some of its attributes. In place of the * of the SELECT clause, we may list any of the attributes of the relation mentioned in the FROM clause. The result will be projected onto the attributes listed.[1]

Example 5.2 : Suppose we wish to modify the query of Example 5.1 to produce only the movie title and length. We may write

```
SELECT title, length
FROM Movie
WHERE studioName = 'Disney' AND year = 1990;
```

---

[1]Thus, the keyword SELECT in SQL actually corresponds most closely to the projection operator of relational algebra, while the selection operator of the algebra corresponds to the WHERE clause of SQL queries.

The result is a table with two columns, headed `title` and `length`. The tuples in this table are pairs, each consisting of a movie title and its length, such that the movie was produced by Disney in 1990. For instance, the relation schema and one of its tuples looks like:

title	length
Pretty Woman	119

□

Sometimes, we wish to produce a relation with column headers different from the attributes of the relation mentioned in the `FROM` clause. We may follow the name of the attribute by the keyword `AS` and an *alias*, which will be the name appearing in the result relation. `AS` is optional, and some older SQL systems always omit it. That is, an alias can immediately follow the attribute it stands for, without any intervening comma.

Example 5.3: We can modify Example 5.2 to produce a relation with attributes `name` and `duration` in place of `title` and `length` as follows.

```
SELECT title AS name, length AS duration
FROM Movie
WHERE studioName = 'Disney' AND year = 1990;
```

The result is the same set of tuples as in Example 5.2, but with the columns headed by attributes `name` and `duration`. For example, the result relation might begin:

name	duration
Pretty Woman	119

□

Another option in the `SELECT` clause is to use a formula in place of an attribute.

Example 5.4: Suppose we wanted output as in Example 5.3, but with the length in hours. We might replace the `SELECT` clause of that example with

```
SELECT title AS name, length*0.016667 AS lengthInHours
```

Then the same name-length pairs would be produced, but the lengths would be calculated in hours and the second column would be headed by attribute `lengthInHours`. □

Example 5.5: We can even allow a constant as an item in the `SELECT` clause. It might seem pointless, but one application is to put some useful words into the output that SQL displays. The following query:

Case Insensitivity

SQL is *case insensitive*, meaning that it treats upper- and lower-case letters as the same letter. For example, although we have chosen to write keywords like FROM in capitals, it is equally proper to write this keyword as From or from, or even FrOm. Names of attributes, relations, aliases, and so on are similarly case insensitive. Only inside quotes does SQL make a distinction between upper- and lower-case letters. Thus, 'FROM' and 'from' are different character strings; of course neither is the keyword FROM.

```
SELECT title, length*0.016667 AS length, 'hrs.' AS inHours
FROM Movie
WHERE studioName = 'Disney' AND year = 1990;
```

produces tuples such as

title	length	inHours
Pretty Woman	1.98334	hrs.

We have arranged that the third column is called inHours, which fits with the column header length in the second column. Every tuple in the answer will have the constant hrs. in the third column, which thus appears to be the units attached to the value in the second column. □

5.1.2 Selection in SQL

The selection operator of relational algebra, and much more, is available through the WHERE clause of SQL. The expressions that may follow WHERE include conditional expressions like those found in common languages such as C or Pascal.

We may build expressions by comparing values using the six common comparison operators: =, <>, <, >, <=, and >=. These operators are the same as those used in Pascal and have the obvious meanings (<> is "not equal to," if you're not a big Pascal fan).

The values that may be compared include constants and attributes of the relation or relations mentioned after FROM. We may also apply the usual arithmetic operators, +, *, and so on, to numeric values before we compare them. For instance, $(year - 1930) * (year - 1930) < 100$ is true for those years within 9 of 1930. We may apply the concatenation operator || to strings; for example 'foo' || 'bar' has value 'foobar'.

An example comparison is

```
studioName = 'Disney'
```

in Example 5.1. The attribute `studioName` of the relation `Movie` is tested for equality against the constant `'Disney'`. This constant is string-valued; strings in SQL are denoted by surrounding them with single quotes. Numeric constants, integers and reals, are also allowed, and SQL uses the common notations for reals such as `-12.34` or `1.23E45`.

The result of a comparison is a boolean value: either `TRUE` or `FALSE`. boolean values may be combined by the logical operators `AND`, `OR`, and `NOT`, with their usual meanings as in Pascal. For instance, we saw in Example 5.1 how two conditions could be combined by `AND`. The `WHERE` clause of this example evaluates to true if and only if both comparisons are satisfied; that is, the studio name is `'Disney'` and the year is 1990. Here are some more examples of queries with complex `WHERE` clauses.

Example 5.6: The following query asks for all the movies made after 1970 that are in black-and-white.

```
SELECT title
FROM Movie
WHERE year > 1970 AND NOT inColor;
```

In this condition, we again have the `AND` of two booleans. The first is an ordinary comparison, but the second is the attribute `inColor`, negated. This use of an attribute by itself makes sense, because `inColor` is of type boolean.

Next, consider the query

```
SELECT title
FROM Movie
WHERE (year > 1970 OR length < 90)
      AND studioName = 'MGM';
```

This query asks for the titles of movies made by MGM Studios that were either made after 1970 or were less than 90 minutes long. Notice that comparisons can be grouped using parentheses. The parentheses are needed here because the precedence of logical operators in SQL is the same as in most other languages: `AND` takes precedence over `OR`, and `NOT` takes precedence over both. □

5.1.3 Comparison of Strings

Two strings are equal if they are the same sequence of characters. SQL allows declarations of different types of strings, for example fixed-length arrays of characters and variable-length lists of characters.[2] If so, we can expect reasonable coercions among string types. For example, a string like `foo` might be stored

---

[2] At least the strings may be thought of as stored as an array or list, respectively. How they are actually stored is an implementation-dependent matter, not specified in any SQL standard.

Representing Booleans and Bit Strings

We may represent boolean values in SQL as a special case of *bit strings*. A string of bits is represented by B followed by a quoted string of 0's and 1's. Thus, B'011' represents the string of three bits, the first of which is 0 and the other two of which are 1. Hexadecimal notation may also be used, where an X is followed by a quoted string of hexadecimal digits (0 through 9, and *a* through *f*, with the latter representing "digits" 10 through 15). For instance, X'7ff' represents a string of twelve bits, a 0 followed by eleven 1's. Note that each hexadecimal digit represents four bits, and leading 0's are not suppressed.

The boolean value TRUE can be represented by a 1 bit, that is, B'1'. Similarly, FALSE is represented by B'0'.

---

as a fixed-length string of length 10, with 7 "pad" characters, or it could be stored as a variable-length string. We would expect values of both types to be equal to each other and also equal to the constant string 'foo'.

When we compare strings by one of the "less than" operators, such as < or >=, we are asking whether one precedes the other in lexicographic order (i.e., in dictionary order, or alphabetically). That is, if $a_1 a_2 \cdots a_n$ and $b_1 b_2 \cdots b_m$ are two strings, then the first is "less than" the second if either $a_1 < b_1$, or if $a_1 = b_1$ and $a_2 < b_2$, or if $a_1 = b_1$, $a_2 = b_2$, and $a_3 < b_3$, and so on. We also say $a_1 a_2 \cdots a_n < b_1 b_2 \cdots b_m$ if $n < m$ and $a_1 a_2 \cdots a_n = b_1 b_2 \cdots b_n$; that is, the first string is a proper prefix of the second. For instance, 'fodder' < 'foo', because the first two characters of each string are the same, fo, and the third character of fodder precedes the third character of foo. Also, 'bar' < bargain because the former is a proper prefix of the latter. As with equality, we may expect reasonable coercion among different string types.

SQL also provides the capability to compare strings on the basis of a simple pattern match. An alternative form of comparison expression is

    s LIKE p

where s is a string and p is a *pattern*, that is, a string with the optional use of the two special characters % and _. Ordinary characters in p match only themselves in s. But % in p can match any sequence of 0 or more characters in s, and _ in p matches any one character in s. The value of this expression is true if and only if string s matches pattern p. Similarly, s NOT LIKE p has value true if and only if string s does not match pattern p.

Example 5.7: We remember a movie "Star something," and we remember that the something has four letters. What could this movie be? We can retrieve all such names with the query:

Escape Characters in LIKE expressions

What if the pattern we wish to use in a LIKE expression involves the characters % or _? Instead of having a particular character used as the escape character (e.g., the backslash in most UNIX commands), SQL allows us to specify any one character we like as the escape character for a single pattern. We do so by following the pattern by the keyword ESCAPE and the chosen escape character, in quotes. A character % or _ preceded by the escape character in the pattern is interpreted literally as that character, not as a symbol for any sequence of characters or any one character, respectively. For example,

$$s \ \text{LIKE} \ 'x\%\%x\%' \ \text{ESCAPE} \ 'x'$$

makes x the escape character in the pattern x%%x%. The sequence x% is taken to be a single %. Thus, this pattern matches any string that begins and ends with %.

```
SELECT title
FROM Movie
WHERE title LIKE 'Star ____'
```

This query asks if the title attribute of a movie has a value that is nine characters long, the first five characters being Star and a blank. The last four characters may be anything, since any sequence of four characters matches the four _ symbols. The result of the query is the set of complete matching titles, such as *Star Wars* and *Star Trek*.   □

Example 5.8 : Let us search for all movies with a possessive ('s) in their titles. The desired query is

```
SELECT title
FROM Movie
WHERE title LIKE '%''s%'
```

To understand this pattern, we must first observe that the apostrophe, being the character that surrounds strings in SQL cannot also represent itself. The convention taken by SQL is that two consecutive apostrophes in a string represent a single apostrophe and do not end the string. Thus, ''s in a pattern is matched by a single apostrophe and an s in the title of a movie.

The two % characters on either side of the 's match any strings whatsoever. Thus, any title with 's as a substring will match the pattern, and the answer to this query will include films such as *Logan's Run* or *Alice's Restaurant*.   □

5.1.4 Comparing Dates and Times

Implementations of SQL generally support dates and times as special data types. These values are often representable in a variety of formats such as 5/14/1948 or 14 May 1948. Here we shall describe only the SQL2 standard notation, which is very specific about format.

A *date* is represented by the keyword DATE followed by a quoted string of a special form. For example, DATE '1948-05-14' follows the required form. The first four characters are digits representing the year. Then come a hyphen and two digits representing the month. Note that, as in our example, a one-digit month is padded with a leading 0. Finally there is another hyphen and two digits representing the day. As with months, we pad the day with a leading 0 if that is necessary to make a two-digit number.

A *time* is represented similarly by the keyword TIME and a quoted string. This string has two digits for the hour, on the military (24-hour) clock. Then come a colon, two digits for the minute, another colon, and two digits for the second. If fractions of a second are desired, we can continue with a decimal point and as many significant digits as we like. For instance, TIME '15:00:02.5' represents the time at which all students will have left a class that ends at 3 PM: two and a half seconds past three o'clock.

We can compare dates or times using the same comparison operators we use for numbers or strings. That is, < on dates means that the first date is earlier than the second; < on times means that the first is earlier (within the same day) than the second.

5.1.5 Ordering the Output

We may ask that the tuples produced by a query be presented in sorted order. The order may be based on the value of any attribute, with ties broken by the value of a second attribute, remaining ties broken by a third, and so on. To get output in sorted order, we add to the select-from-where statement a clause:

```
ORDER BY <list of attributes>
```

The order is by default ascending, but we can get the output highest-first by appending the keyword DESC (for "descending"). Similarly, we can specify ascending order with the keyword ASC, but that word is unnecessary.

Example 5.9 : The following is a rewrite of our original query of Example 5.1, asking for the Disney movies of 1990 from the relation

```
Movie(title, year, length, inColor, studioName, producerC#)
```

To get the movies listed by length, shortest first, and among movies of equal length, alphabetically, we can say:

```
SELECT *
FROM Movie
WHERE studioName = 'Disney' AND year = 1990
ORDER BY length, title;
```

If there is an order of attributes understood (which there should be, since SQL relations are declared with a list of attributes, as we shall see in Section 5.7.2), then we can use the numbers of the attributes instead of the names if we wish. Thus, the ORDER BY clause above could have been written

```
ORDER BY 3, 1;
```

according to the standard order in which we list the attributes of relation Movie. □

5.1.6   Exercises for Section 5.1

Exercise 5.1.1: If a query has a SELECT clause

```
SELECT A B
```

how do we know whether A and B are two different attributes or B is an alias of A?

Exercise 5.1.2: Write the following queries, based on our running movie database example

```
Movie(title, year, length, inColor, studioName, producerC#)
StarsIn(movieTitle, movieYear, starName)
MovieStar(name, address, gender, birthdate)
MovieExec(name, address, cert#, netWorth)
Studio(name, address, presC#)
```

in SQL.

* a) Find the address of MGM studios.

  b) Find Sandra Bullock's birthdate.

* c) Find all the stars that appeared either in a movie made in 1980 or a movie with "Love" in the title.

  d) Find all executives worth at least $10,000,000.

  e) Find all the stars who either are male or live in Malibu (have Malibu as a part of their address).

Exercise 5.1.3: Write the following queries in SQL. They refer to the database schema of Exercise 4.1.1:

```
Product(maker, model, type)
PC(model, speed, ram, hd, cd, price)
Laptop(model, speed, ram, hd, screen, price)
Printer(model, color, type, price)
```

Show the result of your queries using the data from Exercise 4.1.1.

* a) Find the model number, speed, and hard-disk size for all PC's whose price is under $1600.

* b) Do the same as (a), but rename the speed column megahertz and the hd column gigabytes.

  c) Find the manufacturers of printers.

  d) Find the model number, memory size, and screen size for laptops costing more than $2000.

* e) Find all the tuples in the Printer relation for color printers. Remember that color is a boolean-valued attribute.

  f) Find the model number, speed, and hard-disk size for those PC's that have either a 6x or 8x CD and a price less than $2000. You may regard the cd attribute as having a string type.

Exercise 5.1.4: Write the following queries based on the database schema of Exercise 4.1.3:

```
Classes(class, type, country, numGuns, bore, displacement)
Ships(name, class, launched)
Battles(name, date)
Outcomes(ship, battle, result)
```

and show the result of your query on the data of Exercise 4.1.3.

  a) Find the class name and country for all classes with at least 10 guns.

  b) Find the names of all ships launched prior to 1918, but call the resulting column shipName.

  c) Find the names of ships sunk in battle and the name of the battle in which they were sunk.

  d) Find all ships that have the same name as their class.

  e) Find the names of all ships that begin with the letter "R."

! f) Find the names of all ships whose name consists of three or more words (e.g., King George V).

5.2 Queries Involving More than One Relation

Much of the power of relational algebra comes from its ability to combine two or more relations through joins, products, unions, intersections, and differences. We can use any of these five operations in SQL. The set-theoretic operations — union, intersection, and difference — appear directly in SQL, as we shall learn in Section 5.2.5. First, we shall learn how the select-from-where statement of SQL allows us to use products and joins.

5.2.1 Products and Joins in SQL

SQL has a simple way to couple relations in one query: list each relation in the FROM clause. Then, the SELECT and WHERE clauses can refer to the attributes of any of the relations in the FROM clause.

Example 5.10 : Suppose we want to know the name of the producer of *Star Wars*. To answer this question we need the following two relations from our running example:

```
Movie(title, year, length, inColor, studioName, producerC#)
MovieExec(name, address, cert#, netWorth)
```

The producer certificate number is given in the Movie relation, so we can do a simple query on Movie to get this number. We could then do a second query on the relation MovieExec to find the name of the person with that certificate number.

However, we can phrase both these steps as one query about the pair of relations Movie and MovieExec as follows:

```
SELECT name
FROM Movie, MovieExec
WHERE title = 'Star Wars' AND producerC# = cert#
```

This query asks us to consider all pairs of tuples, one from Movie and the other from MovieExec. The conditions on this pair are stated in the WHERE clause:

1. The title attribute of the tuple from Movie must have value 'Star Wars'.

2. The producerC# attribute of the Movie tuple must be the same certificate number as the cert# attribute in the MovieExec tuple. That is, these two tuples must refer to the same producer.

Whenever we find a pair of tuples satisfying both conditions, we produce the name attribute of the tuple from MovieExec as part of the answer. If the data is what we expect, the only time both conditions will be met is when the tuple from Movie is for *Star Wars*, and the tuple from MovieExec is for George Lucas. Then and only then will the title be correct and the certificate numbers agree. Thus, George Lucas should be the only value produced. □

5.2.2 Disambiguating Attributes

Sometimes we ask a query involving several relations, and among these relations
are two or more attributes with the same name. If so, we need a way to indicate
which of these attributes is meant by a use of their shared name. SQL solves
this problem by allowing us to place a relation name and a dot in front of an
attribute. Thus $R.A$ refers to the attribute A of relation R.

Example 5.11: The two relations

```
MovieStar(name, address, gender, birthdate)
MovieExec(name, address, cert#, netWorth)
```

each have attributes `name` and `address`. Suppose we wish to find pairs consisting of a star and an executive with the same address. The following query does
the job.

```
SELECT MovieStar.name, MovieExec.name
FROM MovieStar, MovieExec
WHERE MovieStar.address = MovieExec.address
```

In this query, we look for a pair of tuples, one from `MovieStar` and the other
from `MovieExec`, such that their address components agree. The `WHERE` clause
enforces the requirement that the `address` attributes from each of the two
tuples agree. Then, for each matching pair of tuples, we extract the two `name`
attributes, first from the `MovieStar` tuple and then from the other. The result
would be a set of pairs such as

MovieStar.name	*MovieExec.name*
Jane Fonda	Ted Turner

□

The relation, followed by a dot, is permissible, even in situations where there
is no ambiguity. For instance, we are free to write the query of Example 5.10
as

```
SELECT MovieExec.name
FROM Movie, MovieExec
WHERE Movie.title = 'Star Wars'
      AND Movie.producerC# = MovieExec.cert#
```

Alternatively, we may use relation names and dots in front of any subset of the
attributes in this query.

Tuple Variables and Relation Names

Technically, references to attributes in SELECT and WHERE clauses are *always* to a tuple variable. However, if a relation appears only once in the FROM clause, then we can use the relation name as its own tuple variable. Thus, we can see a relation name R in the FROM clause as shorthand for R AS R.

5.2.3   Tuple Variables

Disambiguating attributes by prefixing the relation is successful as long as the query involves combining several different relations. However, sometimes we need to ask a query that involves two or more tuples from the same relation. We may list relation R as many times as we need to in the FROM clause, but we need a way to refer to each occurrence of R. SQL allows us to define, for each occurrence of R in the FROM clause, an "alias" which we shall refer to as a *tuple variable*. Each use of R in the FROM clause is followed by the (optional) keyword AS and the name of the tuple variable.

In the SELECT and WHERE clauses, we can disambiguate attributes of R by preceding them by the appropriate tuple variable and a dot. Thus, the tuple variable serves as another name for relation R and can be used in its place when we wish.

Example 5.12 : While Example 5.11 asked for a star and an executive sharing an address, we might similarly want to know about two stars who share an address. The query is essentially the same, but now we must think of two tuples chosen from relation MovieStar, rather than tuples from each of MovieStar and MovieExec. Using tuple variables as aliases for two uses of MovieStar, we can write the query as

```
SELECT Star1.name, Star2.name
FROM MovieStar AS Star1, MovieStar AS Star2
WHERE Star1.address = Star2.address
      AND Star1.name < Star2.name
```

We see in the FROM clause the declaration of two tuple variables, Star1 and Star2, each an alias for relation MovieStar. The tuple variables are used in the SELECT clause to refer to the **name** components of the two tuples. These aliases are also used in the WHERE clause to say that the two MovieStar tuples they represent have the same value in their **address** components.

The second condition in the WHERE clause, Star1.name < Star2.name, says that the name of the first star precedes the name of the second star alphabetically. If this condition were omitted, then tuple variables Star1 and Star2 could both refer to the same tuple. We would find that the addresses of those tuples were equal, of course, and then produce each pair of identical star names.[3] The second condition also forces us to produce each pair of stars with a common address only once, in alphabetical order. If we used <> (not-equal) as the comparison operator, then we would produce pairs of married stars twice, like

Star1.name	*Star2.name*
Alec Baldwin	Kim Basinger
Kim Basinger	Alec Baldwin

□

5.2.4 Interpreting Multirelation Queries

There are several ways to define the meaning of the select-from-where expressions that we have just covered. All are *equivalent*, in the sense that they each give the same answer for each query applied to the same relation instances. We shall consider each in turn.

Nested Loops

The semantics that we have implicitly used in examples so far is that of tuple variables. Recall that an alias of a relation name is a tuple variable that ranges over all tuples of the corresponding relation. A relation name that is not aliased is also a tuple variable ranging over the relation itself. If there are several tuple variables, we may imagine nested loops, one for each tuple variable, in which the variables each range over the tuples of their respective relations. For each assignment of tuples to the tuple variables, we decide whether the WHERE clause is true. If so, we produce a tuple consisting of the values of the terms following SELECT; note that each term is given a value by the current assignment of tuples to tuple variables. The query-answering algorithm is suggested by Fig. 5.2.

Parallel Assignment

There is an equivalent definition in which we do not explicitly create nested loops ranging over the tuple variables. Rather, we consider in arbitrary order or in parallel all possible assignments of tuples from the appropriate relations to the tuple variables. For each such assignment, we consider whether the WHERE clause becomes true. Each assignment that produces a true WHERE clause contributes a tuple to the answer; that tuple is constructed from the attributes of the SELECT clause, evaluated according to that assignment.

---

[3]The same problem would occur in Example 5.11 should the same individual be both a star and an executive. We could solve that problem similarly by requiring that the two names be unequal.

```
LET the tuple variables in the from clause range over
        relations R1, R2,..., Rn;
FOR each tuple t1 in relation R1 DO
    FOR each tuple t2 in relation R2 DO
        ...
        FOR each tuple tn in relation Rn DO
            IF the where clause is satisfied when the values
            from t1, t2,..., tn are substituted for all
            attribute references THEN
                evaluate the attributes of the select clause
                according to t1, t2,..., tn and produce the
                tuple of values that results.
```

Figure 5.2: Answering a simple SQL query

Datalog Interpretation and SQL Interpretation

The reader should notice the similarity between the second approach to interpreting Datalog rules that we described in Section 4.2.4 and the second interpretation we gave for SQL select-from-where statements. For Datalog, we spoke of considering all possible assignments of tuples from the appropriate relation to relational subgoals of the rule body. In SQL, we consider all possible assignments of tuples to the tuple variables. In both cases, arithmetic subgoals (parts of the WHERE clause in SQL) restrict these assignments of tuples, and the tuples of the result are obtained by evaluating the head of the rule (SELECT clause in SQL).

Conversion to Relational Algebra

A third approach is to relate the SQL query to relational algebra. We start with the tuple variables in the FROM clause and take their Cartesian product. If two tuple variables refer to the same relation, then this relation appears twice in the product, and we rename its attributes so all attributes have unique names. Similarly, attributes of the same name from different relations are renamed to avoid ambiguity.

Having created the product, we apply a selection operator to it by converting the WHERE clause to a selection condition in the obvious way. That is, each attribute reference in the WHERE clause is replaced by the attribute of the product to which it corresponds. Finally, we create from the SELECT clause a list of attributes for a final projection operation. The attributes for the projection operation are determined as for the selection operation; we replace each attribute

---

An Unintuitive Consequence of SQL semantics

Suppose R, S, and T are unary (one-component) relations, each having attribute A alone, and we wish to find those elements that are in R and also in either S or T (or both). That is, we want to compute $R \cap (S \cup T)$. We might expect the following SQL query would do the job.

```
SELECT R.A
FROM R, S, T
WHERE R.A = S.A OR R.A = T.A
```

However, consider the situation in which T is empty. Since then $R.A = T.A$ can never be satisfied, we might expect the query to produce exactly $R \cap S$, based on our intuition about how "OR" operates. Yet whichever of the three equivalent definitions of Section 5.2.4 one prefers, we find that the result is empty, regardless of how many elements R and S have in common. If we use the nested-loop semantics of Figure 5.2, then we see that the loop for tuple variable T iterates 0 times, since there are no tuples in the relation for the tuple variable to range over. Thus, the if-statement inside the for-loops never executes, and nothing can be produced. Similarly, if we look for assignments of tuples to the tuple variables, there is no way to assign a tuple to T, so no assignments exist. Finally, if we use the Cartesian-product approach, we start with $R \times S \times T$, which is empty because T is empty.

---

reference in the SELECT clause by the corresponding attribute of the product.[4]

Example 5.13: Let us convert the query of Example 5.12 to relational algebra. First, there are two tuple variables in the FROM clause, both referring to relation MovieStar. Thus, our expression begins

MovieStar × MovieStar

The resulting relation has eight attributes, the first four correspond to attributes name, address, gender, and birthdate from the first copy of relation MovieStar, and the second four correspond to the same attributes from the other copy of MovieStar. We could create names for these attributes with a dot and the aliasing tuple variable — e.g., Star1.gender — but for succinctness, let us invent new symbols and call the attributes simply $A_1, A_2, \ldots, A_8$. Thus, A_1 corresponds to Star1.name, A_5 corresponds to Star2.name, and so on.

---

[4]Technically, relational algebra does not allow arithmetic computations in the SELECT clause, while SQL does (as in Example 5.4). However, the extension to the project operator of relational algebra should be obvious, and it is only for the sake of tradition that projection is defined in the more limited way.

Under this naming strategy for attributes, the selection condition obtained from the WHERE clause is $A_2 = A_6$ and $A_1 < A_5$. The projection list is A_1, A_5. Thus,

$$\pi_{A_1,A_5}\left(\sigma_{A_2=A_6 \text{ AND } A_1<A_5}\left(\rho_{M(A_1,A_2,A_3,A_4)}(\text{MovieStar}) \times \right.\right.$$
$$\left.\left. \rho_{N(A_5,A_6,A_7,A_8)}(\text{MovieStar})\right)\right)$$

renders the entire query in relational algebra.   □

5.2.5   Union, Intersection, and Difference of Queries

Sometimes we wish to combine relations using the set operations of relational algebra: union, intersection, and difference. SQL provides corresponding operators that apply to the results of queries, provided those queries produce relations with the same set of attributes. The keywords used are UNION, INTERSECT, and EXCEPT for $\cup$, $\cap$, and $-$, respectively. Words like UNION are used between two queries, and those queries must be parenthesized.

Example 5.14: Suppose we wanted the names and addresses of all female movie stars who are also movie executives with a net worth over \$10,000,000. Using the following two relations:

```
MovieStar(name, address, gender, birthdate)
MovieExec(name, address, cert#, netWorth)
```

we can write the query in Fig. 5.3. Lines (1) through (3) produce the set of female movie stars in a relation whose schema is the attributes **name** and **address**.

Similarly, lines (5) through (7) produce the set of "rich" executives, those with net worth over \$10,000,000. This query also yields a relation whose schema has the attributes **name** and **address** only. Since the two schemas are the same, we can intersect them, and we do so with the operator of line (4).   □

```
1)   (SELECT name, address
2)    FROM MovieStar
3)    WHERE gender = 'F')
4)         INTERSECT
5)   (SELECT name, address
6)    FROM MovieExec
7)    WHERE netWorth > 10000000);
```

Figure 5.3: Intersecting female movie stars with rich executives

---

Readable SQL Queries

Generally, one writes SQL queries so that each important keyword like FROM or WHERE starts a new line. This style offers the reader visual clues to the structure of the query. However, when a query or subquery is short, we shall sometimes write it out on a single line, as we did in Example 5.15. That style, keeping a complete query compact, also offers good readability.

Example 5.15: In a similar vein, we could take the difference of two sets of persons, each selected from a relation. The query

```
(SELECT name, address FROM MovieStar)
    EXCEPT
(SELECT name, address FROM MovieExec);
```

gives the names and addresses of movie stars who are not also movie executives regardless of gender or net worth. □

In the two examples above, the attributes of the relations whose intersection or difference we took were conveniently the same. However, if necessary to get a common set of attributes, we can rename attributes as in Example 5.3.

Example 5.16: Suppose we wanted all the titles and years of movies that appeared in either the Movie or StarsIn relation of our running example:

```
Movie(title, year, length, inColor, studioName, producerC#)
StarsIn(movieTitle, movieYear, starName)
```

Ideally, these sets of movies would be the same, but in practice it is common for relations to diverge; for instance we might have movies with no listed stars or a StarsIn tuple that mentions a movie not found in the Movie relation.[5] Thus, we might write

```
(SELECT title, year FROM Movie)
    UNION
(SELECT movieTitle AS title, movieYear AS year FROM StarsIn);
```

The result would be all movies mentioned in either relation, with title and year as the attributes of the resulting relation. □

---

[5]There are ways to prevent this divergence; see Chapter 6.

5.2.6   Exercises for Section 5.2

Exercise 5.2.1: Using the database schema of our running movie example

```
Movie(title, year, length, inColor, studioName, producerC#)
StarsIn(movieTitle, movieYear, starName)
MovieStar(name, address, gender, birthdate)
MovieExec(name, address, cert#, netWorth)
Studio(name, address, presC#)
```

write the following queries in SQL.

* a) Who were the male stars in *Terms of Endearment?*

  b) Which stars appeared in movies produced by MGM in 1995?

  c) Who is the president of MGM studios?

*! d) Which movies are longer than *Gone With the Wind?*

 ! e) Which executives are worth more than Merv Griffin?

Exercise 5.2.2: Write the following queries, based on the database schema

```
Product(maker, model, type)
PC(model, speed, ram, hd, cd, price)
Laptop(model, speed, ram, hd, screen, price)
Printer(model, color, type, price)
```

of Exercise 4.1.1, and evaluate your queries using the data of that exercise.

* a) Give the manufacturer and speed of laptops with a hard disk of at least one gigabyte?

* b) Find the model number and price of all products (of any type) made by manufacturer B.

  c) Find those manufacturers that sell Laptops, but not PC's.

 ! d) Find those hard-disk sizes that occur in two or more PC's.

 ! e) Find those pairs of PC models that have both the same speed and RAM. A pair should be listed only once; e.g., list (i, j) but not (j, i).

 !! f) Find those manufacturers of at least two different computers (PC's or laptops) with speeds of at least 133.

Exercise 5.2.3: Write the following queries, based on the database schema

```
Classes(class, type, country, numGuns, bore, displacement)
Ships(name, class, launched)
Battles(name, date)
Outcomes(ship, battle, result)
```

of Exercise 4.1.3, and evaluate your queries using the data of that exercise.

a) Find the ships heavier than 35,000 tons.

b) List the name, displacement, and number of guns of the ships engaged in the battle of Guadalcanal.

c) List all the ships mentioned in the database. (Remember that all these ships may not appear in the Ships relation.)

! d) Find those countries that have both battleships and battlecruisers.

! e) Find those ships that were damaged in one battle, but later fought in another.

! f) Find those battles with at least three ships of the same country.

*! **Exercise 5.2.4:** A general form of relational-algebra query is

$$\pi_L\Big(\sigma_C(R_1 \times R_2 \times \cdots \times R_n)\Big)$$

Here, L is an arbitrary list of attributes, and C is an arbitrary condition. The list of relations $R_1, R_2, \ldots, R_n$ may include the same relation repeated several times, in which case appropriate renaming may be assumed applied to the R_i's. Show how to express any query of this form in SQL.

! **Exercise 5.2.5:** Another general form of relational-algebra query is

$$\pi_L\Big(\sigma_C(R_1 \bowtie R_2 \bowtie \cdots \bowtie R_n)\Big)$$

The same assumptions as in Exercise 5.2.4 apply here; the only difference is that the natural join is used instead of the product. Show how to express any query of this form in SQL.

5.3 Subqueries

In this section, we shall advance our understanding of the expressions that may appear in WHERE clauses. Previously, we saw that conditions may compare *scalar* values (simple values such as integers, reals, strings, or dates, or expressions that represent those values). Now, we shall expand this view and allow the things being compared to be whole tuples or even whole relations. Our first step is to learn how to use subqueries in conditions. A *subquery* is an expression that evaluates to a relation. For example, a select-from-where expression may be a subquery. After seeing how to create values that are relations, we shall consider some operators that SQL provides so we can compare tuples and relations within a WHERE clause.

5.3.1   Subqueries that Produce Scalar Values

A select-from-where expression can produce a relation with any number of attributes in its schema, and there can be any number of tuples in the relation. However, often we are only interested in values of a single attribute. Furthermore, sometimes we can deduce from information about keys that there will be only a single value produced for that attribute.

If so, we can use this select-from-where expression, surrounded by parentheses, as if it were a constant. In particular, it may appear in a WHERE clause any place we would expect to find a constant or an attribute representing a component of a tuple. For instance, we may compare the result of such a subquery to a constant or attribute.

Example 5.17: Let us recall Example 5.10, where we asked for the producer of *Star Wars*. We had to query the two relations

```
Movie(title, year, length, inColor, studioName, producerC#)
MovieExec(name, address, cert#, netWorth)
```

because only the former has movie title information and only the latter has producer names. The information is linked by "certificate numbers." These numbers uniquely identify producers. The query we developed is:

```
SELECT name
FROM Movie, MovieExec
WHERE title = 'Star Wars' AND producerC# = cert#
```

There is another way to look at this query. We only need the Movie relation to get the certificate number for the producer of *Star Wars*. Once we have it, we can query the relation MovieExec to find the name of the person with this certificate. The first problem, getting the certificate number, can be written as a subquery, and the result, which we expect will be a single value, can be used in the "main" query to achieve the same effect as the query above. This query is shown in Fig. 5.4.

```
1) SELECT name
2) FROM MovieExec
3) WHERE cert# =
4)     (SELECT producerC#
5)      FROM Movie
6)      WHERE title = 'Star Wars'
7)     );
```

Figure 5.4: Finding the producer of *Star Wars* by using a nested subquery

Lines (4) through (6) of Fig. 5.4 are the subquery. Looking only at this simple query by itself, we see that the result will be a unary relation with attribute `producerC#`, and we expect to find only one tuple in this relation. The tuple will look like (12345), that is, a single component with some integer, perhaps 12345 or whatever George Lucas' certificate number is. If zero or more than one tuple is produced by the subquery of lines (4) through (6), it is a run-time error.

Having executed this subquery, we can then execute lines (1) through (3) of Fig. 5.4, as if the value 12345 replaced the entire subquery. That is, the "main" query is executed as if it were

```
SELECT name
FROM MovieExec
WHERE cert# = 12345;
```

The result of this query should be `George Lucas`. □

5.3.2 Conditions Involving Relations

There are a number of SQL operators that we can apply to a relation R and produce a boolean result. Typically, the relation R will be the result of a select-from-where subquery. Some of these operators — IN, ALL, and ANY — also involve a scalar value s, in which case the relation R is required to be a one-column relation. Here are the definitions of the operators:

1. EXISTS R is a condition that is true if and only if R is not empty.

2. s IN R is true if and only if s is equal to one of the values in R. Likewise, s NOT IN R is true if and only if s is equal to no value in R. Here, we assume R is a unary relation. We shall discuss extensions to the IN and NOT IN operators where R has more than one attribute in its schema and s is a tuple in Section 5.3.3.

3. s > ALL R is true if and only if s is greater than every value in unary relation R. Similarly, the > operator could be replaced by any of the other five comparison operators, with the analogous meaning. For instance, s <> ALL R is the same as s NOT IN R.

4. s > ANY R is true if and only if s is greater than at least one value in unary relation R. Similarly, any of the other five comparisons could be used in place of >. For instance, s = ANY R is the same as s IN R.

The EXISTS, ALL, and ANY operators can be negated by putting NOT in front of the entire expression, just like any other boolean-valued expression. Thus, NOT EXISTS R is true if and only if R is empty. NOT s > ALL R is true if and only if s is not the maximum value in R, and NOT s > ANY R is true if and only if s is the minimum value in R. We shall see several examples of the use of these operators shortly.

5.3.3 Conditions Involving Tuples

A tuple in SQL is represented by a parenthesized list of scalar values. Examples are (123, 'foo') and (name, address, networth). The first of these has constants as components; the second has attributes as components. Mixing of constants and attributes is permitted.

If a tuple t has the same number of components as a relation R, then it makes sense to compare t and R in expressions of the type listed in above. Examples are t IN R or t <> ANY R. The latter comparison means that there is some tuple in R other than t. Note that when comparing a tuple with members of a relation R, we must compare components using the assumed standard order for the attributes of R.

```
 1) SELECT name
 2) FROM MovieExec
 3) WHERE cert# IN
 4)     (SELECT producerC#
 5)      FROM Movie
 6)      WHERE (title, year) IN
 7)          (SELECT movieTitle, movieYear
 8)           FROM StarsIn
 9)           WHERE starName = 'Harrison Ford'
10)          )
11)     );
```

Figure 5.5: Finding the producers of Harrison Ford's movies

Example 5.18: In Fig. 5.5 is an SQL query on the three relations

```
Movie(title, year, length, inColor, studioName, producerC#)
StarsIn(movieTitle, movieYear, starName)
MovieExec(name, address, cert#, netWorth)
```

asking for all the producers of movies in which Harrison Ford stars. It consists of a "main" query, a query nested within that, and a third query nested within the second.

We should analyze any nested query from the inside out. Thus, let us start with the innermost nested subquery: lines (7) through (9). This query examines the tuples of the relation StarsIn and finds all those tuples whose starName component is 'Harrison Ford'. The titles and years of those movies is returned by this subquery. Recall that title and year, not title alone, is the key for movies, so we need to produce tuples with both attributes to identify a movie uniquely. Thus, we would expect the value produced by lines (7) through (9) to look something like Fig. 5.6.

title	year
Star Wars	1977
Raiders of the Lost Ark	1981
The Fugitive	1993
...	...

Figure 5.6: Title-year pairs returned by inner subquery

Now, consider the middle subquery, lines (4) through (6). It searches the Movie relation for tuples whose title and year are in the relation suggested by Fig. 5.6. For each tuple found, the producer's certificate number is returned, so the result of the middle subquery is the set of certificates of the producers of Harrison Ford's movies.

Finally, consider the "main" query of lines (1) through (3). It examines the tuples of the MovieExec relation to find those whose cert# component is one of the certificates in the set returned by the middle subquery. For each of these tuples, the name of the producer is returned, giving us the set of producers of Harrison Ford's movies, as desired. □

Incidentally, the nested query of Fig. 5.5 can, like many nested queries, be written as a single select-from-where expression with relations in the FROM clause for each of the relations mentioned in the main query or a subquery. The IN relationships are replaced by equalities in the WHERE clause. For instance, the query of Fig. 5.7 is essentially that of Fig. 5.5. There is a difference regarding the way duplicate occurrences of a producer – e.g., George Lucas — are handled, as we shall discuss in Section 5.4.1.

```
SELECT name
FROM MovieExec, Movie, StarsIn
WHERE cert# = producerC# AND
      title = movieTitle AND
      year = movieYear AND
      starName = 'Harrison Ford';
```

Figure 5.7: Ford's producers without nested subqueries

5.3.4 Correlated Subqueries

The simplest subqueries can be evaluated once and for all, and the result used in a higher-level query. A more complicated use of nested subqueries requires the subquery to be evaluated many times, once for each assignment of a value to some term in the subquery that comes from a tuple variable outside the subquery. A subquery of this type is called a *correlated* subquery. Let us begin with an example.

Example 5.19 : We shall find the titles that have been used for two or more movies. We start with an outer query that looks at all tuples in the relation

```
Movie(title, year, length, inColor, studioName, producerC#)
```

For each such tuple, we ask in a subquery whether there is a movie with the same title and a greater year. The entire query is shown in Fig. 5.8.

As with other nested queries, let us begin at the innermost subquery, lines (4) through (6). If `Old.title` in line (6) were replaced by a constant string such as `'King Kong'`, we would understand it quite easily as a query asking for the year or years in which movies titled *King Kong* were made. The present subquery differs little. The only problem is that we don't know what value `Old.title` has. However, as we range over `Movie` tuples of the outer query of lines (1) through (3), each tuple provides a value of `Old.title`. We then execute the query of lines (4) through (6) with this value for `Old.title` to decide the truth of the `WHERE` clause that extends from lines (3) through (6).

```
1) SELECT title
2) FROM Movie AS Old
3) WHERE year < ANY
4)     (SELECT year
5)      FROM Movie
6)      WHERE title = Old.title
7)     )
```

Figure 5.8: Finding movie titles that appear more than once

The condition of line (3) is true if any movie with the same title as `Old.title` has a later year than the movie in the tuple that is the current value of tuple variable `Old`. This condition is true unless the year in the tuple `Old` is the last year in which a movie of that title was made. Consequently, lines (1) through (3) produce a title one fewer times than there are movies with that title. A movie made twice will be listed once, a movie made three times will be listed twice, and so on.[6]   □

When writing a correlated query it is important that we be aware of the *scoping rules* for names. In general, an attribute in a subquery belongs to one

---

[6]This example is the first occasion on which we've had to confront an important difference between relations in relational algebra and relations in SQL. All SQL relations may have duplicates; i.e., they are bags, not sets. There are several ways that duplicates may crop up in SQL relations. We shall discuss the matter in detail in Section 5.4.

of the tuple variables in that subquery's FROM clause if some tuple variable's relation has that attribute in its schema. If not, we look at the immediately surrounding subquery, then to the one surrounding that, and so on. Thus, year on line (4) and title on line (6) of Fig. 5.8 refer to the attributes of the tuple variable that ranges over all the tuples of the copy of relation Movie introduced on line (5) — that is, the copy of the Movie relation addressed by the subquery of lines (4) through (6).

However, we can arrange for an attribute to belong to another tuple variable if we prefix it by that tuple variable and a dot. That is why we introduced the alias Old for the Movie relation of the outer query, and why we refer to Old.title in line (6). Note that if the two relations in the FROM clauses of lines (2) and (5) were different, we would not need an alias. Rather, in the subquery we could refer directly to attributes of a relation mentioned in line (2).

5.3.5 Exercises for Section 5.3

Exercise 5.3.1: Write the following queries, based on the database schema

```
Product(maker, model, type)
PC(model, speed, ram, hd, cd, price)
Laptop(model, speed, ram, hd, screen, price)
Printer(model, color, type, price)
```

of Exercise 4.1.1. You should use at least one subquery in each of your answers and write each query in two significantly different ways (e.g., using different sets of the operators EXISTS, IN, ALL, and ANY).

* a) Find the makers of PC's with a speed of at least 160.

b) Find the printers with the highest price.

! c) Find the laptops whose speed is slower than that of any PC.

! d) Find the model number of the item (PC, laptop, or printer) with the highest price.

! e) Find the maker of the color printer with the lowest price.

!! f) Find the maker of the printer with the fastest processor among all those PC's that have the smallest amount of RAM.

Exercise 5.3.2: Write the following queries, based on the database schema

```
Classes(class, type, country, numGuns, bore, displacement)
Ships(name, class, launched)
Battles(name, date)
Outcomes(ship, battle, result)
```

of Exercise 4.1.3. You should use at least one subquery in each of your answers and write each query in two significantly different ways (e.g., using different sets of the operators EXISTS, IN, ALL, and ANY).

a) Find the countries whose ships had the largest number of guns.

*! b) Find the classes of ships at least one of which was sunk in a battle.

c) Find the names of the ships with a 16-inch bore.

d) Find the battles in which ships of the Kongo class participated.

!! e) Find the names of the ships whose number of guns was the largest for those ships of the same bore.

! **Exercise 5.3.3 :** Write the query of Fig. 5.8 without any subqueries.

! **Exercise 5.3.4 :** Consider expression $\pi_L(R_1 \bowtie R_2 \bowtie \cdots \bowtie R_n)$ of relational algebra, where L is a list of attributes all of which belong to R_1. Show that this expression can be written in SQL using subqueries only. More precisely, write an equivalent SQL expression where no FROM clause has more than one tuple variable in its list.

! **Exercise 5.3.5 :** Write the following queries without using the intersection or difference operators:

* a) The intersection query of Fig. 5.3.

b) The difference query of Example 5.15.

!! **Exercise 5.3.6 :** We have noticed that certain operators of SQL are redundant, in the sense that they always can be replaced by other operators. For example, we saw that s IN R can be replaced by s = ANY R. Show that EXISTS and NOT EXISTS are redundant by explaining how to replace any expression of the form EXISTS R or NOT EXISTS R by an expression that does not involve EXISTS (except perhaps in the expression represented by R). *Hint*: Although rarely used, it is permissible to have a constant in the SELECT clause.

5.4   Duplicates

The operations on relations we have studied so far have largely been tuple-at-a-time operations. The exceptions are the union, intersection, and difference operators discussed in Section 5.2.5. In this and the next section we shall study some operations that act on relations as a whole. Here, we deal with the fact that SQL uses relations that are bags rather than sets, and a tuple can appear more than once in a relation. We shall see how to force the result of an operation to be a set in Section 5.4.1, and in Section 5.4.2 we shall see that it is also possible to prevent the elimination of duplicates.

5.4.1 Eliminating Duplicates

As mentioned in Section 5.3.4, SQL's notion of relations differs from the abstract notion of relations presented in Chapter 3. A relation, being a set, cannot have more than one copy of any given tuple. When an SQL query creates a new relation, the SQL system does not ordinarily eliminate duplicates. Thus, the SQL response to a query may list the same tuple several times.

Recall from Section 5.2.4 that one of several equivalent definitions of the meaning of an SQL select-from-where query is that we begin with the Cartesian product of the relations referred to in the FROM clause. Each such tuple is tested by the condition in the WHERE clause, and the ones that pass the test are given to the output for projection according to the SELECT clause. This projection may cause the same tuple to result from different tuples of the product, and if so, each copy of the resulting tuple is printed in its turn. Further, since there is nothing wrong with an SQL relation having duplicates, the relations from which the Cartesian product is formed may have duplicates, and each identical copy is paired with the tuples from the other relations, yielding a proliferation of duplicates in the product.

If we do not wish duplicates to be created, then we may follow the keyword SELECT by the keyword DISTINCT. That word tells SQL to produce only one copy of any tuple. As a result, the answer is guaranteed to be duplicate-free.

Example 5.20: Let us reconsider the query of Fig. 5.7, where we asked for the producers of Harrison Ford's movies using no subqueries. As written, George Lucas will appear many times in the output. If we want only to see each producer once, we may change line (1) of the query to

```
1) SELECT DISTINCT name
```

Then, the list of producers will have duplicate occurrences of names eliminated before printing.

Incidentally, the query of Fig. 5.5, where we used subqueries, does not necessarily suffer from the problem of duplicate answers. True, the subquery at line (4) of Fig. 5.5 will produce the certificate number of George Lucas several times. However, in the "main" query of line (1), we examine each tuple of MovieExec once. Presumably, there is only one tuple for George Lucas in that relation, and if so, it is only this tuple that satisfies the WHERE clause of line (3). Thus, George Lucas is printed only once.   □

5.4.2 Duplicates in Unions, Intersections, and Differences

Unlike the SELECT statement, which preserves duplicates as a default and only eliminates them when instructed to by the DISTINCT keyword, the union, intersection, and difference operations, which we introduced in Section 5.2.5, normally eliminate duplicates. In order to prevent the elimination of duplicates, we must follow the operator UNION, INTERSECT, or EXCEPT by the keyword ALL.

The Cost of Duplicate Elimination

One might be tempted to place DISTINCT after every SELECT, on the theory that it is harmless. In fact, it is very expensive to eliminate duplicates from a relation. In general, the relation must be sorted so that identical tuples appear next to each other. Only by grouping the tuples in this way can we determine whether or not a given tuple should be eliminated. The time it takes to sort the relation so that duplicates may be eliminated is often greater than the time it takes to execute the query itself. Thus, duplicate elimination should be used judiciously if we want our queries to run fast.

If we do, then we get the bag semantics of these operators as was discussed in Section 4.6.2.

Example 5.21: Consider again the union expression from Example 5.16, but now add the keyword ALL, as:

```
(SELECT title, year FROM Movie)
    UNION ALL
(SELECT movieTitle AS title, movieYear AS year FROM StarsIn);
```

Now, a title and year will appear as many times in the result as it appears in each of the relations Movie and StarsIn put together. For instance, if a movie appeared once in the Movie relation and there were three stars for that movie listed in StarsIn (so the movie appeared in three different tuples of StarsIn), then that movie's title and year would appear four times in the result of the union. □

As for union, the operators INTERSECT ALL and EXCEPT ALL are intersection and difference of bags. Thus, if R and S are relations, then the result of expression

$$R \text{ INTERSECT ALL } S$$

is the relation in which the number of times a tuple t appears is the minimum of the number of times it appears in R and the number of times it appears in S.

The result of expression

$$R \text{ EXCEPT ALL } S$$

has tuple t as many times as the difference of the number of times it appears in R minus the number of times it appears in S, provided the difference is positive. Each of these definitions is what we discussed for bags in Section 4.6.2.

5.4.3 Exercises for Section 5.4

Exercise 5.4.1: Write each of the queries in Exercise 4.1.1 in SQL, making sure that duplicates are eliminated.

Exercise 5.4.2: Write each of the queries in Exercise 4.1.3 in SQL, making sure that duplicates are eliminated.

! **Exercise 5.4.3:** For each of your answers to Exercise 5.3.1, determine whether or not the result of your query can have duplicates. If so, rewrite the query to eliminate duplicates. If not, write a query without subqueries that has the same, duplicate-free answer.

! **Exercise 5.4.4:** Repeat Exercise 5.4.3 for your answers to Exercise 5.3.2.

5.5 Aggregation

Another class of operations that involve relations as a whole are those that aggregate values in a column. By *aggregation*, we mean an operation that forms a single value from the list of values appearing in the column. Examples are the sum or average of the values in a column. SQL not only allows us to aggregate columns, but we may also group the tuples of a relation according to some criterion, such as the value in some other column, and then aggregate within each group.

5.5.1 Aggregation Operators

SQL provides five operators that apply to a column of a relation and produce some summary or aggregation of that column. These operators are:

1. SUM, the sum of the values in this column.

2. AVG, the average of values in this column.

3. MIN, the least value in the column.

4. MAX, the greatest value in the column.

5. COUNT, the number of values (including duplicates unless they are explicitly eliminated with DISTINCT).

These operators are used by applying them to a scalar-valued expression, typically a column name, in a SELECT clause.

Example 5.22: The following query finds the average net worth of all movie executives:

```
SELECT AVG(netWorth)
FROM MovieExec;
```

Note that there is no `WHERE` clause at all, so the keyword `WHERE` is properly omitted. This query examines the `netWorth` column of the relation

```
MovieExec(name, address, cert#, netWorth)
```

sums the values found there, one value for each tuple (even if the tuple is a duplicate of some other tuple), and divides the sum by the number of tuples. If there are no duplicate tuples, then this query gives the average net worth as we expect. If there were duplicate tuples, then a movie executive whose tuple appeared n times would have his or her net worth counted n times in the average. □

Example 5.23: The following query

```
SELECT COUNT(*)
FROM MovieExec;
```

counts the number of tuples in the `MovieExec` relation. On the assumption that `name` is a key for `MovieExec` and that there are no duplicate tuples in the relation, that is the same as counting the number of movie executives mentioned in our database.

The use of the `COUNT` aggregation operator to apply to ∗ — that is, to a whole tuple — is something unique to `COUNT`. It does not make sense to apply any of the other aggregation operators to more than a single column.

If we want to be certain that we do not count duplicate tuples more than once, we can count the `name` attribute only and use the keyword `DISTINCT` before it, as:

```
SELECT COUNT(DISTINCT name)
FROM MovieExec;
```

Even if `name` were not a key (i.e., there could be two different tuples about the same movie executive, or there could be two executives with the same name), the above query would count each name only once. □

5.5.2 Grouping

Often we do not want simply the average or some other aggregation of a column. Rather, we need to consider the tuples of a relation in groups, corresponding to the value of one or more other columns. As an example, suppose we wanted to compute the total number of minutes of movies produced by each studio. Then we must group the tuples of the `Movie` relation according to their studio, and sum the `length` column within a group. We would also like the result to be a table relating studios to their sum, that is, a table like:

studio	SUM(length)
Disney	12345
MGM	54321
. . .	. . .

To produce a table such as the above, we use a `GROUP BY` clause, following the `WHERE` clause. The keywords `GROUP BY` are followed by a list of *grouping* attributes. In the simplest situation, there is only one relation reference in the `FROM` clause, and this relation has its tuples grouped according to their values in the grouping attributes. Whatever aggregation operators are used in the `SELECT` clause are applied only within groups.

Example 5.24: The problem of finding from the relation

    `Movie(title, year, length, inColor, studioName, producerC#)`

the sum of the lengths of all movies for each studio is expressed by

```
SELECT studioName, SUM(length)
FROM Movie
GROUP BY studioName;
```

We may imagine that the tuples of relation `Movie` are reorganized and grouped so that all the tuples for Disney studios are together, all those for MGM are together, and so on, as suggested in Fig. 5.9. The sums of the length components of all the tuples in each group are calculated, and for each group, the studio name is printed along with that sum.   □

studioName	
Disney Disney Disney	
MGM MGM	
○ ○ ○	

Figure 5.9: A relation with imaginary division into groups

Observe in Example 5.24 how the `SELECT` clause has two kinds of terms.

1. Aggregations, where an aggregate operator is applied to an attribute or expression involving an attribute. As mentioned, these terms are evaluated on a per-group basis.

2. Attributes, such as `studioName` in this example, that appear in the `GROUP BY` clause. In a `SELECT` clause that has aggregations, only those attributes that are mentioned in the `GROUP BY` clause may appear unaggregated in the `SELECT` clause.

While queries involving `GROUP BY` generally have both grouping attributes and aggregations in the `SELECT` clause, it is technically not necessary to have both. For example, we could write

```
SELECT studioName
FROM Movie
GROUP BY studioName
```

This query would group the tuples of `Movie` according to their studio name and then print the studio name for each group, no matter how many tuples there are with a given studio name. Thus, the above query has the same effect as

```
SELECT DISTINCT studioName
FROM Movie
```

It is also possible to use a `GROUP BY` clause in a query about several relations. Such a query is interpreted by the following sequence of steps:

1. Evaluate the relation R implied by the `FROM` and `WHERE` clauses. That is, relation R is the Cartesian product of the relations mentioned in the `FROM` clause, to which the selection of the `WHERE` clause is applied.

2. Group the tuples of R according to the attributes in the `GROUP BY` clause.

3. Produce as a result the attributes and aggregations of the `SELECT` clause, as if the query were about relation R.

Example 5.25: Suppose we wish to print a table listing each producer's total length of film produced. We need to get information from the two relations

```
Movie(title, year, length, inColor, studioName, producerC#)
MovieExec(name, address, cert#, netWorth)
```

so we begin by taking their theta-join, equating the certificate numbers from the two relations. That step gives us a relation in which each `MovieExec` tuple is paired with the `Movie` tuples for all the movies of that producer. Now, we can group the selected tuples of this relation according to the name of the producer. Finally, we sum the lengths of the movies in each group. The query is shown in Fig. 5.10. □

5.5.3 HAVING Clauses

Suppose that we did not wish to include all of the producers in our table of Example 5.25. We could restrict the tuples prior to grouping in a way that would make undesired groups empty. For instance, if we only wanted the total length of movies for producers with a net worth of more than $10,000,000, we could change line (3) of Fig. 5.10 to

```
1) SELECT name, SUM(length)
2) FROM MovieExec, Movie
3) WHERE producerC# = cert#
4) GROUP BY name;
```

Figure 5.10: Computing the length of movies for each producer

```
3) WHERE producerC# = cert# AND networth >= 10000000
```

However, sometimes we want to choose our groups based on some aggregate property of the group itself. Then we follow the GROUP BY clause with a HAVING clause. The latter clause consists of the keyword HAVING followed by a condition about the group.

Example 5.26: Suppose we want to print the total film length for only those producers who made at least one film prior to 1930. We may append to Fig. 5.10 the clause

```
HAVING MIN(year) < 1930
```

The resulting query, shown in Fig. 5.11, would remove from the grouped relation all those groups in which every tuple had a year component 1930 or higher. □

```
SELECT name, SUM(length)
FROM MovieExec, Movie
WHERE producerC# = cert#
GROUP BY name
HAVING MIN(year) < 1930;
```

Figure 5.11: Computing the total length of film for early producers

5.5.4 Exercises for Section 5.5

Exercise 5.5.1: Write the following queries, based on the database schema

```
Product(maker, model, type)
PC(model, speed, ram, hd, cd, price)
Laptop(model, speed, ram, hd, screen, price)
Printer(model, color, type, price)
```

of Exercise 4.1.1, and evaluate your queries using the data of that exercise.

Order of Clauses in SQL Queries

We have now met all six clauses that can appear in an SQL "select-from-where" query: SELECT, FROM, WHERE, GROUP BY, HAVING, and ORDER BY. Only the first two are required. Whichever additional clauses appear must be in the order listed above.

---

* a) Find the average speed of PC's.

  b) Find the average speed of laptops costing over $2500.

  c) Find the average price of PC's made by manufacturer "A."

! d) Find the average price of PC's and laptops made by manufacturer "D."

  e) Find, for each different speed the average price of a PC.

*! f) Find for each manufacturer, the average screen size of its laptops.

! g) Find the manufacturers that make at least three different models of PC.

! h) Find for each manufacturer the maximum price of a PC.

*! i) Find for each speed of PC above 150 the average price.

!! j) Find the average hard disk size of a PC for all those manufacturers that make printers.

Exercise 5.5.2 : Write the following queries, based on the database schema

```
Classes(class, type, country, numGuns, bore, displacement)
Ships(name, class, launched)
Battles(name, date)
Outcomes(ship, battle, result)
```

of Exercise 4.1.3, and evaluate your queries using the data of that exercise.

  a) Find the number of battleship classes.

  b) Find the average number of guns of battleship classes.

! c) Find the average number of guns of battleships. Note the difference between (b) and (c); do we weight a class by the number of ships of that class ot not?

! d) Find for each class the year in which the first ship of that class was launched.

! e) Find for each class the number of ships of that class sunk in battle.

!! f) Find for each class with at least three ships the number of ships of that class sunk in battle.

!! g) The weight (in pounds) of the shell fired from a naval gun is approximately one half the cube of the bore (in inches). Find the average weight of the shell for each country's ships.

5.6 Database Modifications

To this point, we have focused on the normal SQL query form: the select-from-where statement. There are a number of other statement forms that do not return a result, but rather change the state of the database. In this section, we shall focus on three types of statements that allow us to

1. Insert tuples into a relation.

2. Delete certain tuples from a relation.

3. Update values of certain components of certain existing tuples.

We refer to these three types of operations collectively as *modifications*.

5.6.1 Insertion

The basic form of insertion statement consists of:

1. The keywords INSERT INTO,

2. The name of a relation R,

3. A parenthesized list of attributes of the relation R,

4. The keyword VALUES, and

5. A tuple expression, that is, a parenthesized list of concrete values, one for each attribute in the list (3).

That is, the basic insertion form is

$$\text{INSERT INTO } R(A_1, \ldots, A_n) \text{ VALUES } (v_1, \ldots, v_n);$$

A tuple is created using the value v_i for attribute A_i, for $i = 1, 2, \ldots, n$. If the list of attributes does not include all attributes of the relation R, then the tuple created has default values for all missing attributes. Default values are discussed in Section 5.7.5. The most common default value is NULL, as we discussed earlier is Section 4.7.4, and which we discuss further in the context of SQL in Section 5.9. For the moment we can think of NULL as a value that serves as a placeholder when the correct value of a component is unknown.

Example 5.27: Suppose we wish to add Sydney Greenstreet to the list of stars of *The Maltese Falcon*. We say:

```
1) INSERT INTO StarsIn(movieTitle, movieYear, starName)
2) VALUES('The Maltese Falcon', 1942, 'Sydney Greenstreet');
```

The effect of executing this statement is that a tuple with the three components on line (2) is inserted into the relation `StarsIn`. Since all attributes of `StarsIn` are mentioned on line (1), there is no need to add default components. The values on line (2) are matched with the attributes on line (1) in the order given, so `'The Maltese Falcon'` becomes the value of the component for attribute `movieTitle`, and so on. □

If, as in Example 5.27, we provide values for all attributes of the relation, then we may omit the list of attributes that follows the relation name. That is, we could just say:

```
INSERT INTO StarsIn
VALUES('The Maltese Falcon', 1942, 'Sydney Greenstreet');
```

However, if we take this option, we must be sure that the order of the values is the same as the standard order of attributes for the relation. We shall see in Section 5.7 how relation schemas are declared, and we shall see that as we do so we provide an order for the attributes. This order is assumed when matching values to attributes, if the list of attributes is missing from an `INSERT` statement. If you are not sure of the standard order for the attributes, it is best to list them in the order you prefer.

The simple `INSERT` described above only puts one tuple into a relation. Instead of using explicit values for one tuple, we can compute a set of tuples to be inserted, using a subquery. This subquery replaces the keyword `VALUES` and the tuple expression in the `INSERT` statement form described above.

Example 5.28: Suppose we want to add to the relation

```
Studio(name, address, presC#)
```

all movie studios that are mentioned in the relation

```
Movie(title, year, length, inColor, studioName, producerC#)
```

but do not appear in `Studio`. Since there is no way to determine an address or a president for such a studio, we shall have to be content with value `NULL` for attributes `address` and `presC#` in the inserted `Studio` tuples. A way to make this insertion is shown in Fig. 5.12.

Like most nested SQL statements, Fig. 5.12 is easiest to examine from the inside out. Lines (5) and (6) generate all the studio names in the relation `Studio`. Thus, line (4) tests that a studio name from the `Movie` relation is none of these studios.

```
1) INSERT INTO Studio(name)
2)     SELECT DISTINCT studioName
3)     FROM Movie
4)     WHERE studioName NOT IN
5)         (SELECT name
6)          FROM Studio);
```

Figure 5.12: Adding new studios

Now, we see that lines (2) through (6) produce the set of studio names found in Movie but not in Studio. The use of DISTINCT on line (2) assures that each studio will appear only once in this set, no matter how many movies it is associated with. Finally, line (1) inserts each of these studios, with NULL for the attributes address and presC#, into relation Studios. □

5.6.2 Deletion

A deletion statement consists of:

1. The keywords DELETE FROM,

2. The name of a relation, say R,

3. The keyword WHERE, and

4. A condition.

That is, the form of a deletion is

DELETE FROM R WHERE <condition>;

The effect of executing this statement is that every tuple satisfying the condition (4) will be deleted from relation R.

Example 5.29: We can delete from relation

StarsIn(movieTitle, movieYear, starName)

the fact that Sydney Greenstreet was a star in *The Maltese Falcon* by the SQL statement:

```
DELETE FROM StarsIn
WHERE movieTitle = 'The Maltese Falcon' AND
      movieYear = 1942 AND
      starName = 'Sydney Greenstreet';
```

The Timing of Insertions

Figure 5.12 illustrates a subtle point about the semantics of SQL statements. In principle, the evaluation of the query of lines (2) through (6) should be accomplished prior to executing the insertion of line (1). Thus, there is no possibility that new tuples added to Studio at line (1) will affect the condition on line (4). However, for efficiency purposes, it is possible that an implementation will execute this statement so that changes to Studio are made as soon as new studios are found, during the execution of lines (2) through (6).

In this particular example, it does not matter whether or not insertions are delayed until the query is completely evaluated. However, there are other queries where the result can be changed by varying the timing of insertions. For cxample, supposed DISTINCT were removed from line (2) of Fig. 5.12. If we evaluate the query of lines (2) through (6) before doing any insertion, then a new studio name appearing in several Movie tuples would appear several times in the result of this query and therefore would be inserted several times into relation Studio. However, if we inserted new studios into Studio as soon as we found them during the evaluation of the query of lines (2) through (6), then the same new studio would not be inserted twice. Rather, as soon as the new studio was inserted once, its name would no longer satisfy the condition of lines (4) through (6), and it would not appear a second time in the result of the query of lines (2) through (6).

Notice that unlike the insertion statement of Example 5.27, we cannot simply specify a tuple to be deleted. Rather, we must describe the tuple exactly by a WHERE clause.   □

Example 5.30: Here is another example of a deletion. This time, we delete from relation

```
MovieExec(name, address, cert#, netWorth)
```

several tuples at once by using a condition that can be satisfied by more than one tuple. The statement

```
DELETE FROM MovieExec
WHERE netWorth < 10000000;
```

deletes all movie executives whose net worth is low — less than ten million dollars.   □

Insertion, Deletion, and Duplicates

There are some tricky points about how insertions and deletions interact with the duplicates that are permitted in SQL relations. First, an insertion adds the specified tuple or tuples, regardless of whether they exist in the relation prior to the insertion. Thus, if there were already a `StarsIn` tuple for *The Maltese Falcon* and Sydney Greenstreet, the insertion of Example 5.27 would add another copy of the same tuple. If we followed the insertion by the deletion of Example 5.29, both tuples would satisfy the condition of the `WHERE` clause, and therefore both tuples would be deleted. One surprising consequence is that this insertion followed by this deletion leaves the relation `StarsIn` different from what it was before the two operations. Another is that the deletion statement, which appears to describe a single tuple to be deleted, in fact deletes more than one tuple. In fact, there is no way whatsoever in SQL to delete only one of a pair of identical tuples.

5.6.3 Updates

While we might think of both insertions and deletions of tuples as "updates" to the database, an *update* in SQL is a very specific kind of change to the database: one or more tuples that already exist in the database have some of their components changed. The general form of an update statement is:

1. The keyword UPDATE,

2. A relation name, say R,

3. The keyword SET,

4. A list of formulas that each set an attribute of the relation R equal to the value of an expression or constant,

5. The keyword WHERE, and

6. A condition.

That is, the form of an update is

       UPDATE R SET <new-value assignments> WHERE <condition>;

Each new-value assignment (item 4 above) is an attribute, an equal sign, and a formula. If there is more than one assignment, they are separated by commas.

The effect of this statement is to find all the tuples in R that satisfy the condition (6). Each of these tuples are then changed by having the formulas of (4) evaluated and assigned to the components of the tuple for the corresponding attributes of R.

Example 5.31: Let us modify the relation

```
MovieExec(name, address, cert#, netWorth)
```

by prepending the title **Pres.** in front of every movie executive who is the president of a studio. The condition the desired tuples satisfy is that their certificate numbers appear in the **presC#** component of some tuple in the **Studio** relation. We express this update as:

```
1) UPDATE MovieExec
2) SET name = 'Pres. ' || name
3) WHERE cert# IN (SELECT presC# FROM Studio);
```

Line (3) tests whether the certificate number from the **MovieExec** tuple is one of those that appear as a president's certificate number in **Studio**.

Line (2) performs the update on the selected tuples. Recall that the operator || denotes concatenation of strings, so the expression following the = sign in line (2) places the characters **Pres.** and a blank in front of the old value of the **name** component of this tuple. The new string becomes the value of the **name** component of this tuple; the effect is that '**Pres. '** has been prepended to the old value of **name**.   □

5.6.4   Exercises for Section 5.6

Exercise 5.6.1: Write the following database modifications, based on the database schema

```
Product(maker, model, type)
PC(model, speed, ram, hd, cd, price)
Laptop(model, speed, ram, hd, screen, price)
Printer(model, color, type, price)
```

of Exercise 4.1.1. Describe the effect of the modifications on the data of that exercise.

a) Using two **INSERT** statements store in the database the fact that PC model 1100 is made by manufacturer C, has speed 240, RAM 32, hard disk 2.5, a 12x CD, and sells for $2499.

! b) Insert the facts that for every PC there is a laptop with the same speed, RAM, and hard disk, an 8x CD, a model number 1100 greater, and a price $500 more.

c) Delete all PC's with less that 2 gigabytes of hard disk.

d) Delete all Laptops made by a manufacturer that doesn't make printers.

e) Manufacturer A buys manufacturer B. Change all products made by B so they are now made by A.

f) For each PC, double the amount of RAM and add one gigabyte to the amount of hard disk. (Remember that several attributes can be changed by one UPDATE statement.)

! g) For each laptop made by manufacturer E, add one inch to the screen size and subtract $100 from the price.

Exercise 5.6.2: Write the following database modifications, based on the database schema

```
Classes(class, type, country, numGuns, bore, displacement)
Ships(name, class, launched)
Battles(name, date)
Outcomes(ship, battle, result)
```

of Exercise 4.1.3. Describe the effect of the modifications on the data of that exercise.

* a) The two British battleships of the Nelson class — Nelson and Rodney — were both launched in 1927, had nine 16-inch guns, and a displacement of 34,000 tons. Insert these facts into the database.

 b) Two of the three battleships of the Italian Vittorio Veneto class — Vittorio Veneto and Italia — were launched in 1940; the third ship of that class, Roma, was launched in 1942. Each had nine 15-inch guns and a displacement of 41,000 tons. Insert these facts into the database.

* c) Delete from Ships all ships sunk in battle.

* d) Modify the Classes relation so that gun bores are measured in centimeters (one inch = 2.5 centimeters) and displacements are measured in metric tons (one metric ton = 1.1 tons).

 e) Delete all classes with fewer than three ships.

5.7 Defining a Relation Schema in SQL

In this section we shall begin a discussion of *data definition*, the portions of SQL that involve describing the structure of information in the database. In contrast, the aspects of SQL discussed previously — queries and modifications — are often called *data manipulation*.

The subject of this section is declaration of relation schemas. We shall see how to describe a new relation or *table* as it is called in SQL. Some of the aspects that we shall be able to describe are the attribute names, the data types for attributes, and some limited types of constraints such as keyness. Section 5.8 covers "views," which are virtual relations that are not really stored in the database, while some of the more complex issues regarding constraints on relations are deferred to Chapter 6.

5.7.1   Data Types

To begin, let us introduce the principal data types that are supported by SQL systems. All attributes must have a data type.

1. Character strings of fixed or varying length. The type CHAR(n) denotes a fixed-length string of n characters. That is, if an attribute has type CHAR(n), then in any tuple the component for this attribute will be a string of n characters. VARCHAR(n) denotes a string of up to n characters. Components for an attribute of this type will be strings of between 0 and n characters. SQL permits reasonable coercions between values of character-string types. Normally, a string is padded by trailing blanks if it becomes the value of a component that is a fixed-length string of greater length. For example, the string 'foo', if it became the value of a component for an attribute of type CHAR(5), would assume the value 'foo ' (with two blanks following the second o). The padding blanks can then be ignored if the value of this component were compared (see Section 5.1.3) with another string.

2. Bit strings of fixed or varying length. These are analogous to fixed and varying-length character strings, but their values are strings of bits rather than characters. The type BIT(n) denotes bit strings of length n, while BIT VARYING(n) denotes bit strings of length up to n.

3. The type INT or INTEGER (these names are synonyms) denotes typical integer values. The type SHORTINT also denotes integers, but the number of bits permitted may be less, depending on the implementation (as with the types int and short int in C).

4. Floating-point numbers can be represented in a variety of ways. We may use the type FLOAT or REAL (these are synonyms) for typical floating-point numbers. A higher precision can be obtained with the type DOUBLE PRECISION; again the distinction between these types is as in C. SQL also has types that are real numbers with a fixed decimal point. For example, DECIMAL(n,d) allows values that consist of n decimal digits, with the decimal point assumed to be d positions from the right. Thus, 0123.45 is a possible value of type DECIMAL(6,2).

5. Dates and times can be represented by the data types DATE and TIME, respectively. Recall our discussion of date and time values in Section 5.1.4. These values are essentially character strings of a special form. We may, in fact, coerce dates and times to string types, and we may do the reverse if the string "makes sense" as a date or time.

5.7.2   Simple Table Declarations

The simplest form of declaration of a relation schema consists of the keywords CREATE TABLE followed by the name of the relation and a parenthesized list of the attribute names and their types.

Example 5.32 : The relation schema for our example `MovieStar` relation, which was described informally in Section 3.9, could be created as an SQL table by the statement of Fig. 5.13. The first two attributes, `name` and `address`, have each been declared to be character strings. However, with the name, we have made the decision to use a fixed-length string of 30 characters, padding a name out with blanks at the end if necessary and truncating a name to 30 characters if it is longer. In contrast, we have declared addresses to be variable-length character strings of up to 255 characters.[7] It is not clear that these two choices are the best possible, but we use them to illustrate two kinds of string data types.

```
1)  CREATE TABLE MovieStar (
2)      name CHAR(30),
3)      address VARCHAR(255),
4)      gender CHAR(1),
5)      birthdate DATE
    );
```

Figure 5.13: Declaring the relation schema for the `MovieStar` relation

The `gender` attribute has values that are a single letter, M or F. Thus, we can safely use a single character as the type of this attribute. Finally, the `birthdate` attribute naturally deserves the data type `DATE`. If this type were not available in a system that did not conform to the SQL2 standard, we could use `CHAR(10)` instead, since all `DATE` values are actually strings of 10 characters: eight digits and two hyphens. □

5.7.3 Deleting Tables

A relation that is created as part of a long-lived database is typically created once and populated with tuples over a period of years. The relation might be *bulk loaded* by translating existing data that is in some form other than an SQL table into a sequence of insertion commands; possibly the DBMS provides a bulk-load facility for this purpose. In addition, the relation might evolve over time, accumulating tuples day by day. For example, the `Movie` relation might be bulk loaded initially from some earlier database and then kept up-to-date by `INSERT` operations each time a new movie is released.

---

[7]The number 255 is not the result of some weird notion of what typical addresses look like. A single byte can store integers between 0 and 255, so it is possible to represent a varying-length character string of up to 255 bytes by a single byte for the count of characters plus the bytes to store the string itself. Commercial systems generally support longer varying-length strings, however.

However, there are times when we wish to delete a relation from the database schema. As conditions change, it might become unnecessary to maintain the information in the table. Or the relation might be temporary, perhaps as an intermediate result in some complex query that cannot be expressed as a single SQL statement. If that is the case, we can delete a relation R by the SQL statement

```
DROP R;
```

5.7.4 Modifying Relation Schemas

More frequently than we would drop a relation that is part of a long-lived database, we may be forced to modify the schema of an existing relation. These modifications are done by a statement that begins with the keywords ALTER TABLE and the name of the relation. We then have several options, the most important of which are

1. ADD followed by a column name and its data type.

2. DROP followed by a column name.

Example 5.33: Thus, for instance, we could modify the MovieStar relation by adding an attribute phone with

```
ALTER TABLE MovieStar ADD phone CHAR(16);
```

As a result, the MovieStar scheme now has five attributes, the four mentioned in Fig. 5.13 and the attribute phone, which is a fixed-length string of 16 bytes. In the actual relation, tuples would all have components for phone, but we know of no phone numbers to put there. Thus, the value of each of these components would be NULL. In Section 5.7.5, we shall see how it is possible to choose another "default" value to be used instead of NULL for unknown values.

As another example, we could delete the birthdate attribute by

```
ALTER TABLE MovieStar DROP birthdate;
```

□

5.7.5 Default Values

When we create or modify tuples, we sometimes do not have values for all components. For example, we mentioned above that when we add a column to a relation scheme, the existing tuples do not have a known value, and it was suggested that the special value NULL could be used in place of a "real" value. Or, we suggested in Example 5.28 that we could insert new tuples into the Studio relation knowing only the studio name and not the address or president's certificate number. Again, it would be necessary to use some value that says "I don't know" in place of real values for the latter two attributes.

To address these problems, SQL provides the NULL value. This value becomes the value of any component that is not given a specific value, with the exception of some situations where the NULL value is not permitted (see Section 6.2). However, there are times when we would prefer to use another choice of *default* value, the value that is placed in a component if no other value is known.

In general, any place we declare an attribute and its data type, we may add the keyword DEFAULT and an appropriate value. That value is either NULL or a constant. Certain other values that are provided by the system, such as the current time, may also be options.

Example 5.34: Let us consider Example 5.32. We might wish to use the character ? as the default for an unknown gender, and we might also wish to use the earliest possible date, DATE '0000-00-00' for an unknown birthdate. We could replace lines (4) and (5) of Fig. 5.13 by:

```
4)      gender CHAR(1) DEFAULT '?',
5)      birthdate DATE DEFAULT DATE '0000-00-00'
```

As another example, we could have declared the default value for new attribute phone to be 'unlisted' when we added this attribute in Example 5.33. The alteration statement would then look like:

```
ALTER TABLE MovieStar ADD phone CHAR(16) DEFAULT 'unlisted';
```

□

5.7.6 Domains

So far, we have defined for each attribute a data type. An alternative is to define first a *domain*, which is a new name for a data type. Other information, such as a default value or constraints on values that we shall discuss in Section 6.3.3, may also be declared for a domain. Then, when we declare the attribute, we may follow its name by the domain name instead of a data type. Several attributes may use the same domain, tying them together in a useful way. For example, if we use the same domain for two attributes, then we know a value of one can always be a value of the other.

The form of a domain definition is the keywords CREATE DOMAIN, the name of the domain, the keyword AS, and a datatype. That is, a domain is declared by:

```
CREATE DOMAIN <name> AS <type description>;
```

This material may be followed by a default declaration and also by other constraints on the domain that we shall discuss in Section 6.3.3.

Example 5.35 : Let us define a domain `MovieDomain` for the titles of movies. This domain can be used for attribute `title` of relation `Movie` and also for `movieTitle` in `StarsIn`. Here is a possible definition for this domain.

```
CREATE DOMAIN MovieDomain AS VARCHAR(50) DEFAULT 'unknown';
```

Thus, the values of the domain `MovieDomain` are variable-length character strings of length up to 50, and the default for an unknown title is `'unknown'`.

When we declare the schema for relation `Movie`, we can declare attribute `title` by:

```
title MovieDomain
```

rather than the equivalent

```
title VARCHAR(50) DEFAULT 'unknown'
```

Similarly, we can declare attribute `movieTitle` of relation `StarsIn` by

```
movieTitle MovieDomain
```

☐

It is possible to change the default for a domain with a statement such as

```
ALTER DOMAIN MovieDomain SET DEFAULT 'no such title';
```

This change replaces the default `'unknown'`, which we just declared in Example 5.35 for domain `MovieDomain`, by the string `'no such title'`. Other alteration options are available, for example regarding constraints on the domain, which we discuss in Chapter 6.

We can delete a domain definition with a statement such as

```
DROP DOMAIN MovieDomain;
```

The effect will be to make this domain no longer available for declarations of attributes. However, attributes already defined using this domain will continue to have the same type and default as they had before dropping the domain.

5.7.7 Indexes

An *index* on an attribute A of a relation is a data structure that makes it efficient to find those tuples that have a fixed value for attribute A. Indexes usually help with queries in which their attribute A is compared with a constant, for instance $A = 3$, or even $A \leq 3$. When relations are very large, it becomes expensive to scan all the tuples of a relation to find those (perhaps very few) tuples that match a given condition. For example, consider the first query we examined:

```
SELECT *
FROM Movie
WHERE studioName = 'Disney' AND year = 1990;
```

from Example 5.1. There might be 10,000 Movie tuples, of which only 200 were made in 1990.

The naive way to implement this query is to get all 10,000 tuples and test the condition of the WHERE clause on each. It would be much more efficient if we had some way of getting only the 200 tuples from the year 1990 and testing each of them to see if the studio was Disney. It would be even more efficient if we could obtain directly only the 10 or so tuples that satisfied both the conditions of the WHERE clause — that the studio be Disney and the year be 1990 — but that is more than we can expect from commonly used data structures.

Although the creation of indexes is not part of any SQL standard up to and including SQL2, most commercial systems have a way for the database designer to say that the system should create an index on a certain attribute for a certain relation. The following syntax is typical. Suppose we want to have an index on attribute year for the relation Movie. Then we say:

```
CREATE INDEX YearIndex ON Movie(year);
```

The result will be that an index whose name is YearIndex will be created on attribute year of the relation Movie. Henceforth, SQL queries that specify a year may be executed by the SQL query processor in such a way that only those tuples of Movie with the specified year are ever examined, with a resulting decrease in the time needed to answer the query.

Often, a *multiattribute index* is also available. This index takes values for several variables and efficiently finds the tuples with the given values for these variables. It might seem that multiattribute indexes are less useful than single-attribute indexes, since the latter might be used when the former does not have values a value for each of its attributes. However, multiattribute indexes home in on desired tuples more efficiently when they can be used.

Example 5.36 : Since title and year form a key for Movie, we might expect that it is common that values for both these attributes will be specified, or neither will. The following is a typical declaration of an index on these two attributes:

```
CREATE INDEX KeyIndex ON Movie(title, year);
```

Since (title, year) is a key, then when we are given a title and year, we know the index will find only one tuple, and that will be the desired tuple. In contrast, if the query specifies both the title and year, but only YearIndex is available, then the best the system can do is retrieve all the movies of that year and check through them for the given title.

If we had an index on title alone, we are in better shape than if the index were on year alone. The reason is that there are many movies of a given year but typically very few movies with a given title. In this particular example, retrieving all with a given title and then examining them for the given year takes little more time than using the multiattribute index on both `title` and `year`. □

If we wish to delete the index, we simply use its name in a statement like:

```
DROP INDEX YearIndex;
```

Selection of indexes requires a trade-off by the database designer.

- The existence of an index on an attribute greatly speeds up queries in which a value for that attribute is specified.

- On the other hand, every index built for an attribute of some relation makes insertions, deletions, and updates to that relation more complex and time-consuming.

Index selection is one of the hardest parts of database design, since it requires estimating what the typical mix of queries and other operations on the database will be. If a relation is queried much more frequently than it is modified, then indexes on the attributes most frequently specified makes sense. If modifications are the predominant action, then we should be very conservative about creating indexes. Even then, it may be an efficiency gain to create an index on a frequently used attribute. In fact, since some modification commands involve querying the database (e.g., an `INSERT` with a select-from-where subquery or a `DELETE` with a condition) one must be very careful how one estimates the relative frequency of modifications and queries.

5.7.8 Exercises for Section 5.7

* **Exercise 5.7.1:** In this section, we gave a formal declaration for only the relation `MovieStar` among the five relations of our running example. Give suitable declarations for the other four relations:

```
Movie(title, year, length, inColor, studioName, producerC#)
StarsIn(movieTitle, movieYear, starName)
MovieExec(name, address, cert#, netWorth)
Studio(name, address, presC#)
```

Exercise 5.7.2: Below we repeat once again the informal database schema from Exercise 4.1.1.

```
Product(maker, model, type)
PC(model, speed, ram, hd, cd, price)
Laptop(model, speed, ram, hd, screen, price)
Printer(model, color, type, price)
```

Write the following declarations:

  a) A suitable schema for relation `Product`.

  b) A suitable schema for relation `PC`.

* c) A suitable schema for relation `Laptop`.

  d) A suitable schema for relation `Printer`.

  e) A suitable definition for a domain `ModelType` whose values are model numbers. Show how to use this domain in your schemas of (a) through (d).

* f) An alteration to your `Laptop` schema from (c) to add the attribute `cd`. Let the default value for this attribute be `'none'` if the laptop does not have a CD reader.

  g) An alteration to your `Printer` schema from (d) to delete the attribute `color`.

Exercise 5.7.3: Here is the informal schema from Exercise 4.1.3.

```
Classes(class, type, country, numGuns, bore, displacement)
Ships(name, class, launched)
Battles(name, date)
Outcomes(ship, battle, result)
```

Write the following declarations:

  a) A suitable schema for relation `Classes`.

  b) A suitable schema for relation `Ships`.

  c) A suitable schema for relation `Battles`.

  d) A suitable schema for relation `Outcomes`.

  e) A suitable definition of a domain `ShipNames` that can be used for both ship and class names. Modify your schemas from (a), (b), and (c) to use this domain.

  f) An alteration to your `Ships` relation from (b) to include the attribute `yard` giving the shipyard where the ship was built.

  g) An alteration to your `Classes` relation from (a) to delete the attribute `bore`.

! **Exercise 5.7.4:** Explain the difference between the statement

```
DROP R;
```

and the statement

```
DELETE FROM R;
```

5.8   View Definitions

Relations that are defined with a `CREATE TABLE` statement actually exist in the database. That is, an SQL system stores tables in some physical organization. They are persistent, in the sense that they can be expected to exist indefinitely and not to change unless they are explicitly told to change by an `INSERT` or one of the other modification statements we discussed in Section 5.6.

There is another class of SQL relations, called *views*, that do not exist physically. Rather, they are defined by an expression much like a query. Views, in turn, can be queried as if they existed physically, and in some cases, we can even modify views.

5.8.1   Declaring Views

The simplest form of view definition is

1. The keywords `CREATE VIEW`,

2. The name of the view,

3. The keyword `AS`, and

4. A query Q. This query is the definition of the view. Any time we query the view, SQL behaves as if Q were executed at that time and the query applied to the relation produced by Q.

That is, a simple view declaration has the form

                 `CREATE VIEW` <view-name> `AS` <view-definition>;

Example 5.37: Suppose we want to have a view that is a part of the

        `Movie(title, year, length, inColor, studioName, producerC#)`

relation, specifically, the titles and years of the movies made by Paramount Studios. We can define this view by

```
1)  CREATE VIEW ParamountMovie AS
2)      SELECT title, year
3)      FROM Movie
4)      WHERE studioName = 'Paramount';
```

First, the name of the view is `ParamountMovie`, as we see from line (1). The attributes of the view are those listed in line (2), namely `title` and `year`. The definition of the view is lines (2) through (4).   □

> ## Relations, Tables, and Views
>
> SQL programmers tend to use the term "table" instead of "relation." The reason is that it is important to make a distinction between stored relations, which are "tables," and virtual relations, which are "views." Now that we know the distinction between a table and a view, we shall use "relation" only where either a table or view could be used. When we want to emphasize that a relation is stored, rather than a view, we shall sometimes use the term "base relation" or "base table."
>
> There is also a third kind of relation, one that is neither a view nor stored permanently. These relations are temporary results, as might be constructed for some subquery. Temporaries will also be referred to as "relations" subsequently.

5.8.2 Querying Views

Relation `ParamountMovie` does not contain tuples in the usual sense. Rather, if we query `ParamountMovie`, the appropriate tuples are obtained from the base table `Movie`, so the query can be answered. As a result, we can ask the same query about `ParamountMovie` twice and get different answers, even though we appear not to have changed `ParamountMovie`, because the base table may have changed in the interim.

Example 5.38: We may query the view `ParamountMovie` just as if it were a stored table, for instance:

```
SELECT title
FROM ParamountMovie
WHERE year = 1979;
```

The definition of the view `ParamountMovie` is used to turn the query above into a new query that addresses only the base table `Movie`. We shall illustrate how to convert queries on views to queries on base tables in Section 5.8.5. However, in this simple case it is not hard to deduce what the example query about the view means. We observe that `ParamountMovie` differs from `Movie` in only two ways:

1. Only attributes `title` and `year` are produced by `ParamountMovie`.

2. The condition `studioName = 'Paramount'` is part of any `WHERE` clause about `ParamountMovie`.

Since our query wants only the `title` produced, (1) does not present a problem. For (2), we need only to introduce the condition `studioName = 'Paramount'` into the `WHERE` clause of our query. Then, we can use `Movie` in place of

ParamountMovie in the FROM clause, assured that the meaning of our query is preserved. Thus, the query:

```
SELECT title
FROM Movie
WHERE studioName = 'Paramount' AND year = 1979;
```

is a query about the base table Movie that has the same effect as our original query about the view ParamountMovie. Note that it is the job of the SQL system to do this translation. We show the reasoning process only to indicate what a query about a view means. □

Example 5.39 : It is also possible to write queries involving both views and base tables. An example is

```
SELECT DISTINCT starName
FROM ParamountMovie, StarsIn
WHERE title = movieTitle AND year = movieYear;
```

This query asks for the name of all stars of movies made by Paramount. Note that the use of DISTINCT assures that stars will be listed only once, even if they appeared in several Paramount movies. □

Example 5.40 : Let us consider a more complicated query used to define a view. Our goal is a relation MovieProd with movie titles and the names of their producers. The query defining the view involves both relation

```
Movie(title, year, length, inColor, studioName, producerC#)
```

from which we get a producer's certificate number, and the relation

```
MovieExec(name, address, cert#, netWorth)
```

where we connect the certificate to the name. We may write:

```
1) CREATE VIEW MovieProd AS
2)     SELECT title, name
3)     FROM Movie, MovieExec
4)     WHERE producerC# = cert#;
```

We can query this view as if it were a stored relation. For instance, to find the producer of *Gone With the Wind*, ask:

```
SELECT name
FROM MovieProd
WHERE title = 'Gone With the Wind';
```

As with any view, this query is treated as if it were an equivalent query over the base tables alone, such as:

```
SELECT name
FROM Movie, MovieExec
WHERE producerC# = cert# AND title = 'Gone With the Wind';
```

□

5.8.3 Renaming Attributes

Sometimes, we might prefer to give a view's attributes names of our own choosing, rather than use the names that come out of the query defining the view. We may specify the attributes of the view by listing them, surrounded by parentheses, after the name of the view in the CREATE VIEW statement. For instance, we could rewrite the view definition of Example 5.40 as:

```
CREATE VIEW MovieProd(movieTitle, prodName) AS
    SELECT title, name
    FROM Movie, MovieExec
    WHERE producerC# = cert#;
```

The view is the same, but its columns are headed by attributes movieTitle and prodName instead of title and name.

5.8.4 Modifying Views

In limited circumstances it is possible to execute an insertion, deletion, or update to a view. At first, this idea makes no sense at all, since the view does not exist the way a base table (stored relation) does. What could it mean, say, to insert a new tuple into a view? Where would the tuple go, and how would the database system remember that it was supposed to be in the view?

For many views, the answer is simply "you can't do that." However, for sufficiently simple views, called *updatable views*, it is possible to translate the modification of the view into an equivalent modification on a base table, and the modification can be done to the base table instead. SQL2 provides a formal definition of when modifications to a view are permitted. The SQL2 rules are complex, but roughly, they permit modifications on views that are defined by selecting (using SELECT, not SELECT DISTINCT) some attributes from one relation R (which may itself be an updatable view). Two important technical points:

- The WHERE clause must not not involve R in a subquery.

- The attributes in the SELECT clause must include enough attributes that for every tuple inserted into the view, we can fill the other attributes out with NULL values or the proper default and have a tuple of the base relation that will yield the inserted tuple of the view.

Example 5.41 : Suppose we try to insert into view `ParamountMovie` of Example 5.37 a tuple like:

```
INSERT INTO ParamountMovie
VALUES('Star Trek', 1979);
```

View `ParamountMovie` almost meets the SQL2 updatability conditions, since the view asks only for some components of some tuples of one base table:

```
Movie(title, year, length, inColor, studioName, producerC#)
```

The only problem is that since attribute `studioName` of `Movie` is not an attribute of the view, the tuple we insert into `Movie` would have `NULL` rather than `'Paramount'` as its value for `studioName`.

Thus, to make the view `ParamountMovie` updatable, we shall add attribute `studioName` to its `SELECT` clause, even though it is obvious to us that the studio name will be Paramount. The revised definition of view `ParamountMovie` is:

```
1)  CREATE VIEW ParamountMovie AS
2)      SELECT studioName, title, year
3)      FROM Movie
4)      WHERE studioName = 'Paramount';
```

Then, we write the insertion into updatable view `ParamountMovie` as:

```
INSERT INTO ParamountMovie
VALUES('Paramount', 'Star Trek', 1979);
```

To effect the insertion, we invent a `Movie` tuple that yields the inserted view tuple when the view definition is applied to `Movie`. For the particular insertion above, the `studioName` component is `'Paramount'`, the `title` component is `'Star Trek'`, and the `year` component is 1979.

The other three attributes that do not appear in the view — `length`, `inColor`, and `producerC#` — must exist in the inserted `Movie` tuple. However, we cannot deduce their values. As a result, the new `Movie` tuple must have in the components for each of these three attributes the appropriate default value: either `NULL` or some other default that was declared for an attribute or its domain. For example, if the default value 0 was declared for attribute `length` but the other two use `NULL` for the default, then the resulting inserted `Movie` tuple would be:

title	*year*	*length*	*inColor*	*studioName*	*producerC#*
'Star Trek'	1979	0	NULL	'Paramount'	NULL

□

We may also delete from an updatable view. The deletion, like the insertion, is passed through to the underlying relation R and causes the deletion of every tuple of R that gives rise to a deleted tuple of the view.

Example 5.42: Suppose we wish to delete from the updatable `Paramount-Movie` view all movies with "Trek" in their titles. We may issue the deletion statement

```
DELETE FROM ParamountMovie
WHERE title LIKE '%Trek%';
```

This deletion is translated into an equivalent deletion on the `Movie` base table; the only difference is that the condition defining the view `ParamountMovie` is added to the conditions of the `WHERE` clause.

```
DELETE FROM Movie
WHERE title LIKE '%Trek%' AND studioName = 'Paramount';
```

is the resulting delete statement.   □

Similarly, an update on an updatable view is passed through to the underlying relation. The view update thus has the effect of updating all tuples of the underlying relation that give rise in the view to updated view tuples.

Example 5.43: The view update

```
UPDATE ParamountMovie
SET year = 1979
WHERE title = 'Star Trek the Movie';
```

is turned into the base-table update

```
UPDATE Movie
SET year = 1979
WHERE title = 'Star Trek the Movie' AND
      studioName = 'Paramount';
```

□

A final kind of modification of a view is to delete it altogether. This modification may be done whether or not the view is updatable. A typical `DROP` statement is

```
DROP VIEW ParamountMovie;
```

Note that this statement deletes the definition of the view, so we may no longer make queries or issue modification commands involving this view. However dropping the view does not affect any tuples of the underlying relation `Movie`. In contrast,

```
DROP TABLE Movie
```

would not only make the `Movie` table go away. It would also make the view `ParamountMovie` unusable, since a query that used it would indirectly refer to the nonexistent relation `Movie`.

Why Some Views Are Not Updatable

Consider the view `MovieProd` of Example 5.40, which relates movie titles and producers' names. This view is not updatable according to the SQL2 definition, because there are two relations in the `FROM` clause: `Movie` and `MovieExec`. Suppose we tried to insert a tuple like

          ('Greatest Show on Earth', 'Cecil B. DeMille')

We would have to insert tuples into both `Movie` and `MovieExec`. We could use the default value for attributes like `length` or `address`, but what could be done for the two equated attributes `producerC#` and `cert#` that both represent the unknown certificate number of DeMille? We could use `NULL` for both of these. However, when joining relations with `NULL`'s, SQL does not recognize two `NULL` values as equal (see Section 5.9.1). Thus, 'Greatest Show on Earth' would not be connected with 'Cecil B. DeMille' in the `MovieProd` view, and our insertion would not have been done correctly.

5.8.5 Interpreting Queries Involving Views

While the details of how queries on views are implemented by an SQL system is beyond the scope of this book, we can get good idea of what view queries mean by following the interpretation process. We shall restrict ourselves to queries and views that can be expressed in relational algebra, although complete SQL can be handled by adding operators that correspond to the additional features of SQL, such as grouping and aggregation.

The basic idea is illustrated in Fig. 5.14. A query Q is there represented by its expression tree in relational algebra. This expression tree uses as leaves some relations that are views. We have suggested two such leaves, the views V and W. To interpret Q in terms of base tables, we find the definition of the views V and W. These definitions are also expressed as expression trees of relational algebra.

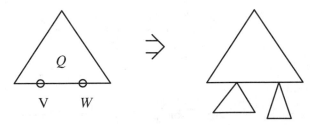

Figure 5.14: Substituting view definitions for view references

To form the query over base tables, we substitute, for each leaf in the tree for Q that is a view, the root of a copy of the tree that defines that view. Thus, in Fig. 5.14 we have shown the leaves labeled V and W replaced by the definitions of these views. The resulting tree is a query over base tables that is equivalent to the original query about views.

Example 5.44: Let us consider the view definition and query of Example 5.38. Recall the definition of view `ParamountMovie` is:

```
1)  CREATE VIEW ParamountMovie AS
2)      SELECT title, year
3)      FROM Movie
4)      WHERE studioName = 'Paramount';
```

An expression tree for the query that defines this view is shown in Fig. 5.15.

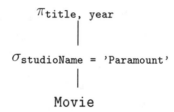

Figure 5.15: Expression tree for view `ParamountMovie`

The query of Example 5.38 is

```
SELECT title
FROM ParamountMovie
WHERE year = 1979;
```

asking for the Paramount movies made in 1979. This query has the expression tree shown in Fig. 5.16. Note that the one leaf of this tree represents the view `ParamountMovie`.

We therefore interpret the query by substituting the tree of Fig. 5.15 for the leaf `ParamountMovie` in Fig. 5.16. The resulting tree is shown in Fig. 5.17.

The tree of Fig. 5.17 is an acceptable interpretation of the query. However, it is expressed in an unnecessarily complex way. An SQL system would apply transformations to this tree in order to make it look like the expression tree for the query we suggested in Example 5.38:

```
SELECT title
FROM Movie
WHERE studioName = 'Paramount' AND year = 1979;
```

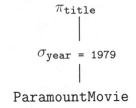

Figure 5.16: Expression tree for the query

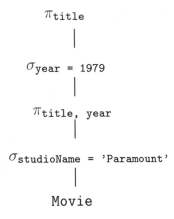

Figure 5.17: Expressing the query in terms of base tables

For example, we can move the projection $\pi_{\texttt{title, year}}$ above the selection $\sigma_{\texttt{year=1979}}$. The reason is that delaying a projection can never change the meaning of an expression. Then, we have two projections in a row, first onto `title` and `year` and then onto `title` alone. Clearly the first of these is redundant, and we can eliminate it. Thus, the two projections can be replaced by a single projection onto `title`.

The two selections can also be combined. In general, two consecutive selections can be replaced by one selection for the AND of their conditions. The resulting expression tree is shown in Fig. 5.18. It is the tree that we would obtain from the query

```
SELECT title
FROM Movie
WHERE studioName = 'Paramount' AND year = 1979;
```

directly.   □

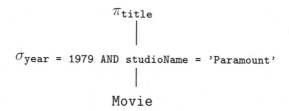

Figure 5.18: Simplifying the query over base tables

5.8.6 Exercises for Section 5.8

Exercise 5.8.1: From the following base tables of our running example

```
MovieStar(name, address, gender, birthdate)
MovieExec(name, address, cert#, netWorth)
Studio(name, address, presC#)
```

Construct the following views:

* a) A view `RichExec` giving the name, address, certificate number and net worth of all executives with a net worth of at least $10,000,000.

  b) A view `StudioPres` giving the name, address, and certificate number of all executives who are studio presidents.

  c) A view `ExecutiveStar` giving the name, address, gender, birth date, certificate number, and net worth of all individuals who are both executives and stars.

Exercise 5.8.2: Which of the views of Exercise 5.8.1 are updatable?

Exercise 5.8.3: Write each of the queries below, using one or more of the views from Exercise 5.8.1 and no base tables.

  a) Find the names of females who are both stars and executives.

* b) Find the names of those executives who are both studio presidents and worth at least $10,000,000.

! c) Find the names of studio presidents who are also stars and are worth at least $50,000,000.

*! **Exercise 5.8.4:** For the view and query of Example 5.40:

  a) Show the expression tree for the view `MovieProd`.

  b) Show the expression tree for the query of that example.

c) Build from your answers to (a) and (b) an expression for the query in terms of base tables.

d) Explain how to change your expression from (c) so it is an equivalent expression that matches the suggested solution in Example 5.40.

! Exercise 5.8.5 : For each of the queries of Exercise 5.8.3, express the query and views as relational-algebra expressions, substitute for the uses of the view in the query expression, and simplify the resulting expressions as best you can. Write SQL queries corresponding to your resulting expressions on the base tables.

Exercise 5.8.6 : Using the base tables

```
Classes(class, type, country, numGuns, bore, displacement)
Ships(name, class, launched)
```

from Exercise 4.1.3:

a) Define a view `BritishShips` that gives for each ship of Great Britain its class, type, number of guns, bore, displacement, and year launched.

b) Write a query using your view from (a) asking for the number of guns and displacements of all British battleships launched before 1919.

! c) Express the query of (b) and view of (a) as relational-algebra expressions, substitute for the uses of the view in the query expression, and simplify the resulting expressions as best you can.

! d) Write an SQL query corresponding to your expression from (c) on the base tables `Classes` and `Ships`.

5.9   Null Values and Outerjoins

In this section we shall learn more about the use of NULL as a value in SQL tuples. An especially important application of NULL values is in defining a variant of the join operation that does not lose information in situations where a tuple of one relation fails to join with any tuple of the other relation. This version of join is called "outerjoin." We shall cover several variants of the outerjoin operator in this section. Although NULL's are present in earlier SQL standards, the outerjoin operator is generally present only in systems that support SQL2.

5.9.1   Operations on Nulls

We have seen several times that SQL supports a special value called NULL. Section 4.7.4 discussed some of the uses of the NULL, such as representing an unknown or nonexistent value. NULL values are created, for example, when we insert a tuple into a relation by a command that specifies some but not all of the

---

Pitfalls Regarding Nulls

It is tempting to assume that NULL in SQL2 can always be taken to mean "a value that we don't know but that surely exists." However, there are several ways that intuition is violated. For instance, suppose x is a component of some tuple, and the domain for that component is the integers. We might reason that $0 * x$ surely has the value 0, since no matter what integer x is, its product with 0 is 0. However, if x has the value NULL, rule (1) of Section 5.9.1 applies, and the product of 0 and a NULL is NULL. Similarly, we might reason that $x - x$ has the value 0, since whatever integer x is, its difference with itself is 0. However, again rule (1) applies and the result is NULL.

---

tuple's components. Unless there is another declared default for a component whose value is not specified, the NULL value appears there. We shall see that outerjoins are another source of NULL values as well.

There are two important rules to remember when we operate upon a NULL value.

1. When we operate on a NULL and any other value, including another NULL, using an arithmetic operator like $\times$ or $+$, the result is NULL.

2. When we compare a NULL value and any value, including another NULL, using a comparison operator like = or >, the result is UNKNOWN. The value UNKNOWN is another truth-value, like TRUE and FALSE; we shall discuss how to manipulate value UNKNOWN shortly.

However, we must remember that, although NULL is a value that can appear in tuples, it is *not* a constant. Thus, while the above rules apply when we try to operate on an expression whose value is NULL, we cannot use NULL explicitly as an operand.

Example 5.45 : Let x have the value NULL. Then the value of $x + 3$ is also NULL. However, NULL + 3 is not a legal SQL expression. Similarly, the value of $x = 3$ is UNKNOWN, because we cannot tell if the value of x, which is NULL, equals the value 3. However, the comparison NULL = 3 is not correct SQL. □

Incidentally, the correct way to ask if x has the value NULL is with the expression x IS NULL. This expression has the value TRUE if x has the value NULL and it has value FALSE otherwise. Similarly, x IS NOT NULL has the value true unless the value of x is NULL.

5.9.2   The Truth-Value UNKNOWN

In Section 5.1.2 we observed that the result of a comparison was either TRUE
or FALSE, and these truth-values were combined in the obvious way using the
logical operators AND, OR, and NOT. We have just seen that when NULL values
occur, comparisons can yield a third truth-value: UNKNOWN. We must now learn
how the logical operators behave on combinations of all three truth-values.

The rule is easy to remember if we think of TRUE as 1 (i.e., fully true), FALSE
as 0 (i.e., not at all true), and UNKNOWN as 1/2 (i.e., somewhere between true
and false). Then:

1. The AND of two truth-values is the minimum of those values. That is,
   x AND y is FALSE if either x or y is FALSE; it is UNKNOWN if neither is FALSE
   but at least one is UNKNOWN, and it is TRUE only when both x and y are
   TRUE.

2. The OR of two truth-values is the maximum of those values. That is,
   x OR y is TRUE if either x or y is TRUE; it is UNKNOWN if neither is TRUE but
   at least one is UNKNOWN, and it is FALSE only when both are FALSE.

3. The negation of a truth-value is 1 minus the truth-value. That is, NOT x
   has the value TRUE when x is FALSE, the value FALSE when x is TRUE, and
   the value UNKNOWN when x has value UNKNOWN.

In Fig. 5.19 is a summary of the result of applying the three logical operators
to the nine different combinations of truth-values for operands x and y. The
value of the last operator, NOT, depends only on x.

x	y	x AND y	x OR y	NOT x
TRUE	TRUE	TRUE	TRUE	FALSE
TRUE	UNKNOWN	UNKNOWN	TRUE	FALSE
TRUE	FALSE	FALSE	TRUE	FALSE
UNKNOWN	TRUE	UNKNOWN	TRUE	UNKNOWN
UNKNOWN	UNKNOWN	UNKNOWN	UNKNOWN	UNKNOWN
UNKNOWN	FALSE	FALSE	UNKNOWN	UNKNOWN
FALSE	TRUE	FALSE	TRUE	TRUE
FALSE	UNKNOWN	FALSE	UNKNOWN	TRUE
FALSE	FALSE	FALSE	FALSE	TRUE

Figure 5.19: Truth table for three-valued logic

SQL conditions, as appear in WHERE clauses of select-from-where statements
or DELETE statements, apply to each tuple in some relation, and for each tuple,
one of the three truth values, TRUE, FALSE, or UNKNOWN is produced. However,
only the tuples for which the condition has the value TRUE become part of the

answer; tuples with either UNKNOWN or FALSE as value are excluded from the answer. That situation leads to another surprising behavior similar to that discussed in the box on "Pitfalls Regarding Nulls."

Example 5.46: Suppose we ask about our running-example relation

```
Movie(title, year, length, inColor, studioName, producerC#)
```

the following query:

```
SELECT *
FROM Movie
WHERE length <= 120 OR length > 120;
```

Untuitively, we would expect to get a copy of the Movie relation, since each movie has a length that is either 120 or less or that is greater than 120.

However, suppose there are Movie tuples with NULL in the length component. Then both comparisons length <= 120 and length > 120 evaluate to UNKNOWN. The OR of two UNKNOWN's is UNKNOWN, by Fig. 5.19. Thus, for any tuple with a NULL in the length component, the WHERE clause evaluates to UNKNOWN. Such a tuple is *not* returned as part of the answer to the query. As a result, the true meaning of the query is "find all the Movie tuples with non-NULL lengths. □

5.9.3 SQL2 Join Expressions

Before introducing the outerjoin operation of SQL2, let us consider the simpler case of a conventional join. There are several kinds of join operators available in SQL2; previous SQL standards did not have these operators explicitly, although it is possible to obtain the same effect by a select-from-where query. In SQL2, the join expressions are an alternative to select-from-where and may be used wherever a select-from-where query is permitted. Moreover, join expressions, since they produce relations, may be used in the FROM clause of a select-from-where expression.

The simplest form of join expression is a *cross join*; that term is a synonym for what we called a Cartesian product or just "product" in Section 4.1.4. For instance, if we want the product of the two relations

```
Movie(title, year, length, inColor, studioName, producerC#)
StarsIn(movieTitle, movieYear, starName)
```

we can say

```
Movie CROSS JOIN StarsIn;
```

and the result will be a nine-column relation with all the attributes of `Movie` and `StarsIn`. Every pair consisting of one tuple of `Movie` and one tuple of `StarsIn` will be a tuple of the resulting relation.

The attributes in the product relation can be called $R.A$, where R is one of the two joined relations and A one of its attributes. If only one of the relations has an attribute named A, then the R and dot can be dropped, as usual. In this instance, since `Movie` and `StarsIn` have no common attributes, the nine attribute names suffice in the product.

However, the product by itself is rarely a useful operation. A more conventional theta-join is obtained with the keyword `ON`. We put `JOIN` between two relation names R and S and follow them by `ON` and a condition. The product of $R \times S$ is followed by a selection for whatever condition follows `ON`.

Example 5.47: Suppose we want to join the relations

```
Movie(title, year, length, inColor, studioName, producerC#)
StarsIn(movieTitle, movieYear, starName)
```

with the condition that the only tuples to be joined are those that refer to the same movie. That is, the titles and years from both relations must be the same. We can ask this query by

```
Movie JOIN StarsIn ON
        title = movieTitle AND year = movieYear;
```

The result is again a nine-column relation with the obvious attribute names. However, now a tuple from `Movie` and one from `StarsIn` combine to form a tuple of the result only if the two tuples agree on both the title and year. As a result, two of the columns are redundant, because every tuple of the result will have the same value in both the `title` and `movieTitle` components and will have the same value in both `year` and `movieYear`. □

As mentioned, join expressions may appear in the `FROM` clause of a select-from-where expression. If so, the relation denoted by the join expression is treated just like base tables or views in the `FROM` clause. An example of this use follows.

Example 5.48: If we are concerned with the fact that Example 5.47 has two redundant components, we can put the whole expression of that example in a `FROM` clause and use a `SELECT` clause to remove the undesired attributes. Thus, we could write

```
SELECT title, year, length, inColor, studioName,
        producerC#, starName
FROM Movie JOIN StarsIn ON
        title = movieTitle AND year = movieYear;
```

to get a seven-column relation which is the `Movie` relation's tuples, each extended in all possible ways with a star of that movie. □

5.9.4 Natural Joins

As we recall from Section 4.1.5, a natural join differs from a theta-join in that

1. The join condition is that all pairs of attributes from the two relations having a common name are equated, and there are no other conditions.

2. One of each pair of equated attributes is projected out.

The SQL2 natural join behaves exactly this way. Keywords `NATURAL JOIN` appear between the relations to express the $\bowtie$ operator.

Example 5.49: Suppose we want to compute the natural join of the relations

```
MovieStar(name, address, gender, birthdate)
MovieExec(name, address, cert#, netWorth)
```

The result will be a relation whose schema includes attributes `name` and `address` plus all the attributes that appear in one or the other of the two relations. A tuple of the result will represent an individual who is both a star and an executive and will have all the information pertinent to either: a name, address, gender, birthdate, certificate number, and net worth. The expression

```
MovieStar NATURAL JOIN MovieExec;
```

succinctly describes the desired relation. □

5.9.5 Outerjoins

The outerjoin is a variant of the join provided by the SQL2 standard to handle the following problem with certain joins. Suppose we wish to compute the join $R \bowtie S$. If a tuple t of R does not match any tuple of S, then all trace of t will disappear from the relation $R \bowtie S$. That situation could be awkward for a variety of reasons. For example, if this join were a view, and we queried the view about attributes belonging to the schema of R only, then we would intuitively expect to see t represented in the query result. But in fact, t is not visible through the view $R \bowtie S$, so the same query on R might produce a different result from the query on $R \bowtie S$.

An outerjoin differs from an ordinary (or "inner") join by adding to the result any tuple of either relation that does not join with at least one tuple of the other relation. Recall from Example 4.6 that tuples that fail to join with any tuple from the other relation are called *dangling tuples*. Since tuples in the joined relation must have all the attributes of both relations, we "pad out" each of the dangling tuples with NULL's in those attributes belonging only to the other relation before adding them to the relation that is the result of the join.

Example 5.50: Suppose we wish to take the join of the two relations

```
MovieStar(name, address, gender, birthdate)
MovieExec(name, address, cert#, netWorth)
```

but to retain those individuals who are stars and not executives or executives and not stars. We could perform what SQL2 calls a "natural full outerjoin" on these relations. The syntax is unsurprising:

```
MovieStar NATURAL FULL OUTER JOIN MovieExec;
```

The result of this operation is a relation with the same six-attribute schema as Example 5.49. The tuples of this relation are of three kinds. Those representing individuals who are both stars and executives have tuples with all six attributes non-NULL. These are the tuples that are also in the result of Example 5.49.

The second kind of tuple is one for an individual who is a star but not an executive. These tuples have values for attributes `name`, `address`, `gender`, and `birthdate` taken from their tuple in `MovieStar`, while the attributes belonging only to `MovieExec`, namely `cert#` and `netWorth`, have NULL values.

The third kind of tuple is for an executive who is not also a star. These tuples have values for the attributes of `MovieExec` taken from their `MovieExec` tuple and NULL's in the attributes `gender` and `birthdate` that come only from `MovieStar`. For instance, the three tuples of the result relation shown in Fig. 5.20 correspond to the three types of individuals, respectively. □

name	address	gender	birthdate	cert#	networth
Mary Tyler Moore	Maple St.	'F'	9/9/99	12345	$100···
Tom Hanks	Cherry Ln.	'M'	8/8/88	NULL	NULL
George Lucas	Oak Rd.	NULL	NULL	23456	$200···

Figure 5.20: Three tuples in the outerjoin of `MovieStar` and `MovieExec`

There are many variations on the outerjoin available in SQL2. First, in addition to the full outerjoin, where dangling tuples of both relations are padded with nulls, we can have a *left* outerjoin, where the dangling tuples of only the left (first) relation are padded with NULL's and included in the result. For instance,

```
MovieStar NATURAL LEFT OUTER JOIN MovieExec;
```

would yield the first two tuples of Fig. 5.20 but not the third.

Similarly, a *right* outerjoin pads and includes only the dangling tuples from the right (second) relation. Thus,

```
MovieStar NATURAL RIGHT OUTER JOIN MovieExec;
```

would yield the first and third tuples of Fig. 5.20 but not the second.

The second kind of variation on outerjoins is how we specify the condition that matching tuples must satisfy. Instead of using the keyword NATURAL, we may follow the join by ON and a condition that matching tuples must follow. If we also specify FULL OUTER JOIN, then after matching tuples from the two joined relations, we pad dangling tuples of either relation with NULL's and include the padded tuples in the result.

Example 5.51: Let us reconsider Example 5.47, where we joined the relations Movie and StarsIn using the conditions that the title and movieTitle attributes of the two relations agree and that the year and movieYear attributes of the two relations agree. If we modify that example to call for a full outerjoin:

```
Movie FULL OUTER JOIN StarsIn ON
    title = movieTitle AND year = movieYear;
```

then we shall get not only tuples for movies that have at least one star mentioned in StarsIn, but we shall get tuples for movies with no listed stars, padded with NULL's in attributes movieTitle, movieYear, and starName. Likewise, for stars not appearing in any movie listed in relation Movie we get a tuple with NULL's in the six attributes of Movie. □

The keyword FULL can be replaced by either LEFT or RIGHT in outerjoins of the type suggested by Example 5.51. For instance,

```
Movie LEFT OUTER JOIN StarsIn ON
    title = movieTitle AND year = movieYear;
```

gives us the Movie tuples with at least one listed star and NULL-padded Movie tuples without a listed star, but will not include stars without a listed movie. Conversely,

```
Movie RIGHT OUTER JOIN StarsIn ON
    title = movieTitle AND year = movieYear;
```

will omit the tuples for movies without a listed star but will include tuples for stars not in any listed movies, padded with NULL's.

5.9.6 Exercises for Section 5.9

Exercise 5.9.1: For these relations from our running movie database schema

```
StarsIn(movieTitle, movieYear, starName)
MovieStar(name, address, gender, birthdate)
MovieExec(name, address, cert#, netWorth)
Studio(name, address, presC#)
```

describe the tuples that would appear in the following SQL expressions:

    a) `Studio CROSS JOIN MovieExec;`

    b) `StarsIn FULL NATURAL OUTER JOIN MovieStar;`

    c) `StarsIn FULL OUTER JOIN MovieStar ON name = starName;`

*! Exercise 5.9.2: Using the database schema

```
Product(maker, model, type)
PC(model, speed, ram, hd, cd, price)
Laptop(model, speed, ram, hd, screen, price)
Printer(model, color, type, price)
```

write an SQL query that will produce information about all products — PC's, laptops, and printers — including their manufacturer if available, and whatever information about that product is relevant (i.e., found in the relation for that type of product).

Exercise 5.9.3: Using the two relations

```
Classes(class, type, country, numGuns, bore, displacement)
Ships(name, class, launched)
```

from our database schema of Exercise 4.1.3, write an SQL query that will produce all available information about ships, including that information available in the `Classes` relation. You need not produce information about classes if there are no ships of that class mentioned in `Ships`.

! Exercise 5.9.4: Repeat Exercise 5.9.3, but also include in the result, for any class C that is not mentioned in `Ships`, information about the ship that has the same name C as its class.

! Exercise 5.9.5: In Example 5.46 we discussed the query

```
SELECT *
FROM Movie
WHERE length <= 120 OR length > 120;
```

which behaves unintuitively when the length of a movie is `NULL`. Find a simpler, equivalent query, one with a single condition in the `WHERE` clause (no `AND` or `OR` of conditions).

! Exercise 5.9.6: The join operators we learned in this section are redundant, in the sense that they can always be replaced by select-from-where expressions. Explain how to write expressions of the following forms using select-from-where:

  * a) `R CROSS JOIN S;`

    b) `R NATURAL JOIN S;`

c) R JOIN S ON C;, where C is an SQL condition.

!! Exercise 5.9.7: Outerjoin operators also can be replaced by SQL queries involving other operators of SQL. Show how to rewrite the following without using join or outerjoin operators explicitly:

a) R NATURAL LEFT OUTER JOIN S;

b) R NATURAL FULL OUTER JOIN S;

c) R FULL OUTER JOIN S ON C;, where C is an SQL condition.

5.10 Recursion in SQL3

In this section, we shall focus on a feature of SQL3 — recursive queries — that is just beginning to appear in commercial systems. In comparison, the previous sections of this chapter were based on features of SQL2 that are present in, or similar to, features found in almost all commercial systems. Further, while the SQL2 standard has been formally adopted, the description of recursive queries in this section is based on a draft of the SQL3 standard and might evolve from that draft.

The SQL3 approach to recursion is based on the recursive Datalog rules described in Section 4.4. However, there are several modifications. First, the SQL3 standard suggests that only *linear* recursion, that is, rules with at most one recursive subgoal, is mandatory. Second, the requirement of stratification, which we discussed for the negation operator in Section 4.4.4, applies also to other operators of SQL that can cause similar problems, such as aggregations.

5.10.1 Defining IDB Relations in SQL3

Recall from Section 4.4 that it is useful to distinguish between EDB (extensional database) relations that are stored tables and IDB (intensional database) relations that are defined by Datalog rules. SQL3 has a statement introduced by the keyword WITH that allows us to define its equivalent of IDB relations. These definitions can then be used within the WITH statement itself. A simple form of the WITH statement is:

$$\text{WITH } R \text{ AS } \text{<definition of } R\text{> <query involving } R\text{>}$$

That is, one defines a temporary relation named R, and then uses R in some query. More generally, one can define several relations after the WITH, separating their definitions by commas. Any of these definitions may be recursive. Several defined relations may be *mutually* recursive; that is, each may be defined in terms of some of the other relations, optionally including itself. However, any relation that is involved in a recursion must be preceded by the keyword RECURSIVE. Thus, a WITH statement has the form:

1. The keyword WITH.

2. One or more definitions. Definitions are separated by commas, and each definition consists of

    (a) An optional keyword RECURSIVE, which is required if the relation being defined is recursive.

    (b) The name of the relation being defined.

    (c) The keyword AS.

    (d) The query that defines the relation.

3. A query, which may refer to any of the prior definitions, and forms the result of the WITH statement.

It is important to note that, unlike other definitions of relations, the definitions inside a WITH statement are only available within that statement and cannot be used elsewhere. If one wants a persistent relation, one should define that relation in the database schema, outside any WITH statement.

Example 5.52: Let us reconsider the airline flights information that we used as an example in Section 4.4. The data about flights is in a relation[8]

```
Flights(airline, frm, to, departs, arrives)
```

The actual data for our example was given in Fig. 4.19, which we reproduce here as Fig. 5.21.

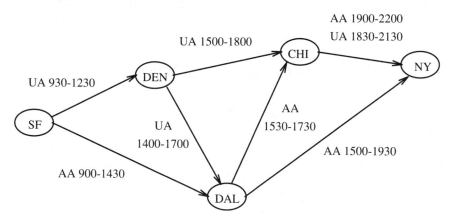

Figure 5.21: Airline flights (repeat of Fig. 4.19)

In Example 4.37, we computed the set of pairs of cities such that it is possible to fly from the first to the second using the flights represented by Fig. 5.21. In that example, we computed an IDB relation Flights, that gave us the desired information, using the two rules:

---

[8]We changed the name of the second attribute to frm, since from in SQL is a keyword.

```
1. Reaches(x,y) ← Flights(a,x,y,d,r)
2. Reaches(x,y) ← Reaches(x,z) AND Reaches(z,y)
```

From these rules, we can develop an SQL definition of `Reaches` that means the same. This SQL query becomes the definition of `Reaches` in a WITH statement, and we complete the WITH statement with the desired query. In Example 4.37, that result was the entire `Reaches` relation, but we could also ask some query about `Reaches`, for instance the set of cities reachable from Denver.

```
1)    WITH RECURSIVE Reaches(frm, to) AS
2)          (SELECT frm, to FROM Flights)
3)       UNION
4)          (SELECT R1.frm, R2.to
5)           FROM Reaches AS R1, Reaches AS R2
6)           WHERE R1.to = R2.frm)
7)    SELECT * FROM Reaches;
```

Figure 5.22: SQL3 query for pairs of reachable cities

Figure 5.22 shows how to compute `Reaches` as an SQL3 query.[9] Line (1) introduces the definition of `Reaches`, while the actual definition of this relation is in lines (2) through (6).

That definition is a union of two queries, corresponding to the two rules by which `Reaches` was defined in Example 4.37. Line (2) is the first term of the union and corresponds to the first, or basis rule. It says that for every tuple in the `Flights` relation, the second and third components (the `frm` and `to` components) are a tuple in `Reaches`.

Lines (4) through (6) correspond to the second, or inductive, rule in the definition of `Reaches`. The two `Reaches` subgoals are represented in the FROM clause by two aliases R1 and R2 for `Reaches`. The first component of R1 corresponds to x in Rule (2), and the second component of R2 corresponds to y. Variable z is represented by both the second component of R1 and the first component of R2; note that these components are equated in line (6).

Finally, line (7) describes the relation produced by the entire query. It is a copy of the `Reaches` relation. As an alternative, we could replace line (7) by a more complex query. For instance,

```
7)    SELECT to
      FROM Reaches
      WHERE frm = 'DEN';
```

---

[9]There is a technicality that the SQL3 standard requires only that linear recursions, where the query defining a recursive relation has only one occurrence of a recursive relation in the FROM clause, be supported by the DBMS. Line (5) of Fig. 5.52 has two uses of the recursive relation `Reaches`. However, this query best mimics Example 4.37 and is probably most natural. It might or might not be supported by an SQL3 DBMS as written.

Mutual Recursion

There is a graph-theoretic way to check whether two relations or predicates are mutually recursive. Construct a *dependency graph* whose nodes correspond to the relations (or predicates if we are using Datalog rules). Draw an arc from relation A to relation B if the definition of B depends directly on the definition of A. That is, if Datalog is being used, then A appears in the body of a rule with B at the head. In SQL, A would appear somewhere in the definition of B, normally in a FROM clause, but possibly as a term in a union, intersection, or difference.

If there is a cycle involving nodes R and S, then R and S are *mutually recursive*. The most common case will be a loop from R to R, indicating that R depends recursively upon itself.

Note that the dependency graph is similar to the graph we introduced in Section 4.4.4 to define stratified negation. However, there we had to distinguish between positive and negative dependence, while here we do not make that distinction.

---

would produce all those cities reachable from Denver.   □

5.10.2 Linear Recursion

As we mentioned in connection with Example 5.52, there is a technical flaw in our solution, because the SQL3 standard only requires that *linear* recursion be supported by implementations of SQL3. Formally, a recursion is linear if the FROM clause for any defined relation has at most one occurrence of a relation that is mutually recursive with the relation being defined. In the most common case, the relation being defined will itself appear once in the FROM clause, but it is also possible that the one occurrence of a recursive relation will be some other relation that is mutually recursive with the relation being defined.

Example 5.53: Interestingly, we can fix the code in Fig. 5.22 by simply replacing either one of the uses of Reaches in line (5) by Flights. That would make the recursion take the form of either the left-recursive or right-recursive rules discussed in the box in Section 4.4.3. Another way is to define an additional relation Pairs in the WITH statement, representing the projection of Flights onto its frm and to components, and use this relation in both parts of the union.

The recoding of Fig. 5.22 is shown in Fig. 5.23. There, we have chosen to make the definition right-recursive, although we could alternatively have interchanged the order of Pairs and Reaches in line (7) and made it left-recursive.

```
1)   WITH
2)       Pairs AS SELECT frm, to FROM Flights,

3)       RECURSIVE Reaches(frm, to) AS
4)              Pairs
5)          UNION
6)              (SELECT Pairs.frm, Reaches.to
7)               FROM Pairs, Reaches
8)               WHERE Pairs.to = Reaches.frm)

9)   SELECT * FROM Reaches;
```

Figure 5.23: Linear-recursive query for pairs of reachable cities

Note that the iterative fixedpoint calculation outlined in Section 4.4.2 can be used for SQL queries such as this one, just as it can be used for Datalog rules. Because the recursion is linear, `Reaches` facts may be discovered in a somewhat different order, but all pairs of cities (x, y) such that one can fly from x to y are eventually discovered.

Consider the first round with our sample data. Since `Reaches` is initially empty, only the first term of the union — `Pairs` on line (4) — contributes the basis pairs of cities represented by the map of Fig. 5.21. On the second round, `Pairs` provides single hops and `Reaches` also contributes single hops, so we get the two-hop pairs such as (SF, CHI). On the next round, `Reaches` contributes double hops as well, but there are no more pairs to be added. In general, on the ith round we would get all pairs (x, y) such that the shortest route from x to y consisted of i arcs. □

5.10.3 Use of Views in With-Statements

Views as well as tables can be defined within a WITH statement. The only syntactic difference is that we use the keyword VIEW in the definition of the relation.

Example 5.54: The relation `Pairs` on line (2) of Fig. 5.23 could just as well have been defined to be a view. We need only modify line (2) to be:

```
2)       VIEW Pairs AS SELECT frm, to FROM Flights
```

There is even some good reason to make `Pairs` a view. If we make it a true relation, then it will be first constructed in its entirety when the WITH statement is executed, independent of its use to start off the construction of `Reaches` in line (4). If it is a view, then its use in constructing `Reaches` can be replaced by the use of components from tuples in `Flights`. □

5.10.4   Stratified Negation

The queries that can appear as the definition of a recursive relation are not arbitrary SQL queries. Rather, they must be restricted in certain ways; one of the most important requirements is that negation of mutually recursive relations be stratified, as discussed in Section 4.4.4. In Section 5.10.5, we shall see how the principle of stratification extends to other constructs that we find in SQL but not in Datalog or relational algebra, such as aggregation.

Example 5.55: Let us reexamine Example 4.39, where we asked for those pairs of cities (x, y) such that it was possible to travel from x to y on the airline UA, but not on AA. We need recursion to express the idea of traveling on one airline through an indefinite sequence of hops. However, the negation aspect appears in a stratified way: after using recursion to compute the two relations UAreaches and AAreaches in Example 4.39, we took their difference.

We could adopt the same strategy to write the query in SQL3, although we would have to replace the nonlinear recursion in that example by a left- or right-linear form as we did in Example 5.53. However, to illustrate a different way of proceeding, we shall instead define recursively a single relation Reaches(airline,frm,to), whose triples (a, f, t) mean that one can fly from city f to city t, perhaps using several hops but using only flights of airline a. We shall also use a relation Triples(airline,frm,to) that is the projection of Flights onto the three relevant components. The query is shown in Fig. 5.24.

The definition of relation Reaches in lines (3) through (9) is the union two two terms. The basis term is the relation Triples at line (4). The inductive term is the query of lines (6) through (9) that produces the join of Triples with Reaches itself. The effect of these two terms is to put into Reaches all tuples (a, f, t) such that one can travel from city f to city t using one or more hops, but with all hops on airline a.

The query itself appears in lines (10) through (12). Line (10) gives the city pairs reachable via UA, and line (12) gives the city pairs reachable via AA. The result of the query is the difference of these two relations.   □

Example 5.56: In Fig. 5.24, the negation represented by EXCEPT in line (11) is clearly stratified, since it applies only after the recursion of lines (3) through (9) has been completed. On the other hand, the use of negation in Example 4.40, which we observed was unstratified, is translated into a use of EXCEPT within the definition of a recursive relation. The straightforward translation of that example into SQL3 is shown in Fig. 5.25. This query only asks for the value of P, although we could have asked for Q, or some function of P and Q.

The two uses of EXCEPT, in lines (4) and (8) of Fig. 5.25 are illegal in SQL3, since in each case the second argument is a relation that is mutually recursive with the relation being defined. Thus, these uses of negation are not stratified negation and therefore not permitted. In fact, there is no work-around for this problem in SQL3, nor should there be, since the recursion of Fig. 5.25 does not really define the values of relations P and Q.   □

```
1) WITH
2)     Triples AS SELECT airline, frm, to FROM Flights,

3)     RECURSIVE Reaches(airline, frm, to) AS
4)             Triples
5)         UNION
6)             (SELECT Triples.airline, Triples.frm, Reaches.to
7)             FROM Triples, Reaches
8)             WHERE Triples.to = Reaches.frm AND
9)                     Triples.airline = Reaches.airline
            )

10)     (SELECT frm, to FROM Reaches WHERE airline = 'UA')
11) EXCEPT
12)     (SELECT frm, to FROM Reaches WHERE airline = 'AA');
```

Figure 5.24: Stratified query for cities reachable by one of two airlines

5.10.5 Problematic Expressions in Recursive SQL3

We have seen in Example 5.56 that the use of EXCEPT in a recursive definition violates SQL3's requirement that negation be stratified. However, there are other unacceptable forms of query that do not use EXCEPT.[10] For instance, negation of a relation can also be expressed by the use of NOT IN. Thus, lines (2) through (5) of Fig. 5.25 could also have been written

```
RECURSIVE P(x) AS
    SELECT x FROM R WHERE x NOT IN Q
```

This rewriting still leaves the recursion unstratified and therefore illegal.

On the other hand, simply using NOT in a WHERE clause, such as NOT x=y (which could be written x<>y anyway) does not automatically violate the condition that negation be stratified. What then is the general rule about what sorts of SQL queries can be used to define recursive relations in SQL3?

The principle is that to be a legal SQL3 recursion, the definition of a recursive relation R can only involve the use of a mutually recursive relation S (S can be R itself) if that use is *monotone* in S. A use of S is monotone if adding an arbitrary tuple to S might add one or more tuples to R, or it might leave R unchanged, but it can never cause any tuple to be deleted from R.

This rule makes sense when one considers the least-fixedpoint computation outlined in Section 4.4.2. We start with our recursively defined IDB relations

---

[10]Technically, nonlinear recursion, even without negation is also unacceptable in SQL3, although the SQL3 document promises nonlinear recursion "in SQL4." However, here we are concerned with forms of recursion that are meaningless or paradoxical, rather than forms that are merely not part of the SQL3 standard.

```
1)   WITH
2)        RECURSIVE P(x) AS
3)                (SELECT * FROM R)
4)            EXCEPT
5)                (SELECT * FROM Q),

6)        RECURSIVE Q(x) AS
7)                (SELECT * FROM R)
8)            EXCEPT
9)                (SELECT * FROM P)

10)   SELECT * FROM P;
```

Figure 5.25: Unstratified query, illegal in SQL3

empty, and we repeatedly add tuples to them in successive rounds. If adding a tuple in one round could cause us to have to delete a tuple at the next round, then there is the risk of oscillation, and the fixedpoint computation might never converge. In the following examples, we shall see some constructs that are nonmonotone and therefore are outlawed in SQL3 recursion.

Example 5.57 : Figure 5.25 is an implementation of the Datalog rules of Example 4.40, which we should recall was an example of unstratified negation. There, the rules allowed two different minimal fixedpoints. As expected, the definitions of P and Q in Fig. 5.25 are not monotone. Look at the definition of P in lines (2) through (5) for instance. P depends on Q, with which it is mutually recursive, but adding a tuple to Q can delete a tuple from P. To see why, suppose that R consists of the two tuples (a) and (b), and Q consists of the tuples (a) and (c). Then $P = \{(b)\}$. However, if we add (b) to Q, then P becomes empty. Addition of a tuple has caused the deletion of a tuple, so we have a nonmonotone, illegal construct.

This lack of monotonicity leads directly to an oscillating behavior when we try to evaluate the relations P and Q by computing a minimal fixedpoint.[11] For instance, suppose that R has the two tuples $\{(a), (b)\}$. Initially, both P and Q are empty. Thus, in the first round, lines (3) through (5) of Fig. 5.25 compute P to have value $\{(a), (b)\}$. Lines (7) through (9) compute Q to have the same value, since the old, empty value of P is used at line (9).

Now, both R, P, and Q have the value $\{(a), (b)\}$. Thus, on the next round, P and Q are each computed to be empty at lines (3) through (5) and (7)

---

[11] When the recursion is not monotone, then the order in which we evaluate the relations in a WITH clause affects the final answer, although when the recursion is monotone, the result is independent of order. In this and the next example, we shall assume that on each round, P and Q are evaluated "in parallel." That is, the old value of each relation is used to compute the other at each round.

through (9), respectively. On the third round, both would therefore get the value $\{(a), (b)\}$. This process continues forever, with both relations empty on even rounds and $\{(a), (b)\}$ on odd rounds. Therefore, we never obtain clear values for the two relations P and Q from their "definitions" in Fig. 5.25. □

Example 5.58: Aggregation can also lead to nonmonotonicity, although the connection may not be obvious at first. Suppose we have unary (one-attribute) relations P and Q defined by the following two conditions:

1. P is the union of Q and an EDB relation R.

2. Q has one tuple that is the sum of the members of P.

We can express these conditions by a WITH statement, although this statement violates the monotonicity requirement of SQL3. The query shown in Fig. 5.26 asks for the value of P.

```
1)    WITH
2)        RECURSIVE P(x) AS
3)                (SELECT * FROM R)
4)            UNION
5)                (SELECT * FROM Q),

6)        RECURSIVE Q(x) AS
7)            SELECT SUM(x) FROM P

8)    SELECT * FROM P;
```

Figure 5.26: Unstratified query involving aggregation, illegal in SQL3

Suppose that R consists of the tuples (12) and (34), and initially P and Q are both empty, as they must be at the beginning of the fixedpoint computation. Figure 5.27 summarizes the values computed in the first six rounds. Recall that we have adopted the strategy that all relations are computed in one round from the values at the previous round. Thus, P is computed in the first round to be the same as R, and Q is empty, since the old, empty value of P is used in line (7).

At the second round, the union of lines (3) through (5) is the set $R = \{(12), (34)\}$, so that becomes the new value of P. The old value of P was the same as the new value, so on the second round $Q = \{(46)\}$. That is, 46 is the sum of 12 and 34.

At the third round, we get $P = \{(12), (34), (46)\}$ at lines (2) through (5). Using the old value of P, $\{(12), (34)\}$, Q is defined by lines (6) and (7) to be $\{(46)\}$ again.

Round	P	Q
1)	$\{(12),(34)\}$	$\emptyset$
2)	$\{(12),(34)\}$	$\{(46)\}$
3)	$\{(12),(34),(46)\}$	$\{(46)\}$
4)	$\{(12),(34),(46)\}$	$\{(92)\}$
5)	$\{(12),(34),(92)\}$	$\{(92)\}$
6)	$\{(12),(34),(92)\}$	$\{(148)\}$

Figure 5.27: Iterative calculation of fixedpoint for a nonmonotone aggregation

---

Using New Values in Fixedpoint Calculations

One might wonder why we used the old values of P to compute Q in Examples 5.57 and 5.58, rather than the new values of P. The result then might depend on the order in which we listed the definitions of the recursive predicates in the WITH clause. In Example 5.57, P and Q would converge to one of the two possible fixedpoints, depending on the order of evaluation. In Example 5.58, P and Q would still not converge, and in fact they would change at every round, rather than every other round.

At the fourth round, P has the same value, $\{(12),(34),(46)\}$, but Q gets the value $\{(92)\}$, since 12+34+46=92. Notice that Q has lost the tuple (46), although it gained the tuple (92). That is, adding the tuple (46) to P has caused a tuple (by coincidence the same tuple) to be deleted from Q. That behavior is the nonmonotonicity that SQL3 prohibits in recursive definitions, confirming that the query of Fig. 5.26 is illegal. In general, at the $2i$th round, P will consist of the tuples (12), (34), and $(46i - 46)$, while Q consists only of the tuple $(46i)$. □

5.10.6   Exercises for Section 5.10

Exercise 5.10.1: In Example 4.36 we discussed a relation

```
SequelOf(movie, sequel)
```

that gives the immediate sequels of a movie. We also defined an IDB relation FollowOn whose pairs (x,y) were movies such that y was either a sequel of x, a sequel of a sequel, or so on.

a) Write the definition of FollowOn as an SQL3 recursion.

b) Write a recursive SQL3 query that returns the set of pairs (x, y) such that movie y is a follow-on to movie x, but not a sequel of x.

c) Write a recursive SQL3 query that returns the set of pairs (x, y) meaning that y is a follow-on of x, but neither a sequel nor a sequel of a sequel.

! d) Write a recursive SQL3 query that returns the set of movies x that have at least two follow-ons. Note that both could be sequels, rather than one being a sequel and the other a sequel of a sequel.

! e) Write a recursive SQL3 query that returns the set of pairs (x, y) such that movie y is a follow-on of x but y has at most one follow-on.

Exercise 5.10.2: In Exercise 4.4.3, we introduced a relation

```
Rel(class, eclass, mult)
```

that describes how one ODL class is related to other classes. Specifically, this relation has tuple (c, d, m) if there is a relation from class c to class d. This relation is multivalued if $m = $ 'multi' and it is single-valued if $m = $ 'single'. We also suggested in Exercise 4.4.3 that it is possible to view Rel as defining a graph whose nodes are classes and in which there is an arc from c to d labeled m if and only if (c, d, m) is a tuple of Rel.

a) Write a recursive SQL3 query that produces the set of pairs (c, d) such that there is a path from class c to class d in the graph described above.

* b) Write a recursive SQL3 query that produces the set of pairs (c, d) such that there is a path from c to d along which every arc is labeled single.

*! c) Write a recursive SQL3 query that produces the set of pairs (c, d) such that there is a path from c to d along which at least one arc is labeled multi.

d) Write a recursive SQL3 query that produces the set of pairs (c, d) such that there is a path from c to d but no path along which all arcs are labeled single.

! e) Write a recursive SQL3 query that produces the set of pairs (c, d) such that there is a path from c to d along which arc labels alternate single and multi.

f) Write a recursive SQL3 query that produces the set of pairs (c, d) such that there are paths from c to d and from d to c along which every arc is labeled single.

*! **Exercise 5.10.3:** Suppose we modified the Reaches calculation of Fig. 5.23 to use nonlinear recursion. Specifically, lines (6) through (8) could be replaced by:

```
6)                    (SELECT First.frm, Second.to
7)                      FROM Reaches AS First, Reaches AS Second
8)                      WHERE First.to = Second.frm)
```

in which two copies of Reaches, represented by tuple variables First and Second, are joined to get new pairs. On the ith round of the fixedpoint calculation, how long are the new paths added to Reaches?

5.11 Summary of Chapter 5

✦ *SQL*: The language SQL is the principal query language for relational database systems. The standard with the greatest influence on commercial systems in 1997 is called SQL2. An emerging standard for the language, SQL3, is expected to be finalized shortly.

✦ *Select-From-Where Queries*: The most common form of SQL query has the form select-from-where. It allows us to take the product of several relations (the FROM clause), apply a condition to the tuples of the result (the WHERE clause), and produce desired components (the SELECT clause).

✦ *Subqueries*: Select-from-where queries can also be used as subqueries within a WHERE clause of another query. The operators EXISTS, IN, ALL, and ANY may be used to express boolean-valued conditions about the relations that are the result of a subquery.

✦ *Set Operations on Relations*: We can take the union, intersection, or difference of relations by connecting the relations, or connecting queries defining the relations, with the keywords UNION, INTERSECT, and EXCEPT, respectively.

✦ *The Bag Model of Relations*: SQL actually regards relations as bags of tuples, not sets of tuples. We can force elimination of duplicate tuples with the keyword DISTINCT, while keyword ALL allows the result to be a bag in certain circumstances where bags are not the default.

✦ *Aggregations*: The values appearing in one column of a relation can be summarized (aggregated) by using one of the keywords SUM, AVG (average value), MIN, MAX, or COUNT. Tuples can be partitioned prior to aggregation with the keywords GROUP BY. Certain groups can be eliminated with a clause introduced by the keyword HAVING.

✦ *Modification Statements*: SQL allows us to change the tuples in a relation. We may INSERT (add new tuples), DELETE (remove tuples), or UPDATE (change some of the existing tuples), by writing SQL statements using one of these three keywords.

✦ *Data Definition*: SQL has statements to declare elements of a database
  schema. The `CREATE TABLE` statement allow us to declare the schema for
  stored relations (called tables), specifying the attributes and their types.
  We can also use a `CREATE DOMAIN` statement to define a name for a data
  type, which can then be used in relation schema declarations. These
  `CREATE` statements also allow us to declare default values for attributes
  and domains.

✦ *Altering Schemas*: We can change aspects of the database schema with an
  `ALTER` statement. These changes include adding and removing attributes
  from relation schemas and changing the default value associated with an
  attribute or domain. We may also use a `DROP` statement to completely
  eliminate relations, domains, or other schema elements.

✦ *Indexes*: While not part of the SQL standard, commerical SQL systems
  allow the declaration of indexes on attributes; these indexes speed up
  certain queries or modifications that involve specification of a value for
  the indexed attribute.

✦ *Views*: A view is a definition of how one relation (the view) may be
  constructed from tables stored in the database. Views may be queried as
  if they were tables, and an SQL system modifies queries about a view so
  the query is instead about the tables that are used to define the view.

✦ *Null Values*: SQL provides a special value `NULL` that appears in components of tuples for which no concrete value is available. The arithmetic
  and logic of `NULL` is unusual. Comparison of any value to `NULL`, even
  another `NULL`, gives the truth value `UNKNOWN`. That truth value, in turn,
  behaves in boolean-valued expressions as if it were half way between `TRUE`
  and `FALSE`.

✦ *Join Expressions*: SQL has operators such as `NATURAL JOIN` that may be
  applied to relations, either as queries by themselves or to define relations
  in a `FROM` clause.

✦ *Outerjoins*: SQL also provides an `OUTER JOIN` operator that joins relations but also includes in the result dangling tuples from one or both
  relations; the dangling tuples are padded with `NULL`'s in the resulting
  relation.

✦ *SQL3 Recursion*: The SQL3 standard will include a way of defining temporary relations recursively and using these relations in queries. The
  proposed standard requires that negations and aggregations involved in
  a recursion be stratified; that is, a recursively defined relation can not be
  defined in terms of a negation or aggregation of itself.

5.12   References for Chapter 5

The SQL2 and SQL3 standards are obtainable on-line through the National Institute of Science and Technology (NIST, formerly the National Bureau of Standards). These documents may be obtained either by anonymous FTP or by HTTP. The host name is `speckle.ncsl.nist.gov`. The SQL2 standard and current versions of the SQL3 standard are found in directory

```
isowg3/dbl/BASEdocs
```

Of special interest is the formal syntax for SQL2, found in file

```
isowg3/dbl/BASEdocs/sql-92.bnf
```

The directory `isowg3/x3h2` contains many working and historical documents explaining the SQL2 and SQL3 standards. These documents all have report numbers beginning X3H2.

To access SQL documents by HTTP, use URL

```
http://speckle.ncsl.nist.gov/~ftp/
```

followed by the path for one of the directories mentioned above.

Several books are available that give more details of SQL programming. Some of our favorites are [2], [3], and [6].

SQL was first defined in [4]. It was implemented as part of System R [1], one of the first generation of relational database prototypes. Reference [5] is the source for the material on SQL3 recursion.

1. Astrahan, M. M. et al., "System R: a relational approach to data management," *ACM Transactions on Database Systems* **1**:2, pp. 97–137, 1976.

2. Celko, J., *SQL for Smarties*, Morgan-Kaufmann, San Francisco, 1995.

3. Date, C. J. and H. Darwen, *A Guide to the SQL Standard*, Addison-Wesley, Reading, MA, 1993.

4. Chamberlin, D. D., et al., "SEQUEL 2: a unified approach to data definition, manipulation, and control," *IBM Journal of Research and Development* **20**:6, pp. 560–575, 1976.

5. Finkelstein, S. J., N. Mattos, I. S. Mumick, and H. Pirahesh, "Expressing recursive queries in SQL," ISO WG3 report X3H2–96–075, March, 1996.

6. Melton, J. and A. R. Simon, *Understanding the New SQL: A Complete Guide*, Morgan-Kaufmann, San Francisco, 1993.

Chapter 6

Constraints and Triggers in SQL

In this chapter we shall cover those aspects of SQL that let us create "active" elements. An *active* element is an expression or statement that we write once, store in the database, and expect the element to execute at appropriate times. The time of action might be when a certain event occurs, such as an insertion into a particular relation, or it might be whenever the database changes so that a certain boolean-valued condition becomes true.

One of the serious problems faced by writers of applications that update the database is that the new information may be wrong in a variety of ways. The most straightforward way to make sure that database modifications do not allow inappropriate tuples in relations is to write application programs so every insertion, deletion, and update command has associated with it the checks necessary to assure correctness. Unfortunately, the correctness requirements are frequently complex, and they are always repetitive; application programs must make the same tests after every modification.

Fortunately, SQL2 provides a variety of techniques for expressing *integrity constraints* as part of the database schema. In this chapter we shall study the principal methods. First are key constraints, where an attribute or set of attributes is declared to be a key for a relation. Next, we consider *referential integrity*, the requirement that a value in an attribute or attributes of one relation (e.g., a presC# in Studio) must also appear as a value in an attribute or attributes of another relation (e.g., cert# of MovieExec). We then look at some of the constraints that can be placed on domains, including uniqueness ("keyness"), restrictions of the domain to specific values, and a prohibition against NULL's. Next, we consider constraints on tuples or relations as a whole and interrelation constraints called "assertions." These constraints are tested every time a modification to the relevant relation or relations is made.

Finally, we discuss "triggers," which are a form of active element that is called into play on certain specified events, such as insertion into a specific relation. Triggers are not present in the SQL2 standard, but the follow-on standard, SQL3, includes triggers. Although SQL3 has not been finalized as this book is written, several commercial database systems offer the user a form of trigger.

6.1   Keys in SQL

Perhaps the most important kind of constraint in a database is a declaration that a certain attribute or set of attributes forms a key for a relation. That is, two tuples of the relation are forbidden to agree on an attribute declared to be a key, or on all of a set of attributes that are together declared to form a key. A key constraint, like many other constraints, is declared within the CREATE TABLE command of SQL. There are two similar ways to declare keys: using the keywords PRIMARY KEY or the keyword UNIQUE. However, a table may have only one primary key but any number of "unique" declarations.

6.1.1   Declaring Keys

The primary key may consist of one or more attributes of the relation. There are two ways to declare a primary key in the CREATE TABLE statement that defines a stored relation.

1. We may declare an attribute to be a primary key when that attribute is listed in the relation schema.

2. We may add to the list of items declared in the schema (which so far have only been attributes) an additional declaration that says a particular attribute or set of attributes forms the primary key.

For method (1), we append the keywords PRIMARY KEY after the attribute and its type. For method (2), we introduce a new element in the list of attributes consisting of the keywords PRIMARY KEY and a parenthesized list of the attribute or attributes that form this key. Note that if the key is more than one attribute, we need to use method (2).

Example 6.1 : Let us reconsider the schema for relation MovieStar from Example 5.32. The primary key for this relation is name. Thus, we can add this fact to the line declaring name. Figure 6.1 is a revision of Fig. 5.13 that reflects this change.

Alternatively, we can use a separate definition of the primary key. After line (5) of Fig. 5.13 we add a declaration of the primary key, and we have no need to declare it in line (2). The resulting schema declaration would look like Fig. 6.2.   □

Note that in Example 6.1, the form of either Fig. 6.1 or Fig. 6.2 is acceptable, because the primary key is a single attribute. However, in a situation where

```
1)  CREATE TABLE MovieStar (
2)      name CHAR(30) PRIMARY KEY,
3)      address VARCHAR(255),
4)      gender CHAR(1),
5)      birthdate DATE
    );
```

Figure 6.1: Making name the primary key

```
1)  CREATE TABLE MovieStar (
2)      name CHAR(30),
3)      address VARCHAR(255),
4)      gender CHAR(1),
5)      birthdate DATE,
6)      PRIMARY KEY (name)
    );
```

Figure 6.2: A separate declaration of the primary key

the primary key has more than one attribute, we must use the style of Fig. 6.2. For instance, if we declare the schema for relation Movie, whose key is the pair of attributes title and year, we should add, after the list of attributes, the line

```
PRIMARY KEY (title, year)
```

Another way to declare a key is to use the keyword UNIQUE. This word can appear exactly where PRIMARY KEY can appear: either following an attribute and its type or as a separate item within a CREATE TABLE statement. It has the same significance as a primary-key declaration. However, we may have any number of UNIQUE declarations for a table but only one primary key.

Example 6.2: Line (2) of Fig. 6.1 could have been written

```
2)      name CHAR(30) UNIQUE,
```

We could also change line (3) to

```
3)      address VARCHAR(255) UNIQUE,
```

if we felt that two movie stars could not have the same address (a dubious assumption). Similarly, we could change line (6) of Fig. 6.2 to

```
6)      UNIQUE (name)
```

should we choose.   □

A *key constraint* is a constraint declared with either PRIMARY KEY or UNIQUE. See the box on "Primary Keys and Unique Attributes" in Section 6.2.2 for an outline of the differences between these two types of declarations.

6.1.2   Enforcing Key Constraints

Recall our discussion of indexes in Section 5.7.7, where we learned that although they are not part of any SQL standard, each SQL implementation has a way of creating indexes as part of the database schema definition. It is normal to build an index on the primary key, in order to support the common type of query that specifies a value for the primary key. We may also want to build indexes on other attributes declared to be UNIQUE.

Then, when the WHERE clause of the query includes a condition that equates a key to a particular value — for instance name = 'Audrey Hepburn' in the case of the MovieStar relation of Example 6.1 — the matching tuple will be found very quickly, without a search through all the tuples of the relation.

Many SQL implementations offer an index-creation statement using the keyword UNIQUE that declares an attribute to be a key at the same time it creates an index on that attribute. For example, the statement

```
CREATE UNIQUE INDEX YearIndex ON Movie(year);
```

would have the same effect as the example index-creation statement in Section 5.7.7, but it would also declare a uniqueness constraint on attribute year of the relation Movie (not a reasonable assumption).

Let us consider for a moment how an SQL system would enforce a key constraint. In principle, the constraint must be checked every time we try to change the database. However, it should be clear that the only time a key constraint for a relation R can become violated is when R is modified. In fact, a deletion from R cannot cause a violation; only an insertion or update can. Thus, it is normal practice for the SQL system to check a key constraint only when an insertion or update to that relation occurs.

An index on the attribute(s) declared to be keys is vital if the SQL system is to enforce a key constraint efficiently. If the index is available, then whenever we insert a tuple into the relation or update a key attribute in some tuple, we use the index to check that there is not already a tuple with the same value in the attribute(s) declared to be a key. If so, the system must prevent the modification from taking place.

If there is no index on the key attribute(s), it is still possible to enforce a key constraint. However, then the system must search the entire relation for a tuple with the same key value. That process is extremely time-consuming and would virtually render database modification of large relations impossible.

6.1.3 Exercises for Section 6.1

* **Exercise 6.1.1:** Our running example movie database of Section 3.9 has keys defined for all its relations. Modify your SQL schema declarations of Exercise 5.7.1 to include declarations of the keys for each of these relations. Recall that all three attributes are the key for `StarsIn`.

Exercise 6.1.2: Suggest suitable keys for the relations of the PC database of Exercise 4.1.1. Modify your SQL schema from Exercise 5.7.2 to include declarations of these keys.

Exercise 6.1.3: Suggest suitable keys for the relations of the battleships database of Exercise 4.1.3. Modify your SQL schema from Exercise 5.7.3 to include declarations of these keys.

6.2 Referential Integrity and Foreign Keys

A second important kind of constraint on a database schema is that values for certain attributes must make sense. That is, an attribute like `presC#` of relation `Studio` is expected to refer to a particular movie executive. The implied "referential integrity" constraint is that if a studio's tuple has a certain certificate number c in the `presC#` component, then c is not bogus: it is the certificate of a real movie executive. In terms of the database, a "real" executive is one mentioned in the `MovieExec` relation. Thus, there must be some `MovieExec` tuple that has c in the `cert#` attribute.

6.2.1 Declaring Foreign-Key Constraints

In SQL we may declare an attribute or attributes of one relation to be a *foreign key*, referencing some attribute(s) of a second relation (possibly the same relation). The implication of this declaration is twofold:

1. The referenced attribute(s) of the second relation must be declared the primary key for their relation.

2. Any value appearing in an attribute of the foreign key in the first relation must also appear in the corresponding attribute of the second relation. That is, there is a referential integrity constraint connecting the two attributes or sets of attributes.

   As for primary keys, we have two ways to declare a foreign key.

a) If the foreign key is a single attribute we may follow its name and type by a declaration that it "references" some attribute (which must be the primary key) of some table. The form of the declaration is

REFERENCES <table>(<attribute>)

b) Alternatively, we may append to the list of attributes in a CREATE TABLE statement one or more declarations stating that a set of attributes is a foreign key. We then give the table and its attributes (which must be the primary key) to which the foreign key refers. The form of this declaration is:

```
FOREIGN KEY <attributes> REFERENCES <table>(<attributes>)
```

Example 6.3 : Suppose we wish to declare the relation

```
Studio(name, address, presC#)
```

whose primary key is name and which has a foreign key presC# that references cert# of relation

```
MovieExec(name, address, cert#, netWorth)
```

We may declare presC# directly to reference cert# as follows:

```
CREATE TABLE Studio (
    name CHAR(30) PRIMARY KEY,
    address VARCHAR(255),
    presC# INT REFERENCES MovieExec(cert#)
);
```

An alternative form is to add the foreign key declaration separately, as

```
CREATE TABLE Studio (
    name CHAR(30) PRIMARY KEY,
    address VARCHAR(255),
    presC# INT,
    FOREIGN KEY presC# REFERENCES MovieExec(cert#)
);
```

Notice that the referenced foreign key, cert# in MovieExec, is in fact the primary key of that relation. It is necessary that cert# be declared the primary key of MovieExec if we are legally to declare presC# to be a foreign key in Studio referencing cert# of MovieExec.

The meaning of either of these two foreign key declarations is that whenever a value appears in the presC# component of a Studio tuple, that value must also appear in the cert# component of some MovieExec tuple. One exception is that, should a particular Studio tuple have NULL as the value of its presC# component, there is no requirement that NULL appear as the value of a cert# component (in fact, it is sound practice not to allow NULL's in a primary-key attribute anyway; see Section 6.3.1).   □

Primary Keys and Unique Attributes

A `PRIMARY KEY` declaration is almost a synonym for a `UNIQUE` declaration. The most obvious difference is that there can be only one primary key for a table but any number of `UNIQUE` attributes or sets of attributes. However, there are several subtle differences as well.

1. A foreign key can only reference the primary key of a relation.

2. The implementor of a database management system has the option to attach to the concept "primary key" some special meaning that is not part of the SQL2 standard. For instance, a database vendor might always place an index (as discussed in Section 6.1.2) on a key declared to be a primary key (even if that key consisted of more than one attribute), but require the user to call for an index explicitly on other attributes. Alternatively, a table might always be kept sorted on its primary key, if it had one.

6.2.2 Maintaining Referential Integrity

We have seen how to declare a foreign key, and we learned that this declaration implies that any non-NULL value in the foreign key must also appear in the corresponding attribute(s) of the referenced relation. But how is this constraint to be maintained in the face of modifications to the database? The database implementor may choose from among three alternatives.

The Default Policy: Reject Violating Modifications

SQL has a default policy that any update violating the referential integrity constraint is rejected by the system. For instance, consider Example 6.3, where it is required that a `presC#` value in relation Studio also be a `cert#` value in MovieExec. The following actions will be rejected by the system (i.e., a run-time error will be generated).

1. We try to insert a new Studio tuple whose `presC#` value is not NULL and is not the `cert#` component of any MovieExec tuple. The insertion is rejected by the system and the tuple is never inserted into Studio.

2. We try to update a Studio tuple to change the `presC#` component to a non-NULL value that is not the `cert#` component of any MovieExec tuple. The update is rejected and the tuple is unchanged.

3. We try to delete a MovieExec tuple, and its `cert#` component appears as the `presC#` component of one or more Studio tuples. The deletion is

rejected and the tuple remains in `MovieExec`.

4. We try to update a `MovieExec` tuple in a way that changes the `cert#` value, and the old `cert#` is the value of `presC#` of some movie studio. We again reject the change and leave `MovieExec` as it was.

The Cascade Policy

There is another approach to handling deletions or updates to a referenced relation like `MovieExec` (i.e., the third and fourth types of modifications described above), called the *cascade policy*. Under this policy, when we delete the `MovieExec` tuple for the president of a studio, then to maintain referential integrity the system will delete the referencing tuple(s) from `Studio`. Updates are handled analogously. If we change the `cert#` for some movie executive from c_1 to c_2, and there was some `Studio` tuple with c_1 as the value of its `presC#` component, then the system will also update this `presC#` component to have value c_2.

The Set-Null Policy

Yet another approach to handling the problem is to change the `presC#` value from that of the deleted or updated studio president to NULL; this policy is called *set-null*.

These options may be chosen for deletes and updates, independently, and they are stated with the declaration of the foreign key. We declare them with `ON DELETE` or `ON UPDATE` followed by our choice of `SET NULL` or `CASCADE`.

Example 6.4: Let us see how we might modify the declaration of

        Studio(name, address, presC#)

in Example 6.3 to specify the handling of deletes and updates in the

        MovieExec(name, address, cert#, netWorth)

relation. Figure 6.3 takes the first of the `CREATE TABLE` statements in that example and expands it with an `ON DELETE` and `ON UPDATE` clause. Line (5) says that when we delete a `MovieExec` tuple, we set the `presC#` of any studio of which he or she was the president to NULL. Line (6) says that if we update the `cert#` component of a `MovieExec` tuple, then any tuples in `Studio` with the same value in the `presC#` component are changed similarly.

Note that in this example, the set-null policy makes more sense for deletes, while the cascade policy seems preferable for updates. We would expect that if, for instance, a studio president retires, the studio will exist with a "null" president for a while. However, an update to the certificate number of a studio president is most likely a clerical change. The person continues to exist and to be the president of the studio, so we would like the `presC#` attribute in `Studio` to follow the change. □

```
1) CREATE TABLE Studio (
2)     name CHAR(30) PRIMARY KEY,
3)     address VARCHAR(255),
4)     presC# INT REFERENCES MovieExec(cert#)
5)         ON DELETE SET NULL
6)         ON UPDATE CASCADE
   );
```

Figure 6.3: Choosing policies to preserve referential integrity

6.2.3 Exercises for Section 6.2

Exercise 6.2.1: Declare the following referential integrity constraints for the movie database

```
Movie(title, year, length, inColor, studioName, producerC#)
StarsIn(movieTitle, movieYear, starName)
MovieStar(name, address, gender, birthdate)
MovieExec(name, address, cert#, netWorth)
Studio(name, address, presC#)
```

a) The producer of a movie must be someone mentioned in MovieExec. Modifications to MovieExec that violate this constraint are rejected.

b) Repeat (a), but violations result in the producerC# in Movie being set to NULL.

c) Repeat (a), but violations result in the deletion of the offending Movie tuple.

d) A movie that appears in StarsIn must also also appear in Movie. Handle violations by rejecting the modification.

e) A star appearing in StarsIn must also appear in MovieStar. Handle violations by deleting violating tuples.

*! **Exercise 6.2.2:** We would like to declare the constraint that every movie in the relation Movie must appear with at least one star in StarsIn. Can we do so with a foreign-key constraint? Why or why not?

Exercise 6.2.3: Write the following referential integrity constraints, based on the database schema

```
Classes(class, type, country, numGuns, bore, displacement)
Ships(name, class, launched)
Battles(name, date)
Outcomes(ship, battle, result)
```

Dangling Tuples and Modification Policies

A tuple with a foreign key value that does not appear in the referenced relation is said to be a *dangling tuple*. Recall that a tuple which fails to participate in a join is also called "dangling." The two ideas are closely related. If a tuple's foreign-key value is missing from the referenced relation, then the tuple will not participate in a join of its relation with the referenced relation.

    The dangling tuples are exactly the tuples that violate referential integrity for this foreign-key constraint.

- The default policy for deletions and updates to the referenced relation is that the action is forbidden if and only if it creates one or more dangling tuples in the referencing relation.

- The cascade policy is to delete or update all dangling tuples created (depending on whether the modification is a delete or update to the referenced relation, respectively).

- The set-null policy is to set the foreign key to NULL in each dangling tuple.

---

of Exercise 4.1.3. Make reasonable assumptions about keys and handle all violations by setting the referencing attribute value to NULL.

* a) Every class mentioned in Ships must be mentioned in Classes.

  b) Every battle mentioned in Outcomes must be mentioned in Battles.

  c) Every ship mentioned in Outcomes must be mentioned in Ships.

6.3 Constraints on the Values of Attributes

We have seen key constraints, which force certain attributes to have distinct values among all the tuples of a relation, and we have seen foreign-key constraints, which enforce referential integrity between attributes of two relations. Now, we shall see a third important kind of constraint: one that limits the values that may appear in components for some attribute. These constraints may be expressed as either:

1. A constraint on the attribute in the definition of its relation's schema, or

2. A constraint on a domain, which is then declared to be the domain for the attribute in question.

In Section 6.3.1 we shall introduce a simple type of constraint on an attribute's value: the constraint that the attribute not have a NULL value. Then in Section 6.3.2 we cover the principal form of constraints of type (1): *attribute-based* CHECK *constraints*. Constraints of the second type — on domains — are covered in Section 6.3.3. There are other, more general kinds of constraints that we shall meet in Section 6.4. These constraints can be used to restrict changes to whole tuples or even a whole relation or several relations, as well as to constrain the value of a single attribute.

6.3.1 Not-Null Constraints

One simple constraint to associate with an attribute is NOT NULL. The effect is to disallow tuples in which this attribute is NULL. The constraint is declared by the keywords NOT NULL following the declaration of the attribute in a CREATE TABLE statement.

Example 6.5 : Suppose relation Studio required presC# not to be NULL, perhaps by changing line (4) of Fig. 6.3 to:

```
4)      presC# INT REFERENCES MovieExec(cert#) NOT NULL
```

This change has several consequences. For instance:

- We could not update the value of the presC# component of a tuple to be NULL.

- We could not insert a tuple into Studio by specifying only the name and address, because the inserted tuple would have NULL in the presC# component.

- We could not use the set-null policy in situations like line (5) of Fig. 6.3, which tells the system to fix foreign-key violations by making presC# be NULL.

□

6.3.2 Attribute-Based CHECK Constraints

More complex constraints can be attached to an attribute declaration by the keyword CHECK, followed by a parenthesized condition that must hold for every value of this attribute. In practice, an attribute-based CHECK constraint is likely to be a simple limit on values, such as an enumeration of legal values or an arithmetic inequality. However, in principle the condition can be anything that could follow WHERE in an SQL query. This condition may refer to the attribute being constrained. However, if it refers to any other relations or attributes of relations, then the relation must be introduced in the FROM clause of a subquery (even if the relation referred to is the one to which the checked attribute belongs).

An attribute-based CHECK constraint is checked whenever any tuple gets a new value for this attribute. The new value could be introduced by an update for the tuple, or it could be part of an inserted tuple. If the constraint is violated by the new value, then the modification is rejected. As we shall see in Example 6.7, the attribute-based CHECK constraint is not necessarily checked if a database modification does not change a value of the attribute with which the constraint is associated, and this limitation can result in the constraint becoming violated. First, let us consider a simple example of an attribute-based check.

Example 6.6 : Suppose we want to require that certificate numbers be at least six digits. We could modify line (4) of Fig. 6.3, a declaration of the schema for relation

```
    Studio(name, address, presC#)
```

to be

```
4)      presC# INT REFERENCES MovieExec(cert#)
                CHECK (presC# >= 100000)
```

For another example, the attribute gender of relation

```
    MovieStar(name, address, gender, birthdate)
```

was declared in Fig. 5.13 to be of data type CHAR(1) — that is, a single character. However, we really expect that the only characters that will appear there are 'F' and 'M'. The following substitute for line (4) of Fig. 5.13 serves.

```
4) gender CHAR(1) CHECK (gender IN ('F', 'M')),
```

The above condition uses an explicit relation with two values, and says that the value of any gender component must be in this set.   □

It is permitted for the condition being checked to mention other attributes or tuples of the relation, or even to mention other relations, but doing so requires a subquery in the condition. As we said, the condition can be anything that could follow WHERE in a select-from-where SQL statement. However, we should be aware that the checking of the constraint is associated with the attribute in question only, not with every relation or attribute mentioned by the constraint. As a result, the condition can become false, if some element other than the checked attribute changes.

Example 6.7 : We might suppose that we could simulate a referential integrity constraint by an attribute-based CHECK constraint that requires the existence of the referred-to value. The following is an *erroneous* attempt to simulate the requirement that the presC# value in a

```
Studio(name, address, presC#)
```

tuple must appear in the **cert#** component of some

```
MovieExec(name, address, cert#, netWorth)
```

tuple. Suppose line (4) of Fig. 6.3 were replaced by

```
4)      presC# INT CHECK
            (presC# IN (SELECT cert# FROM MovieExec))
```

This statement is a legal attribute-based **CHECK** constraint, but let us look at its effect.

- If we attempt to insert a new tuple into **Studio**, and that tuple has a **presC#** value that is not the certificate of any movie executive, then the insertion is rejected.

- If we attempt to update the **presC#** component of a **Studio** tuple, and the new value is not the **cert#** of a movie executive, the update is rejected.

- However, if we change the **MovieExec** relation, say by deleting the tuple for the president of a studio, this change is invisible to the above **CHECK** constraint. Thus, the deletion is permitted, even though the attribute-based **CHECK** constraint on **presC#** is now violated.

We shall see in Section 6.4.2 how more powerful constraint forms can correctly express this condition. □

6.3.3 Domain Constraints

We can also constrain the values of an attribute by declaring a domain (see Section 5.7.6) with a similar constraint and then declaring that domain to be the data type for the attribute. The only important difference is that when we try to write a constraint about a value in a domain, we do not have anything to call that value. In comparison, when we wrote a constraint about an attribute, we had the name of that attribute to refer to its value. SQL2 solves this problem by providing the special keyword **VALUE** to refer to a value in the domain.

Example 6.8: We could declare a domain **GenderDomain** to have only the two characters 'F' and 'M' as values by:

```
CREATE DOMAIN GenderDomain CHAR(1)
    CHECK (VALUE IN ('F', 'M'));
```

Then, we could revise line (4) of Fig. 5.13 to read:

```
4) gender GenderDomain,
```

When Should a Constraint Be Checked?

Under normal circumstances, an SQL system will not allow a database modification that causes a constraint to be violated. However, sometimes several related modifications need to be done, and one will cause a violation while the other repairs the problem. For instance, in Example 6.3 we established that `presC#` is a foreign key of `Studio`, referencing `cert#` of `MovieExec`. If we want to add a new studio and its president, then adding the studio first will violate the foreign-key constraint.

 It seems we could fix the problem by adding the president to `MovieExec` first. However, suppose there were also a constraint that tuples in `MovieExec` had to have certificates that appeared either as a studio president or a producer (in `Movie`). Then, no order would be proper.

 Fortunately, SQL2 gives us the ability to declare a constraint to be `DEFERRED`. Then, the checking of the constraint will not take place until the "transaction" (a basic unit of operation on the database; see Section 7.2) is completed. We can include the insertion of both a studio and its president in a single transaction, thus avoiding this spurious constraint violation.

Similarly, the same effect as in Example 6.6, where we required six-digit certificates for the attribute `presC#`, can be had by declaring a domain

```
CREATE DOMAIN CertDomain INT
    CHECK (VALUE >= 100000);
```

If we then write the declaration of attribute `presC#`:

```
4)     presC# CertDomain REFERENCES MovieExec(cert#)
```

we have the desired constraint. □

6.3.4 Exercises for Section 6.3

Exercise 6.3.1: Write the following constraints for attributes of the relation

```
Movie(title, year, length, inColor, studioName, producerC#)
```

* a) The year cannot be before 1895.

 b) The length cannot be less than 60 nor more than 250.

* c) The studio name can only be Disney, Fox, MGM, or Paramount.

Exercise 6.3.2: Write the following constraints on attributes from our example schema

```
Product(maker, model, type)
PC(model, speed, ram, hd, cd, price)
Laptop(model, speed, ram, hd, screen, price)
Printer(model, color, type, price)
```

of Exercise 4.1.1.

a) The speed of a laptop must be at least 100.

b) The speed of a CD can be only 4x, 6x, 8x, or 12x.

c) The only types of printers are laser, ink-jet, and dry.

d) The only types of products are PC's, laptops, and printers.

e) The amount of RAM a PC has must be at least 1% of the amount of hard disk it has.

6.4 Global Constraints

Now, we shall take up the declaration of more complex constraints that involve relationships between several attributes or even several different relations. The subject is divided into two parts:

1. *Tuple-based* CHECK *constraints*, which restrict any aspect of the tuples of a single relation, and

2. *Assertions*, which are constraints that may involve entire relations or several tuple-variables ranging over the same relation.

6.4.1 Tuple-Based CHECK Constraints

To declare a constraint on the tuples of a single table R, when we define that table with a CREATE TABLE statement, we may add to the list of attributes and key or foreign key declarations the keyword CHECK followed by a parenthesized condition. This condition can be anything that could appear in a WHERE clause. It is interpreted as a condition about a tuple in the table R. However, as for attribute-based CHECK constraints, the condition may mention, in subqueries, other relations or other tuples of the same relation R.

The condition of a tuple-based CHECK constraint is checked every time a tuple is inserted into R and every time a tuple of R is updated. The condition of the check is evaluated for every new or updated tuple. If it is false for that tuple, then the constraint is violated and the insertion or update that caused the violation is rejected. However, if the condition mentions R some relation (even R itself) in a subquery, and a change to that relation causes the condition to become false for some tuple of R, the check does not inhibit this change. That is, like the attribute-based CHECK discussed in Example 6.7, a tuple-based CHECK is invisible to other relations.

Although tuple-based checks can involve some very complex conditions, it is often best to leave complex checks to SQL's "assertions," which we discuss in Section 6.4.2. The reason is that, as discussed above, tuple-based checks can be violated under certain conditions. However, if the tuple-based check involves only attributes of the tuple being checked and has no subqueries, then its constraint will always hold. Here is one example of a simple tuple-based CHECK constraint that involves several attributes of one tuple.

Example 6.9: Recall Example 5.32, where we declared the schema of table MovieStar. Figure 6.4 repeats the CREATE TABLE statement with the addition of a key declaration using the keyword UNIQUE and one other constraint, which is one of several possible "consistency conditions" that we might wish to check. This constraint says that if the star's gender is male, then his name must not begin with 'Ms.'.

```
1) CREATE TABLE MovieStar (
2)     name CHAR(30) UNIQUE,
3)     address VARCHAR(255),
4)     gender CHAR(1),
5)     birthdate DATE,
6)     CHECK (gender = 'F' OR name NOT LIKE 'Ms.%')
   );
```

Figure 6.4: A constraint on the table MovieStar

In line (2), name is declared a key for the relation. Then line (6) declares a constraint. The condition of this constraint is true for every female movie star and for every star whose name does not begin with 'Ms.'. The only tuples for which it is *not* true are those where the gender is male and the name *does* begin with 'Ms.'. Those are exactly the tuples we wish to exclude from MovieStar. □

6.4.2 Assertions

We have advanced from constraints on attributes to constraints on tuples. But sometimes even these forms are not enough. We sometimes need a constraint that involves a relation as a whole, for example a constraint on the sum or another aggregation of the values in one column. There is also use for a constraint that involves more than one relation. In fact, foreign-key constraints are an example we have already seen of a constraint connecting two relations, but foreign-key constraints have a limited form.

SQL2's *assertions* (also called "general constraints") allow us to enforce any condition (expression that can follow WHERE). While other types of constraints

Writing Constraints Correctly

Many constraints are like Example 6.9, where we want to forbid tuples that satisfy two or more conditions. The expression that should follow the check is the OR of the negations, or opposites, of each condition. Thus, in Example 6.9 the first condition was that the star be male, and we used gender = 'F' as a suitable negation (although perhaps gender <> 'M' would be the more normal way to phrase the negation). The second condition is that the name begin with 'Ms.', and for this negation we used the NOT LIKE comparison. This comparison negates the condition itself, which would be name LIKE 'Ms.%' in SQL.

are associated with other schema elements, usually base tables or domains, assertions are themselves schema elements.

Like other schema elements, we declare an assertion with a CREATE statement. The form of an assertion is:

1. The keywords CREATE ASSERTION,

2. The name of the assertion,

3. The keyword CHECK, and

4. A parenthesized condition.

That is, the form of this statement is

CREATE ASSERTION <name> CHECK (<condition>)

The condition in an assertion must always be true, and any database modification whatsoever that causes it to become false will be rejected. Recall that the other types of CHECK constraints we have covered can be violated under certain conditions, if they involve subqueries.

There is a difference between the way we write tuple-based CHECK constraints and the way we write assertions. Tuple-based checks can refer to the attributes of that relation in whose declaration they appear. For instance, in line (6) of Fig. 6.4 we used attributes gender and name without saying where they came from. They refer to components of a tuple of the table MovieStar, because that table is the one being declared in the CREATE statement.

The condition of an assertion has no such privilege. Any attributes referred to in the condition must be introduced in the assertion, typically by mentioning their relation in a select-from-where expression. Since the condition must have a boolean value, it is normal to aggregate the results of the condition in some way to make a single true/false choice. For example, we might write the condition as an expression producing a relation, to which NOT EXISTS is applied; that

---

Limited Constraint Checking: Bug or Feature?

One might wonder why attribute- and tuple-based checks are allowed to be violated if they refer to other relations or other tuples of the same relation. The reason is that such constraints can be implemented more efficiently than assertions can. With attribute- or tuple-based checks, we only have to evaluate that constraint for the tuple(s) that are inserted or updated. On the other hand, assertions must be evaluated every time any one of the relations they mention is changed. Whether the extra evaluations are worth the additional running time of database modifications is a judgement for the database designer to make. However, we recommend, for the sake of long-term reliability of code, that the designer *not* use an attribute- or tuple-based check that can become violated.

```
CREATE ASSERTION RichPres CHECK
    (NOT EXISTS
        (SELECT *
         FROM Studio, MovieExec
         WHERE presC# = cert# AND netWorth < 10000000
         )
    );
```

Figure 6.5: Assertion guaranteeing rich studio presidents

is, the constraint is that this relation is always empty. Alternatively, we might apply an aggregate operator like SUM to a column of a relation and compare it to a constant. For instance, this way we could require that a sum always be less than some limiting value.

Example 6.10: Suppose we wish to require that no one can become the president of a studio unless their net worth is at least $10,000,000. We declare an assertion to the effect that the set of movie studios with presidents having a net worth less than $10,000,000 is empty. This assertion involves the two relations

```
MovieExec(name, address, cert#, netWorth)
Studio(name, address, presC#)
```

The assertion is shown in Fig. 6.5.

Incidentally, it is worth noting that even though this constraint involves two relations, we could write it as tuple-based CHECK constraints on the two relations rather than as a single assertion. For instance, we can add to the CREATE TABLE statement of Example 6.3 a constraint on Studio as shown in Fig. 6.6.

```
1) CREATE TABLE Studio (
2)     name CHAR(30) PRIMARY KEY,
3)     address VARCHAR(255),
4)     presC# INT REFERENCES MovieExec(cert#),
5)     CHECK (presC# NOT IN
6)         (SELECT cert# FROM MovieExec
7)         WHERE netWorth < 10000000)
        )
    );
```

Figure 6.6: A constraint on `Studio` mirroring an assertion

Note, however, that the constraint of Fig. 6.6 will only be checked when a change to its relation, `Studio` occurs. It would not catch a situation where the net worth of some studio president, as recorded in relation `MovieExec`, dropped below $10,000,000. To get the full effect of the assertion, we would have to add another constraint to the declaration of the table `MovieExec`, requiring that the net worth be at least $10,000,000 if that executive is the president of a studio. □

Example 6.11: Here is another example of an assertion. It affects only relation

```
Movie(title, year, length, inColor, studioName, producerC#)
```

and says the total length of all movies by a given studio shall not exceed 10,000 minutes.

```
CREATE ASSERTION SumLength CHECK (10000 >= ALL
    (SELECT SUM(length) FROM Movie GROUP BY studioName);
)
```

This constraint happens to involve only the relation `Movie`. It could have been expressed as a tuple-based `CHECK` constraint in the schema for `Movie` rather than as an assertion. That is, we could add to the definition of table `Movie` the tuple-based `CHECK` constraint

```
CHECK (10000 >= ALL
    (SELECT SUM(length) FROM Movie GROUP BY studioName));
```

Notice that in principle this condition applies to every tuple of table `Movie`. However, it does not mention any attributes of the tuple explicitly, and all the work is done in the subquery.

Comparison of Constraints

The following table lists the principal differences among attribute-based checks, tuple-based checks, and assertions.

Type of Constraint	Where Declared	When Activated	Guaranteed to Hold?
Attribute-based CHECK	With attribute	On insertion to relation or attribute update	Not if subqueries
Tuple-based CHECK	Element of relation schema	On insertion to relation or tuple update	Not if subqueries
Assertion	Element of database schema	On change to any mentioned relation	Yes

---

Also observe that if implemented as a tuple-based constraint, the check would not be made on deletion of a tuple from the relation Movie. In this example, that difference causes no harm, since if the constraint was satisfied before the deletion, then it is surely satisfied after the deletion. However, if the constraint were a lower bound on total length, rather than an upper bound as in this example, then we could find the constraint violated had we written it as a tuple-based check rather than an assertion. □

6.4.3 Exercises for Section 6.4

Exercise 6.4.1: We mentioned in Example 6.10 that the tuple-based CHECK constraint of Fig. 6.6 does only half the job of the assertion of Fig. 6.5. Write the CHECK constraint on MovieExec that is necessary to complete the job.

Exercise 6.4.2: Write the following constraints as tuple-based CHECK constraints on one of the relations of our running movies example:

```
Movie(title, year, length, inColor, studioName, producerC#)
StarsIn(movieTitle, movieYear, starName)
MovieStar(name, address, gender, birthdate)
MovieExec(name, address, cert#, netWorth)
Studio(name, address, presC#)
```

If the constraint actually involves two relations, then you should put constraints in both relations so that whichever relation changes, the constraint will be checked on insertions and updates. Assume no deletions; it is not possible to maintain tuple-based constraints in the face of deletions.

* a) A movie may not be in color if it was made before 1939.

b) A star may not appear in a movie made before they were born.

! c) No two studios may have the same address.

*! d) A name that appears in `MovieStar` must not also appear in `MovieExec`.

! e) A studio name that appears in `Studio` must also appear in at least one `Movie` tuple.

!! f) If a producer of a movie is also the president of a studio, then he or she must be the president of the studio that made the movie.

Exercise 6.4.3: Express the following constraints as SQL assertions. The constraints are based on the relations of Exercise 4.1.1:

```
Product(maker, model, type)
PC(model, speed, ram, hd, cd, price)
Laptop(model, speed, ram, hd, screen, price)
Printer(model, color, type, price)
```

* a) No manufacturer of PC's may also make laptops.

*! b) A manufacturer of a PC must also make a laptop with at least as great a processor speed.

! c) If a laptop has a larger main memory than a PC, then the laptop must also have a higher price than the PC.

!! d) No model number may appear twice among the relations PC, `Laptop`, and `Printer`.

!! e) If the relation `Product` mentions a model and its type, then this model must appear in the relation appropriate to that type.

Exercise 6.4.4: Write the following as tuple-based CHECK constraints about our "PC" schema.

a) A PC with a processor speed less than 150 must not sell for more than $1500.

b) A laptop with a screen size less than 11 inches must have at least a 1 gigabyte hard disk or sell for less than $2000.

Exercise 6.4.5: Express the following constraints as SQL assertions. The constraints are based on the relations of Exercise 4.1.3:

```
Classes(class, type, country, numGuns, bore, displacement)
Ships(name, class, launched)
Battles(name, date)
Outcomes(ship, battle, result)
```

a) No class may have more than 2 ships.

! b) No country may have both battleships and battlecruisers.

! c) No ship with more than 9 guns may be in a battle with a ship having fewer than 9 guns that was sunk.

! d) No ship may be launched before the ship that bears the name of that ship's class.

! e) For every class, there is a ship with the name of that class.

Exercise 6.4.6: Write the following as tuple-based CHECK constraints about our "battleships" schema.

a) No class of ships may have guns with larger than 16-inch bore.

b) If a class of ships has more than 9 guns, then their bore must be no larger than 14 inches.

! c) No ship can be in battle before it is launched.

6.5 Modification of Constraints

It is possible to add, modify, or delete constraints at any time. The way to express such modifications depends on whether the constraint involved is associated with a domain, an attribute, a table, or a database schema.

6.5.1 Giving Names to Constraints

In order to modify or delete an existing constraint, it is necessary that the constraint have a name. Assertions, which are part of the database schema, are always given names as part of their CREATE ASSERTION statement. However, other constraints may also be given names. To do so, we precede the constraint by the keyword CONSTRAINT and a name for the constraint.

Example 6.12: Even a declaration of a primary or foreign key can be named. For instance, we could rewrite line (2) of Fig. 6.1 to name the constraint that says attribute name is a primary key, as

```
2)     name CHAR(30) CONSTRAINT NameIsKey PRIMARY KEY,
```

Similarly, we could name the attribute-based CHECK constraint that appeared in Example 6.6 by:

```
4) gender CHAR(1) CONSTRAINT NoAndro
              CHECK (gender IN ('F', 'M')),
```

The domain constraint from Example 6.8 can be given a name as

```
CREATE DOMAIN CertDomain INT
    CONSTRAINT SixDigits CHECK (VALUE >= 100000);
```

Finally, the following constraint:

```
6)    CONSTRAINT RightTitle
         CHECK (gender = 'F' OR name NOT LIKE 'Ms.\%')
```

is a rewriting of the tuple-based CHECK constraint in line (6) of Fig. 6.4 to give that constraint a name. □

6.5.2 Altering Constraints on Tables

We can modify the set of constraints associated with a domain, an attribute, or a table with an ALTER statement. We discussed some uses of the ALTER TABLE statement in Section 5.7.4, where we used it to add and delete attributes. Similarly, we discussed ALTER DOMAIN in Section 5.7.6, where we used it to change the default value.

These statements can also be used to alter constraints; ALTER TABLE is used for both attribute-based and tuple-based checks. We may drop a constraint with keyword DROP and the name of the constraint to be dropped. We may also add a constraint with the keyword ADD, followed by the constraint to be added.

Example 6.13: Let us see how we would drop and add the constraints of Example 6.12. First, the constraint that name is the primary key for relation MovieStar can be dropped by

```
ALTER TABLE MovieStar DROP CONSTRAINT NameIsKey;
```

The attribute-based CHECK constraint for the same relation that restricts the values for the **gender** attribute is dropped by

```
ALTER TABLE MovieStar DROP CONSTRAINT NoAndro;
```

. Also, the constraint on relation MovieStar that restricted the title 'Ms.' to female stars can be dropped by

```
ALTER TABLE MovieStar DROP CONSTRAINT RightTitle;
```

Should we wish to reinstate these constraints, we would alter the schema for relation MovieStar by adding the same constraints, for example:

Name Your Constraints

Remember, it is a good idea to give each of your constraints a name, even if you do not believe you will ever need to refer to it. Once the constraint is created without a name, it is too late to give it one later, should you need to alter it in any way.

```
ALTER TABLE MovieStar ADD CONSTRAINT NameIsKey
    PRIMARY KEY (name);
ALTER TABLE MovieStar ADD CONSTRAINT NoAndro
    CHECK (gender IN ('F', 'M'));
ALTER TABLE MovieStar ADD CONSTRAINT RightTitle
    CHECK (gender = 'F' OR name NOT LIKE 'Ms.\%')
```

These constraints are now tuple-based, rather than attribute-based checks. We could not bring them back as attribute constraints, although if the attributes' types were domains, we could alter the constraints on those domains instead of altering the MovieStar table.

The name is optional for these reintroduced constraints. However, we cannot rely on SQL remembering the constraints that were associated with the constraint names. Thus, when we add a former constraint we need to write the constraint again; we cannot refer to it only by name. □

6.5.3   Altering Domain Constraints

We drop and add constraints on a domain in essentially the same way that we drop or add tuple-based checks. To drop a domain constraint, we use an ALTER statement, where the keyword DROP is followed by the name of the constraint. To add a constraint for a domain, the ALTER statement has the keyword ADD, the name of the constraint, and a CHECK condition that defines the constraint.

Example 6.14: The domain constraint that certificate numbers have at least six digits can be deleted by:

```
ALTER DOMAIN CertDomain DROP CONSTRAINT SixDigits;
```

Conversely, we can reinstate that constraint by

```
ALTER DOMAIN CertDomain ADD CONSTRAINT SixDigits
    CHECK (VALUE >= 100000);
```

□

6.5.4 Altering Assertions

An assertion may be dropped by a statement consisting of the keywords DROP ASSERTION followed by the name of the assertion.

Example 6.15: The assertion from Example 6.10 may be deleted by the statement

```
DROP ASSERTION RichPres;
```

To reinstate the constraint, declare it again, as we did in Example 6.10. □

6.5.5 Exercises for Section 6.5

Exercise 6.5.1: Show how to alter your relation schemas for the movie example:

```
Movie(title, year, length, inColor, studioName, producerC#)
StarsIn(movieTitle, movieYear, starName)
MovieStar(name, address, gender, birthdate)
MovieExec(name, address, cert#, netWorth)
Studio(name, address, presC#)
```

in the following ways.

* a) Make title and year the key for Movie.

 b) Require the referential integrity constraint that the producer of every movie appear in MovieExec.

 c) Require that no movie length be less than 60 nor greater than 250.

*! d) Require that no name appear as both a movie star and movie executive (this constraint need not be maintained in the face of deletions).

! e) Require that no two studios have the same address.

Exercise 6.5.2: Show how to alter the schemas of the "battleships" database:

```
Classes(class, type, country, numGuns, bore, displacement)
Ships(name, class, launched)
Battles(name, date)
Outcomes(ship, battle, result)
```

to have the following tuple-based constraints.

 a) Class and country form a key for relation Classes.

 b) Require the referential integrity constraint that every ship appearing in Battles also appears in Ships.

c) Require the referential integrity constraint that every ship appearing in `Outcomes` appears in `Ships`.

d) Require that no ship has more than 14 guns.

! e) Disallow a ship being in battle before it is launched.

6.6 Triggers in SQL3

The various forms of constraints that we have studied in this chapter follow the SQL2 standard. They have an execution model in which they are called whenever the element that they are constraining is changed. For example, an attribute-based check would be called whenever this attribute changes in some tuple (including the situation where a tuple is inserted).

Since the implementation of constraints involves "triggering" the check on appropriate events, one might naturally ask whether the selection of triggering events could be given to the database programmer, rather than the system. That approach might give the user some added options to trigger database operations for purposes other than preventing constraint violations. Thus, the proposed SQL3 standard also includes "triggers," which are reminiscent of constraints but have explicitly specified triggering events as well as explicitly specified actions to take based on the result of the condition. Interestingly, current commercial systems are often closer to SQL3 than to SQL2 in their approach to powerful active elements. A possible explanation is that triggers are in a sense easier for the commercial vendors to implement than are assertions.

6.6.1 Triggers and Constraints

Triggers, sometimes called *event-condition-action rules* or *ECA rules*, differ from the kinds of constraints discussed previously in three ways.

1. Triggers are only tested when certain *events*, specified by the database programmer, occur. The sorts of events allowed are usually insert, delete, or update to a particular relation. Another kind of event allowed in many SQL systems is a transaction end (see Section 7.2 for a discussion of the atomic work units called transactions that are used for the bulk of database operations).

2. Instead of immediately preventing the event that woke it up, a trigger tests a *condition*. If the condition does not hold, then nothing else associated with the trigger happens in response to this event.

3. If the condition of the trigger is satisfied, the *action* associated with the trigger is performed by the DBMS. The action may then prevent the event from taking place, or it could undo the event (e.g., delete the tuple inserted). In fact, the action could be any sequence of database operations, perhaps even operations not connected in any way to the triggering event.

In what follows, we shall first consider triggers in SQL3. Then, we shall discuss briefly SQL3's extension to the SQL2 constraints called "assertions." These constraints also incorporate some aspects of triggers.

6.6.2 SQL3 Triggers

The SQL3 trigger statement gives the user a number of different options in the event, condition, and action parts. Here are the principal features.

1. The action can be executed before, after, or instead of the triggering event.

2. The action can refer to both old and new values of tuples that were inserted, deleted, or updated in the event that triggered the action.

3. Update events may specify a particular column or set of columns.

4. A condition may be specified by a WHEN clause, and the action is only executed if the rule is triggered *and* the condition holds when the triggering event occurs.

5. The programmer has an option of specifying that the action is performed either:

   (a) Once for each modified tuple, or

   (b) Once for all the tuples that are changed in one database operation.

Before giving the details of the syntax for triggers, let us consider an example that will illustrate the most important syntactic as well as semantic points. In this example, the trigger executes once for each tuple that is updated.

Example 6.16: We shall write an SQL3 trigger that applies to the

```
MovieExec(name, address, cert#, netWorth)
```

table. It is triggered by updates to the netWorth attribute. The effect of this rule is to restore any attempt to lower the net worth of a studio president. The trigger declaration appears in Fig. 6.7.

Line (1) introduces the declaration with the keywords CREATE TRIGGER and the name of the trigger. Line (2) then gives the triggering event, namely the update of the netWorth attribute of the MovieExec relation. Lines (3) through (5) set up a way for the condition and action portions of this trigger to talk about both the old tuple (the tuple before the update) and the new tuple (the tuple after the update). These tuples will be referred to as OldTuple and NewTuple, according to the declarations in lines (4) and (5), respectively. In the condition and action, these names can be used as if they were tuple variables declared in the FROM clause of an ordinary SQL query.

```
1)   CREATE TRIGGER NetWorthTrigger
2)   AFTER UPDATE OF netWorth ON MovieExec
3)   REFERENCING
4)       OLD AS OldTuple,
5)       NEW AS NewTuple
6)   WHEN(OldTuple.netWorth > NewTuple.netWorth)
7)       UPDATE MovieExec
8)       SET netWorth = OldTuple.netWorth
9)       WHERE cert# = NewTuple.cert#
10)  FOR EACH ROW
```

Figure 6.7: An SQL3 trigger

Line (6) is the condition part of the trigger. It says that we only perform the action when the new net worth is lower than the old net worth; i.e., the net worth of an executive has shrunk.

Lines (7) through (9) form the action portion; they are an ordinary SQL update statement, and they have the effect of restoring the net worth of this executive to what it was before the update. Note that in principle, every tuple of MovieExec is considered, but the WHERE-clause of line (9) guarantees that only the updated tuple (the one with the proper cert#) will be affected.

Finally, Line (10) expresses the requirement that this triggering occurs once for each updated tuple. If it is missing, then the triggering would occur once for an SQL statement, no matter how many triggering-event changes to tuples it made. □

Of course Example 6.16 illustrates only some of the features of SQL3 triggers. In the points that follow, we shall outline the options that are offered by triggers and how to express these options.

- Line (2) of Fig. 6.7 says that the action of the rule is executed after the triggering event, as indicated by the keyword AFTER. Alternatives to AFTER are

  1. BEFORE. The WHEN condition is tested before the triggering event. If the condition is true, then the action of the trigger is executed. Then, the event that triggered the update is executed, regardless of whether the condition was true.

  2. INSTEAD OF. The action is executed (if the WHEN condition is met), and the triggering event is never executed.

- Besides UPDATE, other possible triggering events are INSERT and DELETE. The OF netWorth clause in line (2) of Fig. 6.7 is optional for UPDATE events, and if present defines the event to be only an update of the attribute(s) listed after the keyword OF. An OF clause is not permitted for INSERT or DELETE events; these events make sense for entire tuples only.

- While we showed a single SQL statement as an action, there can be any number of such statements, separated by semicolons.

- When the triggering event is an update, then there will be old and new tuples, which are the tuple before the update and after, respectively. We give these tuples names by the OLD AS and NEW AS clauses seen in lines (4) and (5). If the triggering event is an insertion, then we may use a NEW AS clause to give a name for the inserted tuple, and OLD AS is disallowed. Conversely, on a deletion OLD AS is used to name the deleted tuple and NEW AS is disallowed.

- If we omit the FOR EACH ROW on line (10), then a *row-level trigger* such as Fig. 6.7 becomes a *statement-level trigger*. A statement-level trigger is executed once for each statement that generates one or more triggering events. For instance, if we update an entire table with an SQL update statement, a statement-level update trigger would execute only once, while a tuple-level trigger would execute once for each tuple. In a statement-level trigger, we cannot refer to old and new tuples directly, as we did in lines (4) and (5). Rather, we can refer to the set of *old tuples* (deleted tuples or old versions of updated tuples) and the set of *new tuples* (inserted tuples or new versions of updated tuples) as two relations. We use declarations such as OLD_TABLE AS OldStuff and NEW_TABLE AS NewStuff in place of the declarations in lines (4) and (5) of Fig. 6.7. OldStuff names a relation containing all the new tuples as defined above, while NewStuff refers to a relation containing the new tuples.

Example 6.17: Suppose we want to prevent the average net worth of movie executives from dropping below $500,000. This constraint could be violated by an insertion, a deletion, or an update to the netWorth column of

```
MovieExec(name, address, cert#, netWorth)
```

We need to write one trigger for each of these three events. Figure 6.8 shows the trigger for the update event. The triggers for the insertion and deletion of tuples are similar but slightly simpler.

Lines (3) through (5) declare that NewStuff and OldStuff are the names of relations containing the new tuples and old tuples that are involved in the database operation that triggered our rule. Note that one database statement can modify many tuples of a relation, and if such a statement executes, there can be many tuples in NewStuff and OldStuff.

If the operation is an update, then NewStuff and OldStuff are the new and old versions of the updated tuples, respectively. If an analogous trigger were written for deletions, then the deleted tuples would be in OldStuff, and there

```
1)   CREATE TRIGGER AvgNetWorthTrigger
2)   INSTEAD OF UPDATE OF netWorth ON MovieExec
3)   REFERENCING
4)       OLD_TABLE AS OldStuff
5)       NEW_TABLE AS NewStuff

6)   WHEN(500000 <=
7)       (SELECT AVG(netWorth)
8)        FROM ((MovieExec EXCEPT OldStuff) UNION NewStuff)
         )

9)   DELETE FROM MovieExec
10)  WHERE (name, address, cert#, netWorth) IN OldStuff;

11)  INSERT INTO MovieExec
12)      (SELECT * FROM NewStuff);
```

Figure 6.8: Constraining the average net worth

would be no declaration of a relation name like NewStuff for NEW_TABLE in this trigger. Likewise, in the analogous trigger for insertions, the new tuples would be in NewStuff, and there would be no declaration of OldStuff.

Lines (6) through (8) are the condition. This condition is satisfied if the average net worth *after* the modification is at least $500,000. Notice that the expression on line (8) computes the relation that MovieExec would be if the modification had been made.

However, since line (2) stipulates INSTEAD OF, any attempt to update the netWorth column of MovieExec is intercepted. The modification is never performed. Instead, the trigger uses its condition to decide what to do. In our example, if the modification leaves the average net worth of movie executives at least half a million, then the action has the effect of doing what the modification intended to do. That is, lines (9) and (10) delete the tuples that the modification intended to update, and lines (11) and (12) insert the new versions of these tuples. □

6.6.3 Assertions in SQL3

SQL3 also extends SQL2 assertions in two important ways.

1. Assertions are triggered by programmer-specified events, rather than by events that the system decides might violate the constraint.

2. Optionally, the assertion may refer to each tuple of a table, like a tuple-level check, rather than to the table or tables as a whole.

Example 6.18: The assertion `RichPres` of Example 6.10 is shown in Fig. 6.9, using SQL3's notation. Line (1) begins the declaration, as usual. In lines (2) through (6) we see a number of events that can trigger the checking of the assertion.

```
1)   CREATE ASSERTION RichPres
2)   AFTER
3)       INSERT ON Studio,
4)       UPDATE OF presC# ON Studio,
5)       UPDATE OF netWorth ON MovieExec,
6)       DELETE ON MovieExec
7)   CHECK(NOT EXISTS
8)       (SELECT * FROM Studio, MovieExec
9)        WHERE presC# = cert# AND netWorth < 10000000
         )
     )
```

Figure 6.9: An SQL3 assertion

Recall that in order to intercept all possible changes to the database that could violate the constraint of lines (7) through (9), we need to watch for either a new studio president or a change in the net worth of some executive. Thus, lines (3) and (4) cause the assertion to be checked any time a `Studio` tuple is inserted or the certificate number of the studio's president is updated (i.e., the president changes). Lines (5) and (6) trigger the check when either the net worth of any executive is updated, or an executive is deleted, either of which could cause the constraint to become false. The constraint to be checked is in lines (7) through (9) and is essentially the same as that of Example 6.10. □

The major difference between the SQL3 approach to assertions and the SQL2 approach is that the assertion of Fig. 6.9 makes it explicit when the check needs to be performed. That situation makes the SQL3 assertion easier for the system implementors, but harder for the user, who:

1. Must discover all the events that might trigger the constraint, and

2. Runs the risk of allowing the database to enter an inconsistent state if the events are chosen incorrectly.

6.6.4 Exercises for Section 6.6

Exercise 6.6.1: Write the SQL3 triggers analogous to Fig. 6.8 for the insertion and deletion events on `MovieExec`.

Exercise 6.6.2: Write the following SQL3 triggers or assertions based on the "PC" example of Exercise 4.1.1:

```
Product(maker, model, type)
PC(model, speed, ram, hd, cd, price)
Laptop(model, speed, ram, hd, screen, price)
Printer(model, color, type, price)
```

* a) When updating the price of a PC, check that there is no lower priced PC with the same speed.

  b) When inserting a new printer, check that the model number exists in `Product`.

! c) When making any modification to the `Laptop` relation, check that the average price of laptops for each manufacturer is at least $2000.

! d) When updating the RAM or hard disk of any PC, check that the updated PC has at least 100 times as much hard disk as RAM.

! e) When inserting a new PC, laptop, or printer, make sure that the model number did not previously appear in PC, `Laptop`, or `Printer`.

Exercise 6.6.3: Based on the database schema

```
Classes(class, type, country, numGuns, bore, displacement)
Ships(name, class, launched)
Battles(name, date)
Outcomes(ship, battle, result)
```

of Exercise 4.1.3, write one or more SQL3 triggers or assertions to accomplish the following:

* a) When a new class is inserted into `Classes`, also insert a ship with the name of that class and a `NULL` launch date.

  b) When a new class is inserted with a displacement greater than 35,000 tons, allow the insertion, but change the displacement to 35,000.

! c) If a tuple is inserted into `Outcomes`, check that the ship and battle are listed in `Ships` and `Battles`, respectively, and if not, insert tuples into one or both of these relations, with `NULL` components where necessary.

! d) When there is an insertion into `Ships` or an update of the `class` attribute of `Ships`, check that no country has more than 20 ships and undo the insertion if so.

!! e) Check, under all circumstances that could cause a violation, that no ship fought in a battle that was at a later date than another battle in which that ship was sunk. Prevent the modification from taking place, if so.

! **Exercise 6.6.4:** Write the following either as SQL3 triggers or SQL3 assertions, as appropriate. The problems are based on our running movie example:

```
Movie(title, year, length, inColor, studioName, producerC#)
StarsIn(movieTitle, movieYear, starName)
MovieStar(name, address, gender, birthdate)
MovieExec(name, address, cert#, netWorth)
Studio(name, address, presC#)
```

You may assume that the desired condition holds before any change to the database is attempted. Also, prefer to modify the database, even if it means inserting tuples with NULL or default values, rather than rejecting the attempted modification.

a) Assure that at all times, any star appearing in StarsIn also appears in MovieStar.

b) Assure that at all times every movie executive appears as either a studio president, a producer of a movie, or both.

c) Assure that every movie has at least one male and one female star.

d) Assure that the number of movies made by any studio in any year is no more than 100.

e) Assure that the average length of all movies made in any year is no more than 120.

! **Exercise 6.6.5:** In Example 6.17 we handled bad modifications by checking first and then doing the modification if it did not violate the condition. Another approach is to allow the modification to take place and then undo it if it violates the condition. Write this trigger.

6.7 Summary of Chapter 6

✦ *Key Constraints*: We can declare an attribute or set of attributes to be a key with a UNIQUE or PRIMARY KEY declaration in a relation schema.

✦ *Referential Integrity Constraints*: We can declare that a value appearing in some attribute or set of attributes must also appear in the primary key attributes of some tuple of another relation with a REFERENCES or FOREIGN KEY declaration in a relation schema.

✦ *Value-Based Check Constraints*: We can check a constraint on the value for some attribute by adding the keyword CHECK and the condition to be checked after the declaration of that attribute in its relation schema. Alternatively, we can use a domain for the type of that attribute and specify the condition to be checked in the declaration of the domain.

✦ *Tuple-Based Check Constraints*: We can check a condition about any or all of the components of tuples in a relation by adding the keyword CHECK and the condition to be checked to the declaration of the relation itself.

✦ *Assertions*: We may declare an assertion as an element of a database schema with the keyword CHECK and the condition to be checked. This condition may involve one or more relations of the database schema, and may involve the relation as a whole, e.g., with aggregation, as well as conditions about individual tuples.

✦ *Invoking the Checks*: Assertions are checked whenever a change to one of the relations involved makes it possible that there is a violation of the constraint. Value- and tuple-based checks are only checked when the attribute or relation to which they apply changes by insertion or update of tuples. Thus, these constraints can be violated if they have subqueries that involve other relations or other tuples of the same relation.

✦ *SQL3 Triggers*: The SQL3 proposed standard includes triggers that specify certain events (e.g., insertion, deletion, or update to a particular relation) that call them into play. Once triggered, a condition can be checked, and if true, a specified sequence of actions (SQL statements such as queries and database modifications) will be executed.

✦ *SQL3 Assertions*: The SQL3 standard includes a notion of assertion different from the SQL2 assertion. Like SQL3 triggers, these assertions are called into play by one or more events such as insertion into a relation. When invoked, the SQL3 assertion checks a condition about either relations or tuples and rejects the modification if the condition is not met.

6.8 References for Chapter 6

The reader should go to the bibliographic notes for Chapter 5 for information about how to get the SQL2 or SQL3 standards documents. Reference [4] is a source for information about all aspects of active elements in database systems. [1] discusses recent thinking regarding active elements in SQL3 and future standards. References [2] and [3] discuss HiPAC, an early prototype system that offered active database elements.

1. Cochrane, R. J., H. Pirahesh, and N. Mattos, "Integrating triggers and declarative constraints in SQL database systems," *Intl. Conf. on Very Large Database Systems*, pp. 567–579, 1996.

2. Dayal, U., et al., "The HiPAC project: combining active databases and timing constraints," *SIGMOD Record* **17**:1, pp. 51–70, 1988.

3. McCarthy, D. R., and U. Dayal, "The architecture of an active database management system," *Proc. ACM SIGMOD Intl. Conf. on Management of Data*, pp. 215–224, 1989.

4. Widom, J. and S. Ceri, *Active Database Systems*, Morgan-Kaufmann, San Francisco, 1996.

Chapter 7

System Aspects of SQL

We now turn to the question of how SQL fits into a complete programming environment. For each of the issues mentioned below, we follow the SQL2 standard. In Section 7.1 we see that SQL is most commonly used inside programs that are written in an ordinary programming language, such as C. There are a number of features of SQL that allow us to move data between its own relations and the variables of the surrounding, or "host," language.

Then, Section 7.2 introduces us to the "transaction," an atomic unit of work. Many database applications, such as banking, require that operations on the data appear atomic, or indivisible, even though a large number of concurrent operations may be in progress at once. SQL provides features to allow us to specify transactions, and SQL systems have mechanisms to make sure that what we call a transaction is indeed executed atomically.

Section 7.3 covers additional system issues, such as support for a client-server model of computing. Then, Section 7.4 discusses how SQL controls unauthorized access to data, and how we can tell the SQL system what accesses are authorized.

7.1 SQL in a Programming Environment

To this point, we have used *direct* SQL in our examples. That is, we have assumed that there is an SQL interpreter, which accepts and executes the sorts of SQL queries and commands that we have learned. This mode of operation is actually rare. In practice, most SQL statements are part of some larger program or collection of functions. A more realistic view is that there is a program in some conventional *host* language such as C, but some of the functions in this program or some of the statements within C programs are actually SQL statements. In this section we shall describe the way SQL can be made to operate within a conventional program.

A sketch of a typical programming system that involves SQL statements is in Fig. 7.1. There, we see the programmer writing programs in a host language, but with some special "embedded" SQL statements that are not part of the host language. The entire program is sent to a preprocessor, which changes the embedded SQL statements into something that makes sense in the host language. The representation of the SQL could be as simple as a call to a function that takes the SQL statement as a character-string argument and executes that SQL statement. We also show in Fig. 7.1 the possibility that the programmer writes code directly in the host language, using these function calls as needed.

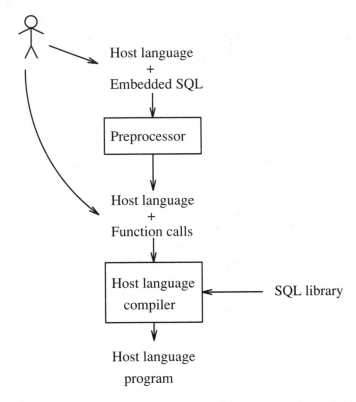

Figure 7.1: Processing programs with SQL statements embedded

The preprocessed host-language program is then compiled in the usual manner. The vendor of the database management system normally provides a library that supplies the necessary function definitions. Thus, the functions that implement SQL can be executed, and the whole program behaves as one unit.

7.1.1 The Impedance Mismatch Problem

The basic problem of connecting SQL statements with those of a conventional programming language is *impedance mismatch*, the fact that the data model of SQL differs so much from the models of other languages. As we know, SQL uses

---

The Languages of the SQL2 Standard

SQL2 implementations are required to support at least the following seven host languages: ADA, C, Cobol, Fortran, M (formerly called Mumps), Pascal, and PL/I. Each of these should be familiar to the student of computer science, with the possible exception of M or Mumps, which is a language used primarily in the medical community. We shall use C in our examples.

---

the relational data model at its core. However, C and other common programming languages use a data model with integers, reals, arithmetic, characters, pointers, record structures, arrays, and so on. Sets are not represented directly in C or these other languages, while SQL does not directly use pointers, arrays, or many other common programming-language constructs. As a result, jumping between SQL and other languages is not straightforward, and a mechanism must be devised to allow the development of programs that use both SQL and another language.

One might first suppose that it is preferable to use a single language; either do all computation in SQL or forget SQL and do all computation in a conventional language. However, we can quickly dispense with the idea of omitting SQL when there are database operations involved. SQL systems greatly aid the programmer in writing database operations that can be executed efficiently, yet that can be expressed at a very high level. SQL takes from the programmer's shoulders the need to understand how data is organized in storage or how to exploit that storage structure to operate efficiently on the database.

On the other hand, there are many important things that SQL cannot do at all. For example, one cannot write an SQL query to compute the factorial of a number n [$n! = n \times (n-1) \times \cdots \times 2 \times 1$], something that is an easy exercise in C or similar languages. SQL cannot directly format its output into a convenient form such as a graphic. Thus, real database programming requires both SQL and a conventional language; the latter is often referred to as the *host language*.

7.1.2 The SQL/Host Language Interface

The transfer of information between the database, which is accessed only by SQL statements, and the host-language program is through variables of the host language that can be read or written by SQL statements. All such *shared variables* are prefixed by a colon when they are referred to by an SQL statement, but they appear without the colon in host-language statements.

When we wish to use an SQL statement within a host-language program, we warn that SQL code is coming with the keywords EXEC SQL in front of the statement. A typical system will preprocess those statements and replace them by suitable function calls in the host language, making use of an SQL-related library of functions.

A special variable, called SQLSTATE in the SQL2 standard serves to connect the host-language program with the SQL execution system.[1] The type of SQLSTATE is an array of five characters. Each time a function of the SQL library is called, a code is put in the variable SQLSTATE that indicates any problems found during that call. For example, '00000' (five zeroes) indicates that no error condition occurred, and '02000' indicates that a tuple requested as part of the answer to an SQL query could not be found. The value of SQLSTATE can be read by the host language program and a decision made on the basis of the value found there.

7.1.3   The DECLARE Section

To declare shared variables, we place their declarations between two embedded SQL statements:

```
EXEC SQL BEGIN DECLARE SECTION;
    ...
EXEC SQL END DECLARE SECTION;
```

What appears between them is called the *declare section*. The form of variable declarations in the declare section is whatever the host language requires. Moreover, it only makes sense to declare variables to have types that both the host language and SQL can deal with, such as integers, reals, and character strings or arrays.

Example 7.1: The following statements might appear in a C function that updates the Studio relation.

```
EXEC SQL BEGIN DECLARE SECTION;
    char studioName[15], studioAddr[50];
    char SQLSTATE[6];
EXEC SQL END DECLARE SECTION;
```

The first and last statements are the required beginning and end of the declare section. In the middle is a statement declaring two variables studioName and studioAddr. These are both character arrays and, as we shall see, they can be used to hold a name and address of a studio that are made into a tuple and inserted into the Studio relation. The third statement declares SQLSTATE to be a six-character array.[2]   □

---

[1] Systems not implementing the SQL2 standard may use a name other than SQLSTATE, but we can expect to find some variable that plays this role.

[2] We shall use six characters for the five-character value of SQLSTATE because in programs to follow we want to use the C function strcmp to test whether SQLSTATE has a certain value. Since strcmp expects strings to be terminated by '\0', we need a sixth character for this endmarker. The sixth character must be set initially to '\0', but we shall not show this assignment in programs to follow.

7.1.4   Using Shared Variables

A shared variable can be used in SQL statements in place of a concrete value. Recall that shared variables are preceded by a colon when so used. Here is an example in which we use the variables of Example 7.1 as components of a tuple to be inserted into relation `Studio`.

Example 7.2: In Fig. 7.2 we find the sketch of a C function `getStudio` that prompts the user for the name and address of a studio, reads the answers, and inserts the appropriate tuple into `Studio`. Lines (1) through (4) are the declarations we learned about in Example 7.1. We omit the C code that prints requests and scans entered text to fill the two arrays `studioName` and `studioAddr`.

```
void getStudio() {

    1) EXEC SQL BEGIN DECLARE SECTION;
    2)     char studioName[15], studioAddr[50];
    3)     char SQLSTATE[6];
    4) EXEC SQL END DECLARE SECTION;

       /* print request that studio name and address be
          entered and read response into variables
          studioName and studioAddr */

    5) EXEC SQL INSERT INTO Studio(name, address)
    6)     VALUES (:studioName, :studioAddr);
}
```

Figure 7.2: Using shared variables to insert a new studio

Then, in lines (5) and (6) is an embedded SQL statement that is a conventional `INSERT` statement. This statement is preceded by the keywords `EXEC SQL` to indicate that it is indeed an embedded SQL statement rather than ungrammatical C code. The preprocessor suggested in Fig. 7.1 will look for `EXEC SQL` to detect statements that must be preprocessed.

The values inserted by lines (5) and (6) are not explicit constants, as they were in previous examples such as in Example 5.27. Rather, the values appearing in line (6) are shared variables whose current values become components of the inserted tuple.   □

There are many kinds of SQL statements besides an `INSERT` statement that can be embedded into a host language, using shared variables as an interface. Each embedded SQL statement is preceded by `EXEC SQL` in the host-language program and may refer to shared variables in place of constants. Any SQL statement that does not return a result (i.e., is not a query) can be embedded. Examples of embeddable of SQL statements include delete- and update-statements and those statements that create, modify, or drop schema elements such as tables and views.

However, select-from-where queries are not embeddable. The reason queries cannot be embedded simply into a host language is the impedance mismatch. Queries produce sets of tuples as a result, while none of the major host languages supports a set data type directly. Thus, embedded SQL must use one of two mechanisms for connecting the result of queries with a host-language program.

1. A query that produces a single tuple can have that tuple stored in shared variables, one variable for each component of the tuple. To do so, we use a modified form of select-from-where statement called a *single-row select*.

2. Queries producing more than one tuple can be executed if we declare a *cursor* for the query. The cursor ranges over all tuples in the answer relation, and each tuple in turn can be fetched into shared variables and processed by the host-language program.

We shall consider each of these mechanisms in turn.

7.1.5 Single-Row Select Statements

The form of a single-row select is the same as an ordinary select-from-where statement, except that following the SELECT clause is the keyword INTO and a list of shared variables. These shared variables are preceded by colons, as is the case for all shared variables within an SQL statement. If the result of the query is a single tuple, this tuple's components become the values of these variables. If the result is either no tuple or more than one tuple, then no assignment to the shared variables are made, and an appropriate code is written in the variable SQLSTATE.

Example 7.3: We shall write a C function to read the name of a studio and print the net worth of the studio's president. A sketch of this function is shown in Fig. 7.3. It begins with a declare section, lines (1) through (5), for the variables we shall need. Next, C statements that we do not show explicitly obtain a studio name from the standard input. Then, lines (6) through (9) are the single-row select statement. It is quite similar to queries we have already seen. The two differences are that the value of variable studioName is used in place of a constant string in the condition of line (9), and there is an INTO clause at line (7) that tells us where to put the result of the query. In this case, we expect a single tuple, and tuples have only one component, that for attribute netWorth. The value of this one component of one tuple is stored in the shared variable presNetWorth of type integer. ☐

```
void printNetWorth() {

1)  EXEC SQL BEGIN DECLARE SECTION;
2)      char studioName[15];
3)      int presNetWorth;
4)      char SQLSTATE[6];
5)  EXEC SQL END DECLARE SECTION;

        /* print request that studio name be entered.
           read response into studioName */

6)  EXEC SQL SELECT netWorth
7)  INTO :presNetWorth
8)  FROM Studio, MovieExec
9)  WHERE presC# = cert# AND Studio.name = :studioName;

        /* check that SQLSTATE has all 0's and if so, print
           the value of presNetWorth */
}
```

Figure 7.3: A single-row select embedded in a C function

7.1.6 Cursors

The most versatile way to connect SQL to a host language is with a cursor that runs through the tuples of a relation. This relation can be a stored table, or it can be something that is generated by a query. To create and use a cursor, we need the following statements:

1. A cursor declaration. The simplest form of a cursor declaration consists of:

   (a) An introductory EXEC SQL, like all embedded SQL statements.

   (b) The keyword DECLARE.

   (c) The name of the cursor.

   (d) The keywords CURSOR FOR.

   (e) An expression such as a relation name or a select-from-where expression, whose value is a relation. The declared cursor *ranges* over the tuples of this relation; that is, the cursor refers to each tuple of this relation, in turn, as the cursor is "fetched."

That is, the form of a cursor declaration is

```
EXEC SQL DECLARE <cursor> CURSOR FOR <query>
```

2. A statement EXEC SQL OPEN, followed by the cursor name. This statement initializes the cursor to a position where it is ready to retrieve the first tuple of the relation over which the cursor ranges.

3. One or more uses of a *fetch statement*. The purpose of a fetch statement is to get the next tuple of the relation over which the cursor ranges. If the tuples have been exhausted, then no tuple is returned, and the value of SQLSTATE is set to '02000', a code that means "no tuple found." The fetch statement consists of the following components:

   (a) The keywords EXEC SQL FETCH FROM.
   (b) The name of the cursor.
   (c) The keyword INTO.
   (d) A list of shared variables, separated by commas. If there is a tuple to fetch, then the components of this tuple are placed in these variables, in order.

That is, the form of a fetch statement is:

    EXEC SQL FETCH FROM <cursor> INTO <list of variables>

4. The statement EXEC SQL CLOSE followed by the name of the cursor. This statement closes the cursor, which now no longer ranges over tuples of the relation. It can, however, be reinitialized by another OPEN statement, in which case it ranges anew over the tuples of this relation.

Example 7.4: Suppose we wish to determine the number of movie executives whose net worths fall into a sequence of exponentially growing bands, each band corresponding to the number of digits in their net worth. We shall design a query that retrieves the netWorth field of all the MovieExec tuples into a shared variable called worth. A cursor called execCursor will range over all these one-component tuples. Each time a tuple is fetched, we compute the number of digits in the integer worth and increment the appropriate element of an array counts.

The C function worthRanges begins in line (1) of Fig. 7.4. Line (2) declares some variables used only by the C function, not by the embedded SQL. The array counts holds the counts of executives in the various bands, digits counts the number of digits in a net worth, and i is an index ranging over the elements of array counts.

Lines (3) through (6) are an SQL declare section in which shared variable worth and the usual SQLSTATE are declared. Lines (7) and (8) declare execCursor to be a cursor that ranges over the values produced by the query on line (8). This query simply asks for the netWorth components of all the tuples in MovieExec. This cursor is then opened at line (9). Line (10) completes the initialization by zeroing the elements of array counts.

```
1) void worthRanges() {

2)      int i, digits, counts[15];

3)      EXEC SQL BEGIN DECLARE SECTION;
4)          int worth;
5)          char SQLSTATE[6];
6)      EXEC SQL END DECLARE SECTION;

7)      EXEC SQL DECLARE execCursor CURSOR FOR
8)          SELECT netWorth FROM MovieExec;

9)      EXEC SQL OPEN execCursor;

10)     for(i=0; i<15; i++) counts[i] = 0;
11)     while(1) {
12)         EXEC SQL FETCH FROM execCursor INTO :worth;
13)         if(NO_MORE_TUPLES) break;
14)         digits = 1;
15)         while((worth /= 10) > 0) digits++;
16)         if(digits <= 14) counts[digits]++;
        }
17)     EXEC SQL CLOSE execCursor;
18)     for(i=0; i<15; i++)
19)         printf("digits = %d: number of execs = %d\n",
                i, counts[i]);
    }
```

Figure 7.4: Grouping executive net worths into exponential bands

The main work is done by the loop of lines (11) through (16). At line (12) a tuple is fetched into shared variable worth. Since tuples produced by the query of line (8) have only one component, we only need one shared variable, although in general there would be as many variables as there are components of the retrieved tuples. Line (13) tests whether the fetch has been successful. Here, we use a macro NO_MORE_TUPLES, which we may suppose is defined by

```
#define NO_MORE_TUPLES !(strcmp(SQLSTATE,"02000"))
```

Recall that "02000" is the contents of SQLSTATE that means no tuple was found. Thus, line (13) tests if all the tuples returned by the query had previously been found and there was no "next" tuple to be obtained. If so, we break out of the loop and go to line (17).

If a tuple has been fetched, then at line (14) we initialize the number of digits in the net worth to 1. Line (15) is a loop that repeatedly divides the net worth by 10 and increments `digits` by 1. When the net worth reaches 0 after division by 10, `digits` holds the correct number of digits in the value of `worth` that was originally retrieved. Finally, line (16) increments the appropriate element of the array `counts` by 1. We assume that the number of digits is no more than 14. However, should there be a net worth with 15 or more digits, line (16) will not increment any element of the `counts` array, since there is no appropriate range; i.e., enormous net worths are thrown away and do not affect the statistics.

Line (17) begins the wrap-up of the function. The cursor is closed, and lines (18) and (19) print the values in the `counts` array. □

7.1.7   Modifications by Cursor

When a cursor ranges over the tuples of a base table (i.e., a relation that is stored in the database, rather than a view or a relation constructed by a query), then one can not only read and process the value of each tuple, but one can update or delete the tuple. The syntax of these UPDATE and DELETE statements are the same as we encountered in Section 5.6, with the exception of the WHERE clause. That clause may only be WHERE CURRENT OF followed by the name of the cursor. Of course it is possible for the host-language program reading the tuple to apply whatever condition it likes to the tuple before deciding whether to delete or update it.

Example 7.5 : In Fig. 7.5 we see a C function similar to that of Fig 7.4. Both declare a cursor `execCursor` to range over the tuples of `MovieExec`. However, Fig. 7.5 looks at each tuple and decides either to delete the tuple or to double the net worth.

We have again used the macro NO_MORE_TUPLES for the condition that variable SQLSTATE has the "no more tuples" code "02000". In the test of line (12) we ask if the net worth is under $1000. If so, the tuple is deleted by the DELETE statement of line (13). If the net worth is at least $1000, then the net worth is doubled at line (15). □

7.1.8   Cursor Options

SQL2 offers a variety of options for cursors. Below is a summary. Details are found in Sections 7.1.9 through 7.1.11.

1. The order in which tuples are fetched from the relation can be specified.

2. The effect of changes to the relation that the cursor ranges over can be limited.

3. The motion of the cursor through the list of tuples can be varied.

```
1) void changeWorth() {

2)      EXEC SQL BEGIN DECLARE SECTION;
3)          int worth;
4)          char SQLSTATE[6];
5)      EXEC SQL END DECLARE SECTION;

6)      EXEC SQL DECLARE execCursor CURSOR FOR
7)          SELECT netWorth FROM MovieExec;

8)      EXEC SQL OPEN execCursor;

9)      while(1) {
10)         EXEC SQL FETCH FROM execCursor INTO :worth;
11)         if(NO_MORE_TUPLES) break;
12)         if (worth < 1000)
13)             EXEC SQL DELETE FROM MovieExec
                        WHERE CURRENT OF execCursor;
14)         else
15)             EXEC SQL UPDATE MovieExec
                        SET netWorth = 2 * netWorth
                        WHERE CURRENT OF execCursor;
        }
16)     EXEC SQL CLOSE execCursor;
    }
```

Figure 7.5: Modifying executive net worths

7.1.9 Ordering Tuples for Fetching

Let us first consider the order of tuples. We may fetch tuples in sorted order according to the value of any component. To specify an order, we follow the definition of the relation over which the cursor ranges with the keywords ORDER BY and a list of components to be used in the sort, just as we did for queries in Section 5.1.5. The sort is on the first component of the list, with ties broken by the value in the second component, remaining ties broken by the third component, and so on. Components may be specified either by an attribute or by a number. In the latter case, the number is the position of the attribute among all the attributes of the relation.

Example 7.6: Suppose we wish to examine the tuples of the relation that is constructed by joining the Movie and StarsIn relations and projecting the relation to yield only the movie title, year, star, and studio. We also wish to order these tuples by year, and among tuples of the same year, we shall group

the tuples by title, in alphabetical order. Figure 7.6 declares `movieStarCursor`
to be a cursor that ranges over this constructed relation.

```
1) EXEC SQL DECLARE movieStarCursor CURSOR FOR
2)          SELECT title, year, studio, starName
3)          FROM Movie, StarsIn
4)          WHERE title = movieTitle AND year = movieYear
5)          ORDER BY year, title;
```

Figure 7.6: Using an `ORDER BY` clause to control order of fetched tuples

Lines (2) through (4) are a conventional `SELECT` clause, and line (1) declares a cursor to range over the tuples of this relation. Line (5) says that
when we fetch tuples through the cursor `movieStarCursor`, we shall get the
tuples earliest-year-first. Tuples with the same year are grouped by the second
attribute, `title`. Titles within a year will be ordered alphabetically, since that
is how character string values are sorted. Nothing is stipulated about the order
in which tuples representing different stars from the same movie are ordered.
□

7.1.10 Protecting Against Concurrent Updates

Next, let us consider the possibility that as some function is reading tuples via
the cursor `movieStarCursor` of Example 7.6, some concurrently executing function (or even the same function) is changing the underlying `Movie` or `StarsIn`
relation. We shall have more to say about several processes are accessing a
single database simultaneously in Section 7.2. However, for the moment, let us
simply accept the possibility that there are other processes that could modify
a relation as we use it.

What should we do about this possibility? Perhaps nothing. It may be that
we only want to search the tuples for a certain star or stars, and whether or
not we see a star for whom tuples are being inserted or deleted is not critical.
Then, we simply accept what tuples we get through the cursor.

However, we may not wish to allow concurrent changes to affect the tuples we
see through this cursor. For example, if the tuples our function saw caused it to
add new tuples to `StarsIn`, we might get into a feedback loop where the new
tuples generated additional tuples through the cursor, which in turn created
more new tuples, endlessly. If there is a risk of this or another undesirable
behavior, we may declare the cursor *insensitive* to concurrent changes.

Example 7.7: We could modify line (1) of Fig. 7.6 to be:

```
1) EXEC SQL DECLARE movieStarCursor INSENSITIVE CURSOR FOR
```

If `movieStarCursor` is so declared, then the SQL system will guarantee that changes to relations `Movie` or `StarsIn` made between one opening and closing of `movieStarCursor` would not affect the set of tuples fetched. □

An insensitive cursor could be expensive, in the sense that the SQL system might spend a lot of time managing data accesses to assure that the cursor is insensitive.. Again, a discussion of managing concurrent operations on the database is deferred to Section 7.2. However, one simple way to support an insensitive cursor is for the SQL system to hold up any process that could access underlying relations like `Movie` or `StarsIn`, should we wish our cursor to be insensitive.

There are certain cursors ranging over a relation R about which we may say with certainty that they will not change R. Such a cursor can run simultaneously with an insensitive cursor for R, without risk of changing the relation R that the insensitive cursor sees. If we declare a cursor `FOR READ ONLY`, then the database system can be sure that the underlying relation will not be modified because of access to the relation through this cursor.

Example 7.8: We could append after line (5) of Fig. 7.6 a sixth line

```
6)      FOR READ ONLY;
```

If we did, then any attempt to execute an `UPDATE` or `DELETE` through cursor `movieStarCursor` would cause an error. □

7.1.11 Scrolling Cursors

The last type of cursor option is a choice of how we move through the tuples of the relation. The default and most common choice is to start at the beginning, fetch the tuples in order, until the end. However, there are other orders in which tuples may be fetched, and tuples could be scanned several times before the cursor is closed. To take advantage of these options, we need to do two things.

1. When declaring the cursor, put the keyword `SCROLL` before the keyword `CURSOR`. This change tells the SQL system that the cursor may be used in a manner other than moving forward in the order of tuples.

2. In a `FETCH` statement, follow the keyword `FETCH` by one of several options that tell where to find the desired tuple. These options are:

   (a) `NEXT` or `PRIOR` to get the next or previous tuple in the order. Recall that these tuples are relative to the current position of the cursor. `NEXT` is the default if no option is specified and is the usual choice.

   (b) `FIRST` or `LAST` to get the first or last tuple in the order.

    (c) RELATIVE followed by a positive or negative integer, which indicates how many tuples to move forward (if the integer is positive) or backward (if negative) in the order. For instance, RELATIVE 1 is a synonym for NEXT, and RELATIVE -1 is a synonym for PRIOR.

    (d) ABSOLUTE followed by a positive or negative integer, which indicates the position of the desired tuple counting from the front (if positive) or back (if negative). For instance, ABSOLUTE 1 is a synonym for FIRST and ABSOLUTE -1 is a synonym for LAST.

Example 7.9: Let us rewrite the function of Fig. 7.5 to begin at the last tuple and move forward through the list of tuples. First, we need to declare cursor execCursor to be scrollable, which we do by adding the keyword SCROLL in line (6), as:

```
6)      EXEC SQL DECLARE execCursor SCROLL CURSOR FOR
7)          SELECT netWorth FROM MovieExec;
```

Also, we need to initialize the fetching of tuples with a FETCH LAST statement, and in the loop we use FETCH PRIOR. The loop that was lines (9) through (15) in Fig. 7.5 is rewritten as follows.

```
EXEC SQL FETCH LAST FROM execCursor INTO :worth;
while(1) {
    /* same as lines (11) through (15) */
    EXEC SQL FETCH PRIOR FROM execCursor INTO :worth;
}
```

The reader should not assume that there is any advantage to reading tuples in the reverse of the order in which the

```
SELECT netWorth FROM MovieExec
```

query generates them. In fact, it could be more expensive for the system to provide them backwards, since they might all have to be generated and stored before the first fetch from execCursor. □

7.1.12 Dynamic SQL

Our model of SQL embedded in a host language has been that of specific SQL queries and commands within a larger host-language program. However, there is a more general mode of embedding SQL into another language. The statements themselves could be computed by the host language. Such statements are not known at compile time, and thus cannot be handled by an SQL preprocessor or a host-language compiler.

    An example of such a situation is a program that prompts the user for an SQL query, reads the query, and then executes that query. The interpreter for ad-hoc SQL queries that we assumed in Chapter 5 is an example of such a program; every commercial SQL system provides this type of interpreter. If queries are read and executed at run-time, there is nothing that can be done at compile-time. The query has to be parsed and a suitable way to execute the query found by the SQL system, immediately after the query is read.

The host-language program must instruct the SQL system to take the character string just read, turn it into an executable SQL statement, and finally execute that statement. There are two *dynamic SQL* statements that perform these two steps.

1. EXEC SQL PREPARE, followed by an SQL variable V, the keyword FROM, and a host-language variable or expression of character string type. This statement causes the string to become an SQL statement, and V's value becomes that SQL statement. Presumably, the SQL statement is parsed and a good way to execute it is found by the SQL system, but the statement is not executed.

2. EXEC SQL EXECUTE followed by an SQL variable such as V in (1). This statement causes the SQL statement denoted by V to be executed.

Both steps can be combined into one, with the statement:

    EXEC SQL EXECUTE IMMEDIATE

followed by a string-valued, shared variable or a string-valued expression. The disadvantage of combining these two parts is seen if we prepare a statement once and then execute it many times. With EXECUTE IMMEDIATE the cost of preparing the statement is borne each time the statement is executed, rather than borne only once.

Example 7.10: In Fig. 7.7 is a sketch of a C program that reads text from standard input into a variable **query**, prepares it, and executes it. The SQL variable **SQLquery** holds the prepared query. Since the query is only executed once, it would be acceptable to replace lines (6) and (7) of Fig. 7.7 by the single statement:

    EXEC SQL EXECUTE IMMEDIATE :query;

□

7.1.13 Exercises for Section 7.1

Exercise 7.1.1: Write the following embedded SQL queries, based on the database schema

```
1) void readQuery() {
2)     EXEC SQL BEGIN DECLARE SECTION;
3)         char *query;
4)     EXEC SQL END DECLARE SECTION;
5)     /* prompt user for a query, allocate space (e.g., use
          malloc) and make shared variable :query point to
          the first character of the query */
6)     EXEC SQL PREPARE SQLquery FROM :query;
7)     EXEC SQL EXECUTE SQLquery;
   }
```

Figure 7.7: Preparing and executing a dynamic SQL query

```
Product(maker, model, type)
PC(model, speed, ram, hd, cd, price)
Laptop(model, speed, ram, hd, screen, price)
Printer(model, color, type, price)
```

of Exercise 4.1.1. You may use any host language with which you are familiar, and details of host-language programming may be replaced by clear comments if you wish.

* a) Ask the user for a price and find the PC whose price is closest to the desired price. Print the maker, model number, and speed of the PC.

  b) Ask the user for minimum values of the speed, RAM, hard-disk size, and screen size that he or she will accept. Find all the laptops that satisfy these requirements. Print their specifications (all attributes of laptop) and their manufacturer.

! c) Ask the user for a manufacturer. Print the specifications of all products by that manufacturer. That is, print the model number, type, and all the attributes of whichever relation is appropriate to that type.

!! d) Ask the user for a "budget" (total price of a PC and printer), and a minimum speed of the PC. Find the cheapest "system" (PC plus printer) that is within the budget and minimum speed, but make the printer a color printer if possible. Print the model numbers for the chosen system.

  e) Ask the user for a manufacturer, model number, speed, RAM, hard-disk size, CD speed, and price of a new PC. Check that there is no PC with that model number. Print a warning if so, and otherwise insert the information into tables Product and PC.

*! f) Lower the price of all "old" PC's by $100. Make sure that any "new" PC inserted during the time that your program is running does not have its price lowered.

Exercise 7.1.2: Write the following embedded SQL queries, based on the database schema

    Classes(class, type, country, numGuns, bore, displacement)
    Ships(name, class, launched)
    Battles(name, date)
    Outcomes(ship, battle, result)

of Exercise 4.1.3.

  a) The firepower of a ship is roughly proportional to the number of guns times the cube of the bore of the guns. Find the class with the largest firepower.

! b) Ask the user for the name of a battle. Find the countries of the ships involved in the battle. Print the country with the most ships sunk and the country with the most ships damaged.

  c) Ask the user for the name of a class and the other information required for a tuple of table **Classes**. Then ask for a list of the names of the ships of that class and their dates launched. However, the user need not give the first name, which must be the name of the class.

! d) Examine the **Battles**, **Outcomes**, and **Ships** relations for ships that were in battle before they were launched. Prompt the user when there is an error found, offering the option to change the date of launch or the date of the battle. Make whichever change is requested.

*! **Exercise 7.1.3:** In this exercise, our goal is to find all PC's in the relation

    PC(model, speed, ram, hd, cd, price)

for which there are at least two more expensive PC's of the same speed. While there are many ways we could approach the problem, you should use a scrolling cursor in this exercise. Read the tuples of PC ordered first by **speed** and then by **price**. *Hint*: For each tuple read, skip ahead two tuples to see if the speed has not changed.

!! **Exercise 7.1.4:** We mentioned in Section 7.1.1 that it is impossible to write a factorial program in SQL. That claim is correct for SQL2. However, SQL3 recursion, as described in Section 5.10, allows us to do something close. Write a recursive SQL3 query that applies to a relation M that contains a single tuple (m), where m is an integer. The result of the query should be the set of tuples $(n, n!)$, where $1 \leq n \leq m$.

7.2   Transactions in SQL

To this point, our model of operations on the database has been that of one user querying or modifying the database. Thus, operations on the database are executed one at a time, and the database state left by one operation is the state upon which the next operation acts. Moreover, we assume that operations are carried out in their entirety; that is, it is impossible for the hardware or software to fail in the middle of an operation, leaving the database in a state that cannot be explained as the result of the operations performed on it.

Real life is often considerably more complicated. We shall first consider what can happen to leave the database in a state that doesn't reflect the operations performed on it, and then we shall consider the tools SQL gives the user to assure that these problems do not occur.

7.2.1   Serializability

In applications like banking or airline reservations, hundreds of operations per second may be performed on the database. The operations initiate at any of hundreds or thousands of sites, such as automatic teller machines or machines on the desks of travel agents, airline employees, or airline customers themselves. It is entirely possible that we could have two operations affecting the same account or flight, and for those operations to overlap in time. If so, they might interact in strange ways. Here is an example of what could go wrong if the database management system were completely unconstrained as to the order in which it operated upon the database. We emphasize that database systems do not normally behave in this manner, and that one has to go out of one's way to make these sorts of errors occur when using a commercial database management system.

Example 7.11: Suppose that we write a function `chooseSeat()` to read a relation about flights and seats available, find if a particular seat is available, and set it to unavailable if so. The relation upon which we operate will be called `Flights`, and it has attributes `fltNum`, `fltDate`, `fltSeat`, and `occupied` with the obvious meanings. The seat-choosing program is sketched in Fig. 7.8.

Lines (9) through (11) of Fig. 7.8 are a single-row selection that sets shared variable `occ` to true or false (1 or 0) depending on whether the specified seat is or is not occupied. Line (12) tests whether that seat is occupied, and if not, the tuple for that seat is updated to make it occupied. The update is done by lines (13) through (15), and at line (16) the seat is assigned to the user who requested it. In practice, we would probably store seat-assignment information in another relation. Finally, at line (17), if the seat was unavailable the user is told that.

Now, remember that the function `chooseSeat()` may be executed simultaneously by two or more users. Suppose by coincidence that two agents are trying to book the same seat for the same flight and date at approximately the same time, as suggested by Fig. 7.9. They both get to line (9) at the same

```
1) EXEC SQL BEGIN DECLARE SECTION;
2)      int flight; /* flight number */
3)      char date[10]; /* flight date in SQL format */
4)      char seat[3]; /* two digits and a letter represents
                         a seat */
5)      int occ; /* a boolean to tell if seat is occupied */
6) EXEC SQL END DECLARE SECTION;

7) void chooseSeat() {
8)      /* C code to prompt the user to enter a flight,
           date, and seat and store these in the three
           variables with those names */
9)      EXEC SQL SELECT occupied INTO :occ
10)             FROM Flights
11)             WHERE fltNum = :flight AND fltDate = :date
                   AND fltSeat = :seat;
12)     if (!occ) {
13)         EXEC SQL UPDATE Flights
14)                 SET occupied = 'B1'
15)                 WHERE fltNum = :flight
                       AND fltDate = :date
                       AND fltSeat = :seat;
16)         /* C and SQL code to record the seat assignment
               and inform the user of the assignment */
        }
17)     else /* C code to notify user of unavailability and
               ask for another seat selection */
    }
```

Figure 7.8: Choosing a seat

time, and their copies of local variable occ both get value 0; that is, the seat is currently unassigned. At line (12), each execution of chooseSeat() decides to update the bit to 1, that is, make the seat occupied. These updates execute, perhaps one after the other, and each execution tells its user at line (16) that the seat belongs to them. □

As we see from Example 7.11, it is conceivable that two operations could each be performed correctly, and yet the global result not be correct: both users believe they have been granted the seat in question. The problem can be solved by several SQL mechanisms that serve to *serialize* the execution of the two function executions. We say an execution of functions operating on the same database is *serial* if one function executes completely before any other function begins. We say the execution is *serializable* if they behave as if they were run

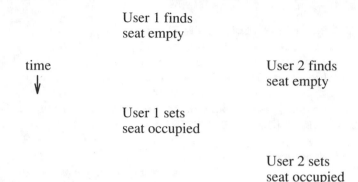

Figure 7.9: Two users trying to book the same seat simultaneously

serially, even though their executions may overlap in time.

Clearly, if the two invocations of `chooseSeat()` are run serially (or serializably), then the error we saw cannot occur. One user's invocation occurs first. This user sees an empty seat and books it. The other user's invocation then begins and sees that the seat is already occupied. It may matter to the users who gets the seat, but to the database all that is important is that a seat is assigned only once.

7.2.2   Atomicity

In addition to nonserialized behavior that can occur if two or more database operations are performed about the same time, it is possible for a single operation to put the database in an unacceptable state if there is a hardware or software "crash" while the operation is executing. Here is another example suggesting what might occur. As in Example 7.11, we should remember that real database systems do not allow this sort of error to occur in properly designed application programs.

Example 7.12: Let us picture another common sort of database: a bank's account records. We can represent the situation by a relation `Accounts` with attributes `acctNo` and `balance`. Pairs in this relation are an account number and the balance in that account.

We wish to write a function `transfer()` that reads two accounts and an amount of money, checks that the first account has at least that much money, and if so moves the money from the first account to the second. Figure 7.10 is a sketch of the function `transfer()`.

The working of Fig. 7.10 is straightforward. Lines (8) through (10) retrieve the balance of the first account. At line (11) it is determined whether this balance is sufficient to allow the desired amount to be subtracted from it. If so, then lines (12) through (14) add the amount to the second account, and lines (15) through (17) subtract the amount from the first account. If the amount

```
1) EXEC SQL BEGIN DECLARE SECTION;
2)      int acct1, acct2; /* the two accounts */
3)      int balance1; /* the amount of money in the
                              first account */
4)      int amount; /* the amount of money to transfer */
5) EXEC SQL END DECLARE SECTION;

6) void transfer() {
7)      /* C code to prompt the user to enter accounts
           1 and 2 and an amount of money to transfer,
           in variables acct1, acct2, and amount */
8)      EXEC SQL SELECT balance INTO :balance1
9)              FROM Accounts
10)             WHERE acctNo = :acct1;
11)     if (balance1 >= amount) {
12)         EXEC SQL UPDATE Accounts
13)                 SET balance = balance + :amount
14)                 WHERE acctNo = :acct2;
15)         EXEC SQL UPDATE Accounts
16)                 SET balance = balance - :amount
17)                 WHERE acctNo = :acct1;
        }
18)     else /* C code to print a message that there
                 were insufficient funds to make the
                 transfer. */
    }
```

Figure 7.10: Transferring money from one account to another

in the first account is insufficient, then no transfer is made, and a warning is printed at line (18).

Now, consider what happens if there is a failure after line (14); perhaps the computer fails or the network connecting the database to the processor that is actually performing the transfer fails. Then the database is left in a state where money has been transferred into the second account, but the money has not been taken out of the first account. The bank has in effect given away the amount of money that was to be transferred. □

The problem illustrated by Example 7.12 is that certain combinations of database operations, like the two updates of Fig. 7.10, need to be done *atomically*; that is, either they are both done or neither is done. For example, a common solution is to have all changes to the database done in a local workspace, and only after all work is done do we *commit* the changes to the database,

---

Assuring Serializable Behavior

In practice it is often impossible to require that operations run serially; there are just too many of them and some parallelism is required. Thus, database management systems adopt a mechanism for assuring serializable behavior; even if the execution is not serial, the result looks to users as if operations were executed serially.

As we discussed in Section 1.2.4, one common approach is for the database management system to *lock* elements of the database so that two functions cannot access them at the same time. For example, if the function `chooseSeat()` of Example 7.11 were written to lock other operations out of the `Flights` relation, then operations that did not access `Flights` could run in parallel with this invocation of `chooseSeat()`, but no other invocation of `chooseSeat()` could run. In fact, as mentioned in Section 1.2.4, locking smaller elements than whole relations, such as single disk blocks or single tuples, will allow even more parallelism, including the ability of certain invocations of `chooseSeat()` to run simultaneously.

---

whereupon all changes become part of the database and visible to other operations.

7.2.3 Transactions

The solution to the problems of serialization and atomicity posed in Sections 7.2.1 and 7.2.2 is to group database operations into *transactions*. A transaction is a collection of one or more operations on the database that must be executed atomically; that is, either all operations are performed or none are. Further, early SQL standards also require that transactions be executed as if they were run serially; that is, they are *serializable*. However, SQL2 takes a more flexible view. In SQL2, serializability is the default,[3] but the user may specify a less stringent constraint on the interleaving of operations from two or more transactions. We shall discuss these modifications to the serializability condition in later sections.

Transactions begin when any SQL statement that queries or manipulates either the database or the schema begins. We do not have to issue any special transaction-begin statement in SQL. However, we must end a transaction explicitly. We can do so in two ways.

1. The SQL statement `COMMIT` causes the transaction to end successfully. Whatever changes to the database were caused by the SQL statement or statements since the current transaction began are installed permanently

---

[3]Although some implementations use a less restrictive default.

How the Database Changes During Transactions

Different systems may do different things to implement transactions. It is possible that as a transaction executes, it makes changes to the database. If the transaction then aborts, it is possible that these changes were seen by some other transaction. The most common solution is for the database system to lock the changed items until COMMIT or ROLLBACK is chosen, thus preventing other transactions from seeing the tentative change. Locks or an equivalent would surely be used if the user wants the transactions to run in a serializable fashion.

However, as we shall see starting in Section 7.2.4, SQL2 offers us several options regarding the treatment of tentative database changes. It is possible that the changed data is not locked and becomes visible even though a subsequent rollback makes the change disappear. It is up to the designer of the transactions to decide whether visibility of tentative changes needs to be avoided. If so, all SQL implementations provide a method, such as locking, to keep changes invisible before commitment.

---

in the database (i.e., they are *committed*). Before the COMMIT statement is executed, changes are tentative and may or may not be visible to other transactions.

2. The SQL statement ROLLBACK causes the transaction to *abort*, or terminate unsuccessfully. Any changes made in response to the SQL statements of the transaction are undone (i.e., they are *rolled back*), so they no longer appear in the database.

Example 7.13: Suppose we want an execution of function transfer() of Fig. 7.10 to be a single transaction. The transaction begins at line (8) when we read the balance of the first account. If the test of line (11) is true, and we perform the transfer of funds, then we would like to commit the changes made. Thus, we put at the end of the if-block of lines (12) through (17) the additional SQL statement

```
EXEC SQL COMMIT;
```

If the test of line (11) is false — that is, there are insufficient funds to make the transfer — then we might prefer to abort the transaction. We can do so by placing

```
EXEC SQL ROLLBACK;
```

at the end of the else-block suggested by line (18). Actually, since in this branch there were no database modification statements executed, it doesn't matter whether we commit or abort, since there are no changes to be committed. □

7.2.4   Read-Only Transactions

Examples 7.11 and 7.12 each involved a transaction that read and then (possibly) wrote some data into the database. This sort of transaction is prone to serialization problems. Thus we saw in Example 7.11 what could happen if two executions of the function tried to book the same seat at the same time, and we saw in Example 7.12 what could happen if there was a crash in the middle of function execution. However, when a transaction only reads data and does not write data, we have more freedom to let the transaction execute in parallel with other transactions.[4]

Example 7.14: Suppose we wrote a function that read data to determine whether a certain seat was available; this function would behave like lines (1) through (11) of Fig. 7.8. We could execute many invocations of this function at once, without risk of permanent harm to the database. The worst that could happen is that while we were reading the availability of a certain seat, that seat was being booked or was being released by the execution of some other function. Thus, we might get the answer "available" or "unavailable," depending on microscopic differences in the time at which we executed the query, but the answer would make sense at some time.   □

If we tell the SQL execution system that our current transaction is *read-only*, that is, it will never change the database, then it is quite possible that the SQL system will be able to take advantage of that knowledge. While we shall not discuss the detailed mechanism here, it will generally be possible for many read-only transactions accessing the same data to run in parallel, while they would not be allowed to run in parallel with a transaction that wrote the same data.

We tell the SQL system that the next transaction is read-only by:

```
SET TRANSACTION READ ONLY;
```

This statement must be executed before the transaction begins. For example, if we had a function consisting of lines (1) through (11) of Fig. 7.8, we could declare it read-only by placing

```
EXEC SQL SET TRANSACTION READ ONLY;
```

just prior to line (9), which begins the transaction. It would be too late to make the read-only declaration after line (9).

We can also inform SQL that the coming transaction will or may write data by the statement

```
SET TRANSACTION READ WRITE;
```

However, this option is normally the default and thus unnecessary.

---

[4]There is a comparison to be made between transactions on one hand and the management of cursors on the other. For example, we noted in Section 7.1.10 that more parallelism was possible with read-only cursors than with general cursors. Similarly, read-only transactions enable parallelism.

7.2.5 Dirty Reads

Dirty data is a common term for data that has been written by a transaction that has not yet committed. A *dirty read* is a read of dirty data. The risk of reading dirty data is that the transaction that wrote it may eventually abort. If so, then the dirty data will be removed from the database, and the world is supposed to behave as if that data never existed. If some other transaction has read the dirty data, then that transaction might commit or take some other action that reflects its knowledge of the dirty data.

Sometimes the dirty read matters, and sometimes it doesn't. Other times it matters sufficiently little that it is worth the risk to avoid time-consuming work by the database management system that would be necessary to prevent dirty reads. Here are some examples of what might happen when dirty reads are allowed.

Example 7.15: Let us reconsider the account transfer of Example 7.12. However, suppose that transfers are implemented by a program P that executes the following sequence of steps:

1. Add money to account 2.

2. Test if account 1 has enough money.

   (a) If there is not enough money, remove the money from account 2 and abort.

   (b) If there is enough money, subtract the money from account 1 and commit.

If program P is executed serializably, then it doesn't matter that we have put money temporarily into account 2. No one will see that money, and it gets removed if the transfer can't be made.

However, suppose dirty reads are possible. Imagine there are three accounts: $A1$, $A2$, and $A3$, with \$100, \$200, and \$300, respectively. Suppose transaction T_1 executes program P to transfer \$150 from $A1$ to $A2$. At roughly the same time, transaction T_2 runs program P to transfer \$250 from $A2$ to $A3$. Here is a possible sequence of events:

1. T_2 executes step 1 and adds \$250 to $A3$, which now has \$550.

2. T_1 executes step 1 and adds \$150 to $A2$, which now has \$350.

3. T_2 executes the test of step 2 and finds that $A2$ has enough funds (\$350) to allow the transfer of \$250 from $A2$ to $A3$.

4. T_1 executes the test of step 2 and finds that $A1$ does not have enough funds (\$100) to allow the transfer of \$150 from $A1$ to $A2$.

5. T_2 executes step 2b. It subtracts \$250 from $A2$, which now has \$100, so T_2 commits.

6. T_1 executes step 2a. It subtracts \$150 from $A2$, which now has $-\$50$. Then, T_1 aborts.

The total amount of money has not changed; there is still \$600 among the three accounts. But because T_2 read dirty data at the third of the six steps above, we have not protected against an account going negative, which supposedly was the purpose of testing the first account to see if it had adequate funds.   □

Example 7.16: Let us imagine a variation on the seat-choosing function of Example 7.11. In the new approach:

1. We find an available seat and reserve it by setting `occupied` to 1 for that seat. If there is none, abort.

2. We ask the customer for approval of the seat. If so, we commit. If not, we release the seat by setting `occupied` to 0 and repeat step 1 to get another seat.

If two transactions are executing this algorithm at about the same time, one might reserve a seat S, which later is rejected by the customer. If the second transaction executes step 1 at a time when seat S is marked unavailable, the customer for that transaction is not given the option to take seat S.

As in Example 7.15, the problem is that a dirty read has occurred. The second transaction saw a tuple (with S marked unavailable) that was written by the first transaction and later modified by the first transaction.   □

How important is the fact that a read was dirty? In Example 7.15 it was very important; it caused an account to go negative despite apparent safeguards against that happening. In Example 7.16, the problem does not look too serious. Indeed, the second traveler might not get his or her favorite seat, or even be told that no seats existed. However, in the latter case, running the transaction again will almost certainly reveal the availability of seat S. It might well make sense to implement this seat-choosing function in a way that allowed dirty reads, in order to speed up the average processing time for booking requests.

SQL2 allows us to specify that dirty reads are acceptable for a given transaction. We use the `SET TRANSACTION` statement that we discussed in Section 7.2.4. The appropriate form for a transaction like that described in Example 7.16 is

```
1) SET TRANSACTION READ WRITE
2)                     ISOLATION LEVEL READ UNCOMMITTED;
```

The statement above does two things:

1. Line (1) declares that the transaction both reads and writes data.

2. Line (2) declares that the following transaction may run with the "isolation level" read-uncommitted. We shall discuss the four isolation levels in Section 7.2.6. So far, we have seen two of them: serializable and read-uncommitted.

Note that if the transaction is not read-only (i.e., it writes at least one item of data into the database), and we specify isolation level `READ UNCOMMITTED`, then we must also specify `READ WRITE`. Recall from Section 7.2.4 that the default assumption is that transactions are read-write. However, SQL2 makes an exception for the case where dirty reads are allowed. Then, the default assumption is that the transaction is read-only, because read-write transactions with dirty reads entail significant risks, as we saw. If we want a read-write transaction to run with read-uncommitted as the isolation level, then we need to specify `READ WRITE` explicitly, as above.

7.2.6 Other Isolation Levels

SQL2 provides a total of four *isolation levels*. Two of them we have already seen: serializable and read-uncommitted (dirty reads allowed). The other two are *read-committed* and *repeatable-read*. They can be specified for a given transaction by

```
SET TRANSACTION ISOLATION LEVEL READ COMMITTED;
```

or

```
SET TRANSACTION ISOLATION LEVEL REPEATABLE READ;
```

respectively. For each, the default is that transactions are read-write, so we can add `READ ONLY` to either statement, if appropriate. Incidentally, we also have the option of specifying

```
SET TRANSACTION ISOLATION LEVEL SERIALIZABLE;
```

However, that is the SQL2 default and need not be stated explicitly.

The read-committed isolation level, as its name implies, forbids the reading of dirty (uncommitted) data. However, it does allow one transaction to issue the same query several times and get different answers, as long as the answers reflect data that has been written by transactions that already committed.

Example 7.17: Let us reconsider the seat-choosing function of Example 7.16, but suppose we declare it to run with isolation level read-committed. Then when it searches for a seat at step 1, it will not see seats as booked if some other transaction is reserving them but not committed.[5] However, if the traveler rejects seats, and one execution of the function queries for available seats many times, it may see a different set of available seats each time it queries, as other transactions successfully book seats or cancel seats in parallel with our transaction. □

---

[5] What actually happens may seem mysterious, since we have not addressed the algorithms for enforcing the various isolation levels. Possibly, should two transactions both see a seat as available and try to book it, one will be forced by the system to abort even if it doesn't wish to execute a `ROLLBACK` statement.

Now, let us consider isolation level repeatable-read. It is something of a misnomer, since the same query issued more than once is not quite guaranteed to get the same answer. Under repeatable-read isolation, if a tuple is retrieved the first time, then we can be sure that tuple will be retrieved again if the query is repeated. However, it is also possible that a second or subsequent execution of the same query will retrieve *phantom* tuples. The latter are tuples that are the result of insertions into the database while our transaction is executing.

Example 7.18: Let us continue with the seat-choosing problem of Examples 7.16 and 7.17. If we execute this function under isolation level repeatable-read, then a seat that is available on the first query at step 1 will remain available at subsequent queries.

However, suppose some new tuples enter the relation `Flights`. For example, the airline may have switched the flight to a larger plane, creating some new tuples that weren't there before, or a reservation may have been cancelled. Then under repeatable-read isolation, a subsequent query for available seats may also retrieve the new seats.   □

7.2.7   Exercises for Section 7.2

Exercise 7.2.1: This and the next exercises involve certain programs that operate on the two relations

```
Product(maker, model, type)
PC(model, speed, ram, hd, cd, price)
```

from our running PC exercise. Sketch the following programs, using embedded SQL and an appropriate host language. Do not forget to issue `COMMIT` and `ROLLBACK` statements at the proper times and to tell the system your transactions are read-only if they are.

a) Given a speed and amount of RAM (as arguments of the function), look up the PC's with that speed and RAM, printing the model number and price of each.

* b) Given a model number, delete the tuple for that model from both `PC` and `Product`.

c) Given a model number, decrease the price of that model PC by $100.

d) Given a maker, model number, processor speed, RAM size, hard-disk size, CD speed, and price, check that there is no product with that model. If there is such a model, print an error message for the user. If no such model existed, enter the information about that model into the `PC` and `Product` tables.

! **Exercise 7.2.2:** For each of the programs of Exercise 7.2.1, discuss the atomicity problems, if any, that could occur should the system crash in the middle of an execution of the program.

! **Exercise 7.2.3 :** Suppose we execute as a transaction T one of the four programs of Exercise 7.2.1, while other transactions that are executions of the same or a different one of the four programs may also be executing at about the same time. What behaviors of transaction T may be observed if all the transactions run with isolation level READ UNCOMMITTED that would not be possible if they all ran with isolation level SERIALIZABLE? Consider separately the case that T is any of the programs (a) through (d) of Exercise 7.2.1.

*!! **Exercise 7.2.4 :** Suppose we have a transaction T that is a function which runs "forever," and at each hour checks whether there is a PC that has a speed of 200 or more and sells for under $1000. If it finds one, it prints the information and terminates. During this time, other transactions that are executions of one of the four programs described in Exercise 7.2.1 may run. For each of the four isolation levels — serializable, repeatable read, read committed, and read uncommitted — tell what the effect on T of running at this isolation level is.

7.3 The SQL Environment

In this section we shall take the broadest possible view of a database management system and the databases and programs it supports. We shall see how databases are defined and organized into clusters, catalogs, and schemas. We shall also see how programs are linked with the data they need to manipulate. Many of the details depend on the particular implementation, so we shall concentrate on the general ideas that are contained in the SQL2 standard.

7.3.1 Environments

An *SQL environment* is the framework under which data may exist and SQL operations on data may be executed. In practice, we should think of an SQL environment as a database management system running at some installation. For example, ABC company buys a license for Dandy-DB Corporation's SQL database management system to run on a collection of ABC's machines. The system running on these machines constitutes an SQL environment.

All the database elements we have discussed — tables, views, domains, and assertions — are defined within an SQL environment. These elements are organized into a hierarchy of structures, each of which plays a distinct role in the organization. The structures defined by the SQL2 standard are indicated in Fig. 7.11.

Briefly, the organization consists of the following structures:

1. *Schemas.*[6] These are collections of tables, views, assertions, domains, and some other types of information that we do not discuss in this book (but see the box on "What Else Is in a Schema" in Section 7.3.2). Schemas

---

[6]Note that the term "schema" in this context refers to a database schema, not a relation schema.

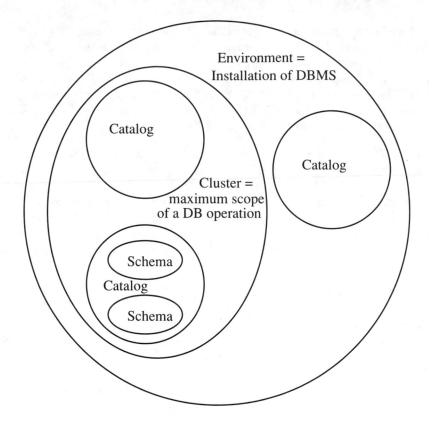

Figure 7.11: Organization of database elements within the environment

are the basic units of organization, close to what we might think of as a "database," but in fact somewhat less than a database as we shall see in point (3) below.

2. *Catalogs.* These are collections of schemas. They are the basic unit for supporting unique, accessible terminology. Each catalog has one or more schemas; the names of schemas within a catalog must be unique, and each catalog contains a special schema called INFORMATION_SCHEMA that contains information about all the schemas in the catalog.

3. *Clusters.* These are collections of catalogs. Each user has an associated cluster: the set of all catalogs accessible to the user (see Section 7.4 for an explanation of how access to catalogs and other elements is controlled). SQL2 is not very precise about what a cluster is, e.g., whether clusters for various users can overlap without being identical. A cluster is the maximum scope over which a query can be issued, so in a sense, a cluster is "the database" as seen by a particular user.

7.3.2 Schemas

The simplest form of schema declaration consists of:

1. The keywords `CREATE SCHEMA`.

2. The name of the schema.

3. A list of declarations for schema elements such as base tables, views, assertions, and domains.

That is, a schema may be declared by:

> `CREATE SCHEMA` <schema name> <element declarations>

The element declarations are of the forms discussed in Sections 5.7, 5.8, and Chapter 6. There are also some kinds of elements whose nature we have not described but that SQL2 allows to be declared in a schema; see the box on "What Else is in a Schema" that follows.

Example 7.19: We could declare a schema that includes the five relations about movies that we have been using in our running example, plus some of the other elements we have introduced, such as views. Figure 7.12 sketches the form of such a declaration. □

```
CREATE SCHEMA MovieSchema
CREATE DOMAIN CertDomain ... as in Example 6.8
    Other domain declarations
CREATE TABLE MovieStar ... as in Fig. 6.4
    Create-table statements for the four other tables
CREATE VIEW MovieProd ... as in Example 5.40
    Other view declarations
CREATE ASSERTION RichPres ... as in Example 6.10
```

Figure 7.12: Declaring a schema

It is not necessary to declare the schema all at once. One can modify or add to a schema using the appropriate `CREATE`, `DROP`, or `ALTER` statement, e.g., `CREATE TABLE` followed by the declaration of a new table for the schema. One problem is that the SQL system needs to know in which schema the new table belongs. If we alter or drop a table or other schema element, we may also need to disambiguate the name of the element, since two or more schemas may have distinct elements of the same name.

We change the "current" schema with a `SET SCHEMA` statement. For example,

```
SET SCHEMA MovieSchema;
```

makes the schema described in Fig. 7.12 the current schema, so any declarations of schema elements are added to that schema or modify elements already in that schema.

What Else Is in a Schema?

In addition to the tables, views, domains, and assertions already mentioned, there are four other kinds of schema elements. First, a schema can specify a *character set*, which is a set of symbols and a method for encoding them. ASCII is the best known character set, but an SQL2 implementation may support many others, such as sets for various foreign languages.

Second, schemas may specify a *collation* for a character set. Recall from Section 5.1.3 that character strings are compared lexicographically, assuming that any two characters can be compared by a "less than" relation we denoted <. A collation specifies which characters are "less than" which others. For example, we might use the ordering implied by the ASCII code, or we might treat lower-case and capital letters the same and not compare anything that isn't a letter.

Third, schemas may have *translations*, which are methods to convert characters of one character set into those of another. The last kind of element that may appear in a schema is a "grant statement" that concerns who has access to the schema. We shall discuss grants of privileges in Section 7.4.

7.3.3 Catalogs

Just as schema elements like tables are created within a schema, schemas are created and modified within a catalog. In principle, we would expect the process of creating and populating catalogs to be analogous to the process of creating and populating schemas. Unfortunately, SQL2 does not define a standard way to do so, such as a statement

$$\text{CREATE CATALOG} <\text{catalog name}>$$

followed by a list of schemas belonging to that catalog and the declarations of those schemas.

However, SQL2 does stipulate a statement

$$\text{SET CATALOG} <\text{catalog name}>$$

This statement allows us to set the "current" catalog, so new schemas will go into that catalog and schema modifications will refer to schemas in that catalog should there be a name ambiguity.

7.3.4 Clients and Servers in the SQL Environment

An SQL environment is more than a collection of catalogs and schemas. It contains elements whose purpose is to support operations on the database or

---

Complete Names for Schema Elements

Formally, the name for a schema element such as a table is its catalog name, its schema name, and its own name, connected by dots in that order. Thus, the table `Movie` in the schema `MovieSchema` in the catalog `MovieCatalog` can be referred to as

`MovieCatalog.MovieSchema.Movie`

If the catalog is the default or current catalog, then we can omit that component of the name. If the schema is also the default or current schema, then that part too can be omitted, and we are left with the element's own name, as is usual. However, we have the option to use the full name if we need to access something outside the current schema or catalog.

---

databases represented by those catalogs and schemas. Within an SQL environment are two special kinds of processes: SQL clients and SQL servers. A server supports operations on the database elements, and a client allows a user to connect to a server. It is envisioned that the server runs on a large host that stores the database and the client runs on another host, perhaps a personal workstation remote from the server. However, it is also possible that both client and server run on the same host.

7.3.5 Connections

If we wish to run some program involving SQL at a host where an SQL client exists, then we may open a connection between the client and server by executing an SQL statement

CONNECT TO <server name> AS <connection name>

The server name is something that depends on the installation. The word `DEFAULT` can substitute for a name and will connect the user to whatever SQL server the installation treats as the "default server."

The connection name can be used to refer to the connection later on. The reason we might have to refer to the connection is that SQL2 allows several connections to be opened by the user, but only one can be active at any time. To switch among connections, we can make `conn1` become the active connection by statement

    SET CONNECTION conn1;

Whatever connection was currently active becomes *dormant* until it is reactivated with another `SET CONNECTION` statement that mentions it explicitly.

We also use the name when we drop the connection. We can drop connection conn1 by

```
DISCONNECT conn1;
```

Now, conn1 is terminated; it is not dormant and cannot be reactivated.

However, if we shall never need to refer to the connection being created, then AS and the connection name may be omitted from the CONNECT TO statement. It is also permitted to skip the connection statements altogether. If we simply execute SQL statements at a host with an SQL client, then a default connection will be established on our behalf.

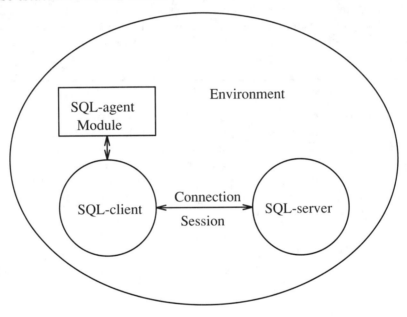

Figure 7.13: The SQL client-server interactions

7.3.6 Sessions

The SQL operations that are performed while a connection is active form a *session*. The session is coextensive with the connection that created it. For example, when a connection is made dormant, its session also becomes dormant, and reactivation of the connection by a SET CONNECTION statement also makes the session active. Thus, we have shown the session and connection as two aspects of the link between client and server in Fig. 7.13.

Each session has a current catalog and a current schema within that catalog. These may be set with statements SET SCHEMA and SET CATALOG, as discussed in Sections 7.3.2 and 7.3.3. There is also an authorized user for every session, as we shall discuss in Section 7.4.

7.3.7 Modules

A *module* is the SQL2 term for an application program. The SQL2 standard suggests that there are three kinds of modules, but insists only that an SQL implementation offer the user at least one of these types.

1. *Generic SQL Interface.* The user may sit and type SQL statements that are executed by an SQL server. In this mode, each query or other statement is a module by itself. It is this mode that we imagined for most of our examples in this book, although in practice it is rarely used.

2. *Embedded SQL.* This style was discussed in Section 7.1, where SQL statements appear within host-language programs and are introduced by `EXEC SQL`. Presumably, a preprocessor turns the embedded SQL statements into suitable function or procedure calls to the SQL system, and these calls are executed at the appropriate time when the compiled host-language program executes.

3. *True Modules.* The most general style of modules envisioned by SQL2 is one in which there are a collection of stored functions or procedures, some of which are host-language code and some of which are SQL statements. They communicate among themselves by passing parameters and perhaps via shared variables.

An execution of a module is called an *SQL agent.* In Fig. 7.13 we have shown both a module and an SQL agent, as one unit, calling upon an SQL client to establish a connection. However, we should remember that the distinction between a module and an SQL agent is analogous to the distinction between a program and a process; the first is code, the second is an execution of that code.

7.4 Security and User Authorization in SQL2

SQL2 postulates the existence of *authorization ID's*, which are essentially user names. SQL also has a special authorization ID, `PUBLIC`, which includes any user. Authorization ID's may be granted privileges, much as they would be in the file system environment maintained by an operating system. For example, a UNIX system generally controls three kinds of privileges: read, write, and execute. That list of privileges makes sense, because the protected objects of a UNIX system are files, and these three operations characterize well the things one typically does with files. However, databases are much more complex than file systems, and the kinds of privileges used in SQL2 are correspondingly more complex.

In this section, we shall first learn what privileges SQL2 allows on database elements. We shall then see how privileges may be acquired by users (by authorization ID's, that is). Finally, we shall see how privileges may be taken away.

7.4.1 Privileges

SQL2 defines six types of privileges:

1. SELECT

2. INSERT

3. DELETE

4. UPDATE

5. REFERENCES

6. USAGE

The first four of these apply to a relation, which may be either a base table or a view. As their names imply, they give the holder of the privilege the right to query (select from) the relation, insert into the relation, delete from the relation, and update tuples of the relation, respectively. A module containing an SQL statement cannot be executed without the privilege appropriate to that statement; e.g., a select-from-where statement requires the SELECT privilege on every table it accesses. We shall see how the module can get those privileges shortly.

The REFERENCES privilege is the right to refer to the relation in an integrity constraint. These constraints may take any of the forms mentioned in Chapter 6, such as assertions, attribute- or tuple-based checks, or referential integrity constraints. A constraint cannot be checked unless the schema in which the constraint appears has the REFERENCES privilege on all data involved in the constraint.

The USAGE privilege on a domain, or on several other kind of schema elements other than relations and assertions (see Section 7.3.2), is the right to use that element in one's own declarations.

Three of the privileges — INSERT, UPDATE, and REFERENCES — may also be given a single attribute as an argument. In that case, the privilege refers to the mentioned attribute only. Several privileges, each mentioning one attribute, may be held; in that way we may authorize access to any subset of the columns of a relation.

Example 7.20: Let us consider what privileges are needed to execute the insertion statement of Fig. 5.12, which we reproduce here as Fig. 7.14. First, it is an insertion into the relation Studio, so we require an INSERT privilege on Studio. However, since the insertion specifies only the component for attribute name, it is acceptable to have either the privilege INSERT or the privilege INSERT(name) on relation Studio. The latter privilege allows us to insert Studio tuples that specify only the name component and leave other components to take their default value or NULL, which is what Fig. 7.14 does.

```
1)  INSERT INTO Studio(name)
2)      SELECT DISTINCT studioName
3)      FROM Movie
4)      WHERE studioName NOT IN
5)          (SELECT name
6)           FROM Studio);
```

Figure 7.14: Adding new studios

However, notice that the insertion statement of Fig. 7.14 involves two subqueries, starting at lines (2) and (5). To carry out these selections we require the privileges needed for the subqueries. Thus, we need the **SELECT** privilege on both relations involved in **FROM** clauses: **Movie** and **Studio**. Note that just because we have the **INSERT** privilege on **Studio** doesn't mean we have the **SELECT** privilege on **Studio**, or vice versa. □

7.4.2 Creating Privileges

We have seen what the SQL2 privileges are and observed that they are required to perform SQL operations. Now we must learn how one obtains the privileges needed to perform an operation. There are two aspects to the awarding of privileges: how they are created initially, and how they are passed from user to user. We shall discuss initialization here and the transmission of privileges in Section 7.4.4.

First, SQL elements such as schemas or modules have an owner. The owner of something has all privileges associated with that thing. There are three points at which ownership is established in SQL2.

1. When a schema is created, it and all the tables and other schema elements in it are assumed owned by the user who created it. This user thus has all possible privileges on elements of the schema.

2. When a session is initiated by a **CONNECT** statement, there is an opportunity to indicate the user with a **USER** clause. For instance, the connection statement

   ```
   CONNECT TO Starfleet-sql-server AS conn1 USER kirk;
   ```

   would create a connection called **conn1** to an SQL server whose name is **Starfleet-sql-server**, on behalf of a user **kirk**. Presumably, the SQL implementation would verify that the user name is valid, for example by asking for a password.

3. When a module is created, there is an option to give it an owner by using an **AUTHORIZATION** clause. We shall not go into the details of module

creation, since the SQL2 standard allows implementations a great deal of flexibility in this regard. However, we can imagine that a clause

```
AUTHORIZATION picard;
```

in a module-creation statement would make user `picard` the owner of the module. It is also acceptable to specify no owner for a module, in which case the module is publicly executable, but the privileges necessary for executing any operations in the module must come from some other source, such as the user associated with the connection and session during which the module is executed.

7.4.3 The Privilege-Checking Process

As we saw above, each module, schema, and session has an associated user; in SQL terms, there is an associated authorization ID for each. Any SQL operation has two parties:

1. The database elements upon which the operation is performed and

2. The agent that causes the operation.

The privileges available to the agent derive from a particular authorization ID called the *current authorization ID*. That ID is either

a) The module authorization ID, if the module that the agent is executing has an authorization ID, or

b) The session authorization ID if not.

We may execute the SQL operation only if the current authorization ID possesses all the privileges needed to carry out the operation.

Example 7.21: To see the mechanics of checking privileges, let us reconsider Example 7.20. We might suppose that the referenced tables — `Movie` and `Studio` — are part of a schema called `MovieSchema` that was created by, and owned by, user `janeway`. At this point, user `janeway` has all privileges on these tables and any other elements of the schema `MovieSchema`. She may choose to grant some privileges to others by the mechanism to be described in Section 7.4.4, but let us assume none have been granted yet. There are several ways that the insertion of Example 7.20 can be executed.

1. The insertion could be executed as part of a module created by user `janeway` and containing an `AUTHORIZATION janeway` clause. The module authorization ID, if there is one, always becomes the current authorization ID. Then, the module and its SQL insertion statement have exactly the same privileges user `janeway` has, which includes all privileges on the tables `Movie` and `Studio`.

2. The insertion could be part of a module that has no owner. User janeway opens a connection with a USER janeway clause in the CONNECT TO statement. Now, janeway is again the current authorization ID, so the insertion statement has all the privileges needed.

3. User janeway grants all privileges on tables Movie and Studio to user sisko, or perhaps to the special user PUBLIC, which stands for "all users." The insertion statement is in a module with the clause

    AUTHORIZATION sisko

    Since the current authorization ID is now sisko, and this user has the needed privileges, the insertion is again permitted.

4. As in (3), user janeway has given user sisko the needed privileges. The insertion statement is in a module without an owner; it is executed in a session whose authorization ID was set by a USER sisko clause. The current authorization ID is thus sisko, and that ID has the needed privileges.

□

There are several principles that are illustrated by Example 7.21. We shall summarize them below.

- The needed privileges are always available if the data is owned by the same user as the user whose ID is the current authorization ID. Scenarios (1) and (2) above illustrate this point.

- The needed privileges are available if the user whose ID is the current authorization ID has been granted those privileges by the owner of the data, or if the privileges have been granted to user PUBLIC. Scenarios (3) and (4) illustrate this point.

- Executing a module owned by the owner of the data, or by someone who has been granted privileges on the data, makes the needed privileges available. Scenarios (1) and (3) illustrate this point.

- Executing a publicly available module during a session whose authorization ID is that of a user with the needed privileges is another way to execute the operation legally. Scenarios (2) and (4) illustrate this point.

7.4.4 Granting Privileges

We saw in Example 7.21 the importance to a user (i.e., an authorization ID) of having the needed privileges. But so far, the only way we have seen to have privileges on a database element is to be the creator and owner of that element. SQL2 provides a GRANT statement to allow one user to give a privilege to another. The first user retains the privilege granted, as well; thus GRANT can be thought of as "copy a privilege."

There is one important difference between granting privileges and copying. Each privilege has an associated *grant option*. That is, one user may have a privilege like SELECT on table Movie "with grant option," while a second user may have the same privilege, but without the grant option. Then the first user may grant the privilege SELECT on Movie to a third user, and moreover that grant may be with or without the grant option. However, the second user, who does not have the grant option, may not grant the privilege SELECT on Movie to anyone else. If the third user later gets this same privilege with the grant option, then that user may grant the privilege to a fourth user, again with or without the grant option, and so on. A *grant statement* consists of the following elements:

1. The keyword GRANT.

2. A list of one or more privileges, e.g., SELECT or INSERT(name). Optionally, the keywords ALL PRIVILEGES may appear here, as a shorthand for all the privileges that the grantor may legally grant on the database element in question (the element mentioned in item 4 below).

3. The keyword ON.

4. A database element. This element is typically a relation, either a base table or a view. It may also be a domain or other element we have not discussed (see the box "What Else Is in a Schema" in Section 7.3.2), but in these cases the element name must be preceded by the keyword DOMAIN or another appropriate keyword.

5. The keyword TO.

6. A list of one or more users (authorization ID's).

7. Optionally, the keywords WITH GRANT OPTION

That is, the form of a grant statement is:

> GRANT <privilege list> ON <database element> TO <user list>

possibly followed by WITH GRANT OPTION.

In order to execute this grant statement legally, the user executing it must possess the privileges granted, and these privileges must be held with the grant option. However, the grantor may hold a more general privilege (with the grant option) than the privilege granted. For instance, the privilege INSERT(name) on table Studio might be granted, while the grantor holds the more general privilege INSERT on Studio, with grant option.

Example 7.22: User `janeway`, who is the owner of the `MovieSchema` schema that contains tables

```
Movie(title, year, length, inColor, studioName, producerC#)
Studio(name, address, presC#)
```

grants the `INSERT` and `SELECT` privileges on table `Studio` and privilege `SELECT` on `Movie` to users `kirk` and `picard`. Moreover, she includes the grant option with these privileges. The grant statements are:

```
GRANT SELECT, INSERT ON Studio TO kirk, picard
    WITH GRANT OPTION;
GRANT SELECT ON Movie TO kirk, picard
    WITH GRANT OPTION;
```

Now, `picard` grants to user `sisko` the same privileges, but without the grant option. The statements are:

```
GRANT SELECT, INSERT ON Studio TO sisko;
GRANT SELECT ON Movie TO sisko;
```

Also, `kirk` grants to `sisko` the minimal privileges needed for the insertion of Fig. 7.14, namely `SELECT` and `INSERT(name)` on `Studio` and `SELECT` on `Movie`. The statements are:

```
GRANT SELECT, INSERT(name) ON Studio TO sisko;
GRANT SELECT ON Movie TO sisko;
```

Note that `sisko` has received the `SELECT` privilege on `Movie` and `Studio` from two different users. He has also received the `INSERT(name)` privilege on `Studio` twice: directly from `kirk` and via the generalized privilege `INSERT` from `picard`. □

7.4.5 Grant Diagrams

Because of the complex web of grants and overlapping privileges that may result from a sequence of grants, it is useful to represent grants by a *grant diagram*. An SQL system maintains a representation of this diagram to keep track of both privileges and their origins (in case a privilege is revoked; see Section 7.4.6). This diagram is a graph whose nodes correspond to a user and a privilege. If user U grants privilege P to user V, and this grant was based on the fact that U holds privilege Q (Q could be P with the grant option, or it could be some generalization of P, again with the grant option), then we draw an arc from the node for U/Q to the node for V/P.

Example 7.23: Figure 7.15 shows the grant diagram that results from the sequence of grant statements of Example 7.22. We use the convention that a ∗ after a user-privilege combination indicates that the privilege includes the grant option. Also, ∗∗ after a user-privilege combination indicates that the privilege derives from ownership of the database element in question and was not due to a grant of the privilege from elsewhere. This distinction will prove important when we discuss revoking privileges in Section 7.4.6. A doubly starred privilege automatically includes the grant option. □

7.4.6 Revoking Privileges

A granted privilege can be revoked at any time. In fact, the revoking of privileges may be required to *cascade*, in the sense that revoking a privilege with the grant option that has been passed on to other users may require those privileges to be revoked too. The simple form of a *revoke statement* is:

1. The keyword `REVOKE`.

2. A list of one or more privileges.

3. The keyword `ON`.

4. A database element, as discussed in item (4) in the description of a grant statement.

5. The keyword `FROM`.

6. A list of one or more users (authorization ID's).

That is, the following is the form of a revoke statement:

> `REVOKE` <privilege list> `ON` <database element> `FROM` <user list>

However, the following items may also be included in the statement:

- The statement can end with the word `CASCADE`. If so, then when the specified privileges are revoked, we also revoke any privileges that were granted only because of the revoked privileges. More precisely, if user U has revoked privilege P from user V, based on privilege Q belonging to U, then we delete the arc in the grant diagram from U/Q to V/P. Now, any node that is not accessible from some ownership node (doubly starred node) is also deleted.

- The statement can instead end with `RESTRICT`, which means that the revoke statement cannot be executed if the cascading rule described in the previous item would result in the revoking of any privileges due to the revoked privileges having been passed on to others.

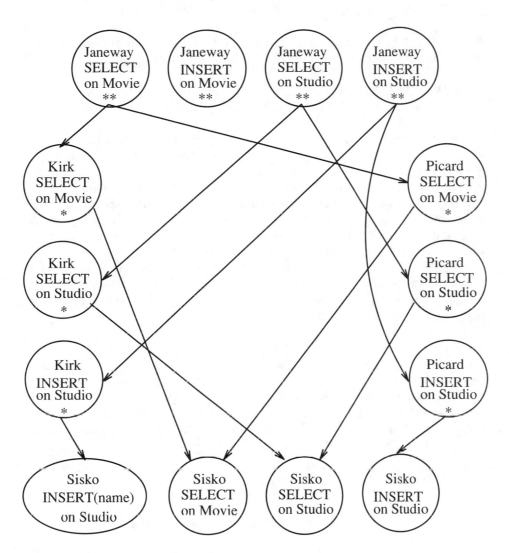

Figure 7.15: A grant diagram

- It is permissible to replace REVOKE by REVOKE GRANT OPTION FOR, in which case the privileges themselves remain, but the option to grant them to others is removed. This choice may be made in combination with either CASCADE or RESTRICT, in which case the grant diagram is examined to see if any other granted privileges need to be revoked.

Example 7.24: Continuing with Example 7.22, suppose that janeway revokes the privileges she granted to picard with the statements:

```
REVOKE SELECT, INSERT ON Studio FROM picard CASCADE;
REVOKE SELECT ON Movie FROM picard CASCADE;
```

We delete the arcs of Fig. 7.15 from these janeway privileges to the corresponding picard privileges. Since CASCADE was stipulated, we also have to see if there are any privileges that are not reachable in the graph from a doubly starred (ownership-based) privilege. Examining Fig. 7.15, we see that picard's privileges are no longer reachable from a doubly starred node (they might have been, had there been another path to a picard node). Also, sisko's privilege to INSERT into Studio is no longer reachable. We thus delete not only picard's privileges from the grant diagram, but we delete sisko's INSERT privilege.

Note that we do not delete sisko's SELECT privileges on Movie and Studio or his INSERT(name) privilege on Studio, because these are all reachable from janeway's ownership-based privileges via kirk's privileges. The resulting grant diagram is shown in Fig. 7.16.   □

Example 7.25: There are a few subtleties that we shall illustrate with abstract examples. First, when we revoke a general privilege p, we do not also revoke a privilege that is a special case of p. For instance, consider the following sequence of steps, whereby user U, the owner of relation R, grants the INSERT privilege on relation R to user V, and also grants the INSERT(A) privilege on the same relation.

Step	By	Action
1	U	GRANT INSERT ON R TO V
2	U	GRANT INSERT(A) ON R TO V
3	U	REVOKE INSERT ON R FROM V RESTRICT

When U revokes INSERT from V, the INSERT(A) privilege remains. The grant diagrams after steps (2) and (3) are shown in Fig. 7.17.

Notice that after step (2) there are two separate nodes for the two similar but distinct privileges that user V has. Also observe that the RESTRICT option in step (3) does not prevent the revocation, because V had not granted the option to any other user. In fact, V could not have granted either privilege, because V obtained them without grant option.   □

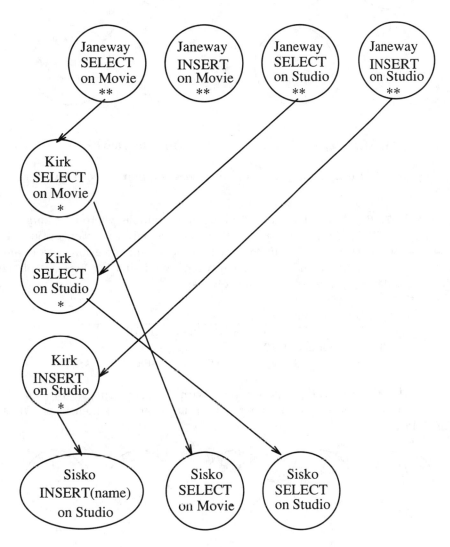

Figure 7.16: Grant diagram after revocation of `picard`'s privileges

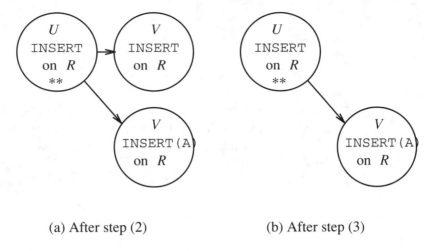

(a) After step (2)   (b) After step (3)

Figure 7.17: Revoking a general privilege leaves a more specific privilege

Example 7.26: Now, let us consider a similar example where U grants V a privilege p with the grant option and then revokes only the grant option. In this case, we must change V's node to reflect the loss of the grant option, and any grants of p made by V must be cancelled by eliminating arcs out of the V/p node. The sequence of steps is as follows:

Step	By	Action
1	U	GRANT p TO V WITH GRANT OPTION
2	V	GRANT p TO W
3	U	REVOKE GRANT OPTION FOR p FROM V CASCADE

In step (1), U grants the privilege p to V with the grant option. In step (2), V uses the grant option to grant p to W. The diagram is then as shown in Fig. 7.18(a).

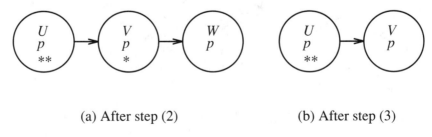

(a) After step (2)   (b) After step (3)

Figure 7.18: Revoking a grant option leaves the underlying privilege

Then in step (3), U revokes the grant option for privilege p from V, but does not revoke the privilege itself. Thus, the star is removed from the node for V and p. However, a node without a $*$ may not have an arc out, because such a node cannot be the source of the granting of a privilege. Thus, we must also remove the arc out of the node V/p that goes to the node for W/p.

Now, the node W/p has no path to it from a ** node that represents the origin of privilege p. As a result, node W/p is deleted from the diagram. However, node V/p remains; it is just modified by removing the * that represents the grant option. The resulting grant diagram is shown in Fig. 7.18(b). □

7.4.7 Exercises for Section 7.4

Exercise 7.4.1: Indicate what privileges are needed to execute the following queries. In each case, mention the most specific privileges as well as general privileges that are sufficient.

a) The query of Fig. 5.3.

b) The query of Fig. 5.5.

* c) The insertion of Fig. 5.12.

d) The deletion of Example 5.29.

e) The update of Example 5.31.

f) The tuple-based check of Fig. 6.4.

g) The assertion of Example 6.10.

* **Exercise 7.4.2:** Show the grant diagrams after steps (4) through (6) of the sequence of actions listed in Fig. 7.19. Assume A is the owner of the relation to which privilege p refers.

Step	By	Action
1	A	GRANT p TO B WITH GRANT OPTION
2	A	GRANT p TO C
3	B	GRANT p TO D WITH GRANT OPTION
4	D	GRANT p TO B, C, E WITH GRANT OPTION
5	B	REVOKE p FROM D CASCADE
6	A	REVOKE p FROM C CASCADE

Figure 7.19: Sequence of actions for Exercise 7.4.2

Exercise 7.4.3: Show the grant diagrams after steps (5) and (6) of the sequence of actions listed in Fig. 7.20. Assume A is the owner of the relation to which privilege p refers.

Step	By	Action
1	A	GRANT p TO B, E WITH GRANT OPTION
2	B	GRANT p TO C WITH GRANT OPTION
3	C	GRANT p TO D WITH GRANT OPTION
4	E	GRANT p TO C
5	E	GRANT p TO D WITH GRANT OPTION
6	A	REVOKE GRANT OPTION FOR p FROM B CASCADE

Figure 7.20: Sequence of actions for Exercise 7.4.3

! Exercise 7.4.4: Show the final grant diagram after the following steps, assuming A is the owner of the relation to which privilege p refers.

Step	By	Action
1	A	GRANT p TO B WITH GRANT OPTION
2	B	GRANT p TO B WITH GRANT OPTION
3	A	REVOKE p FROM B CASCADE

7.5   Summary of Chapter 7

✦ *Embedded SQL*: Instead of using a generic query interface to express SQL queries and modifications, it is often more effective to write programs that embed SQL queries in a conventional host language.

✦ *Impedance Mismatch*: The data model of SQL is quite different from the data models of conventional host languages. Thus, information passes between SQL and the host language through shared variables that can represent components of tuples in the SQL portion of the program.

✦ *Cursors*: A cursor is an SQL variable that indicates one of the tuples of a relation. Connection between the host language and SQL is facilitated by having the cursor range over each tuple of the relation, while the components of the current tuple are retrieved into shared variables and processed using the host language.

✦ *Dynamic SQL*: Instead of embedding particular SQL statements in a host-language program, the host program may create character strings that are interpreted by the SQL system as SQL statements and executed.

✦ *Concurrency Control*: SQL2 provides two mechanisms to prevent concurrent operations from interfering with one another: transactions and restrictions on cursors. Restrictions on cursors include the ability to declare a cursor to be "insensitive," in which case no changes to its relation will be seen by the cursor.

✦ *Transactions*: SQL allows the programmer to group SQL statements into transactions, which may be committed or rolled back (aborted). In the latter case, any changes made by the transaction to the database are cancelled.

✦ *Isolation Levels*: SQL2 allows transactions to run with four isolation levels called, from most stringent to least stringent: "serializable" (the transaction must appear to run either completely before or completely after each other transaction), "repeatable read" (every tuple read in response to a query will appear if the query is repeated), "read committed" (only tuples written by transactions that have already committed may be seen by this transaction), and "read uncommitted" (no constraint on what the transaction may see).

✦ *Read-Only Cursors and Transactions*: Either a cursor or a transaction may be declared read-only. This declaration is a guarantee that the cursor or transaction will not change the database, thus informing the SQL system that it will not affect other transactions or cursors in ways that may violate insensitivity, serializability, or other requirements.

✦ *Organization of a Database*: An installation using an SQL2 DBMS creates an SQL environment. Within the environment, database elements such as relations are grouped into (database) schemas, catalogs, and clusters. A catalog is a collection of schemas, and a cluster is the largest collection of elements that one user may see.

✦ *Client/Server Systems*: An SQL client connects to an SQL server, creating a connection (link between the two processes) and a session (sequence of operations). The code executed during the session comes from a module, and the execution of the module is called an SQL agent.

✦ *Privileges*: For security purposes, SQL2 systems allow many different kinds of privileges to be obtained on database elements. These privileges include the right to select (read), insert, delete, or update relations and the right to reference relations (refer to them in a constraint). The insert, update, and reference privileges may also be obtained on particular columns of a relation.

✦ *Grant Diagrams*: Privileges may be granted by owners to other users or to the general user PUBLIC. If granted with the grant option, then these privileges may be passed on to others. Privileges may also be revoked. The grant diagram is a useful way to remember enough about the history of grants and revokes to keep track of who has what privilege and from whence they obtained those privileges.

7.6 References for Chapter 7

Again, the reader is referred to the bibliographic notes of Chapter 5 for information on obtaining the SQL2 standard. There is a discussion of problems with this standard in the area of transactions and cursors in [1].

The most important idea for implementing transactions, called "two-phase locking," was proposed in [3]. For more on transaction management and implementation, see [2] and [5]. The ideas behind SQL2 authorization originated in [6] and [4].

1. Berenson, H., P. A. Bernstein, J. N. Gray, J. Melton, E. O'Neil, and P. O'Neil, "A critique of ANSI SQL isolation levels," *Proceedings of ACM SIGMOD Intl. Conf. on Management of Data*, pp. 1–10, 1995.

2. Bernstein, P. A., V. Hadzilacos, and N. Goodman, *Concurrency Control and Recovery in Database Systems*, Addison-Wesley, Reading, MA, 1987.

3. Eswaran, K. P., J. N. Gray, R. A. Lorie, and I. L. Traiger, "The notions of consistency and predicate locks in a database system," *Communications of the ACM* **19**:11, pp. 624–633, 1976.

4. Fagin, R., "On an authorization mechanism," *ACM Transactions on Database Systems* **3**:3, pp. 310–319, 1978.

5. Gray, J. N. and A. Reuter, *Transaction Processing: Concepts and Techniques*, Morgan-Kaufmann, San Francisco, 1993.

6. Griffiths, P. P. and B. W. Wade, "An authorization mechanism for a relational database system," *ACM Transactions on Database Systems* **1**:3, pp. 242–255, 1976.

Chapter 8

Object-Oriented Query Languages

In this chapter, we shall discuss two attempts to introduce object-oriented programming into the database world. Both languages — OQL and SQL3 — are emerging standards, rather than widely implemented languages, but both are gaining acceptance and their ideas are filtering into commercial systems rapidly.

OQL, or *Object Query Language* is an attempt to standardize object-oriented query languages into a language that combines the high-level, declarative programming of SQL with the object-oriented programming paradigm. We begin this chapter with a discussion of methods and extents ODL, the object definition language introduced as a modeling tool in Chapter 2. These two features impact the query language OQL in important ways. We then cover various aspects of programming in OQL.

If OQL is an attempt to bring the best of SQL into the object-oriented world, then SQL3 can be characterized as bringing the best of object-orientation into the relational world. In some senses, the two languages "meet in the middle," but there are also significant differences in approach that make certain things easier in one language than the other. Thus, after introducing the object-oriented features of the proposed SQL3 standard, we shall compare capabilities of the two languages.

In essence, the two approaches to object orientation differ in their answer to the question: "how important is the relation?" For the object-oriented community centered around ODL and OQL, the answer is "not very." Thus, in this approach, we find objects of all types, some of which are sets or bags of structures (i.e., relations). For the SQL3 community, the answer is that relations are still the fundamental data structuring concept. In the SQL3 approach, often called *object-relational*, the relational model is extended by allowing more complex types for the tuples of relations and for the domains belonging to the attributes of relations. Thus, objects and classes are introduced into the relational model, but always within a relation.

8.1   Query-Related Features of ODL

In this section we shall continue our discussion of ODL from Chapter 2. We first discuss the matter of ways in which ODL classes can interact with the larger programming environment in which they are placed. Then we take up the matter of "extents" for a class, which play for OQL a role similar to that of relations in SQL.

8.1.1   Operations on ODL Objects

As we shall soon see, OQL is a language that allows us to express operations that have a relational, or set-based flavor, much like SQL does. However, there is often the need to perform other operations that are not set-based. For example, if objects are documents, we might wish to test whether a given document contains a given keyword. If an object is an element of a map or picture, we might wish to display the object in its proper position. Even conventional, record-oriented data such as our running movies example could benefit some special operations, such as generating a graph of the number of movies a given star performed in for each year.

In SQL, these operations are performed by a program in a conventional or *host* programming language such as C, in which the SQL statements are embedded. Values are passed between SQL variables and host-language variables by the mechanism introduced in Section 7.1.

The coupling of ODL definitions and the host language is tighter. It is assumed that the host language will be an object-oriented language, C++ or Smalltalk for example. Each of these languages is sufficiently ODL-like that the ODL declarations can be translated directly into declarations of the host language. Further, the variables of the host language, representing objects, can easily represent objects that are declared in the ODL statements.[1]

To make the coupling of the host language to ODL declarations and to OQL queries even more convenient, ODL allows a third kind of property (besides attributes and relationships): methods. A *method* is a function associated with a class. It is applied to an object in the class and may also take one or more other arguments. As we shall see, methods can be used in OQL almost as if they were attributes of the class.

8.1.2   Declaring Method Signatures in ODL

In ODL, we can declare the names of the methods associated with a class and the input/output types of those methods. These declarations, called *signatures*, are like function declarations in C or C++ (as opposed to function *definitions*, which give the code to implement the function). The actual code for a method

---

[1]Recall that for SQL the types of host-language variables, such as integers, are a bad match for the fundamental data types of SQL: tuples and relations. Thus, the coupling of SQL and the host language is rather awkward, as we saw in Section 7.1.

Why Signatures?

The value of providing signatures is that when we implement the schema in a real programming language, we can check automatically that the implementation matches the design as was expressed in the schema. We cannot check that the implementation correctly implements the "meaning" of the operations, but we can at least check that the input and output parameters are of the correct number and of the correct type.

---

would be written in the host language; the code for a method is not part of ODL.

Declarations of methods appear along with the attributes and relationships in an interface declaration. As is normal for object-oriented languages, each method is associated with a class (i.e., with an interface), and methods are invoked on an object of that class. Thus, the object is a "hidden" argument of the method. This style allows the same method name to be used for several different classes, because the object upon which the operation is performed determines the particular method meant. Such a method name is said to be *overloaded* (appears as a method for more than one class).

The syntax of method declarations is similar to that of function declarations in C, with two important additions:

1. Function parameters are specified to be `in`, `out`, or `inout`, meaning that they are used as input parameters, output parameters, or both, respectively. The last two types of parameters can be modified by the function; `in` parameters cannot be modified. In effect, `out` and `inout` parameters are passed by reference, while `in` parameters may be passed by value. Note that a function may also have a return value, which is a way that a result can be produced by a function other than by assigning a value to an `out` or `inout` parameter.

2. Functions may raise *exceptions*, which are special responses that are outside the normal parameter-passing and response mechanism by which functions communicate. An exception usually indicates an abnormal or unexpected condition that will be "handled" by some function that called it (perhaps indirectly through a sequence of calls). Division by zero is an example of a condition that might be treated as an exception. In ODL, a function declaration can be followed by the keyword `raises`, followed by a parenthesized list of one or more exceptions that the function can raise.

Example 8.1: In Fig. 8.1 we see the evolution of the interface definition for class `Movie`, last seen in Fig. 2.6. There are two changes not related to methods.

1. At line (2), we see an "extent declaration." The purpose of this statement will be covered next, in Section 8.1.3.

2. At line (3) is the declaration of `title` and `year` as the key for `Movie`.

The methods included with the interface declaration are as follows. Line (10) declares a method `lengthInHours`. We might imagine that it produces as a return value the length of the movie object to which it is applied, but converted from minutes (as the attribute `length` represents) to a floating-point number that is the equivalent in hours. Note that the function takes no parameters. The `Movie` object to which the method is applied is the "hidden" argument, and it is from this object that a possible implementation of `lengthInHours` would obtain the length of the movie in minutes.

We also see that the function may raise an exception called `noLengthFound`. Presumably this exception would be raised if the `length` attribute of the object to which the method `lengthInHours` was applied had an undefined value or a value that could not represent a valid length (e.g., a negative number).

```
1)    interface Movie
2)       (extent Movies
3)        key (title, year))
    {
4)      attribute string title;
5)      attribute integer year;
6)      attribute integer length;
7)      attribute enumeration(color,blackAndWhite) filmType;
8)      relationship Set<Star> stars
                    inverse Star::starredIn;
9)      relationship Studio ownedBy
                    inverse Studio::owns;
10)     float lengthInHours() raises(noLengthFound);
11)     starNames(out Set<String>);
12)     otherMovies(in Star, out Set<Movie>)
                    raises(noSuchStar);
    };
```

Figure 8.1: Adding method signatures to the `Movie` class

Remember, there is nothing in the declaration that *requires* the method to do what its name implies. For example, it would be correct to implement the method `lengthInHours` by a function that always returned 3.14159, regardless of the `Movie` object to which it was applied. We might also implement it to return the square of the length, converted to floating point. Any function that takes no argument (except the object to which it is applied), returns a float, and raises no exception other than `noLengthFound`, is acceptable.

In line (11) we see another method signature; this signature is for a function called `starNames`. This function has no return value but has an output parameter whose type is a set of strings. We presume that the value of the output parameter is computed by the function to be the set of strings that are the values of the attribute `name` for the stars of the movie to which the method is applied. However, as always there is no guarantee that the implemented function behaves in this particular way.

Finally, at line (12) is a third method, `otherMovies`. This function has an input parameter of type `Star`. A possible implementation of this function is as follows. We may suppose that `otherMovies` expects this star to be one of the stars of the movie; if it is not, then the exception `noSuchStar` is raised. If it is one of the stars of the movie to which the method is applied, then the output parameter, whose type is a set of movies, is given as its value the set of all the other movies of this star. □

8.1.3 The Extent of a Class

For every ODL class (interface) there may be a declared *extent*, which is a name for the current set of objects of that class. The form of the declaration is the keyword `extent`, followed by the name chosen for the extent. This declaration must appear immediately after the declaration of the interface (class) name.

In a sense, the extent for a class is analogous to the name of a relation, while the class definition itself is analogous to a declaration of the types of the attributes of that relation. As we shall see, OQL queries refer to the extent of a class, not to the class name itself.

Example 8.2: Line (2) of Fig. 8.1 illustrates the definition of an extent for class `Movie`. The name of the extent is `Movies`. The value of `Movies` at any time is the set of all `Movie` objects that exist in the database at that time. □

8.1.4 Exercises for Section 8.1

Exercise 8.1.1: In Fig. 8.2 is an ODL description of our running products exercise. We have made each of the three types of products subclasses of the main `Product` class. The reader should observe that a type of a product can be obtained either from the attribute `type` or from the subclass to which it belongs. This arrangement is not an excellent design, since it allows for the possibility that, say, a PC object will have its `type` attribute equal to `"laptop"` or `"printer"`. However, the arrangement gives you some interesting options regarding how one expresses queries.

Because `type` is inherited by `Printer` from the superclass `Product`, we have had to rename the `type` attribute of `Printer` to be `printerType`. The latter attribute gives the process used by the printer (e.g., laser or inkjet), while `type` of `Product` will have values such as PC, laptop, or printer.

Add to the ODL code of Fig. 8.2 method signatures appropriate for functions that do the following:

```
interface Product
    (extent Products
     key model)
  {
    attribute integer model;
    attribute string manufacturer;
    attribute string type;
    attribute real price;
  };

interface PC : Product
    (extent PCs)
  {
    attribute integer speed;
    attribute integer ram;
    attribute integer hd;
    attribute string cd;
  };

interface Laptop : Product
    (extent Laptops)
  {
    attribute integer speed;
    attribute integer ram;
    attribute integer hd;
    attribute real screen;
  };

interface Printer : Product
    (extent Printers)
  {
    attribute boolean color;
    attribute string printerType;
  };
```

Figure 8.2: Product schema in ODL

* a) Subtract x from the price of a product. Assume x is provided as an input parameter of the function.

* b) Return the speed of a product if the product is a PC or laptop and raise the exception `notComputer` if not.

  c) Set the screen size of a laptop to a specified input value x.

! d) Given an input product p, determine whether the product q to which the method is applied has a higher speed and a lower price than p. Raise the exception `badInput` if p is not a product with a speed (i.e., neither a PC nor laptop) and the exception `noSpeed` if q is not a product with a speed.

Exercise 8.1.2: In Fig. 8.3 is an ODL description of our running "battleships" database. Add the following method signatures:

  a) Compute the firepower of a ship, that is, the number of guns times the cube of the bore.

  b) Find the sister ships of a ship. Raise the exception `noSisters` if the ship is the only one of its class.

  c) Given a battle b as a parameter, and applying the method to a ship s, find the ships sunk in the battle b, provided s participated in that battle. Raise the exception `didNotParticipate` if ship s did not fight in battle b.

  d) Given a name and a year launched as parameters, add a ship of this name and year to the class to which the method is applied.

8.2 Introduction to OQL

In this section we introduce the Object Query Language, or OQL. Our coverage in this section and the next two sections will be less extensive than our SQL coverage. We shall explain the most important kinds of statements and features, but there are many other capabilities of OQL, as well. Often these capabilities are similar to corresponding features either in SQL or in typical object-oriented, conventional programming languages.

OQL does not allow us to express arbitrary functions, the way conventional programming languages like C do. Rather, OQL gives us an SQL-like notation for expressing certain queries at a higher level of abstraction than the typical statement of a conventional language. It is intended that OQL will be used as an extension to some object-oriented *host* language, such as C++, Smalltalk, or Java. Objects will be manipulated both by OQL queries and by the conventional statements of the host language. The ability to mix host-language statements and OQL queries without explicitly transferring values between the two languages is an advance over the way SQL is embedded into a host language, as was discussed in Section 7.1.

```
interface Class
    (extent Classes
     key name)
 {
    attribute string name;
    attribute string country;
    attribute integer numGuns;
    attribute integer bore;
    attribute integer displacement;
    relationship Set<Ship> ships inverse Ship::classOf;
 };

interface Ship
    (extent Ships
     key name)
 {
    attribute name;
    attribute integer launched;
    relationship Class classOf inverse Class::ships;
    relationship Set<Outcome> inBattles
                inverse Outcome::theShip;
 };

interface Battle
    (extent Battles
     key name)
 {
    attribute name;
    attribute Date dateFought;
    relationship Set<Outcome> results
                inverse Outcome::theBattle;
 };

interface Outcome
    (extent Outcomes)
 {
    attribute enum Stat {ok,sunk,damaged} status;
    relationship Ship theShip inverse Ship::inBattles;
    relationship Battle theBattle inverse Battle::results;
 };
```

Figure 8.3: Battleships database in ODL

```
interface Star
    (extent Stars
     key name)
{
    attribute string name;
    attribute Struct Addr
        {string street, string city} address;
    relationship Set<Movie> starredIn
                inverse Movie::stars;
}


interface Studio
    (extent Studios
     key name)
{
    attribute string name;
    attribute string address;
    relationship Set<Movie> owns
                inverse Movie::ownedBy;
}
```

Figure 8.4: Part of an object-oriented movie database

8.2.1 An Object-Oriented Movie Example

In order to illustrate the dictions of OQL, we need a running example. It will involve the familiar classes Movie, Star, and Studio. We shall use the definition of Movie from Fig. 8.1. The definitions of Star and Studio, on the other hand, we have carried over from Fig. 2.6, augmenting them with key and extent declarations but no methods; see Fig. 8.4.

8.2.2 The OQL Type System

Types in OQL are built much as they are for ODL declarations (see Section 2.1.7). However, there are no limits in OQL on the depth of nesting of type constructors.

When discussing a type system for a programming language, we need to distinguish between declaring a type for a variable (sometimes referred to as a *mutable object*) and expressing a constant value (sometimes called an *immutable object*). Variables used in OQL statements will be declared in the surrounding host language, probably using the ODL notation of Section 2.1.7 or something similar. ODL, being a data-definition language, has no need for constants, but OQL programs do. Thus, we need to see how to construct constants of arbitrary type in OQL. Constants are constructed from the following basis and type constructors:

1. *Basic types*, which are either

    (a) *Atomic types*: integers, floats, characters, strings, and booleans. These are represented as in SQL, with the exception that double-quotes are used to surround strings.

    (b) *Enumerations*. The values in an enumeration are actually declared in ODL. Any one of these values may be used as a constant.

2. *Complex types* built from the following type constructors:

    (a) `Set(...)`.
    (b) `Bag(...)`.
    (c) `List(...)`.
    (d) `Array(...)`.
    (e) `Struct(...)`.

The first four of these are called *collection types*. The collection types and `Struct` may be applied at will to any values of the appropriate type(s), basic or complex. However, when applying the `Struct` operator, one needs to specify the field names and their corresponding values. Each field name is followed by a colon and the value, and field-value pairs are separated by commas.

Example 8.3 : The expression `bag(2,1,2)` denotes the bag in which integer 2 appears twice and integer 1 appears once. The expression

```
struct(foo: bag(2,1,2), bar: "baz")
```

denotes a structure with two fields. One, named `foo`, has the bag described above as its value, and the other, named `bar`, has the string `"baz"` for its value. □

8.2.3   Path Expressions

We access components of variables with a complex type using a dot notation that is similar to the dot used in C and also related to the dot used in SQL. The general rule is as follows. If a denotes an object belonging to class C, and p is some property of the class — either an attribute, relationship, or method of the class — then $a.p$ denotes the result of "applying" p to a. That is:

1. If p is an attribute, then $a.p$ is the value of that attribute in object a.

2. If p is a relationship, then $a.p$ is the object or collection of objects related to a by relationship p.

Arrows Instead of Dots

OQL uses the arrow `->` as a synonym for the dot. This convention is partly in the spirit of C, where the dot and arrow both obtain components of a structure. However, in C, the arrow and dot operators have slightly different meanings; in OQL they are the same. In C, expression `a.f` expects `a` to be a structure, while `p->f` expects `p` to be a pointer to a structure. Both produce the value of the field `f` of that structure.

---

3. If p is a method (perhaps with parameters), then $a.p$ is the result of applying p to a.

Example 8.4: Suppose `myMovie` is a host-language variable whose value is a `Movie` object. Then

- The value of `myMovie.length` is the length of the movie, that is, the value of the `length` attribute for the `Movie` object denoted by `myMovie`.

- The value of `myMovie.lengthInHours()` is a real number, the length of the movie in hours, computed by applying the method `lengthInHours` to object `myMovie`.

- The value of `myMovie.stars` is the set of `Star` objects related to the movie `myMovie` by the relationship `stars`.

- Expression `myMovie.starNames(myStars)` returns no value (i.e., in C++ the type of this expression is `void`). As a side effect, however, it sets the value of the output variable `myStars` of the method `starNames` to be a set of strings; those strings are the names of the stars of the movie.

□

If it makes sense, we can form expressions with several dots. For example, if `myMovie` denotes a movie object, then `myMovie.ownedBy` denotes the `Studio` object that owns the movie, and `myMovie.ownedBy.name` denotes the string that is the name of that studio.

8.2.4 Select-From-Where Expressions in OQL

OQL permits us to write expressions using a select-from-where syntax similar to SQL's familiar query form. Here is an example asking for the year of the movie *Gone With the Wind*.

```
SELECT m.year
FROM Movies m
WHERE m.title = "Gone With the Wind"
```

Notice that, except for the double-quotes around the string constant, this query could be SQL rather than OQL. The only nonobvious point is that we would expect the FROM clause in SQL to be written

    FROM Movies AS m

However, the keyword AS is optional in OQL, just as it is in SQL. It appears to make more sense to leave it out in OQL, because the meaning of the phrase "Movies m is that m is a variable that takes on in turn each object that is in the extent Movies; the latter extent is the current set of objects of the Movie class.

In general, the OQL select-from-where expression consists of:

1. The keyword SELECT followed by a list of expressions.

2. The keyword FROM followed by a list of one or more variable declarations. A variable is declared by giving

   (a) An expression whose value has a collection type, e.g. a set or bag.

   (b) The optional keyword AS, and

   (c) The name of the variable.

   Typically, the expression of (a) is the extent of some class, such as the extent Movies for class Movie in the example above. An extent is the analog of a relation in an SQL FROM clause. However, it is possible to use in a variable declaration any collection-producing expression, such as another select-from-where expression. There is no direct analog of this capability in SQL2, although some commercial SQL's permit subqueries in FROM clauses.

3. The keyword WHERE and a boolean-valued expression. This expression, like the expression following the SELECT, may only use as operands constants and those variables declared in the FROM clause. The comparison operators are like SQL's, except that !=, rather than <>, is used for "not equal to." The logical operators are AND, OR, and NOT, like SQL's.

The query produces a bag of objects. We compute this bag by considering all possible values of the variables in the FROM clause, in nested loops. If any combination of values for these variables satisfies the condition of the WHERE clause, then the object described by the SELECT clause is added to the bag that is the result of the select-from-where statement.

Example 8.5: Here is a more complex OQL query that illustrates the select-from-where structure.

    SELECT s.name
    FROM Movies m, m.stars s
    WHERE m.title = "Casablanca"

This query asks for the names of the stars of *Casablanca*. Notice the sequence of terms in the FROM clause. First we define m to be an arbitrary object in the class Movie, by saying m is in the extent of that class, which is Movies. Then, for each value of m we let s be a Star object in the set m.stars of stars of movie m. That is, we consider in two nested loops all pairs (m, s) such that m is a movie and s a star of that movie. The evaluation can be sketched as:

```
FOR each m in Movies DO
    FOR each s in m.stars DO
        IF m.title = "Casablanca" THEN
            add s.name to the output bag
```

The WHERE clause restricts our consideration to those pairs that have m equal to the Movie object whose title is *Casablanca*. Then, the SELECT clause produces the bag (which should be a set in this case) of all the name attributes of star objects s in the (m, s) pairs that satisfy the WHERE clause. These names are the names of the stars in the set m_c.stars, where m_c is the *Casablanca* movie object. □

8.2.5 Eliminating Duplicates

Technically a query like that of Example 8.5 produces a bag, rather than a set as an answer. That is, OQL follows the SQL default of not eliminating duplicates in its answer unless directed to do so. As in SQL, the way we eliminate duplicates is with the keyword DISTINCT following SELECT.

Example 8.6: Let us ask for the names of the stars of Disney movies. The following query does the job, eliminating duplicate names in the situation where a star appeared in several Disney movies.

```
SELECT DISTINCT s.name
FROM Movies m, m.stars s
WHERE m.ownedBy.name = "Disney"
```

The strategy of this query is similar to that of Example 8.5. We again consider all pairs of a movie and a star of that movie in two nested loops as in Example 8.5. But now, the condition on that pair (m, s) is that "Disney" is the name of the studio whose Studio object is m.ownedBy. □

8.2.6 Complex Output Types

The expression or expressions in the SELECT clause need not be simple variables. They can be any expression, including expressions built using type constructors. For example, we can apply the Struct type constructor to several expressions and get a select-from-where query that produces a set or bag of structures.

Example 8.7: Suppose we want the set of pairs of stars living at the same address. We can get this set with the query:

```
SELECT DISTINCT Struct(star1: s1, star2: s2)
FROM Stars s1, Stars s2
WHERE s1.addr = s2.addr AND s1.name < s2.name
```

That is, we consider all pairs of stars, s1 and s2. The WHERE clause checks that they have the same address. It also checks that the name of the first star precedes the name of the second in alphabetic order, so we don't produce pairs consisting of the same star twice and we don't produce the same pair of stars in two different orders.

For every pair that passes the two tests, we produce a record structure. The type of this structure is a record with two fields, named star1 and star2. The type of each field is the class Star, since that is the type of the variables s1 and s2 that provide values for the two fields. That is, formally, the type of the structure is

```
Struct N {star1: Star, star2: Star}
```

for some name N. The type of the result of the query is a set of these structures of type N, that is,

```
Set<Struct N {star1: Star, star2: Star}>
```

Notice that the result type for this query is an example of a type that can appear in OQL programs but not as the type of an attribute or relationship in an ODL declaration. □

Incidentally, we can get the same effect as Example 8.7 without explicitly defining a structure type, if we just list the components and field names after the keyword SELECT. That is, we could have written the first line in Example 8.7 as

```
SELECT star1: s1, star2: s2
```

8.2.7 Subqueries

We can use a select-from-where expression anywhere a collection (e.g., a set) is appropriate. One surprising place for subqueries is in the FROM clause, where a collection that is the range of a variable may be constructed by a select-from-where expression. Incidentally, the same sort of capability — use of an expression defining a table in place of a table name — is part of the proposed SQL3 standard and is available in some commercial SQL systems.

Example 8.8: Let us redo the query of Example 8.6, which asked for the stars of the movies made by Disney. First, the set of Disney movies could be obtained by the query

```
SELECT m
FROM Movies m
WHERE m.ownedBy.name = "Disney"
```

We can now use this query as a subquery to define the set over which a variable d, representing the Disney movies, can range.

```
SELECT DISTINCT s.name
FROM (SELECT m
      FROM Movies m
      WHERE m.ownedBy.name = "Disney") d,
     d.stars s
```

This expression of the query "Find the stars of Disney movies" is no more succinct than that of Example 8.6, and perhaps less so. However, it does illustrate a new form of building queries available in OQL. In the query above, the FROM clause has two nested loops. In the first, the variable d ranges over all Disney movies, the result of the subquery in the FROM clause. In the second loop, nested within the first, the variable s ranges over all stars of the movie d. Notice that no WHERE clause is needed. □

8.2.8 Ordering the Result

The result of a select-from-where expression in OQL is either a bag, or (if DISTINCT is used) a set. We can make the output be a list, and at the same time select an order for the elements of that list, if we use an ORDER BY clause at the end of the select-from-where. The ORDER BY clause in OQL is quite similar to the same clause in SQL. Keywords ORDER BY are followed by a list of expressions. The first of these expressions is evaluated for each object in the result of the query, and objects are ordered by this value. Ties, if any, are broken by the value of the second expression, then the third, and so on.

Example 8.9 : Let us find the set of Dinsey movies, but let the result be a list of movies, ordered by length. If there are ties, let the movies of equal length be ordered alphabetically. The query is:

```
SELECT m
FROM Movies m
WHERE m.ownedBy.name = "Disney"
ORDER BY m.length, m.title
```

The first three lines are identical to the subquery in Example 8.8. The fourth line specifies that the objects m produced by the select-from-where query are to be ordered first by the value of m.length (i.e., the length of the movie) and then, if there are ties, by the value of m.title (i.e., the title of the movie). The value produced by this query is thus a list of Movie objects. By default, the order is ascending, but a choice of ascending or descending order can be indicated by the keyword ASC or DESC, respectively, at the end of the ORDER BY clause, as in SQL.   □

8.2.9   Exercises for Section 8.2

Exercise 8.2.1: Using the ODL schema of Exercise 8.1.1 and Fig. 8.2, write the following queries in OQL:

* a) Find the model numbers of all products that are PC's with a price under $2000.

  b) Find the model numbers of all the PC's with at least 32 megabytes of RAM.

*! c) Find the manufacturers that make at least two different models of laser printer.

  d) Find the set of pairs (r, h) such that some PC or laptop has r megabytes of RAM and h gigabytes of hard disk.

  e) Create a list of the PC's (objects, not model numbers) in ascending order of processor speed.

! f) Create a list of the model numbers of the laptops with at least 16 megabytes of RAM, in descending order of screen size.

! **Exercise 8.2.2:** Repeat each part of Exercise 8.2.1 using at least one subquery in each of your queries.

Exercise 8.2.3: Using the ODL schema of Exercise 8.1.2 and Fig. 8.3, write the following queries in OQL:

  a) Find the names of the classes of ships with at least nine guns.

  b) Find the ships (objects, not ship names) with at least nine guns.

  c) Find the names of the ships with a displacement under 30,000 tons. Make the result a list, ordered by earliest launch year first, and if there are ties, alphabetically by ship name.

  d) Find the pairs of objects that are sister ships (i.e., ships of the same class). Note that the objects themselves are wanted, not the names of the ships.

! e) Find the names of the battles in which ships of at least two different countries were sunk.

!! f) Find the names of the battles in which no ship was listed as damaged.

8.3   Additional Forms of OQL Expressions

In this section we shall see some of the other operators, besides select-from-where, that OQL provides for us to build expressions. These operators include logical quantifiers — for-all and there-exists — aggregation operators, the group-by operator, and set operators — union, intersection, and difference.

8.3.1   Quantifier Expressions

We can test whether all, or at least one, member of a set satisfies some condition. To test whether all members of a set S satisfy condition $C(x)$, where x is a variable, we use the OQL expression

$$\text{FOR ALL } x \text{ IN } S : \ C(x)$$

The result of this expression is TRUE if every x in S satisfies $C(x)$ and FALSE otherwise.

Similarly, the expression

$$\text{EXISTS } x \text{ IN } S : \ C(x)$$

has value TRUE if there is at least one x in S such that $C(x)$ is TRUE and it has value FALSE otherwise.

Example 8.10 : Another way to express the query "find all the stars of Disney movies" is shown in Fig. 8.5. Here, we focus on a star s and ask if they are the star of some movie m that is a Disney movie. Line (3) tells us to consider all movies m in the set of movies `s.starredIn`, which is the set of movies in which star s appeared. Line (4) then asks us whether movie m is a Disney movie. If we find even one such movie m, the value of the EXISTS expression in lines (3) and (4) is TRUE; otherwise it is FALSE.   □

```
1)      SELECT s
2)      FROM Stars s
3)      WHERE EXISTS m IN s.starredIn :
4)         m.ownedBy.name = "Disney"
```

Figure 8.5: Using an existential subquery

Example 8.11 : Let us use the for-all operator to write a query asking for the stars that have appeared only in Disney movies. Technically, that set includes stars who appear in no movies at all (as far as our database is concerned). It is possible to add another condition to our query, requiring that the star appear in at least one movie, but we leave that improvement as an exercise. Figure 8.6 shows the query.   □

```
1)     SELECT s
2)     FROM Stars s
3)     WHERE FOR ALL m IN s.starredIn :
4)        m.ownedBy.name = "Disney"
```

Figure 8.6: Using a subquery with universal quantification

8.3.2   Aggregation Expressions

OQL uses the same five aggregation operators that SQL does: `AVG`, `COUNT`, `SUM`, `MIN`, and `MAX`. However, while these operators in SQL may be thought of as applying to a designated column of a table, the same operators in OQL apply to collections whose members are of a suitable type. That is, `COUNT` can apply to any collection; `SUM` and `AVG` can be applied to collections of arithmetic types such as integers, and `MIN` and `MAX` can be applied to collections of any type that can be compared, e.g., arithmetic values or strings.

Example 8.12 : To compute the average length of all movies, we need to create a bag of all movie lengths. Note that we don't want the set of movie lengths, because then two movies that had the same length would count as one. The query is:

```
AVG(SELECT m.length FROM Movies m)
```

That is, we use a subquery to extract the length components from movies. Its result is the bag of lengths of movies, and we apply the `AVG` operator to this bag, giving the desired answer.   □

8.3.3   Group-By Expressions

The `GROUP BY` clause of SQL carries over to OQL, but with an interesting twist in perspective. The form of a `GROUP BY` clause in OQL is:

1. The keywords `GROUP BY`.

2. A comma-separated list of one or more *partition attributes*. Each of these consists of

   (a) A field name,

   (b) A colon, and

   (c) An expression.

That is, the form of a `GROUP BY` clause is:

$$\text{GROUP BY } f_1{:}e_1, \ f_2{:}e_2, \ldots, f_n{:}e_n$$

A GROUP BY clause follows a select-from-where query. The expressions

$$e_1, e_2, \ldots, e_n$$

may refer to variables mentioned in the FROM clause. To facilitate the explanation of how GROUP BY works, let us restrict ourselves to the common case where there is only one variable x in the from clause. The value of x ranges over some collection, C. For each member of C, say i, that satisfies the condition of the WHERE clause, we evaluate all the expressions that follow the GROUP BY, to obtain values $e_1(i), e_2(i), \ldots, e_n(i)$. This list of values is the group to which value i belongs.

The actual value returned by the GROUP BY is a set of structures. The members of this set have the form

$$\texttt{Struct}(f_1:v_1,\ f_2:v_2, \ldots, f_n:v_n,\ \texttt{partition}:P)$$

The first n fields indicate the group. That is, $v_1, v_2, \ldots, v_n$ are a list of values that comes from evaluating $e_1(i), e_2(i), \ldots, e_n(i)$ for at least one value of i in the collection C that meets the condition of the WHERE clause.

The last field has the special name partition. Its value P is, intuitively, the values i that belong in this group. More precisely, P is a bag consisting of structures of the form

$$\texttt{Struct(x:i)}$$

where x is the variable of the FROM clause.

The SELECT clause of a select-from-where expression that has a GROUP BY clause may refer only to the fields in the result of the GROUP BY, namely $f_1, f_2, \ldots, f_n$ and partition. Through partition, we may refer to the field x that is present in the structures that are members of the bag P that forms the value of partition. Thus, we may refer to the variable x that appears in the FROM clause, but we may only do so within an aggregation operator that aggregates over all the members of a bag P.

Example 8.13: Let us build a table of the total length of movies for each studio and for each year. In OQL, what we actually construct is a bag of structures, each with three components — a studio, a year, and the total length of movies for that studio and year. The query is shown in Fig. 8.7.

```
SELECT std, yr, sumLength: SUM(SELECT p.m.length
                                 FROM partition p)
FROM Movies m
GROUP BY std: m.studio, yr: m.year
```

Figure 8.7: Grouping movies by studio and year

To understand this query, let us start at the FROM clause. There, we find that variable m ranges over all Movie objects. Thus, m here plays the role of x in our general discussion. In the GROUP BY clause are two fields std and yr, corresponding to the expressions m.studio and m.year, respectively.

For instance, *Pretty Woman* is a movie made by Disney in 1990. When m is the object for this movie, the value of m.studio is "Disney" and the value of m.year is 1990. As a result, the set constructed by the GROUP BY clause has as one member the structure

$$\texttt{Struct(std:"Disney", yr:1990, partition:} P\texttt{)}$$

Here, P is a set of structures. In contains the structure:

$$\texttt{Struct(m:} m_{pw} \texttt{)}$$

where m_{pw} is the Movie object for *Pretty Woman*. Also in P are one-component structures with field name m for every other Disney movie of 1990.

Now, let us examine the SELECT clause. For each structure in the set that is the result of the GROUP BY clause, we build one structure that is in the bag result of the query. The first component is std. That is, the field name is std and its value is the value of the std field of the structure resulting from the GROUP BY. Similarly, the second component of the result has field name yr and a value equal to the yr component in the result of the GROUP BY.

The third component of each structure in the output is

```
SUM(SELECT p.m.length FROM partition p)
```

To understand this select-from expression we first realize that variable p ranges over the members of the partition field of the structure in the GROUP BY result. Each value of p, recall, is a structure of the form Struct(m:o), where o is a movie object. The expression p.m therefore refers to this object o. Thus, p.m.length refers to the length component of this Movie object.

As a result, the select-from query produces the bag of lengths of the movies in a particular group. For instance, if std has the value "Disney" and yr has the value 1990, then the result of the select-from is the bag of the lengths of the movies made by Disney in 1990. When we apply the SUM operator to this bag we get the sum of the lengths of the movies in the group. Thus, one of the structures in the output bag might be

$$\texttt{Struct(std:"Disney", yr:1990, sumLength:1234)}$$

if 1234 is the correct total length of all the Disney movies of 1990. $\square$

In the event that there is more than one variable in the FROM clause, a few changes to the interpretation of the query are necessary, but the principles remain the same as in the description of the one-variable case above. Suppose that the variables appearing in the FROM clause are $x_1, x_2, \ldots, x_k$. Then:

1. All variables $x_1, x_2, \ldots, x_k$ may be used in the expressions $e_1, e_2, \ldots, e_n$ of the GROUP BY clause.

2. Structures in the bag that is the value of the **partition** field have fields named $x_1, x_2, \ldots, x_k$.

3. Suppose $i_1, i_2, \ldots, i_k$ are values for variables $x_1, x_2, \ldots, x_k$, respectively, that make the WHERE clause true. Then there is a structure in the set that is the result of the GROUP BY of the form

$$\text{Struct}(f_1:e_1(i_1, \ldots, i_k), \ldots, f_n:e_n(i_1, \ldots, i_k), \text{ partition:P})$$

and in bag P is the structure:

$$\text{Struct}(x_1:i_1, \ x_2:i_2, \ldots, x_k:i_k)$$

8.3.4 HAVING Clauses

A GROUP BY clause of OQL may be followed by a HAVING clause, with a meaning like that of SQL's HAVING clause. That is, a clause of the form

$$\text{HAVING} <\text{condition}>$$

serves to eliminate some of the groups created by the GROUP BY. The condition applies to the value of the **partition** field of each structure in the result of the GROUP BY. If true, then the structure is passed to the output for processing as in Section 8.3.3. If false, then the structure is not used in the result of the query.

Example 8.14: Let us repeat Example 8.13, but ask for the sum of the lengths of movies for only those studios and years such that the studio produced at least one movie of over 120 minutes. The query of Fig. 8.8 does the job. Notice that in the HAVING clause we used the same query as in the SELECT clause to obtain the bag of lengths of movies for a given studio and year. In the HAVING clause, we take the maximum of those lengths and compare it to 120. □

```
SELECT std, yr, sumLength: SUM(SELECT p.m.length
                                FROM partition p)
FROM Movies m
GROUP BY std: m.studio, yr: m.year
HAVING MAX(SELECT p.m.length FROM partition p) > 120
```

Figure 8.8: Restricting the groups considered

8.3.5 Set Operators

We may apply the union, intersection, and difference operators to two objects of set or bag type. These three operators are represented as in SQL, by the keywords UNION, INTERSECT, and EXCEPT, respectively.

```
1)        (SELECT DISTINCT m
2)          FROM Movies m, m.stars s
3)          WHERE s.name = "Harrison Ford")
4)    EXCEPT
5)        (SELECT DISTINCT m
6)          FROM Movies m
7)          WHERE m.ownedBy.name = "Disney")
```

Figure 8.9: Query using the difference of two sets

Example 8.15: We can find the set of movies starring Harrison Ford that were not made by Disney with the difference of two select-from-where queries shown in Fig. 8.9. Lines (1) through (3) find the set of movies starring Ford, and lines (5) through (7) find the set of movies made by Disney. The EXCEPT at line (4) takes their difference. □

We should notice the DISTINCT keywords in lines (1) and (5) of Fig. 8.9. This keyword forces the results of the two queries to be of set type; without DISTINCT, the result would be of bag (multiset) type. In OQL, the operators UNION, INTERSECT, and EXCEPT operate on either sets or bags. When both arguments are sets, then the operators have their usual set meaning.

However, when both arguments are of bag type, or one is a bag and one is a set, then the bag meaning of the operators is used. Recall from Section 4.6.2 that a bag allows an object to appear any number of times within it. The rules for operating on bags are as follows. Suppose that B_1 and B_2 are two bags, and x is an object that appears n_1 times in B_1 and n_2 times in B_2. Either n_1 or n_2 or both could be 0.

- In $B_1 \cup B_2$, x appears $n_1 + n_2$ times.

- In $B_1 \cap B_2$, x appears $\min(n_1, n_2)$ times.

- In $B_1 - B_2$, x appears

    1. If $n_1 \leq n_2$, then 0 times.

    2. If $n_1 > n_2$, then $n_1 - n_2$ times.

For the particular query of Fig. 8.9, the number of times a movie appears in the result of either subquery is zero or one, so the result is the same regardless of whether DISTINCT is used. However, the *type* of the result differs. If DISTINCT is used, then the type of the result is Set<Movie>, while if DISTINCT is omitted in one or both places, then the result is of type Bag<Movie>.

8.3.6 Exercises for Section 8.3

Exercise 8.3.1: Using the ODL schema of Exercise 8.1.1 and Fig. 8.2, write the following queries in OQL:

* a) Find the manufacturers that make both PC's and printers.

* b) Find the manufacturers of PC's that only make PC's with at least 2 gigabytes of hard disk.

  c) Find the manufacturers that make PC's but not laptops.

* d) Find the average speed of PC's.

* e) For each CD speed, find the average amount of RAM on a PC.

! f) Find the manufacturers that make some product with at least 16 megabytes of RAM and also make a product costing under $1000.

!! g) For each manufacturer that makes PC's with an average speed of at least 150, find the maximum amount of RAM that they offer on a PC.

Exercise 8.3.2: Using the ODL schema of Exercise 8.1.2 and Fig. 8.3, write the following queries in OQL:

  a) Find those classes of ship all of whose ships were launched prior to 1919.

  b) Find the maximum displacement of any class.

! c) For each gun bore, find the earliest year in which any ship with that bore was launched.

*!! d) For each class of ships at least one of which was launched prior to 1919, find the number of ships of that class sunk in battle.

! e) Find the average number of ships in a class.

! f) Find the average displacement of a ship.

!! g) Find the battles (objects, not names) in which at least one ship from Great Britain took part and in which at least two ships were sunk.

! **Exercise 8.3.3:** We mentioned in Example 8.11 that the OQL query of Fig. 8.6 would return stars who starred in no movies at all, and therefore, technically appeared "only in Disney movies." Rewrite the query to return only those stars who have appeared in at least one movie and all movies they appeared in where Disney movies.

8.4 Object Assignment and Creation in OQL

In this section we shall consider how OQL connects to its host language, which we shall take to be C++ in examples, although another object-oriented, general-purpose programming language might be the host language in some systems.

8.4.1 Assigning Values to Host-Language Variables

Unlike SQL, which needs to move data between components of tuples and host-language variables, OQL fits naturally into its host language. That is, the expressions of OQL that we have learned, such as select-from-where, produce objects as values. It is possible to assign any host-language variable of the proper type a value that is the result of one of these OQL expressions.

Example 8.16 : The OQL expression

```
SELECT m
FROM Movies m
WHERE m.year < 1920
```

produces the set of all those movies made before 1920. Its type is `Set<Movie>`. If `oldMovies` is a host-language variable of the same type, then we may write (in C++ extended with OQL):

```
oldMovies = SELECT DISTINCT m
            FROM Movies m
            WHERE m.year < 1920;
```

and the value of `oldMovies` will become the set of these `Movie` objects. □

8.4.2 Extracting Elements of Collections

Since the select-from-where and group-by expressions each produce collections — either sets or bags — we have to do something extra if we want a single element of that set. This statement is true even if we have a collection that we are sure contains only one element. OQL provides the operator `ELEMENT` to turn a singleton set or bag into its lone member. This operator can be applied, for instance, to the result of a query that is known to return a singleton.

Example 8.17 : Suppose we would like to assign to the variable `gwtw`, of type `Movie` (i.e., the `Movie` class is its type) the object representing the movie *Gone With the Wind*. The result of the query

```
SELECT m
FROM Movies m
WHERE m.title = "Gone With the Wind"
```

is the bag containing just this one object. We cannot assign this bag to variable gwtw directly, because we would get a type error. However, if we apply the ELEMENT operator first,

```
gwtw = ELEMENT(SELECT m
               FROM Movies m
               WHERE m.title = "Gone With the Wind"
       );
```

then the type of the variable and the expression match, and the assignment is legal. □

8.4.3 Obtaining Each Member of a Collection

Obtaining each member of a set or bag is more complex, but still simpler than the cursor-based algorithms we needed in SQL. First, we need to turn our set or bag into a list. We do so with a select-from-where expression that uses ORDER BY. Recall from Section 8.2.8 that the result of such an expression is a list of the selected objects or values.

Example 8.18: Suppose we want a list of all the movie objects in the class Movie. We can use the title and (to break ties) the year of the movie, since (title, year) is a key for Movie. The statement

```
movieList = SELECT m
            FROM Movies m
            ORDER BY m.title, m.year;
```

assigns to host-language variable movieList a list of all the Movie objects, sorted by title and year. □

Once we have a list, sorted or not, we can access each element by number; the ith element of the list L is obtained by $L[i-1]$. Note that lists and arrays are assumed numbered starting at 0, as in C or C++.

Example 8.19: Suppose we want to write a C++ function that prints the title, year, and length of each movie. A sketch of the function is shown in Fig. 8.10.

Line (1) sorts the Movie class, placing the result into variable movieList, whose type is List<Movie>. Line (2) computes the number of movies, using the OQL operator COUNT. Then, lines (3) through (7) are a for-loop in which integer variable i ranges over each position of the list. For convenience, the ith element on the list is assigned to variable movie. Then, at lines (5) and (6) the relevant attributes of the movie are printed. □

```
1)    movieList = SELECT m
                  FROM Movies m
                  ORDER BY m.title, m.year;
2)    numberOfMovies = COUNT(Movies);
3)    for(i=0; i<numberOfMovies; i++) {
4)        movie = movieList[i];
5)        cout << movie.title << " " << movie.year << " "
6)            << movie.length << "\n";
7)    }
```

Figure 8.10: Examining and printing each movie

8.4.4   Creating New Objects

We have seen that OQL expressions such as select-from-where allow us to create
new objects. These objects are created by computation on existing objects. It is
also possible to create objects by assembling constants or other expressions into
structures and collections explicitly. We do so by applying the type constructors
to values, in an obvious way. In place of the triangular brackets that are used
to describe types, round parentheses are used when we are constructing values.
We saw an example of this convention in Example 8.7, where the line

```
SELECT DISTINCT Struct(star1: s1, star2: s2)
```

was used to specify that the result of the query is a set of objects whose type is
`Struct{star1:  Star, star2:  Star}`. We gave the field names `star1` and
`star2` to specify the structure, while the types of these fields could be deduced
from the types of the variables `s1` and `s2`.

Example 8.20 : We may also create collections by applying any of the collection type constructors `Set`, `Bag`, `List`, or `Array` to objects of the same type.
For instance, consider the following sequence of assignments:

```
x = Struct(a:1, b:2);
y = Bag(x, x, Struct(a:3, b:4));
```

The first line gives variable x a value of type

```
Struct(a:integer, b:integer)
```

a structure with two integer-valued fields named `a` and `b`. We may think of
values of this type as tuples, with just the integers as components and not the
field names `a` and `b`. Thus, the value of x may be represented by $(1, 2)$. The
second line defines y to be a bag whose members are structures of the same
type as x, above. The pair $(1, 2)$ appears twice in this bag, and $(3, 4)$ appears
once.   □

If we have a type, and a query produces a collection of objects of that type, then we can use the type name instead of an explicit type expression. For instance, we saw in Example 8.7 how to create a set of star-pairs explicitly. We followed the SELECT keyword by an expression that used the type constructor Struct to build objects that included two fields whose values are star objects.

Suppose now that we have defined the type StarPair to be:

```
Struct{star1: Star, star2: Star}
```

Then we could rewrite the query of Example 8.7 to use this type in the SELECT clause as follows.

```
SELECT DISTINCT StarPair(star1: s1, star2: s2)
FROM Stars s1, Stars s2
WHERE s1.addr = s2.addr AND s1.name < s2.name
```

The only change from Example 8.7 is that the result of this query has type Set<StarPair>. The result may thus be assigned to a host-language variable that was declared to have this type.

Applying the type name to arguments is especially useful when that type name is a class. Classes typically have several different forms of *constructor functions*, depending on which properties are initialized explicitly and which are given some default value. For example, methods are certainly not initialized, most attributes will get initial values, and relationships might be initialized to the empty set and augmented later. The name for each of these constructor functions is the name of the class, and they are distinguished by the field names mentioned in their arguments. The details of how these constructor functions are defined depend on the host language.

Example 8.21 : Let us consider a possible constructor function for Movie objects. This function, we suppose, takes values for the attributes title, year, length, and ownedBy, producing an object that has these values in the listed fields and an empty set of stars. Then, if mgm is a variable whose value is the MGM Studio object, we might create a *Gone With the Wind* object by:

```
gwtw = Movie(title: "Gone With the Wind",
             year: 1939,
             length: 239,
             ownedBy: mgm);
```

This statement has two effects:

1. It creates a new Movie object, which becomes part of the extent Movies.

2. It makes this object the value of host-language variable gwtw.

□

8.4.5   Exercises for Section 8.4

Exercise 8.4.1: Assign to a host-language variable x the following constants:

* a) The set $\{1, 2, 3\}$.

  b) The bag $\{1, 2, 3, 1\}$.

  c) The list $(1, 2, 3, 1)$.

  d) The structure whose first component, named a, is the set $\{1, 2\}$ and whose second component, named b, is the bag $\{1, 1\}$.

  e) The bag of structures, each with two fields named a and b. The respective pairs of values for the three structures in the bag are $(1, 2)$, $(2, 1)$, and $(1, 2)$.

Exercise 8.4.2: Using the ODL schema of Exercise 8.1.1 and Fig. 8.2, write statements of C++ (or an object-oriented host language of your choice) extended with OQL to do the following:

* a) Assign to host-language variable x the object for the PC with model number 1000.

  b) Assign to host-language variable y the set of all laptop objects with at least 16 megabytes of RAM.

  c) Assign to host-language variable z the average speed of PC's selling for less than $1500.

! d) Find all the laser printers, print a list of their model numbers and prices, and follow it by a message indicating the model number with the lowest price.

!! e) Print a table giving, for each manufacturer of PC's, the minimum and maximum price.

Exercise 8.4.3: In this exercise, we shall use the ODL schema of Exercise 8.1.2 and Fig. 8.3. We shall assume that for each of the four classes of that schema, there is a constructor function of the same name that takes values for each of the attributes and single-valued relationships, but not the multivalued relationships, which are initialized to be empty. For the single-valued relationships to other classes, you may postulate a host-language variable whose current value is the related object. Create the following objects and assign the object to be the value of a host-language variable in each case.

* a) The battleship Colorado of the Maryland class, launched in 1923.

  b) The battleship Graf Spee of the Lützow class, launched in 1936.

c) An outcome of the battle of Malaya was that the battleship Prince of Wales was sunk.

d) The battle of Malaya was fought Dec. 10, 1941.

e) The Hood class of British battlecruisers had eight 15-inch guns and a displacement of 41,000 tons.

8.5 Tuple Objects in SQL3

OQL has no specific notion of a relation; it is just a set (or bag) of structures. However, in SQL the relation is such a core notion, that objects in SQL3 keep relations as a central concept. Objects in SQL3 thus come in two flavors:

1. *Row objects*, which are essentially tuples, and

2. *Abstract Data Types* (often shortened to *ADT* or, in some SQL3 documents, *value ADT*), which are general objects that can be used only as components of tuples.

We shall introduce row objects in this section and ADT's in Section 8.6.

8.5.1 Row Types

In SQL3, one can define a type of tuple, and this type roughly resembles a class of objects. A row-type declaration consists of

1. The keywords CREATE ROW TYPE,

2. A name for the type, and

3. A parenthesized list of attributes and their types.

That is, the definition of a row type T has the form

$$\text{CREATE ROW TYPE } T \text{ (<component declarations>)}$$

Example 8.22: We can create a row type representing movie stars, analogous to the class Star found in the OQL example of Fig. 8.4. However, we cannot represent directly a set of movies as a field within Star tuples. Thus, we shall start with only the name and address components of Star tuples.

To begin, note that the type of an address in Fig. 8.4 is itself a tuple, with components street and city. Thus, we need two type definitions, one for addresses and the other for stars. In SQL3 it is permissible to use a row type as the type of a component of another row type or relation. The necessary definitions are shown in Fig. 8.11.

A tuple of type AddressType has two components, whose attributes are street and city. The types of these components are character strings of length

```
CREATE ROW TYPE AddressType(
    street  CHAR(50),
    city    CHAR(20)
);

CREATE ROW TYPE StarType(
    name    CHAR(30),
    address AddressType
);
```

Figure 8.11: Two row-type definitions

50 and 20, respectively. A tuple of type StarType also has two components. The first is attribute name, whose type is a 30-character string, and the second is address, whose type is AddressType, that is, a tuple with street and city components. □

8.5.2 Declaring Relations with a Row Type

Having declared a row type, we may declare one or more relations whose tuples are of that type. The form of relation declarations is like that of Section 5.7.2, but we use

$$\text{OF TYPE } <\text{row type name}>$$

in place of the list of attributes and their types in a normal SQL table declaration.

Example 8.23: We could declare MovieStar to be a relation whose tuples were of type StarType by

```
CREATE TABLE MovieStar OF TYPE StarType;
```

As a result, table MovieStar has two attributes, name and address. Note that the type of the latter is itself a row type, not normally permitted by SQL standards prior to SQL3. □

While it is common to have one relation for each row type, and to think of that relation as the extent (in the sense of Section 8.1.3) of the class corresponding to that tuple type, it is permissible to have many relations or none of a given row type.

8.5.3 Accessing Components of a Row Type

Because components in SQL3 can themselves have structure, we need a way to reach into a component for *its* components. SQL3 uses a double-dot notation that corresponds closely to the single-dot notation of OQL or C.

Example 8.24 : The query in Fig. 8.12 finds the name and street address of each star living in Beverly Hills. We have chosen to use the full attribute names `MovieStar.name` and `MovieStar.address`, to illustrate the difference between the single and double dot. However, since `name` and `address` are unambiguous attributes here, the `MovieStar` and the single dot are unnecessary. □

```
SELECT MovieStar.name, MovieStar.address..street
FROM MovieStar
WHERE MovieStar.address..city = 'Beverly Hills';
```

Figure 8.12: Accessing the components of components

8.5.4 References

The effect of object identity in object-oriented languages is obtained in SQL3 through the notion of a *reference*. A component of a row type may have as its type a reference to another row type. If T is a row type, then $\text{REF}(T)$ is the type of a reference to a tuple of type T. If we think of a tuple as an object, then a reference to that object is its object ID.

Example 8.25 : We still cannot record in `MovieStar` the set of all movies they starred in, but let us record their best movie. We first need to declare a `Movie` relation, and we can at the same time declare a row type for this relation if we wish. A simple type for movies, excluding for the moment relationships with stars, studios, or producers, is

```
CREATE ROW TYPE MovieType(
    title  CHAR(30),
    year   INTEGER,
    inColor BIT(1)
);
```

We can then declare a relation of tuples of this type by:

```
CREATE TABLE Movie OF TYPE MovieType;
```

Next, we must modify the type of `MovieStar` tuples to include a reference to the star's best movie.[2] The new definition of `StarType` is:

```
CREATE ROW TYPE StarType(
    name        CHAR(30),
    address     AddressType,
    bestMovie   REF(MovieType)
);
```

□

Example 8.26: Suppose, however, that we want the standard, many-many relationship between movies and stars: a star is in a set of movies and a movie has a set of stars. While ODL allows a set of stars as a component of movies and vice versa, SQL3 retains the relational approach that we have followed throughout the book.[3] However, a many-many relationship may be represented by a separate relation containing pairs of related items.

Figure 8.13 suggests how we could represent the stars-in relationship between movies and stars. In standards prior to SQL3, we could only represent many-many relationships by pairing the keys for the related classes, SQL3 allows us to refer to objects (tuples, to be exact) directly through attributes with a reference type. We begin with definitions of types `MovieType` and `StarType` for relations `Movie` and `MovieStar`, respectively. We have reverted to the original row type `StarType` that does not have a best movie. The row type `StarsInType`, defined for relation `StarsIn`, holds pairs of references; each pair refers to a star and a movie in which that star appeared.

The definitions of the row types are followed by declarations of three tables, `Movie`, `MovieStar`, and `StarsIn`, that use these row types. Note that the row type `AddressType` is not used as the type of a table. Rather, it was used as the type of the attribute `address` within the row type `StarType`.

We should compare the relation called `StarsIn` here with the relation of the same name in the database schema of Section 3.9. The latter relation has attributes `movieTitle` and `movieYear` instead of a reference to a movie tuple and has attribute `starName` in place of a reference to a star tuple.   □

8.5.5   Following References

Once we accept that a component of one tuple can be a reference to a tuple of some other (or the same) relation, it is natural to extend SQL by allowing

---

[2]SQL3 does not include `ALTER TYPE` or similar statements that would allow us to modify existing type definitions. Thus, in practice we would have to drop the row type and any tables defined to have that type, then redefine the type and reconstruct the tables, should we wish to make changes to a previously defined row type.

[3]Although some drafts of the SQL3 standard do allow collection types (e.g., sets or relations) as types of attributes, it is likely that this use of collection types will be deferred to the later SQL4 standard.

```
CREATE ROW TYPE MovieType(
    title   CHAR(30),
    year    INTEGER,
    inColor BIT(1)
);

CREATE ROW TYPE AddressType(
    street  CHAR(50),
    city    CHAR(20)
);

CREATE ROW TYPE StarType(
    name    CHAR(30),
    address AddressType,
);

CREATE ROW TYPE StarsInType(
    star    REF(StarType),
    movie   REF(MovieType)
);

CREATE TABLE Movie OF TYPE MovieType;

CREATE TABLE MovieStar OF TYPE StarType;

CREATE TABLE StarsIn OF TYPE StarsInType;
```

Figure 8.13: Stars, movies, and their relationship

Domains and Row Types

In Section 5.7.6 we learned about domains, which are a kind of type declaration. There are at least two important differences between domains and row types. The first, obvious difference is that domains define types for components, while row types are types for entire tuples.

But there is a more subtle difference. Domains are shorthands. Two domains can represent the same type, and values from those domains will not be distinguished. However, suppose two row types, T_1 and T_2, have identical definitions. Then tuples from relations with those types cannot be interchanged. For example, an attribute whose type is a reference to a T_1 cannot be made to refer to a tuple whose type is T_2.

---

a *dereferencing* operator. In SQL3, `->` is used for dereferencing, and it has the same meaning as this operator does in C. That is, if x is a reference to a tuple t, and a is an attribute of t, then `x->a` is the value of the attribute a in tuple t. This operator is convenient in many SQL3 queries, since it may substitute for certain joins that are necessary in SQL2.

Example 8.27: Let us use the schema of Fig. 8.13 and find the titles of all the movies in which Mel Gibson starred. Our strategy is to examine each pair in `StarsIn`. If the star referred to is Mel Gibson, then we produce as part of the result the title of the movie referred to by the other component of the pair. The SQL3 query is:

```
SELECT movie->title
FROM StarsIn
WHERE star->name = 'Mel Gibson';
```

The query is interpreted as follows. As for all SQL select-from-where queries, we consider each tuple in the relation mentioned in the `FROM` clause, say (s, m). Here, s is a reference to a star tuple and m is a reference to a movie tuple. The `WHERE` clause asks us to determine whether the `name` component of the `MovieStar` tuple referred to by reference s is Mel Gibson. If so, then we obtain the value of the `title` component of the `Movie` tuple referred to by m, and this value is one of the tuples produced by the query. □

8.5.6 Scopes of References

To answer a query such as that of Example 8.27, an SQL3 database system will have to interpret a reference-following expression like `star->name` as a reference to the `name` field of a particular relation. One simple way is to look at every tuple of `StarsIn`, follow its `star` reference, and see if the tuple referred to has

---

Dereferencing and Component-Extraction

One of the differences between SQL3 and OQL can be seen in the way they interpret the `->` and dot operators. Recall from Section 8.2.3 that the dot and `->` operators are synonyms in OQL. Each applies to an OQL object that is a tuple and returns a component of that object. SQL3, like C, distinguishes these operators. We can apply only `->` to a reference to a tuple, and we can apply only the dot operator (which in SQL3 is written with two dots) to tuple variables themselves. As in C, if r is a reference to a tuple t, then `r->a` yields the same value as `t..a`.

---

name "Mel Gibson." However, that could be a very time-consuming way to answer the question, if `StarsIn` is big.

There might be a better way if the DBMS permits the creation of indexes on the `name` attribute of some relation R that takes us from a particular value — e.g., "Mel Gibson" — to those `StarsIn` tuples that refer to tuples of R with `name` equal to "Mel Gibson." But in which relation or relations R should we search using such an index? In this example, we know that the `star` attribute of any `StarsIn` tuple has a value that is a reference to some tuple, and that tuple must be in a relation whose type is `StarType`. We have only shown one such relation, `MovieStar`, so we might expect that it is to this relation that the reference refers.

However, there may be other relations declared to be of type `StarType`, and if so, it is necessary to search indexes belonging to each of them for the name "Mel Gibson." That search can waste time if, for reasons known to the designer of the schema, all the references were to tuples of one particular relation, as should normally be the case. Thus, SQL3 provides a mechanism for specifying which relation a reference attribute refers to. We may add a clause to the declaration of a relation with an attribute whose type is a reference, stating:

$$\text{SCOPE FOR <attribute> IS <relation>}$$

The meaning of this statement is that the named attribute, whose type must be a reference, always refers to a tuple of the named relation.

Example 8.28: To guarantee that in table `StarsIn`, `star` references are always to tuples of `MovieStar`, and `movie` references are always to tuples of `Movie`, we could write the declaration of relation `StarsIn` as shown in Fig. 8.14. □

8.5.7 Object Identifiers as Values

It is a generally held principle of object-oriented languages that object ID's are internal system values, not accessible through the query language. For example,

```
CREATE ROW TYPE StarsInType(
    star    REF(StarType),
    movie   REF(MovieType)
);

CREATE TABLE StarsIn OF TYPE StarsInType
SCOPE FOR star IS MovieStar,
SCOPE FOR movie IS Movie;
```

Figure 8.14: Declaring scopes for reference attributes

OQL makes this assumption. However, there is no reason in principle why we should not be able to refer to object ID's explicitly, and SQL3 gives us this capability. In the declaration of a relation or its row type, we may have an attribute whose value is a reference to tuples of the same type. If we include in the declaration of a row type or table the clause:

`VALUES FOR <attribute> ARE SYSTEM GENERATED`

then the values for the named attribute will be references to the same tuple in which the reference appears. Thus, such an attribute can serve both as the primary key for the relation and as the object ID for its tuples.

Example 8.29: Let us rewrite Fig. 8.13 so that both `MovieStar` and `Movie` have object-ID attributes, which we shall call `star_id` and `movie_id`, respectively. The modified schema is shown in Fig. 8.15. The changes between this figure and Fig 8.13 are:

1. The `movie_id` attribute was added to row type `MovieType`.

2. The `star_id` attribute was added to row type `StarType`.

3. A statement that the value for `movie_id` in the table `Movie` is system generated was added to the declaration of that table.

4. A statement that the value for `star_id` in the table `MovieStar` is system generated was added to the declaration of that table.

5. The `SCOPE` declarations from Example 8.28 have been retained.

We now have a more conventional way of writing the query discussed in Example 8.27, to find the movies in which Mel Gibson starred. We can equate in the `WHERE` clause the references in `StarsIn` to the object-ID attributes of relations `MovieStar` and `Movie` that are self-references to their own tuples. This query is:

```
CREATE ROW TYPE MovieType(
    movie_id REF(MovieType),
    title    CHAR(30),
    year     INTEGER,
    inColor  BIT(1)
);

CREATE ROW TYPE AddressType(
    street   CHAR(50),
    city     CHAR(20)
);

CREATE ROW TYPE StarType(
    star_id  REF(StarType),
    name     CHAR(30),
    address  AddressType,
);

CREATE ROW TYPE StarsInType(
    star     REF(StarType),
    movie    REF(MovieType)
);

CREATE TABLE Movie OF TYPE MovieType
VALUES FOR movie_id ARE SYSTEM GENERATED;

CREATE TABLE MovieStar OF TYPE StarType
VALUES FOR star_id ARE SYSTEM GENERATED;

CREATE TABLE StarsIn OF TYPE StarsInType
SCOPE FOR star IS MovieStar,
SCOPE FOR movie IS Movie;
```

Figure 8.15: Adding object ID's to relations

```
SELECT Movie.title
FROM StarsIn, MovieStar, Movie
WHERE StarsIn.star = MovieStar.star_id AND
      StarsIn.movie = Movie.movie_id AND
      MovieStar.name = 'Mel Gibson';
```

That is, the FROM clause tells us to consider all triples consisting of tuples from the relations StarsIn, MovieStar, and Movie, respectively. The first condition of the WHERE clause is that the tuple from StarsIn must refer (in its star component) to the tuple from MovieStar. Similarly, the second condition of the WHERE clause states that the StarsIn tuple refers (in its movie component) to the tuple from table Movie. The effect of these two conditions is to require that the tuples from MovieStar and Movie represent the star and movie that are paired in the StarsIn tuple.

Then, the third condition of the WHERE clause requires that the star in question be Mel Gibson, and the SELECT clause produces the title of the movie in question. Note that we can still write the query using reference-following, as we did in Example 8.27. In fact, that approach is much simpler for this query, although writing the query as we did served to illustrate some of the possibilities inherent in the use of attributes that are object ID's. □

8.5.8 Exercises for Section 8.5

Exercise 8.5.1: Write row type declarations for the following types:

a) NameType, with components for first, middle, and last names and a title.

* b) PersonType, with a name of the person and references to the persons that are their mother and father. You must use the row type from part (a) in your declaration.

c) MarriageType, with the date of the marriage and references to the husband and wife.

Exercise 8.5.2: Redesign our running products database schema of Exercise 4.1.1 to use row type declarations and reference attributes where appropriate. In particular, in the relations PC, Laptop, and Printer make the model attribute be a reference to the Product tuple for that model.

Exercise 8.5.3: Using your schema from Exercise 8.5.2, write the following queries. Try to use references whenever appropriate.

a) Find the manufacturers of PC's with a hard disk larger than 2 gigabytes.

b) Find the manufacturers of laser printers.

! c) Produce a table giving for each model of laptop, the model of the laptop having the highest processor speed of any laptop made by the same manufacturer.

! **Exercise 8.5.4:** In Exercise 8.5.2 we suggested that model numbers in the tables `PC`, `Laptop`, and `Printer` could be references to tuples of the `Product` table. Is it also possible to make the `model` attribute in `Product` a reference to the tuple in the relation for that type of product? Why or why not?

* **Exercise 8.5.5:** Redesign our running battleships database schema of Exercise 4.1.3 to use row type declarations and reference attributes where appropriate. The schema from Exercise 8.1.2 should suggest where reference attributes are useful. Look for many-one relationships and try to represent them using an attribute with a reference type.

Exercise 8.5.6: Using your schema from Exercise 8.5.5, write the following queries. Try to use references whenever appropriate and avoid joins (i.e., subqueries or more than one tuple variable in the `FROM` clause).

* a) Find the ships with a displacement of more than 35,000 tons.

b) Find the battles in which at least one ship was sunk.

! c) Find the classes that had ships launched after 1930.

!! d) Find the battles in which at least one US ship was damaged.

8.6 Abstract Data Types in SQL3

SQL3's row types and references to row types provide much of the functionality of objects in OQL. In addition, they allow us to modify "objects" using the convenient operators of SQL such as insertion and deletion; in comparison, OQL expects that modifications will be handled in the surrounding object-oriented programming language such as C++.

However, row types do not provide the *encapsulation* available in object-oriented programming languages. Recall from Section 1.3.1 that we "encapsulate" a class to make sure its objects are modified using only a fixed set of operations that are defined with the class. The purpose of encapsulation is to inhibit the programming mistakes that often arise when data is used in ways that the designer of the database did not intend or anticipate.

Row types are not encapsulated; we can operate on tuples of a row type using any operation that we can express in SQL3. ODL interfaces (classes) are not completely encapsulated, since we can access components of objects using the query forms of OQL. On the other hand, querying the inner structure of objects is generally less dangerous than modifying objects in unplanned ways. In OQL, one cannot update objects, except through methods (see Section 8.1.2). These methods, presumably written in the surrounding, conventional language such as C++, apply only to objects of that class.

In SQL3 there is another kind of "class" definition that does support encapsulation: the *abstract data type* or *ADT*. Objects of an ADT are intended to be used as components of tuples, not as tuples themselves. However, these objects typically have a tuple structure themselves, just as ODL objects normally have a structure with components.

8.6.1   Defining ADT's

The form of an ADT definition is shown in Fig. 8.16. Line (1) is the create-statement, introducing the name of the ADT. Line (2) represents the comma-separated list of attribute names and their types.

```
1)    CREATE TYPE <type name> (
2)        list of attributes and their types
3)        optional declaration of = and < functions for the type
4)        declaration of functions (methods) for the type
5)    );
```

Figure 8.16: Defining abstract data types

Line (3) of Fig. 8.16 represents optional declarations for the comparison operators = and <. The form of the declaration of the equality function is

EQUALS <name of function implementing equality>

and the < function is defined similarly, with keywords LESS THAN replacing EQUALS.[4] Note that the other four comparison operators can be built from these and need not be defined explicitly. For instance, ≤ is "= or <," and > is "not <." If = and < are defined, then it is possible to compare values of this ADT in WHERE clauses, just as for the conventional SQL types such as integers or character strings.

Line (4) suggests the declaration of other functions (i.e., methods) for the ADT. SQL3 provides certain "built-in" functions with every ADT, and these do not need to be declared or defined. They include:

1. A *constructor* function that returns a new object of the type. All attributes of this object are initially NULL. If T is the name of the ADT, then $T()$ is the constructor function.

2. *Observer* functions for each attribute that return the value of this attribute. If A is an attribute name, and X is a variable whose value is an object of the ADT, then $A(X)$ is the value of attribute A of object X. We may also use the more conventional notation $X.A$ to mean the same thing.

---

[4]Possibly, as the SQL3 standard evolves, these functions will not be treated specially but will have to be defined and used as any other function for the type.

3. *Mutator* functions for each attribute that set the value of that attribute to a new value. These are normally used on the left side of assignment statements in a manner to be discussed in Section 8.6.2. Note that to achieve encapsulation, it is necessary to block these functions from public use. The approach used by SQL3 is to have an EXECUTE privilege for functions. This privilege may be granted or revoked just like the six privileges of SQL2 discussed in Section 7.4.1.

Other functions may be defined either inside or outside the CREATE TYPE statement. However, if they are outside, they may only use the functions defined inside, including those built-in functions listed above.

Example 8.30 : In Example 8.22 we defined addresses, consisting of street and city components, to be a row type. We could alternatively have declared addresses to be an ADT with the same structure. That approach would have the effect of encapsulating addresses; we could not access the street and city components unless we made their observer and mutator functions public.

```
1)   CREATE TYPE AddressADT (
2)       street  CHAR(50),
3)       city    CHAR(20),
4)       EQUALS addrEq,
5)       LESS THAN addrLT
            other functions could be declared here
    );
```

Figure 8.17: Definition of an address ADT

Figure 8.17 shows the definition of the ADT AddressADT, except for the actual definitions of the functions or methods associated with the ADT. Line (1) gives the name of the ADT.

Lines (2) and (3) define the representation, a tuple with components named street and city. The types of these components are as in Example 8.22: character strings of lengths 50 and 20, respectively.

Lines (4) and (5) tell us that the equality function for AddressADT is called addrEq, while the < comparison function is called addrLT. We do not yet know what these functions do, since we have not provided their definitions. We shall give our choice of definitions for these functions in Example 8.32. There, we shall order addresses lexicographically by city name first, then then by street. □

Our next example illustrates the power of ADT's to introduce into SQL programs data types that were not anticipated by the classical assumptions about what database management systems would be used for. It is now feasible to store very large objects, such as images, audio clips, or movies in databases.

However, the operations we perform on these objects are not like the "standard" SQL operations of comparing, printing, aggregating, and so on. Rather, we need to display these objects, often using a complex decoding algorithm to do so, and it may even be feasible in the future to do complex comparisons of images or identify important features of images.

Example 8.31: Suppose we want to have an ADT `Mpeg` that is the MPEG encoding of a movie (MPEG is a standard form of compressing video; see the box on the subject for details). Technically, an MPEG encoding is a character string, so the type `VARCHAR` might be thought appropriate. However, the length of MPEG-encoded video is often so large (gigabytes) that it is unfeasible to treat videos as character strings.

To support videos and other very large data items, modern database systems support a special data type called a *BLOB* (Binary, Large, OBject), a special kind of bit string that may be very long, even gigabytes long if necessary. In this example, we shall assume that the type BLOB is a built-in type for the database system. Then a suitable definition for the ADT `Mpeg` is shown in Fig. 8.18.

```
1)   CREATE TYPE Mpeg (
2)       video     BLOB,
3)       length    INTEGER,
4)       copyright VARCHAR(255),
5)       EQUALS DEFAULT,
6)       LESS THAN NONE
             definitions of functions go here
     );
```

Figure 8.18: Definition of an MPEG ADT

Line (2) defines attribute `video` to be of type BLOB. This attribute holds the very large MPEG-encoded video. Lines (3) and (4) are two other "ordinary" attributes: a length (running time) for the video and a copyright notice for the video. Line (5) says that the equality comparison on values of type `Mpeg` is the default: identity. That is, two `Mpeg` objects are equal if and only if they are identical, bit for bit, in corresponding attributes. We might contemplate writing a more complex definition of equality, reflecting the idea that two `Mpeg` values are "equal" if they look the same when decoded and displayed on a screen of reasonable resolution, but we shall not pursue the matter here. Line (6) says that there is no definition for $<$ between `Mpeg` values. That is, it is illegal to write $A < B$ if A and B are values of type `Mpeg`. □

MPEG Encoding of Video

Since video requires so much space to store, it is usually encoded by one of several standard compression schemes. The most common such scheme, MPEG, takes advantage of the fact that one frame of a motion picture is very similar to the frame before it. Thus, regions of one frame can be represented by a pointer to a similar region in the previous frame. Note that the region in the previous frame may be at the same position (if it is part of a stationary background) or may be in a different position (if it is part of a moving object).

While MPEG can compress video much better than standard compression schemes for text can, MPEG-compressed video still requires about one gigabyte for an hour of video. Moreover, because slight differences in corresponding regions are tolerated, the quality of the video is often degraded slightly. Decompressing the video for display is also a complex process. Despite these problems, MPEG represents a good tradeoff among picture quality, space used, and computational power required.

8.6.2 Defining Methods for ADT's

After the attribute list of an ADT, we can append any list of function declarations. The form of a function declaration is

```
FUNCTION <name> ( <arguments> ) RETURNS <type> ;
```

Each argument consists of a variable name and a type for the variable. Arguments are separated by commas.

Functions are of two types: internal and external. External functions are written in the host language and only their signature appears in the definition of the ADT. We shall discuss external functions in Section 8.6.3. Internal functions are written in an extended SQL. The following are some options, including extensions both to SQL2 and to the query language portion of SQL3:

- := is used as an assignment operator.

- A variable local to the function can be declared by giving its name, preceded by a colon and followed by its type.

- The dot operator is used to access components of a structure.

- Boolean values can be expressed as in WHERE clauses.

- BEGIN and END are used to collect several statements into the body of a function.

Binary, Large Objects

BLOB's may look like big bit strings to the user, but behind the scenes their implementation is far more complicated than is the implementation of character strings with a small length limit like 255 bytes. For instance, it does not make sense to store huge strings as components of tuples, so they must be stored separately, usually by the surrounding file system.

For another example, the client-server model discussed in Section 7.3.4 assumes that values and tuples are of modest size, and the server will pass to the client entire tuples that answer a query. It does not make sense to pass a whole BLOB to the client immediately. For example, if the client asks the server for a video clip, the server should pass only a small amount at a time, perhaps a few seconds' worth of video. Then, the client can begin playing the movie and not have to store several gigabytes of video locally or wait until the entire video is received before starting to display it.

Example 8.32: Let us continue Example 8.30, where we defined an address ADT. Figure 8.19 gives some functions that we could include with the type-creation statement of Fig. 8.17.

Lines (1) through (6) define a constructor function for the ADT `AddressADT`. Recall that SQL3 provides a zero-argument, built-in constructor whose name is `AddressADT` (the name of the ADT itself). However, we would like another constructor that takes values for the street and city as arguments. We could call it what we like, but it is legal and appropriate to use the same name as the class.

In line (1) we see the declaration of the new constructor function. It takes two arguments, s and c, representing the street and city, respectively. Their types are character strings of length 50 and 20, respectively. The function returns a value of the type `AddressADT`. Line (2) declares a to be a local variable of type `AddressADT`.

The body of the function is lines (3) through (6). In line (3) we use the built-in constructor `AddressADT()` to create a new object and make it the value of variable `:a`. Note that we cannot confuse the built-in constructor function with the one we are writing, because the arguments of the two functions are different. That is, line (3) cannot be misinterpreted as a recursive call. Line (4) copies the first argument into the `street` component of a, while line (5) copies the second argument into the `city` component of a. Finally, line (6) returns the constructed value a.

Lines (7) and (8) define the equality function for ADT `AddressADT`. Recall from line (4) of Fig. 8.17 that the equality function for `AddressADT` was declared to have the name `addrEq`, so this is the name we must use. The function is

```
1)   FUNCTION AddressADT(:s CHAR(50), :c CHAR(20)
             RETURNS AddressADT;
2)        :a AddressADT;
          BEGIN
3)            :a := AddressADT();
4)            :a.street := :s;
5)            :a.city := :c;
6)            RETURN :a;
          END;


7)   FUNCTION addrEq(:a1 AddressADT, :a2 AddressADT)
             RETURNS BOOLEAN;
8)        RETURN (:a1.street = :a2.street AND
             :a1.city = :a2.city);


9)   FUNCTION addrLT(:a1 AddressADT, :a2 AddressADT)
             RETURNS BOOLEAN;
10)       RETURN ((:a1.city<:a2.city) OR
             (:a1.city = :a2.city) AND :a1.street<:a2.street));


11)  FUNCTION fullAddr(:a AddressADT) RETURNS CHAR(82);
12)       :z CHAR(10);
          BEGIN
13)           :z = findZip(:a.street, :a.city);
14)           RETURN(:a.street || ' ' || :a.city || ' ' || :z);
          END;
```

Figure 8.19: Some functions for the address ADT

simple; it returns TRUE if and only if the street components of the two values match and so do their city components. This function is in fact the default equality — identity of values — and could have been defaulted as we did in Example 8.31.

Lines (9) and (10) are the < function, addrLT. Here, we have chosen to say that the first address precedes the second if the city of the first is lexicographically less (precedes in alphabetical order) the city of the second. If the cities are the same, then we compare the street names.

Lines (11) through (14) define a function fullAddr that takes an object of type AddressADT and returns the full address, that is, the street address, city, and 9-digit (plus hyphen) zip code. Line (12) declares a local variable :z to hold the zip code temporarily. At line (13), a function findZip is called. This function is externally defined and takes two string arguments representing the street address and city. We shall discuss the form of external function declarations in Section 8.6.3.

By some complex process, which might be lookup in another database or an elaborate series of decisions, `findZip` returns the correct zip code for that street and city. We shall not try to write `findZip` here. Finally, at line (14), we concatenate the street and city from the object `:a` with the zip code held in `:z`. We place single blanks between the three components of the address to separate them. □

8.6.3 External Functions

ADT's may also have methods that are written in some host language rather than in SQL3. If we use such a function, then only its signature appears in the definition of the ADT, along with information telling the language in which the function is written. The form of an external declaration is:

> DECLARE EXTERNAL <function name> <signature>
> LANGUAGE <language name>

Example 8.33: In order to use the external function `findZip` in Example 8.32, we need to declare it in the definition of ADT `AddressADT`. Since this function takes two arguments, which are character strings of length 50 and 20, respectively, and it returns a character string of length 10, the proper declaration is:

```
DECLARE EXTERNAL findZip
CHAR(50) CHAR(20) RETURNS CHAR(10)
LANGUAGE C;
```

The fact that the language is declared to be C means that the address argument will be passed to `findZip` in a form suitable for a C program. □

8.6.4 Exercises for Section 8.6

* **Exercise 8.6.1:** Define a "PC" abstract data type whose objects represent personal computers, including their processor speed, RAM, hard-disk size, CD speed, and price.

Exercise 8.6.2: Write the following functions for your ADT of Exercise 8.6.1, using the extended SQL for internal functions:

* a) A constructor function called `newPC` that takes values for the five attributes of the PC ADT and returns a new object of that type. Recall that you may (and must) use the built-in constructor `PC()` to define this function.

* b) A function `value` that takes a PC object as argument and returns an "evaluation" of the PC, which is a real number telling how "good" the

PC is. The formula for the "value" of the PC is the processor speed plus 5 times the RAM (in megabytes), plus 50 times the hard disk (in gigabytes), and 10 times the speed of the CD.

c) A function **better** that takes a PC object as argument and returns another PC object with twice the processor speed, RAM, hard disk, and CD speed, and the same price. You may use the constructor **newPC** from part (a).

d) A function **equalPC** that serves as the equality for PC objects. This function reports two PC's are "equal" if they have the same speed and hard disk size, regardless of the values of the other components.

e) A function **ltPC** that serves as the less-than function for ADT PC. This function finds $p_1 < p_2$ if the "value" of PC p_1 is less than that of PC p_2, where "value" is as defined in part (b). You may use the function **value** defined in part (b).

Exercise 8.6.3: Define an abstract data type **Ship** for ships, including the name of the ship, date launched, number of guns, bore of the guns, displacement, an MPEG-encoded video clip of the ship in action, and a postscript document about the history of the ship.

Exercise 8.6.4: Write declarations and definitions for the following functions on your **Ship** ADT from Exercise 8.6.3.

a) Function **firePower** takes a **Ship** object as argument and returns the "firepower," which is the number of guns times the cube of the bore.

b) Function **playVideo** that takes a **Ship** object as argument and plays the video of the ship, using an externally defined function (which you must declare) called **playMpeg** that plays an MPEG file.

c) A constructor function called **newShip** that takes values for the name (and none of the other components), and returns a new **Ship** object with that name.

d) A function **equalShips** that serves as the equality for **Ship** objects. This function reports two ships are "equal" if they have the same name and year launched, regardless of the values of the other components.

e) A function **ltShip** that serves as the less-than function for ADT **Ship**. This function finds $s_1 < s_2$ if the name of ship s_1 is alphabetically less than the name of ship s_2, or, if the names are the same, then s_1 was launched before s_2.

8.7   A Comparison of the ODL/OQL and SQL3 Approaches

Having sampled the two major standards proposed for object-oriented database management — ODL/OQL and SQL3 — we should see a number of ways in which the two approaches differ. It is also true that the similarities outweigh the differences, and even though the two proposals come from widely differing models — object-oriented programming languages versus relational database languages — they have each effectively adopted much of what is fundamental to the other's core model.

In this section, we shall list the principal differences and ways in which the two approaches have selected different points on a spectrum of tradeoffs. At the same time, we shall point out ways in which the SQL3 row types and ADT's differ from each other and from interfaces (classes) in ODL. Thus, we are in fact comparing three different approaches to object-orientation: ODL/OQL, SQL3 row types, and SQL3 value types.

1. *Programming environment.* OQL assumes that its statements are embedded in a programming language that shares the same programming and data model. Presumably this language is object-oriented; for example, C++, Smalltalk, or Java. On the other hand, SQL3 assumes that its objects are not objects of the surrounding host language. As in all SQL standards and implementations, there is a limited interface that allows values to be passed between SQL stored data and host-language variables. The use of external functions in SQL3 ADT's is an additional communication mechanism, which complements the usual SQL/host-language interface that we saw in Section 7.1.

2. *Role of relations.* Relations remain central to the SQL3 view of data. Row types really describe relations, and ADT's describe new types for attributes. On the other hand, sets and bags of objects or structures are fundamental to OQL because of their role in select-from-where statements. Collections of structures in ODL/OQL are very close to relations in SQL3.

3. *Encapsulation.* Row types are not encapsulated. It is normal to be able to query and modify, in all the ways SQL permits, the relations, tuples, and components of a given row type. SQL3 abstract data types are encapsulated in the usual sense. ODL classes are very close to SQL3 ADT's in their approach to encapsulation.

4. *Extents for classes.* OQL assumes that there is a single extent maintained for each class. References (i.e., relationships in OQL terms) always refer to some member or members of this extent. In SQL3, we might maintain an extent for a row type, that is, a relation containing every existing tuple of that type, but we are under no obligation to do so. If we have no extent for a row type, then there can be problems finding the relation

in which the tuple referred to by a given reference resides, as discussed in Section 8.5.6 on reference scopes.

5. *Mutability of objects.* An object is *immutable* if once created, no part of its value can change. Objects of elementary type, such as integers or strings, are immutable in this sense. If the components of an object can change while the object retains its object identity, then the object is said to be *mutable.* ODL classes and SQL3 row types define classes of mutable objects, although in ODL/OQL, it is assumed that object modification occurs within the surrounding programming language, not through OQL. SQL3 ADT's are not exactly immutable. However, mutator functions applied to their values result in a new value, which may replace the old one, much as an SQL `UPDATE` statement on an integer-valued attribute produces a new integer that might replace the old integer in the tuple.

6. *Object identity.* Both ODL and SQL3 ADT's follow the conventional interpretation of object identity: it is a system-generated quantity that cannot be stored or manipulated by the user. However, references in row types of SQL3 do not follow this principle. The user can create a column of a relation in which the object-identity of a tuple is stored in that tuple itself, as if it were an ordinary value. The effect is that tuple object-identities can serve as the key for a relation. There is a certain sense to this capability, although it does invite the introduction of dangling references into the database due to updates or deletions. Without allowing the object-identity to be an attribute, relations would typically have two keys: the object identity and a surrogate value such as Social Security number or the "certificates" that we used in our running movie example.

8.8 Summary of Chapter 8

✦ *Methods in ODL*: In addition to the attributes and relationships that we learned about in Chapter 2, ODL allows us to declare methods as part of an interface specification. We define the signature of the method only, i.e., the types of the input and output parameters. The methods themselves are defined in the surrounding program and written in the object-oriented host language.

✦ *The OQL Type System*: Types in OQL are built from class names and the atomic types (e.g., integers). The type constructors are `Struct` to build structures and the collection types for sets, bags, lists, and arrays. The type system is thus the same as ODL's, except there is no limit on the degree of nesting of type constructors in OQL.

✦ *Select-From-Where Statements in OQL*: OQL offers a select-from-where expression that resembles SQL's. In the `FROM` clause, we can declare variables that range over any collection, including both extents of classes (analogous to relations) and collections that are the values of attributes in objects.

✦ *Common OQL Operators*: OQL offers for-all, there-exists, IN, union, intersection, difference, and aggregation operators that are similar in spirit to SQL's. However, aggregation is always over a collection, not a column of a relation.

✦ *OQL Group-By*: OQL also offers a GROUP BY clause in select-from-where statements that is similar to SQL's. However, in OQL, the collection of objects in each group is explicitly accessible through a field name called partition.

✦ *Extracting Elements From OQL Collections*: We can obtain the lone member of a collection that is a singleton by applying the ELEMENT operator. The elements of a collection with more than one member can be accessed by first turning the collection into a list, using an ORDER BY clause in a select-from-where statement, and then using a loop in the surrounding host-language program to visit each element of the list in turn.

✦ *Objects in SQL3*: There are two kinds of objects provided by SQL3: row types and abstract data types. Row types are types for tuples, and abstract data types are types for components of tuples.

✦ *Object Identity for Row Types*: There is a reference type for each row type, and a value of this reference type is the object ID for a tuple. SQL3 permits an attribute to have a type that is a reference to the row type of its own relation and for this attribute's value to be the object ID for the tuple in which it resides, thus allowing the object ID to serve also as a key attribute for its relation.

✦ *Abstract Data Types in SQL3*: One may declare an ADT in SQL3 with a CREATE TYPE statement. Values of an ADT are record structures with one or more components and may have associated methods.

✦ *Methods in SQL3 ADT's*: Functions (methods) may be declared for an ADT. They can be written either in an SQL-like programming language or declared to be external functions written in the host language.

8.9   References for Chapter 8

The reference for OQL is the same as for ODL: [1]. Material on SQL3 can be obtained as described in the bibliographic notes to Chapter 5. In addition, [3] is a source for row objects and [2] is an early exposition of SQL3 abstract data types, from which the standard has evolved in various ways.

1. Cattell, R. G. G. (ed.), *The Object Database Standard: ODMG–93 Release 1.2*, Morgan-Kaufmann, San Francisco, 1996.

2. Melton, J., J. Bauer, and K. Kulkarni, "Object ADT's (with improvements for value ADT's)," ISO WG3 report X3H2–91–083, April, 1991.

3. Kulkarni, K., M. Carey, L. DeMichiel, N. Mattos, W. Hong, and M. Ubell, "introducing reference types and cleaning up SQL3's object model," ISO WG3 report X3H2–95–456, Nov., 1995.

Index

463